GOLD experience

2ND EDITION

TEACHER'S BOOK

B2

First for Schools

Pearson Education Limited
KAO Two
KAO Park
Harlow
Essex
CM17 9NA
England
and Associated Companies throughout the world.

pearsonELT.com/goldexperience

© Pearson Education Limited 2018

Written by Lynda Edwards and Jacky Newbrook.

All rights reserved; no part of this publication may be reproduced, stored in a retrieval system, or transmitted in any form or by any means, electronic, mechanical, photocopying, recording, or otherwise without the prior written permission of the Publishers.

First published 2018
Third impression 2018

ISBN: 978-1-292-23982-8

Set in Camphor Pro
Printed by CPI Group (UK) Ltd, Croydon CR0 4YY

Acknowledgements
The publishers would like to thank Lindsay Warwick and Jacky Newbrook for the Classroom Teaching Ideas and Lindsay Warwick for the Success Criteria content.

Picture Credits
The publisher would like to thank the following for their kind permission to reproduce their photographs:

Alamy Stock Photo: EyeEm 161; **Getty Images:** Fredrik Clement 87, EyeEm / Katrin Donig 103, marrio31 55, stock_colors 22, AJ Wilhelm 71, Rosmarie Wirz 145; **Plainpicture Ltd:** Hollandse Hoogte / Sabine Joosten 39; **Shutterstock.com:** Fotovika 116, Amir Ridhwan 130

Cover images: *Front:* **Getty Images:** EyeEm / Chris Phillips

All other images © Pearson Education

Every effort has been made to trace the copyright holders and we apologise in advance for any unintentional omissions. We would be pleased to insert the appropriate acknowledgement in any subsequent edition of this publication.

CONTENTS

Introduction to Gold Experience 2nd Edition 4-7

Course components 5-6

Teaching pathways 7

Unit walkthrough 8-12

Student's Book unit 8-11

Workbook unit 12

Classroom teaching ideas 13-21

How to teach for exams 13-15

How to flip the classroom 16-17

How to encourage independent Learning 18-19

How to teach with projects 20

How to teach with Readers 21

Unit 1	Wake up your senses!	22-38
Unit 2	On the bucket list	39-54
Unit 3	All in a day's work	55-70
Unit 4	The heart of the city	71-86
Unit 5	A good sport	87-102
Unit 6	Viewpoints	103-115
Unit 7	The full story	116-129
Unit 8	In it together	130-144
Unit 9	Getting it right	145-160
Unit 10	A matter of taste	161-170

Switch on videoscripts 171-175

Workbook answer key 176-193

Speaking: success criteria 194-196

Writing: success criteria 197-208

INTRODUCTION

GOLD EXPERIENCE 2ND EDITION

Gold Experience second edition is an 8-level course that prepares students for the Cambridge English exams while building their language and real-world skills. The course gives students thorough exam preparation in terms of both strategy and language, while simultaneously developing the life skills that students will need to use English successfully beyond the classroom. Real-world, engaging materials ensure students are switched on and curious to learn more. This second edition is fully updated with new content and a new design.

The B2 level

The B2 level is designed for classes where some or all students are preparing for B2 level exams such as *Cambridge B2 First for Schools*. However, the 'general English' feel and teen-centric topics and texts make it suitable for students at this level who are not studying for the exam. With all-new content for the second edition, Gold Experience B2 will continue its focus on developing students' confidence in using English for communication and extending their knowledge of vocabulary and structures. It also aims to find surprising and engaging ways to introduce some thought-provoking topics and themes, and encourages students to reflect on their own knowledge and experience. Gold Experience second edition will equip students to succeed in the *Cambridge B2 First for Schools* exam, but also to succeed in their upcoming young adult lives.

The principles and methodology

Reliable

First and foremost, you need your course to help you achieve students' core aims of building language skills and passing exams. With Gold Experience second edition, the syllabus is based on a combination of exam requirements and the Global Scale of English, ensuring comprehensive language coverage. Meanwhile, we have brought together highly experienced authors and exam consultants to ensure accuracy and rigor in exam preparation, as well as managing the balance of general English, exam English and life skills. This means you can rest assured that your students will be learning the right language with suitable practice to help them excel in their exams and communicate with confidence.

'Under-the-hood' exam preparation

We believe that students need training and practice to excel in exams, but that this doesn't need to be the overarching feel of a class. In Gold Experience second edition, exam tasks are woven seamlessly into the flow of the lesson, but can be easily identified by the e icon. Each unit includes work on every exam paper, giving students exposure to realistic tasks with a focus on the target language of the unit. Over the course of the book, students build their exam strategies and their confidence through the step-by-step core activities and task-based exam tips. For those classes or individuals wanting more targeted exam preparation we have a full practice test in the Workbook, and an additional Exam Practice book for practice of full papers.

Engagement

Gold Experience second edition aims to bring new experiences to students, and encourage students to bring their own experience to the classroom. We believe that any text or discussion topic should be interesting regardless of the language, and we have tried to balance light, quirky topics that students will have fun with, with more weighty themes to really get them thinking.

Where possible, we have used authentic texts and real people in reading texts allowing students to expand on anything that takes their interest. Authentic broadcast video from a variety of sources, and grammar 'vox pop' interviews with the general public introduce students to authentic accents and real experiences and stories.

As every teacher knows, when students are engaged with the topic and the material, they are engaged with English and everything else is just that little bit easier.

'Whole student' development

As well as language and exams, we know you care about developing your students as citizens of the world. This means helping them develop their ability to think critically, assimilate new information and points of view, and formulate, express and defend their opinions. This means helping them develop research techniques, work both alone and with others, and reflect on their own learning. In Gold Experience second edition, these skills are developed throughout each unit in the Speak up sections, where students are encouraged to discuss and debate, and in a more focused way, at the end of each unit in the Project and Independent Learning strands. The Projects are designed to be flexible and you can decide to do them quickly in class, or expand them into longer-term projects over several classes or weeks. The Independent Learning syllabus builds over the course of the book to help students discover both study tools and techniques, and more about themselves as learners.

Flexible resources

We know that the real classroom can often be far more complex than the ideal classroom we imagine. For that reason, we've provided a wealth of materials to provide extra support or further challenge for students who need it, plenty of additional and alternative ideas and resources for you, and a full suite of components to allow you to tailor your teaching package to your classroom.

COURSE COMPONENTS

For students

Student's Book with App

- **Nine topic-based units** divided into 8 main teaching lessons, plus video, project, independent learning, wordlist and unit check.
- Final **tenth unit review** provides revision of language and skills from the course in exam task format.
- Training and practice for the ***Cambridge B2 First for Schools*** exam is seamlessly integrated into every lesson.
- Students and teachers can easily **identify exam-like tasks** with the e icon.
- Additional examples of vocabulary sets in **Extend vocabulary** in the back of the book.

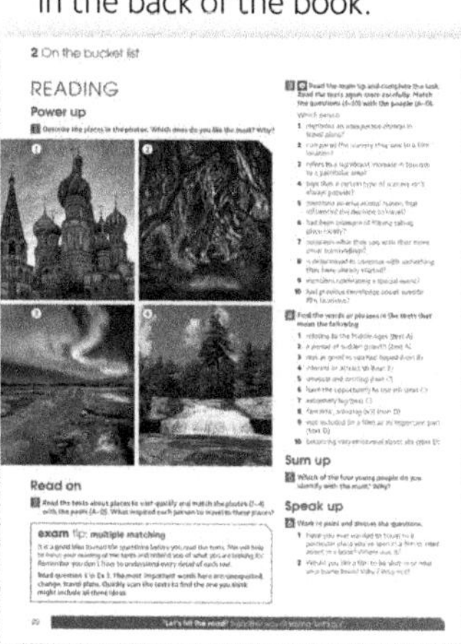
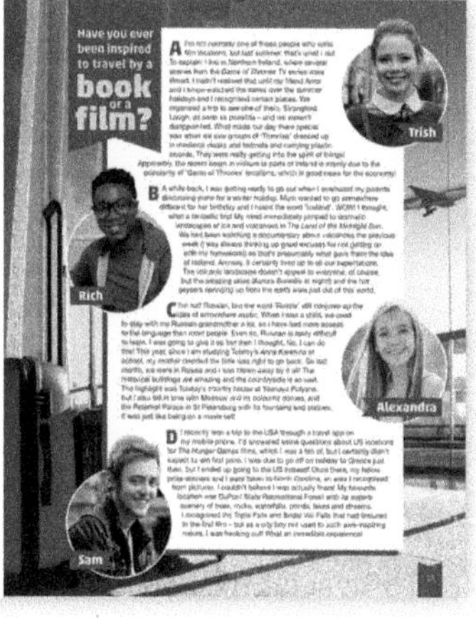

- Students are encouraged to explore their ideas, opinions and knowledge of the world through frequent **discussion opportunities**, for example through Speak up activities.
- **Video clips** expose students to a variety of authentic broadcasting formats, accents and ideas, and encourage students to think critically about what they watch.
- Where appropriate, **grammar vox pop** interviews give authentic examples of target grammar in use.
- End of unit **projects** can be adapted depending on the time available, and encourage students to explore a topic, collaborate and work creatively with classmates, and present back to the class.
- **Independent learning** sections guide students through different aspects of self-reflection and help them become more successful learners.
- The back of book **Grammar file** gives a full page of detailed grammar and language explanation, plus a full page of practice activities for every unit.
- **Writing file** and **Speaking file** give task-by-task exam-related help and useful language for productive tasks.
- **Student's App** gives access to videos and the extensive class and workbook audio, as well as additional fun practice of course vocabulary. Accessed via a code in every Student's Book

eBook for students

- Full Student's Book in digital format with embedded audio, video and interactive activities.
- Suitable for computer or tablet.

Workbook

- **Mirrors the Student's Book** lesson by lesson and consolidates learning with targeted practice.
- Additional **topic-related practice** of reading, writing, speaking, listening and use of English skills.
- Extensive practice of course grammar and vocabulary, including practice of **Extend vocabulary** from the back of the Student's Book for stronger students.
- **Complete practice exam** in Unit 10.
- Designed for either independent study at home or in-class extra practice.
- Audio for listening lessons available on the **Student's App**.

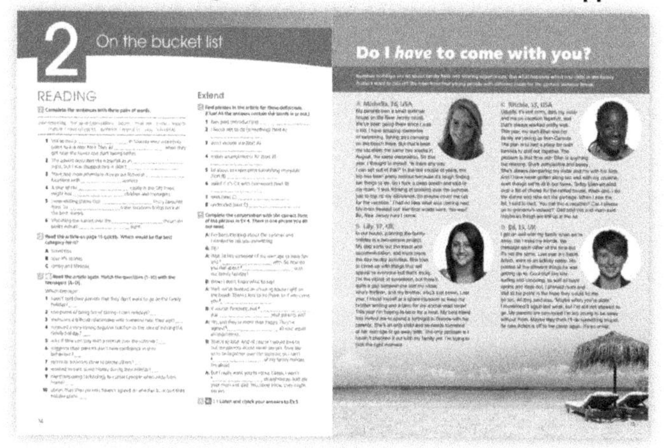

Online Practice for students

- **Fully interactive digital version** of the Workbook, which complements and consolidates the Student's Book material.
- **Remediation** videos and activities powered by MyGrammarLab.
- **Instantly graded** activities with supportive feedback.
- Personal **gradebook** for students to review their performance.
- Access to Student's Book video and audio for students.

Exam practice books

- Additional intensive practice for the *Cambridge B2 First for Schools.*
- Two complete practice tests, one with tips and guidance for every task.
- Extensive support for productive tasks at the back of the book.
- Online answer keys, audio and speaking test videos with teacher's resources.

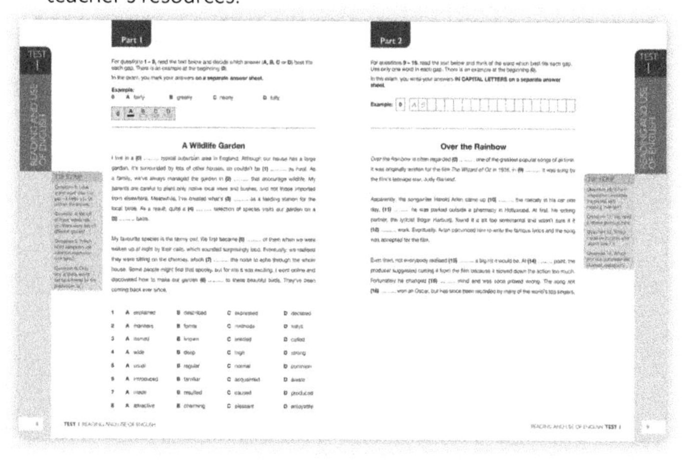

For teachers

Teacher's Book

- Teaching notes with a wealth of additional and alternative classroom ideas, including for mixed ability classes, fast finishers, and additional questions to encourage critical thinking.
- Exam information, including how Student's Book activities may differ from exam tasks (for example, shorter text length, fewer items, a focus on unit language meaning less variety of tested language than in the exam, etc.).
- 'How to' sections in the introduction, giving advice on teaching for exams, flipping the classroom, developing your students as independent learners, teaching with projects and teaching with readers.
- Speaking and Writing Success Criteria at the back of the book to help you and your students understand what a solid answer, a good answer and an 'acing it' answer looks like.
- Photocopiable audio scripts and videoscripts at the back of the book.
- Workbook answer key.
- Access code for all Gold Experience digital teacher tools.

Teacher's Online Resources

All the support a busy teacher needs in one place, accessed via the access code in the back of the Teacher's Book or via your Pearson consultant.

Presentation tool

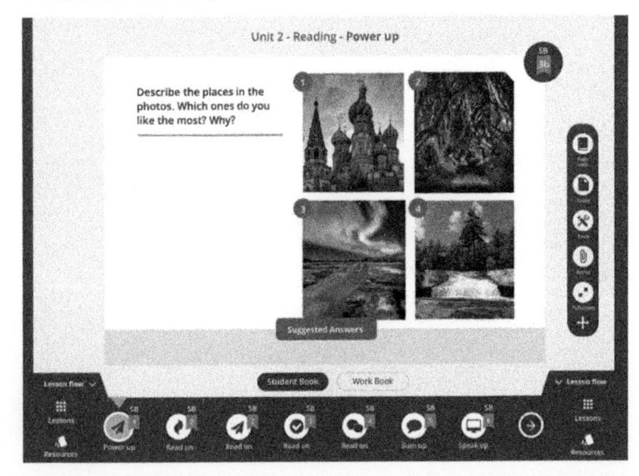

- Front-of-class teacher's tool with fully interactive version of every Student's Book and Workbook activity with integrated audio and video.
- Planning mode, including teacher's notes, and teaching mode.
- Easy navigation via either book page or lesson flow.
- Additional whole-class game activities – plus score and timer tools for teacher-led games.

Resources

- Teaching notes (digital teacher's book).
- Detailed grammar PowerPoint presentations for each unit's grammar points.
- Three photocopiable worksheets (Grammar, Vocabulary + skill or exam focus) per Student's Book unit, with full teaching notes and answer key.
- Class audio and video.
- Assessment package (see below).

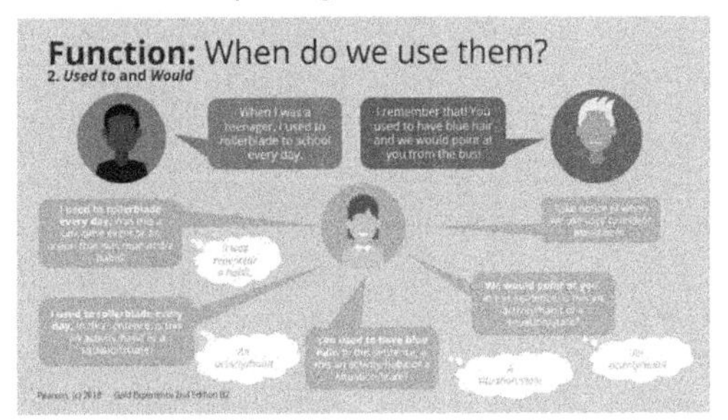

Assessment package

- Extensive range of tests for use throughout the course.
- A/B versions of core tests to prevent cheating.
- Versions for students with special educational needs.
- Available as ready-to-print pdfs or editable word documents.
- Answer keys and audio files.
- Test pack includes:
  - Diagnostic test to help place students and identify strengths or weaknesses.
  - Unit tests with two papers: Grammar, vocabulary and Use of English; Listening and reading.
  - Review tests every three units with three papers: Grammar, vocabulary and use of English; Writing; Speaking.
  - End of Year test with three papers: Listening, Reading and Use of English; Writing; Speaking.

Online Practice for teachers

- Teacher view of Online Practice provides a full learning management system .
- Assign tasks to the whole class, groups or individual students depending on their needs.
- Automatic marking to save time.
- Performance area lets you see how individual students and the whole class are progressing overall and by skill.

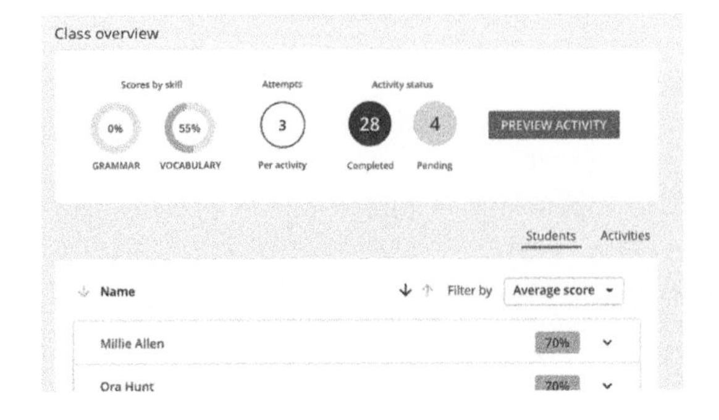

TEACHING PATHWAYS

We know that not every class is the same, and there are many influences, from your course hours, teaching context and personal style to your class size, and the needs of every one of your students. *Gold Experience 2nd Edition* has been designed to be as flexible as possible, allowing you to add relevant sections and support to the core content, and tailor the course to your classes and students.

Component		**To focus on ...**				
Print	**Blended / Digital**	**Core material**	**Grammar and vocabulary**	**Exam preparation**	**21st Century skills**	**Fun activities**
Student's Book + App	Student's eBook	Units 1–9: • core lessons	• Unit checks • Grammar file (reference & practice) • Extended Vocabulary lists • App: Vocab activities • Authentic 'on-the-street' interviews	• Unit 10 (review unit) • Writing file • Speaking file	• Independent Learning section • *Switch on* video project • *Speak up* & extended discussions • *Improve it* writing sections	• *Game on* activities in main units • *Switch on* video & project • Footers in main units
Workbook	Online Practice	Units 1–9: • core lessons	• *Extend vocabulary* sections • Unit checks • Online Practice: MyGrammarLab videos & activities	• Unit 10 (full practice exam)	• Writing tasks	• Puzzles (e.g. crosswords)
Teacher's Book		Units 1–9: • core lessons	• Alternative and extra activities in teaching notes • Additional activities for fast-finishers • Information about common student errors	• How to teach for exams • Writing Success Criteria • Speaking Success Criteria • Extra activities in teaching notes	• How to encourage independent learning • How to flip the classroom • How to teach with projects • How to teach with readers • Critical thinking activities in teaching notes • Project extensions	• How to teach with projects • Extra activities in teaching notes
Teacher's Online Resources (including Teacher's Presentation Tool)		Units 1–9: • audio & video	• Grammar PowerPoint Presentations • Photocopiable activities	• Photocopiable activities		• Photocopiable activities • Presentation Tool games
Assessment package (Word or pdf - part of Online Resources)		Unit tests: Grammar & Vocabulary	• Diagnostic test • Review tests (main)	• Unit tests: Skills • Review tests: Writing • Review tests: Speaking • End of Year tests	Tests used as assessment *for* learning	
Exam practice booklet				Exam booklet • 2 full practice tests • Guidance, tips & reference		

UNIT WALKTHROUGH

STUDENT'S BOOK UNIT

Each unit has a ***lead-in*** photo, quote and discussion questions to get students thinking about the unit theme, and using their existing topic vocabulary.

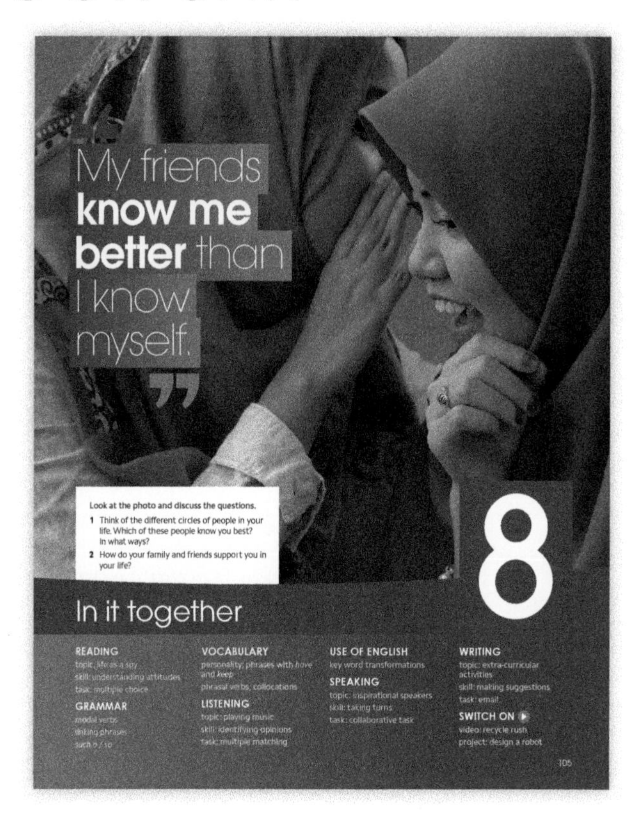

The ***Unit overview*** gives a brief outline of topics, key language, skills focus and exam tasks.

The main reading text **previews grammar** that students will meet in the next lesson.

Power up sections get students thinking about the lesson topic.

Exam skills and strategies are built up through both core activities and **exam tips.**

Exam tasks are easily identified by the **e** symbol.

Sum up sections require students to think about the text as a whole.

8 In it together

READING

Power up

Read on

exam tip: multiple choice

Sum up

Speak up

MI6 hadn't just put him in danger. They'd locked his whole life in a filing cabinet and thrown away the key.

Living life as a spy

An extract from Stormbreaker, by Anthony Horowitz

Speak up sections develop critical **thinking,** asking students to think more deeply about the topic and consider different viewpoints, and provides extra **speaking practice.**

Editable PowerPoint presentations for each core grammar area save valuable preparation time and bring the grammar to life.

Extend vocabulary section in the back of the Student's Book and related Workbook activities provide more useful vocabulary.

Active *explore grammar* boxes require students to engage with the taught grammar.

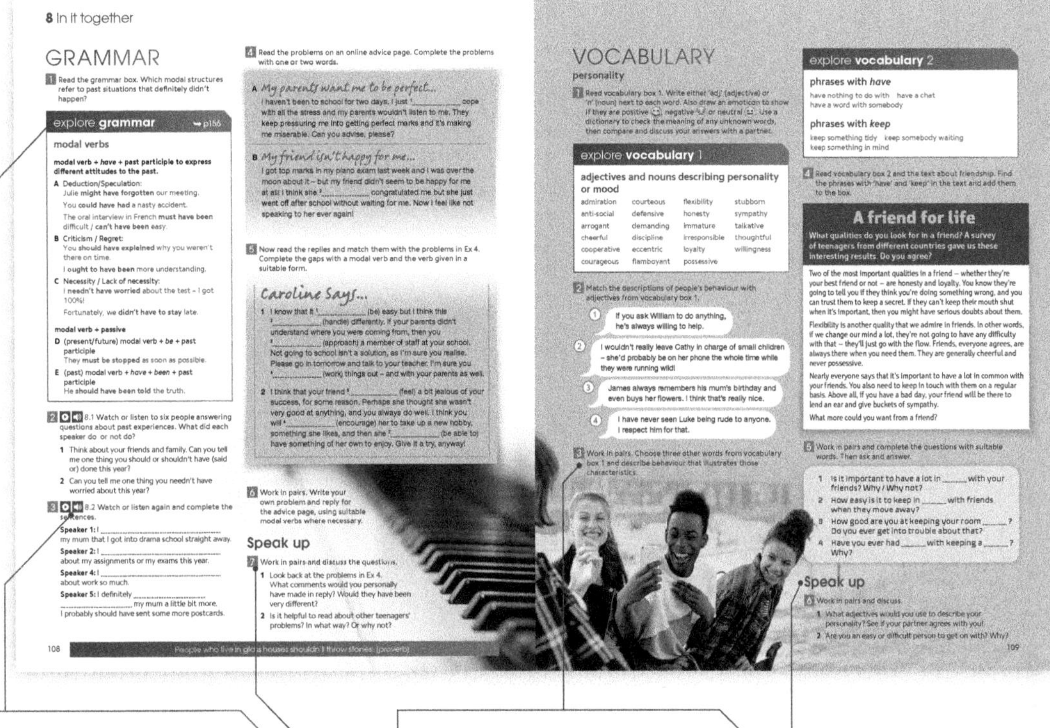
8 In it together

GRAMMAR

explore grammar

modal verbs

Speak up

VOCABULARY

personality

explore vocabulary 1

adjectives and nouns describing personality or mood

explore vocabulary 2

phrases with *have*

phrases with *keep*

A friend for life

Speak up

Language is **contextualised** in authentic **Grammar vox pop** interviews, scripted **conversations** or short texts. Grammar vox pops are provided as both audio and video.

Frequent opportunities for **personalisation** and **discussion** using new language.

Use of English lessons focus on language frequently tested in the exam.

Lesson 1 focuses on more lexical topics,
Lesson 2 on more grammatical topics.

Task **layout** reflects the exam.

All **audioscripts** are printed in the back of the book.

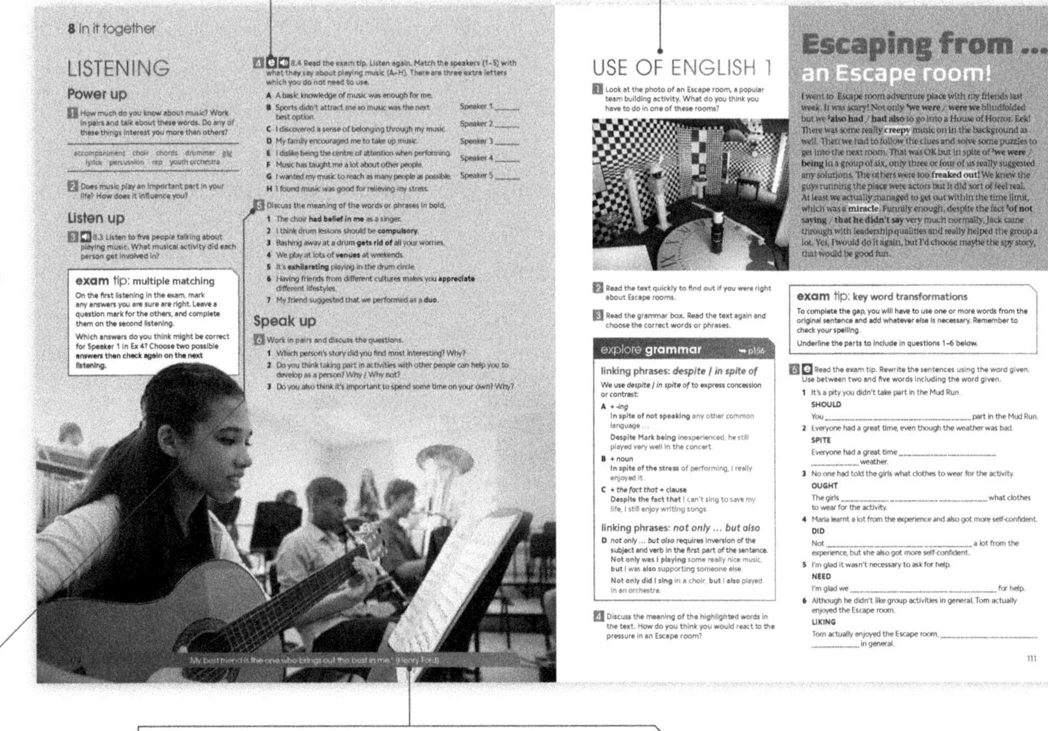
8 In it together

LISTENING

Power up

Listen up

exam tip: multiple matching

Speak up

USE OF ENGLISH 1

Escaping from ... an Escape room!

explore grammar

linking phrases: *despite* / *in spite of*

linking phrases: *not only ... but also*

exam tip: key word transformations

Vocabulary-from-the-text activities encourage students to **notice and absorb** vocabulary they find.

Fun footers, loosely connected to the topic, can be explicitly exploited or left for students to notice.

Useful language boxes provide a wide range of **language options** for a specific function.

Step-by-step approach to exam tasks.

Common examples are presented and practised on the page. Further examples are in ***Extend vocabulary*** at the back of the book.

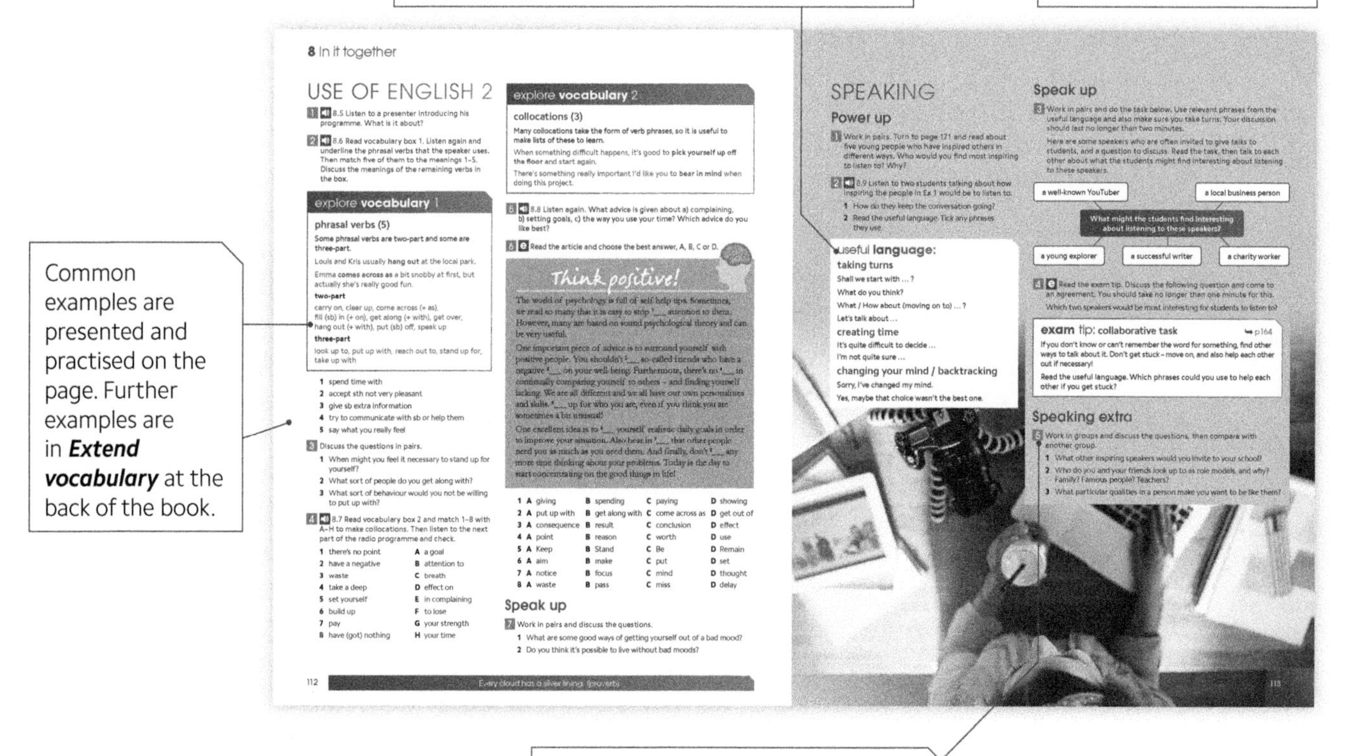

Speaking extra provides more **general** speaking practice on the topic.

Plan on asks students to:

- **analyse** the exam task, with tasks and tips to help them;
- work on **appropriate language**;
- break down tasks such as **how to make an argument** in writing.

The ***explore language*** boxes provide explanation and examples of key language areas.

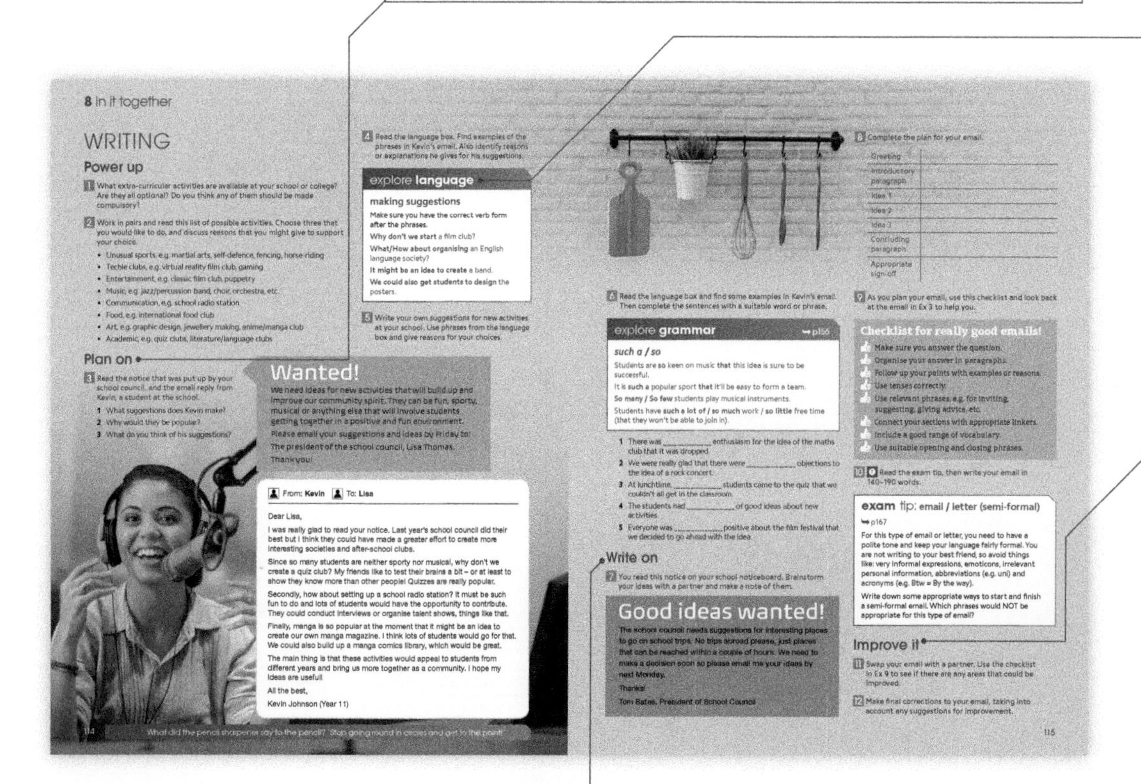

Improve it encourages students to **reflect on** their work and make improvements.

Write on walks students through **planning** and **writing** their own answer.

The ***Switch on*** video lessons provide authentic clips on a variety of engaging and thought-provoking topics.

Unit checks provide two pages of practice to review the unit language.

Activities move from **gist** to **close watching** to general **discussion** questions.

SWITCH ON

Recycle rush

Project

INDEPENDENT LEARNING

Listening and speaking

UNIT CHECK

Wordlist

Practice

Projects involve **research**, **collaboration**, **critical thinking** and **creativity**, and are flexible, allowing teachers to take a quicker or more in-depth approach.

Independent learning sections build through the units and help students reflect on their own learning.

Wordlists include all the explicitly taught **vocabulary** from the unit.

Grammar file at the back of the Student's Book gives detailed explanations for all grammar topics

Each unit has one page of **reference** and one page of **practice,** which can be used for **remediation**, extra **practice** or in a **flipped classroom** scenario.

GRAMMAR FILE UNIT 5

REFERENCE

ways of talking about the future

PRACTICE

LEGO DESIGN

WORKBOOK UNIT

Workbook units mirror the Student's Book with additional practice of all language, skills and exams tasks.

Writing and **Speaking** pages focus on subskills, analysis and useful language, and include an optional productive task in every unit.

Unit check pages at end of each unit help students check they understand the core language from the unit.

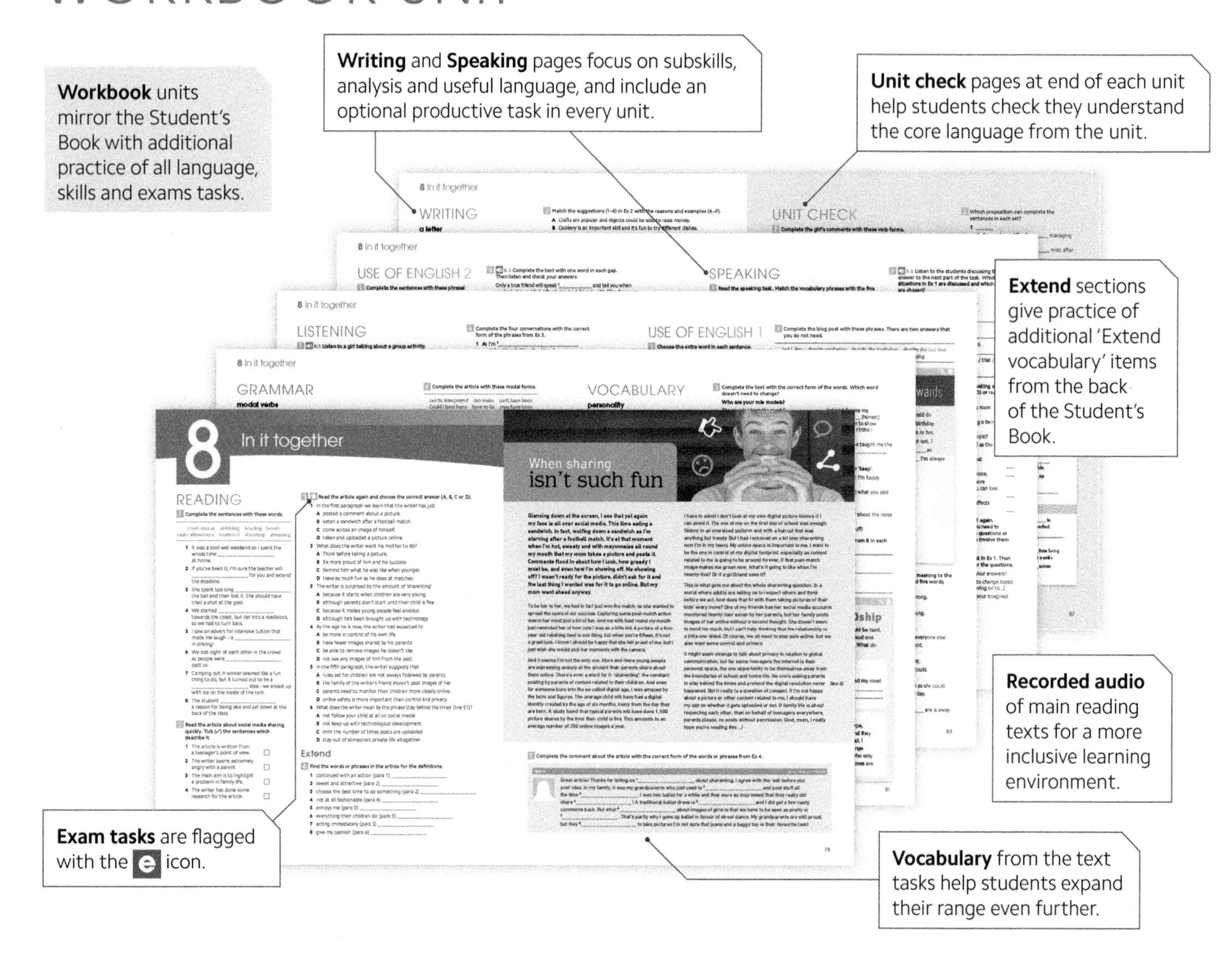

Extend sections give practice of additional 'Extend vocabulary' items from the back of the Student's Book.

Recorded audio of main reading texts for a more inclusive learning environment.

Exam tasks are flagged with the e icon.

Vocabulary from the text tasks help students expand their range even further.

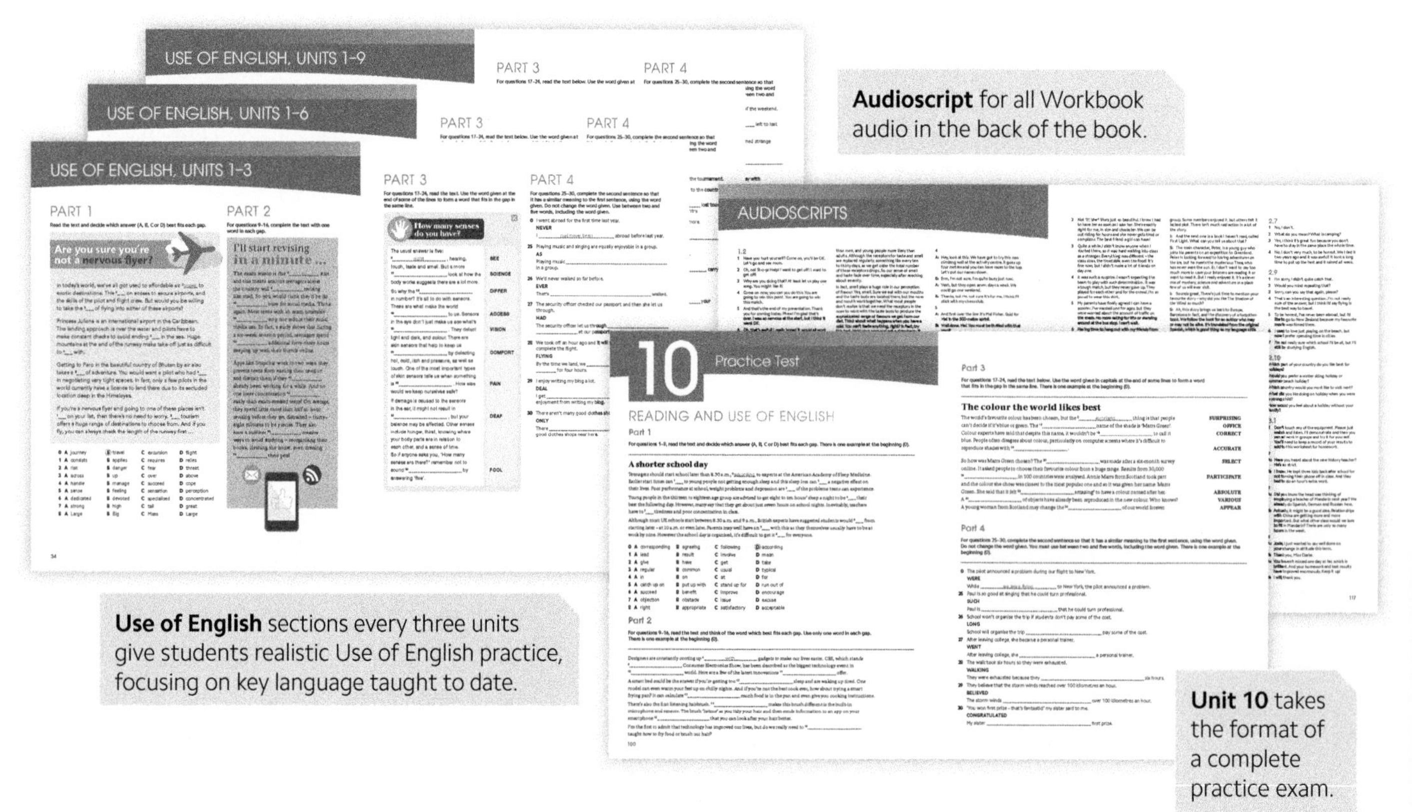

Audioscript for all Workbook audio in the back of the book.

Use of English sections every three units give students realistic Use of English practice, focusing on key language taught to date.

Unit 10 takes the format of a complete practice exam.

HOW TO TEACH FOR EXAMS

What do teachers need to consider?

1 What do you do when not all students in a class are taking the exam?

Teachers should make sure that students who are not taking the exam are still engaged with the work done in class and feel they can benefit from the specific practice that exam students need. This means explaining clearly exactly what is being tested in exam tasks and how these skills also benefit students outside the classroom. Cambridge exams test skills that are transferable to the real world, and this should be explained to students. Once an exam task has been completed, it could be followed by general discussion on the topic or extended vocabulary practice so that non-exam students feel the benefit.

2 How is teaching for exams different from teaching general English classes?

- Exam classes often place more emphasis on reading, writing and grammar. General courses often include more speaking activities and general listening tasks that aim to develop communicative skills and fluency.
- An exam course is fixed, with an exam syllabus that must be completed. This means the teacher may feel there's little time to do many extension activities from the Student's Book that are either optional or not in exam format, even though these are clearly useful. When doing these activities, it's important that teachers explain their value clearly to the students so that they understand how they relate to the exam.
- Exam students may not be interested in learning English for its own sake – they may simply want to pass the exam. This means they may be keen to do exam practice but may not see the value of spending time on communicative or fluency activities. Non-exam students, on the other hand, will want to do fluency work that improves their communicative ability.
- Students may feel under pressure to succeed. This could come from parents, teachers or from the students themselves, and leads to a feeling of frustration if they're not doing well.
- There can be problems if students are not at the level of the exam they're studying for. Students can become demotivated, and teachers can feel frustrated.
- There is a very clear end goal which creates a shared bond among exam students. It also means that non-exam students can see a progression through the course, and gain a sense of progress and achievement in their overall ability.

3 What do exam teachers need to know at the start of a course?

It's vital that teachers know about the exam before they start the course, so they can make crucial decisions about how much time to spend on the different aspects of the exam, when to start exam practice and so on. They also need to know the balance of exam and non-exam students. Teachers should find out about student's priorities and how many students intend to take the exam. They should then find out about individual student's respective strengths and weaknesses in order to focus as much time as possible on those areas students have trouble with. Information they need includes:

a) The format and content of the exam.

- How many papers are there, and what skills does each one test?
- How many different parts are there in each paper? Are they all compulsory or is there a choice?
- What is the grammar syllabus for the exam?
- How are the skills tested – multiple choice questions, gap-fill ... ? What techniques are required for dealing with each one?

b) The practicalities of taking the exam.

- How much time is allowed for each part of the exam? How should students balance their time?
- Where do students write their answers? Is there transfer time?

c) Marking the exam.

- What is the weighting of different papers?
- How many marks are there for each question?
- What are the assessment criteria for each part where there is no 'right' answer, especially when testing the productive skills of writing and speaking?

d) What happens after the exam?

- How are the results presented? Do students receive feedback? Are the grades linked to the CEFR? What level are they linked to?
- What can your students do with the qualification? Is it recognised internationally?
- What is the next exam that your students should progress to?

4 What makes a successful exam teacher?

Teaching for an exam is very rewarding, but it is also challenging. A good exam teacher:

- knows and understands the exam well, including the testing focus of each part and what techniques students need to deal with each one
- understands how to achieve a balance between developing skills and doing exam practice in lessons so as to engage all students in the work
- enjoys teaching towards a goal
- manages their own and their students' time effectively and efficiently
- listens to students' concerns and worries
- gives honest and direct feedback on students' performance
- motivates students and fosters confidence and independent learning

5 How important is balancing teaching and testing?

Students enrolled on an exam course will expect to go through a lot of practice tests and exam practice. However, if this is all you do you will produce excellent test takers but poor language users! You may also risk losing the interest of non-exam students. When time is restricted you need to make the most of the time you choose to teach, and the time you need to be testing. This balance is different with every class.

- **A class below the level**

  The priority is teaching. Students may lack both test taking skills and language knowledge, so you need to identify their needs and try to fill in the gaps. Testing too often might de-motivate them, although you may want to set progress tests for your own assessment of what they need to study more. Make sure that they have realistic aims and that they maintain a sense of progress. You may decide not to mark their work using exam criteria, but to mark constructively which will also benefit non-exam students.

- **A class at the level**

  Students have the basic test-taking and language skills, but they need to consolidate and review these as well as extend the range of structures and language they can use productively. Regular testing can give these students a sense of progress. However, you need to consider how you mark their work in order to provide positive feedback and foster improvement, possibly by not marking to the level of the exam too early.

- **A class above the level**

  The emphasis is on enabling students to achieve the highest mark they can. Their language and test-taking skills should be good, and the problem may be to keep them motivated. Challenge them by setting them tasks above the level of the exam, and involve them in understanding what they have to do to get a higher than average mark in the exam. They should be aiming high, extending their range of language and not settling for 'good enough'.

6 Helping exam students help themselves

Encouraging a collaborative approach to developing exam skills will improve students' confidence, enable them to help each other and make each task seem more familiar and achievable. By involving students in understanding what exam tasks involve, teachers can foster confidence and facilitate success. It is really crucial that students feel comfortable with the tasks, and that there are no surprises when they enter the exam room.

How does Gold Experience second edition help with exam teaching?

Gold Experience works in a graded and supportive way, and provides a number of resources that help to develop the technical skills students need to deal with exam tasks, while also improving and extending their general language skills. The course is beneficial for both exam and non-exam students, and provides supportive and extended practice in real-life skills. The topics are engaging and give students the opportunity to read about and discuss interesting and relevant topics.

Development of language

Exam tasks require students to demonstrate a range of language at the appropriate level. Gold Experience has grammar and vocabulary sections that develop this range in topic related units, which makes it easy for students to apply them to exam tasks and to the real world.

Focus on the process as well as the goal

Learners are helped to understand not just the point of what they are doing but also how to be successful. Understanding the point of each task type, and the process they need to follow in order to complete it, enables student to reach the overall goal.

Graded exam tasks

Exam tasks are introduced to students early in the course, but in a graded way. This may mean that a task has fewer questions or a simpler text, or that it tests a more limited range of structures. This helps them to understand the exam task, and therefore deal with it more effectively.

Developing confidence with exam tasks

The clear learning goals for each skill established at the start of each unit, plus the frequent models throughout the book for the productive skills, show students what they need to do in each task and how to do it.

Students are often nervous about certain parts of the exam, such as the speaking and listening papers. There are often specific reasons for this:

- Speaking – students may be embarrassed about speaking in front of an examiner, or may be nervous so that their mind goes blank and they say too little.
- Listening – students often feel that they are not in control as they can't stop the tape to play it again, and this can cause them to panic if they are unsure of an answer.

Gold Experience provides plenty of practice in these two skills, and clear advice on how to deal with the problems students find with them. In this way students develop confidence.

Regular exam tips

There are exam tips in every unit which deal with specific exam tasks. The tips focus on aspects of the task that will help students deal with it effectively. These often precede practice in that particular task, so that students can see the tip in action. These tips build throughout the Students' Book and help students to understand exactly what is being tested, what to look out for, and develop a bank of appropriate exam techniques that they can refer to. As they work through the Students' Book and become familiar with the tips the tasks will become easier.

Focus on the process of writing

To help students identify good practice in writing tasks, lessons in the Student's Book provide model answers. There are also tasks that encourage students to analyse the model answers, which gives them greater understanding of how to complete the tasks themselves. These analytical tasks focus on the approach, content and language required by the different writing genres. There is a task at the end of each writing section which mirrors the model so that students can practise writing an answer themselves. There is also an *Improve it* section which guides students and helps them review and improve their work. In these sections, students are encouraged to work together to review and analyse each other's writing tasks, and to cooperate in understanding where improvement is required. There is a Writing file with further tips on how to approach the tasks, with further models.

Focus on speaking

Throughout the Student's Book there are discussion questions that encourage students to talk about ideas related to topics they have been reading or writing about. This is particularly beneficial for non-exam students. In sections specifically devoted to exam tasks, there are model answers for students to analyse. These answers give clear models for long turns and give examples of the best ways to interact with a partner.

Explanatory answer keys

There are clear keys provided for the exam tasks. In the reading and listening tasks the lines where the answers can be found are quoted. In the Use of English tasks there are explanations for the answers.

Practice test

As well as working through regular unit tests, students complete the course by doing a full exam practice test in the Workbook, which they can check against the answer key.

Resources for self-study

There are a number of resources which provide opportunities for self-study, and also give supplementary information and further practice. These can be used in class or at home. They include:

- A Wordlist at the end of each unit in the Student's Book
- An Extended Vocabulary section at the back of the Student's Book
- A Speaking file section at the back of the Student's Book
- A Writing file section at the back of the Student's Book
- A Grammar file section at the back of the Student's Book
- A full practice test in the Workbook
- An Exam Practice booklet
- Audioscripts for the listening tasks
- The Workbook
- Online practice activities

Extra activities

Here are five activities that might help your students with their studies for exams.

1 Developing confidence with the Speaking test

If students feel comfortable with the practicalities of taking the Speaking test they only have to think about the language they need, and an activity like this will help them relax.

1 Put students into pairs (A and B). Give out the appropriate worksheets.
2 They read through their own sentences and predict the missing information.
3 They dictate the sentences to each other and complete the gaps.

Student A

1 Arrive .... – don't be late or you will be stressed.
2 Say .... and make yourself comfortable.
3 Listen carefully to the instructions. Ask the examiner .... if you aren't sure.
4 If you're taking the exam with a partner, ...
5 Give .... answers. Don't just say yes or no.
6 Try to use a .... structures and ....
7 Smile! ...., you'll do better.

Student B

1 Arrive in good time – don't be late ....
2 Say hallo to the examiner and ....
3 Listen carefully .... Ask the examiner to repeat if you aren't sure.
4 If you're taking the exam ...., interact with them.
5 Give interesting answers. Don't ....
6 Try to use a range of .... and vocabulary.
7 Smile! If you enjoy it, you'll ....

2 Remind students of the exam tips

Ask students to work in pairs and write down as many exam tips as they can remember. Discuss which tips they have found most useful, and why. You could do this regularly through the course so that students become very familiar with them.

3 Use the marking criteria

The writing tasks are marked under criteria which include organisation, style, language and content. Share these criteria with students early in the course and explain what they mean. Give examples from the models in the Writing file. Ask students to check their own work against these criteria before they hand anything in. This will develop good habits as well as foster understanding of what the tasks require. Use them yourself when you mark students' written work.

4 Share students' experiences

Ask students to share things that they find easy, and anything they have found helpful when they do exam tasks. This will also boost their confidence as they realise how much they do actually know, and will give both exam students and non-exam students a lift!

5 Help students understand what is best for them

Write the incomplete sentences about doing exam tasks on the board. Students should complete them for themselves. Then discuss their answers with the whole class. This activity will also help non-exam students to see the value of exam practice for them.

1 I prefer it when the teacher .... with exam tasks.
2 I understand most when ....
3 I like/don't like doing speaking activities in class because ....
4 When we do practice tests in class I feel .... because ....
5 I feel confident about the exam because ....

HOW TO FLIP THE CLASSROOM

What is it and why is it important?

The flipped classroom is an approach where classroom instruction is given to students at home via a video, and application usually given for homework is completed in class with the teacher's support.

Teachers began flipping their classrooms in subjects such as science when they became frustrated that many of their lessons were taken up with giving students information. Students who struggled to complete their homework without the teacher there to support them were unable to master the topic.

The teachers exploited new technologies by creating short videos that provided classroom instruction. Students watched these in their own time before a lesson and then class time was spent on applying that information with the teacher there to support them. The teacher could differentiate tasks for different learners to ensure that everyone was challenged and supported at an appropriate level.

In language learning terms, flipping the classroom means students listening to or reading information about language at home before a lesson, leaving more time for practice of that language in the classroom. Alternatively, it could be information about an exam technique or how to write an informal letter. Lessons then provide more opportunities for practice of language and skills development with the teacher there to support, correct and challenge the students as they complete tasks. Students can work on the same tasks, or work in groups on different tasks to ensure they work at a level suitable for them.

The flipped classroom is still a fairly new approach and so research on its efficacy is ongoing. Anecdotally, teachers who flip their classrooms believe that the approach allows students to become more independent in their learning. They learn how to learn. Rather than receive information in the classroom, they have to take more control and ensure they learn it outside the classroom, watching the video or re-reading written material several times if necessary. In class, they have time to ask the teacher questions if they still don't understand and choose when they need support. This autonomy motivates students and results in a higher level of engagement according to teachers. In terms of language learning, students can gain more practice time and receive more feedback from the teacher on performance.

Current best practices and methods

The following are the typical stages of a lesson when flipping the classroom.

1 Preparing the homework

Teachers can provide instruction through video or written material. These can be created by the teacher or sourced from an alternative source e.g. their coursebook or online. If teachers make videos, they are usually five to ten minutes long and comprise the teacher recording themselves with their device, standing at the board and explaining the language. Alternatively, a video can be made using screencasting software which allows voice recording over slides.

2 Students watch the video for homework

In the previous lesson, the teacher sets the classroom instruction task as homework, usually with an accompanying activity to check understanding. Students do the tasks at home. The task that checks understanding might be completed online as this allows the teacher to check understanding before the lesson and make adjustments to their lesson plan if students have found the language particularly easy or difficult. Alternatively students may bring the completed task on paper to discuss at the beginning of the lesson.

3 In class review

In the lesson, the teacher begins by checking students' understanding of the content of the video. It could be through checking answers to the homework task, oral questioning or a quick paired quiz. Students are given the opportunity to ask questions.

4 Practice, practice, practice

Students are then given several practice tasks to complete for the rest of the lesson while the teacher monitors and offers support. This practice might be individual at first as they complete written exercises. It can then be communicative as students work in pairs or groups to complete oral tasks. Fast finishers can move onto new tasks so that they are challenged. Weaker students can receive extra support such as prompts.

5 Reflection on performance

Finally, at the end of the lesson, students reflect on what they have learnt to help them identify progress and areas where they still need to improve. These reflections allow students to gain a greater understanding of their strengths and weaknesses, and encourage them to set achievable learning goals for future lessons.

Efficacy

Keeping track of learner progress is one way of finding out whether flipping the classroom is effective or not. This can be through progress tests – or speaking and writing tasks – to assess whether students are improving their use of language. It can also be through self-reflection. For example, you could ask students to feed back using questions such as the following, offering a ranking of 1–5 (1 = not, 5 = very). This can be via a questionnaire or orally in class.

- How useful are the materials you do at home in learning new language?
- How easy is this material to work with?
- How helpful is the extra time for practice in class?
- How helpful is the teacher's support when doing tasks?
- How much do you prefer this approach?
- Are you making more progress using this approach?

How does Gold Experience second edition help me with that?

Gold Experience provides the following resources that will help you to flip your classroom.

Grammar presentations

The Active Teach software contains presentation slides with step-by-step walkthroughs of the grammar points taught in each lesson. These can be used by the teacher in class, when explaining language, but they can also be printed out for students to read at home when flipping the classroom. The slides contain detailed information about the meaning, function and form of the target language with examples. There is a final task that checks students' understanding.

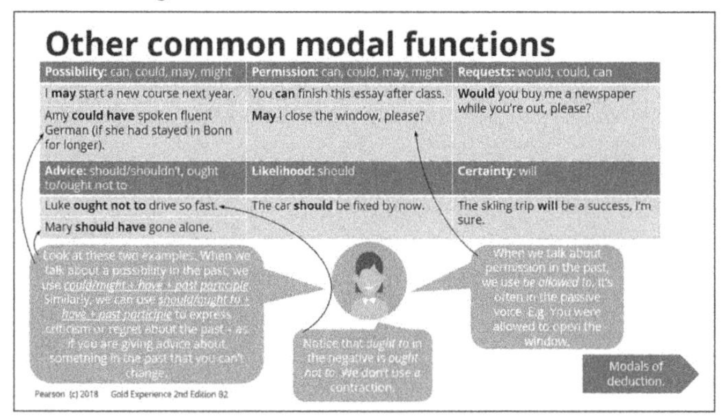

Workbook support

The workbook contains exercises on the grammar points taught in each unit. These can be used as homework prior to the Grammar lesson in order to check what learners already know. With students at this level, the grammar is unlikely to be completely new to them and so a test, teach, test approach can be used.

Alternatively, the workbook exercises can be completed in class to provide as much practice as possible while the teacher is available to offer support and clarify any confusing aspects of the language.

 **Read the sentences and choose the correct meaning.**

1 I'm starting Spanish lessons next term.
This **has already been planned / hasn't been planned yet**.

2 I'm sure you'll do well in the exam.
This is a **prediction / promise**.

3 When does your next class start?
The speaker wants to know about your **plans / timetable**.

Teacher's Book support

In the Teacher's Book, prior to a Grammar lesson, there are notes for the teacher on what materials are available when flipping the classroom.

Explain to students that the next lesson will focus on future forms. Ask them to complete the exercises in the Workbook in preparation for this.

To take it further ...

Here are some tips to help you to flip your classroom effectively:

Tip 1: If you create your own videos, personalise them

Just as we would try to personalise language in class when we clarify it for students, try to personalise it in videos too. For example, give a short anecdote about yourself using the target language. You can then use sentences from that anecdote to explain how the language is used, formed and pronounced.

Tip 2: Motivate student to want to complete the homework tasks

It's important that students complete the homework because if they don't, they'll find it difficult to complete the practice tasks in class. Pose a question and elicit answers but don't give the correct answer. Tell students that they have to do the homework task to find out. For example, before a lesson on future forms, write the following sentence on the board:

By the time we next see each other, you'll have all done your homework, won't you?!

Tell students that this sentence is clearly factually correct (!) but ask if it's grammatically correct.

If you make your own videos, engage students by teasing the context so that they want to know more and have to watch the video to find it out. Let's imagine that you tell a short anecdote in the video using the target language before explaining it. You could show a photo that represents the anecdote or tell the beginning of an anecdote but not the end. Elicit what the anecdote is but don't tell the students the correct answer. They do their homework to find out.

Tip 3: What to do when students don't do the homework

If possible, arrange for students who haven't done their homework to go to the back of the class and do it while the other students start to practise using it. Make technology available there if the homework is a video. Once students get into the habit of a flipped classroom, they tend to do the homework but even the best students sometimes forget or are unable to.

Tip 4: What to do when students don't have the technology

Try to arrange for all students to have access to any online material they need do the homework after school or before school if not everyone in the class has a device or internet access at home. Alternatively, create study pairs or groups where at least one student has a device and can watch the video with someone who does not.

Tip 5: Help learners to become more independent in their learning

As discussed in the section *Independent learning*, students often need to be trained to work independently. To help them do this, make learning goals clear so they know why they are doing the homework before the language lesson and how it will help them. At the end of the lesson, encourage students to reflect on their performance in the lesson so they can identify progress and recognise strengths and weaknesses. This can help them to set personalised learning goals and progress more quickly.

HOW TO ENCOURAGE INDEPENDENT LEARNING

What is it and why is it important?

Independent learning is 'a process, a method and a philosophy of education whereby a learner acquires knowledge by his or her own efforts and develops the ability for enquiry and critical evaluation' (Philip Candy, 1991). In a language learning context, independent learners are those who are able to recognise their learning needs, locate relevant information about language and develop relevant language skills on their own or with other learners. The responsibility for learning is no longer with the teacher but with the learner, who is more actively involved in decision-making.

Reviews of both literature and research suggest that independent learning can result in the following:

- Increased recognition of strengths, weaknesses and progress
- Increased levels of confidence
- Increased motivation
- Better management of learning
- Improved performance

It therefore appears that being an independent learner can be extremely beneficial for students, both at school and beyond. Learning is of course lifelong.

All of us can identify students in our classes who are already quite independent. They have a good understanding of what they are doing in their lessons and why, what their needs are and how to meet those needs. They build on what they learn in class by working independently outside the classroom and are able to achieve appropriate goals. However, many students lack the skills they need to be able to do this and need the opportunity to learn them with the support and encouragement of their teacher. These skills include cognitive skills (i.e. thinking skills), meta-cognitive skills (i.e. an ability to describe how they learn) and affective skills (i.e. management of their feelings) (Meyer et al, 2008).

Current best practices and methods

To help students become more independent, teachers can support them in a number of ways.

Make intended learning goals clear to learners

Sharing intended learning goals with a class helps students to see what they are trying to achieve and then later assess whether they have achieved it. Sharing goals can be done at the beginning of a lesson or series of lessons, or as a lesson progresses. They can be given by the teacher or, if the latter, elicited from the students. Note that they are described as *intended* learning goals. This is because teachers cannot fully determine what students will actually learn in a lesson. However, an intended learning goal can help students to understand what desired goals should be when working towards an advanced level of English.

Help learners to personalise learning goals

This does not mean that every learner will be working on a different goal in each lesson but instead that they are given the opportunity to set goals relevant to their own needs before working outside the classroom or when doing tasks in the classroom. For example, before completing an exam task in a speaking lesson, students could set their own goal in relation to an area of weakness e.g. *In this task, my goal is to speak more fluently/use a wider range of vocabulary/use the third conditional accurately.*

Focus on the process as well as the goal

Learners understand not just what their learning goal is but also how to achieve it. Understanding what success looks like and the process they need to follow in order to be successful will provide them with a greater ability to achieve the goal.

Provide opportunities for reflection on learning

Self- and peer assessment of performance, as well as reflection on whether learning goals have been met, all help students to become more aware of their strengths, weaknesses and progress. Recognition of progress helps to build confidence and motivation. Opportunities for assessment and reflection need not take too much time. Just two minutes after a task or at the end of a lesson answering the question '*What can you do better now that you couldn't at the start of the lesson?*' can give students time to develop important meta-cognitive skills.

Provide feedback on learning

'Feedback is one of the most powerful influences on learning and achievement' (Hattie & Timperley, 2007) and it is certainly something considered to be important in helping learners to develop the skills they need to become independent. Feedback does not only have to come from the teacher though. Peers can often provide useful feedback and suggestions when encouraged to do so in a supportive and sensitive manner. Hattie & Timperley suggest that for feedback to be effective, it must help learners to understand where they are now in their learning, where they are going and how to get there.

Gradually transfer learning decisions to students

Students cannot become independent learners if all of their learning decisions are made for them. Allowing students in a class the opportunity to make some decisions about how they learn gives them a greater level of autonomy. Start with small decisions at first, for example asking students to decide whether to

- do a task alone or in pairs;
- use a set of useful phrases for support or not in a speaking task;
- discuss questions about one topic or a different topic.

This devolvement of responsibility built up over time will help learners to become more independent.

Of course, as with any approach or strategy that you introduce, it is always beneficial to receive some feedback from learners during and at the end of a course to find out if they have been helpful. We could ask our students to rate the following according to how useful they have been (1 = not useful, 5 = very useful) or rank them according to which they have found the most useful (1 = most helpful).

- Clarity of learning goals.
- Self-reflection opportunities.
- Ability to personalise learning goals.
- Feedback on learning from the teacher.
- Ability to make some decisions about the learning process.

Their ratings/rankings can then be a springboard for further discussion.

How does Gold Experience second edition help me with that?

Gold Experience provides a number of resources that will help you to develop more independent learners.

Clear learning goals and models for success

Learning goals for each skill are outlined at the beginning of each unit in both the Student's Book and Teacher's Book. These describe what the student will be able or better able to do at the end of the lesson.

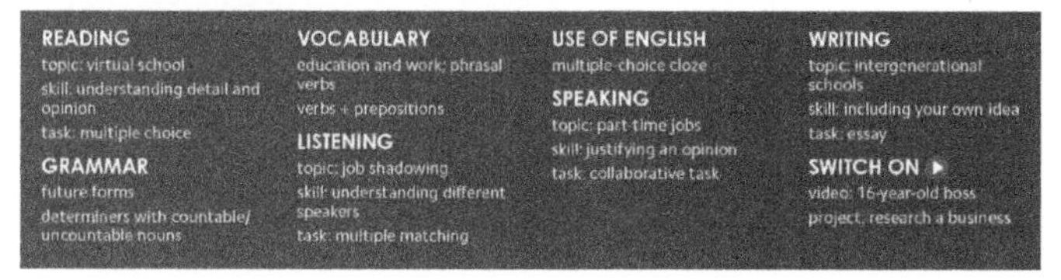

An independent learning section

At the end of each unit is a dedicated section that helps students to become more independent learners. The tasks help students to understand the benefit of self-reflection and encourage them to give better feedback to peers. They help students – and you – to better understand themselves as learners. They also prompt a greater understanding of strengths and weaknesses which then helps students to set realistic, useful, personalised goals.

> **2** Work in pairs. Compare the essays that you both wrote. Are they similar or different? Why? What tips would you give each other for the next essay that you write?

A focus on process

To help students identify good practice in speaking and writing tasks, the Student's Book provides model answers and tasks that encourage students to analyse the answers to better understand how to complete them successfully. Analysis focuses on approach, content and language. The Speaking file and Writing file give further tips on the process and how to achieve success in speaking and writing exam tasks.

Improve it sections in Writing lesson

In each Writing lesson, the *Improve it* section helps students to review work and make improvements. Scaffolded tasks help students to develop the skills they need to do this effectively.

> **11** When you've written your essay, read it carefully and check that you have:
> 1 included all the points in your notes.
> 2 answered the question in the title.
> 3 written well structured paragraphs with clear ideas.

Project work

In each unit there is a group project. These help the students to develop creative skills, and to make decisions about the learning process and how they complete the project.

> **5** Work in groups to prepare a presentation on food in world festivals.
> 1 Research festivals around the world that involve preparing and eating particular foods.
> 2 Choose one festival and create a class presentation.
> 3 Present your work to the class.
> 4 Discuss as a class which festivals you would like to go to.

Resources for self-study

There are a number of resources to help learners to achieve their goals. These can be used in class if the teacher wants to allocate part of a lesson to self-study or they can be used at home. They include:

- A Wordlist at the end of each unit in the Student's Book
- An Extended Vocabulary section at the back of the Student's Book
- Speaking, Writing and Grammar file sections at the back of the Student's Book
- The Workbook
- MyEnglishLab/Online World activities
- Flipped classroom tasks in the Teacher's Book

To take it further ...

Try these activities to help your students become independent learners.

1 Confidence scale

Write the intended learning goal of the lesson on the board (e.g. *understand implied meanings in an academic article*) and draw a confidence scale like the one below. Ask students to note down the number that reflects how confident they are that they can achieve that goal now. Monitor and assess the confidence levels of the class. At the end of the lesson, ask students to assess their confidence levels again, writing the new number next to the old one. Again, monitor confidence levels. In some cases they might go down! Finally, ask students to work in pairs and discuss how they can gain further confidence.

Not confident				Very confident
1	2	3	4	5

2 Selecting the feedback focus

Before students complete a writing task, ask them to identify a personal learning goal e.g. *I'd like to write an essay that is structured effectively*. Encourage them to look back at your feedback on previous written work to help them identify this. Tell them to write this goal at the top of their work when they submit it and that you will provide feedback specifically on that goal when you mark it.

3 Record and reflect

Ask students to use their mobile phone to record themselves completing a speaking task so they can listen back and compare their performance to a model answer. Recording apps are usually free to download or are pre-loaded onto a smartphone.

4 Written feedback

When marking a students' work, provide one comment under each of these headings to help learners identify where they are in their learning now, where they need to go next and how to get there, as well as recognise that they have made progress to boost students' confidence.

A key strength | *An area to work on*
An area of progress | *How you can work on it*

HOW TO TEACH WITH PROJECTS

The benefits

Projects involve students working together to produce something in English. They can require students to research and present information, create something or design something. Students might do two or all of these things. For example, students imagine they are influential bloggers who have decided to promote a product or brand. They choose the product/brand, research it, create a digital marketing campaign and present it to the group.

Projects in the English language classroom provide several benefits:

1 Authentic use of language

Students work on an authentic task which requires them to use English authentically. Projects also often develop all four skills: reading, writing, listening and speaking.

2 Development of personal skills

Projects require learners to collaborate, enabling them to develop skills such as the ability to cooperate, solve problems and communicate.

3 Development of autonomy

As project work involves students making decisions about how to achieve their learning objective, they are able to develop learner autonomy with support and guidance from their teacher.

4 Development of thinking skills

Students can develop information literacy and media literacy when doing research online, determining what information is useful, biased, misinformed, etc. They can also develop critical thinking skills when analysing that information, evaluating it and deciding how to use it.

5 Development of creativity

Many projects require learners to be creative in some way. Creativity, along with collaboration, communication and critical thinking skills are considered to be key skills for 21st century learning.

6 Increased motivation

Project work can provide a break from lessons which have a very specific language or skills focus. In addition to that, all of the other benefits mentioned here can make project work motivating for students.

It is important to note that while project work provides many development opportunities, students are likely to need support in exploiting those opportunities, such as advice from their teacher on how to work independently or feedback on their communication skills.

How to extend Gold Experience projects

At the end of each unit in Gold Experience, there is a Switch on lesson which provides video input and listening tasks followed by a project task. The listening tasks and project can be completed in one lesson, or students can work on them over a longer period of time, e.g. one lesson a week over a month plus homework. By extending the project, students can more fully benefit from it.

Below is the project task from Unit 1.

5 Work in groups to prepare a presentation on food in world festivals.

1. Research festivals around the world that involve preparing and eating particular foods.
2. Choose one festival and create a class presentation.
3. Present your work to the class.
4. Discuss as a class which festivals you would like to go to.

To expand the project over a longer period of time, you could do the following:

Week 1

In class

Students watch the video and complete the listening tasks. Students are put into pairs and set the homework task (see below).

Homework

Each student researches festivals that they have never heard of or do not know well and takes notes.

Week 2

In class

Students share their research with their partners. Pairs then select the one festival they are most interested in.

Homework

Students go away and do more research on the festival they have selected. They take notes. They plan a blog post about the festival.

Week 3

In class

Pairs work together and write their blog posts with feedback from you as they write. Pairs swap blog posts with another pair.

Homework

Students read the other pair's blog post and provide written feedback on it e.g. Is the information organised clearly? Are the festivals explained clearly? Is the language easy to follow?

Week 4

In class

Pairs work together and give each other oral feedback and suggestions on their blog posts. They then edit their own posts. They share them online when finished.

Homework

Students read each other's blog posts and decide which festival is the most interesting.

In class

Students vote on their favourite blog post and discuss why.

HOW TO TEACH WITH READERS

The benefits

Readers are books based on well-known stories which are designed for language learners. They allow learners to read at a level appropriate for them, whether that is A1 or C1. Stories include modern classics, contemporary fiction, short stories and plays. Readers allow learners to read extensively, in contrast to the intensive reading usually done in class. There are questions which help learners to check their comprehension as they read. There is also a wordlist and additional teacher support materials to help teachers create interesting lessons based around readers. Readers come with or without an audio CD.

There are many benefits to students using readers in the English language classroom.

1 Authenticity

Although readers are simplified for different levels of learners, the stories remain authentic as they are based on existing books or films.

2 Skills development

No matter what their level, students can develop all four skills. Students predominantly develop reading skills but they can also develop their listening skills through the use of the audio CD. They can develop speaking and writing skills through classroom or homework tasks and activities.

3 Language input

Students receive language input at a level appropriate to them. They consolidate their existing knowledge of language by seeing it in action. They can also develop their vocabularies by seeing new language. Extra practice materials in the books can help students to notice new vocabulary.

4 Development of autonomy

Students can be encouraged to make decisions about their learning by selecting the book they want to read, deciding when to read it, how often to read it, what kind of vocabulary to note down, etc. When reading takes place outside the classroom learners develop independence.

5 Motivation

When readers have the right book, they are motivated to spend time developing their language skills, whether that is in or outside the classroom. Learners can enjoy using their English skills to experience another time and place, or see the world from a different perspective. The sense of accomplishment when finishing a book in English can help them to recognise their progress in English, as well as motivate them to continue their studies.

How to exploit Readers

There are many ways that readers can be exploited in class. Here are a few of those ideas:

- Students read and summarise a chapter for another student in the class.
- Students note down useful vocabulary and teach it to another student.
- Students write a social media feed from the perspective of one of the characters in the book.
- Students roleplay an interview with one of the characters in the book.
- Students make predictions about what will happen as they read.
- Students write the dialogue for and act out the scene from a book.
- Students write a review of the book.
- Students write a comparison of the book and the film.

Selecting Readers

There are benefits and drawbacks to asking a class to read the same book and encouraging students to choose a book for themselves. With the former, the class can participate more easily in activities based on that book as everyone is reading the same thing. The teacher can create wonderful lessons that encourage analysis, discussion and creation based on that book. However, encouraging students to select a book of their choice may result in more motivation to read that book, as not everyone in the class will have the same interests.

Pearson readers can be found at https://readers.english.com/. On this page you can find access to the catalogue of books as well as sample teaching resources which accompany readers.

Level 5 books are those appropriate for B2 learners, while level 6 books are those appropriate for C1 level learners. You may want to recommend a book such as John Grisham's *The Testament* (level 6), a legal thriller, to the core of the class. Weaker readers may benefit from a more challenging level 5 book such as Charles Dicken's *A Tale of Two Cities*, a drama set during the French Revolution. Stronger readers may prefer Victor Hugo's *Les Misérables* (level 6), about the struggles of Jean Valjean, an ex-convict.

Wake up your senses! 1

READING
topic: trying new things
skill: referencing clues
task: gapped text

GRAMMAR
present tenses
comparative forms: adjectives and adverbs

VOCABULARY
describing experiences and feelings
phrasal verbs
suffixes; introduction to collocations

LISTENING
topic: synaesthesia
skill: listening for specific information
task: sentence completion

USE OF ENGLISH
word formation

SPEAKING
topic: comparison of experiences
skill: comparing photos
task: long turn

WRITING
topic: activities for teens
skill: opinion and recommendation
task: review

SWITCH ON
video: chef tests
project: presentation on food in world festivals

Lead-in SB p7

Read through the Unit Overview before starting the unit. This will give you information about what topics, themes, language points and skills will be focused on in the unit, as well as particular exam preparation and practice. This will be of main benefit to you while preparing your lessons. If you have students who like to know what they will have covered by the end of the unit, you may wish to read through it with them. For students who are preparing for the exam, point out that the items labelled 'task' will give exam-style practice.

The lead-in page allows you to introduce the topic of the unit to your class, and to find out what students know about the topic.

Focus students' attention on the photograph on page 7 and ask the following questions. *What does it show? What is the person doing? How might they be feeling?*

Read the quotation *I love the buzz of doing something for the first time!* Check understanding of the word *buzz* (a feeling of excitement). Ask the class what gives people *a buzz* and give some examples, like *praise for something you've done, an achievement, being driven in a fast car*, etc.

Put students into small groups to discuss the questions. Encourage them to give examples or reasons when answering. Monitor and contribute to the discussions. Ask someone from each group to report back to the class.

Possible answers

1 Visiting a new country or a new city gives me a buzz. It's always exciting to see new things, try new food and meet different kinds of people.
2 I think it's very important to try new things. If we don't, then we just get into a pattern of doing the same things all the time, and then we never learn anything new or grow.

READING SB p8–9

To start

Tell students some things you enjoy doing (for example, reading books, cooking, playing tennis). Put students into small groups to list some of their favourite activities. Then ask someone from each group to report their lists to the class. Collate their results on the board and ask students: *Which of these activities would you like to try? Which would you not like to try?* Encourage students to give reasons.

Tell students that the topic of this lesson is trying new activities, and the aim of the lesson is to complete an exam-style gapped text task.

Power up

1 Ask students to look at the photo. Elicit a description of what the person is doing. Students then discuss these questions in pairs. *1 How do you think the person feels? 2 Would you enjoy the experience? 3 What would the challenges be?* Elicit responses from the class.

Possible answers

The activity in the photo shows someone with a backpack, and it looks like she's been camping in the wild.

1 I think she feels relaxed and free in the countryside. She seems to be enjoying the open space and fresh air.
2 I would enjoy wild camping because I like being in the fresh air. I have done a lot of camping and think it's fun to cook and live outdoors. It's also good not to rely on technology for a while.
3 I think for some people they may not like the dark at night and they may not know how to light a fire. I don't like not having hot water to wash myself every day, but it's OK if you only camp for a few days.

Ask students to compare the photo with the photo on page 7 and discuss the questions in pairs. Elicit a few responses.

Possible answers

1 I think both activities suit people who enjoy being active and outdoors.
2 I like the idea of the zip wire because I've never done it before. I'm not scared of heights and I like sporty activities, so I think I'd enjoy it.
3 I think the camping is more challenging because it lasts overnight and you have to live in the wild. It can be tough camping in the wild when the weather is bad and you get very wet and cold.

Read on

2 Write *a challenge* on the board and elicit the meaning of the word (something that is difficult to try or do). Ask students to read the title and introduction to the blog on page 8 and ask: *What do you think the 7 Day Challenge is?* Check understanding of *step out of our comfort zones* (do something that we would not normally do because it is difficult, or outside our experience).

Ask students to read the rest of the blog to check their ideas. Give them a time limit of 1–2 minutes depending how strong your class is. Tell them that some sentences are missing from the blog (gaps 1–6), but they should ignore these for the moment.

The *7 Day Challenge* is a challenge in which you encourage your friends to try activities they've never tried before.

exam tip

3 Explain this exam task to the class. Six sentences are removed from a text and they have to choose which ones are missing from a list of seven (including one that they do not need). If your class is strong ask: *What do you think can help you find the right sentences?* Then read through the first part of the exam tip with the class (not the final section yet). Check if any students had the right ideas. Give examples of referencing clues (time words such as *before, after, then, later,* etc. and pronouns such as *it, she, he, them,* etc.). Explain that as well as looking for these referencing clues in the gapped text, they should also look for them in the list of sentences.

Ask students to read through sentences A–G in Ex 4 and underline any referencing clues. Ask them to work with a partner to decide which sentence fits gap 1. Elicit the sentence they chose and the reasons why.

1 E *She had a point as we never sign up for anything new.* *She* refers to Sophia who is the person who makes the comment that comes directly before the space. Then, *we* refers to the three friends. The fact that they never sign up for anything new follows on from the idea that they are always moaning about having a dull life.

exam task: gapped text

In the Cambridge exam the reading text does not have a detailed lead-in. Here there is a lead-in to interest and engage the students.

The equivalent reading task in the Cambridge exam does not have a gapped sentence in paragraph 1.

4 **e** Ask students to complete the exam task. Remind them that there will be some unknown vocabulary, but they should not focus on this as the context should make the meanings clear, and that finding the correct answers will not usually depend on understanding single unfamiliar words. If students are at a lower level, allow them to check their answers in pairs before you elicit answers from the class.

2 G *It hasn't actually been that difficult* refers to what is expressed in the previous sentence: *We each come up with an activity we enjoy, but that the other two friends haven't tried before. We* and *close friends* in G refer to *we* in the previous sentence.
3 B *Rob doesn't actually get the part* refers back to the audition challenge set by Sophia, described earlier in this paragraph; *at least he's brave enough to go through with it* compares Rob's bravery in having a go at the difficult challenge with the narrator's own reaction which was not at all brave, described in the previous three sentences – *it's too overwhelming. I leg it … I've fallen at the first hurdle.*

READING (Continued)

4 F *it's not an idea with huge appeal* refers to wild camping, as described in the previous sentence: *not pitching your tent anywhere near a toilet or hot shower*. The writer wouldn't like having no toilet or hot shower as he is someone who *loves his creature comforts*. The following sentence in the blog, *But it's only for one night so I'm willing to give it a go* contrasts with the narrator's dislike of these conditions.
5 A *Once there* refers to arriving at the lake mentioned in the previous sentence. The following sentence about how the people enjoyed cooking and chatting by the lake continues and expands on the idea expressed in A: *I kind of relax into it and my initial reservations start to disappear*.
6 C Sentence C is a summary of the writer's overall positive feelings so far about the challenge, and answers the question before it: *So is the '7 Day Challenge' a worthwhile experience?*

extra: fast finishers 

Ask fast finishers to underline two more sentences that could be removed from the text. Then they should circle any referencing clues in the sentences before and after the 'gapped' sentence, as well as in the sentence they want to gap. This will help give them a better idea of how referencing words connect sentences together.

5 **Put students into pairs to find the words and phrases in the blog. For weaker students, you could divide the list in half and ask different pairs to check for either the first five or the second five items. Elicit answers from the class.**

1 cosy **2** dull **3** nerve-racking **4** overwhelming **5** willing **6** reluctantly **7** pretty **8** worthwhile **9** pigeonhole **10** dismiss

extra: fast finishers 

Ask students to choose three words or phrases and write sentences which include them. However, instead of writing the word or phrase in the sentence, they should leave a gap. Then ask them to swap with another student, who should try and guess what the gapped word or phrase is.

extra 

Give students a chance to check some other unfamiliar phrases from the blog. Put students into small groups. Write these phrases on the board:
1 shy away from
2 take on
3 come across
4 put off by
Students find the items in the blog and discuss what each one means by looking at the context they appear in. Monitor and help where necessary. Elicit answers from the class (1 avoid because of difficulty; 2 accept or agree to do something; 3 find by chance; 4 to be discouraged).

Sum up

6 **Read sentence C again with the class: *OK, I know it's early days, but so far I've found our challenge fun and actually a bit of an eye-opener*. Ask students to write, in one or two sentences, why Tom found the experience an 'eye-opener'. Ask them to compare their ideas in small groups and to choose whose idea summarises the answer best. Elicit each group's best ideas, and ask the class to vote on their favourite.**

Possible answer

Tom describes the experience as being an 'eye opener' because it has made him realise that some things that he thought weren't 'typically him' were really enjoyable. It has made him realise how you shouldn't pigeonhole yourself or others, and that you should be more open-minded about trying new things.

Speak up

7 **Put students into small groups to discuss the questions. Monitor to encourage students to put forward their ideas. This is a fluency activity so do not overcorrect them while they are speaking, but note down common mistakes which you can deal with later.**

Ask students to report their ideas back to the class. Encourage students to notice what similarities and differences there are between each group's ideas.

Possible answers

1 I like to set myself challenges, because I think it's important to have goals.

2 Trying a new sport, like surfing or mountain climbing would make me feel a bit uncomfortable, because I've never done anything like that before, and I think they might be dangerous.

3 I tried riding a motorbike recently. I thought it would be easy, because I know how to ride a bike. But it was completely different, and I realised it will take me a long time before I can ride one properly.

Fun footer

Read the footer with the class and elicit what it means (we need challenges to be able to progress, change or move forward). Ask students to give their own examples of something difficult they have done, which has changed them for the better.

To finish

Ask students to work in small groups to think of a challenge. Point out that it should have a positive effect on the people taking part, for example *Try a day without using your smartphone* or *Give up meat for one week*.

Go round the class and help with ideas. Ask groups to share their ideas with the class, and explain why other people should take up their challenge. Ask the class to vote on the best challenge and, if appropriate, suggest students try it and report back later on how they felt doing the challenge.

Presentation tool: Unit 1, Reading
Workbook / Online Practice: pp4–5
Extra Practice App

GRAMMAR SB p10

To start

Use the start of the lesson to assess students' existing knowledge of the target grammar point. Tell students a fact about yourself, which may be true or false, for example, *I usually have three cups of coffee at breakfast.* Students have to guess if it is true or false. Write some more sentences about yourself on the board, some true, some false. In your sentences, use the present simple and the present continuous rather than other verb forms.

Students guess whether the sentences are true or false. Give feedback, and then ask students to write similar sentences about themselves for their partners to guess whether they are true or not. Elicit some of the students' true sentences and write them on the board. Underline the present tenses in the sentences and elicit the names of the tenses. Elicit that we use the present simple for habits, facts and repeated actions, and that we use the present continuous for actions happening now.

1 Focus on the uses of the present simple and continuous and ask students to check rules A, B and C against their previous ideas. Then read through rule D with the class and explain that although we usually use past tenses to tell a story, if we want to be more dramatic, we can use present tenses.

Ask students to look again at the two sentences in Ex 1 and match them to the correct rules (E or F). Elicit the difference by asking: *Are we still deciding about the challenge?* (No, it's a finished activity.) *Are we still doing the challenge?* (Yes, the activity is still continuing.)

1 E **2** F

extra

Read the sentence in D and say it out loud, to show how using present tenses add dramatic interest. Write another example on the board: *I went home last night. I opened the door. It was windy and the door shut quickly. It hit me on the head and I fell down. My friend was watching me. He didn't do anything. He just laughed!* Elicit how this can be rephrased using present tenses: *I go home. I open the door. It's windy and the door shuts quickly. It hits me on the head and I fall down. My friend is watching me. He doesn't do anything. He just laughs!* Model for students to repeat for dramatic effect. Students write their own stories in pairs to tell each other in small groups.

explore grammar ➥ SB p142

2 Students complete the sentences in rules E and F with the correct verb form. If necessary, check students understand how the present perfect simple is used. Ask: *Do we know when we saw the film?* (No.)

With a lower-level class, remind students that we often use *for* and *since* with the present perfect continuous. Write the following examples on the board: *I've been watching this film <u>for</u> an hour* (a period of time). *I've been watching this film <u>since</u> 8.30* (a point in the past).

1 've (have) seen **2** 's (has) been teaching

The Grammar file covers present tenses, in their simple and continuous aspects. Get students to read the explanations on page 142 and complete Exs 1–3 on page 143. Organise fast finishers into pairs. Ask them to discuss something new they have started in the recent past, what they do now, and what effects it is having.

watch out for

Remind students that some verbs cannot be used with the continuous tenses if they describe states: *I've <u>had</u> the red car since 2017* (not ~~*I've been having*~~ …); *I've known James since we were children* (not ~~*I've been knowing*~~ …).

extra

Tell students three things you have done so far this morning, for example: *I've taught two English classes. I've spoken to the head teacher. I've marked ten essays.* Elicit students' own examples from the class.

Then elicit some things that you (and they) have been doing in the lesson since it started. For example, *We've been learning about present tenses for half an hour.*

3 1.1 Read through the questions with the class. Then play the recording. Students discuss their answers in pairs. Elicit the answers and ask students to give reasons.

Speaker 1: D
Speaker 2: A
Speaker 3: B
Speaker 4: C

4 1.2 With a strong group, ask students to work in pairs to complete the sentences, before playing the recording. With a weaker group, play the recording and ask students to complete the sentences with what they hear. After conducting class feedback, put students into pairs to discuss the questions in Ex 3.

1 've sold, 're moving **2** 're embarking **3** know
4 depends, don't **5** don't do

5 Focus students on the title of the text, as well as the picture, and ask what they think a *gut feeling* is (an instinct, rather than a logical thought). Point out that *gut* is another word for *stomach.* Explain that they need to complete the text with the correct present form of the verbs in the box. Elicit suggestions for the first gap before asking students to complete the task individually. Conduct class feedback.

1 Have, had **2** 's **3** is sending **4** doesn't feel **5** has, said
6 call/have called **7** have **8** have been trying
9 has found **10** don't spend

GRAMMAR (Continued)

Speak up

6 Put students into pairs to discuss different situations. Then, put pairs with other pairs to compare their answers. Conduct feedback with the whole class.

Possible answers

We often have a gut feeling when something is wrong, or something bad might happen. I think it's best to follow these feelings. For example, if you meet someone, and you don't trust them, then you should trust your instincts instead, even if they're very well-dressed or polite.

Fun footer

As a follow-up to Ex 6, read through the quote in the fun footer. Ask students whether following a gut feeling is always a good idea.

game on

Read through the task with the class and give students five minutes to write down their statements, individually. Then put students into small groups to play the game. Go round and monitor for correct use of the present perfect simple and continuous.

To finish

Tell students you are a famous person and they must guess who you are. Give them some information using grammar structures from the lesson, for example: *I'm a singer. I'm in a band. We go on tour a lot. I'm English but I've been living in the USA for a long time. I've made lots of albums. At the moment I'm working on ....*

Ask students to think of a famous person, or someone in the news at the moment. Give them some time to think about or write similar information about this person. In pairs, they give their partner the information for them to guess the person.

extra

Ask students to go online to research someone they admire. They should note down some facts about this person's life at the moment, and about their experiences, and then write a short profile, summarising who the person is and what he or she does. Point out that students should try to use all the present tenses covered in this lesson. In the next lesson, students can present the profile to the group, or hand it in to you to check their use of present tenses.

Presentation tool:	Unit 1, Grammar
Workbook / Online Practice:	p6
Photocopiable activity:	1A
Grammar reference and practice:	SB p142
Audioscript:	SB p175

VOCABULARY SB p11

describing experiences and feelings

To start

Tell students about an experience you have had recently and how you felt at the time. For example, *I lost a favourite earring and I was really upset.* Ask students to work in pairs and think of experiences they have had recently and an adjective to describe how they felt. They can talk about positive or negative feelings. Nominate a few students to say what adjectives they used to talk about feelings.

1 1.3 Focus students' attention on the words in the box. Model the pronunciation of the words for students to repeat chorally and individually. With a strong group, play the recording for them to choose the adjective that best describes the feelings of each person. With a weaker group, elicit a definition of each adjective, then play the recording for them to match them with the speakers. You could also ask students to give other examples of situations when people might feel these different ways.

1 relieved **2** offended **3** sympathetic **4** petrified **5** determined **6** tense

2 Check understanding of *take a penalty* (have a free kick at goal after a rule has been broken in football), *give someone a hug* (put your arms round someone) and *make a speech* (talk for a period of time, usually at a formal occasion). Students complete the gaps individually and then compare answers in pairs. Conduct class feedback.

1 determined **2** tense **3** petrified **4** thrilled **5** moved **6** sympathetic **7** relieved **8** offended

3 Students match the words from Ex 2 with the synonyms.

anxious – tense
delighted – thrilled
insulted – offended
strong-willed – determined
terrified – petrified
understanding – sympathetic

4 In pairs, students ask and answer the question. Encourage them to use as many words from Ex 3 as they can.

Possible answers

I'm quite a strong-willed person. If I know I want to do something, then I'm usually determined to try and achieve it. Sometimes, I get tense or anxious if someone or something tries to stop me.

explore vocabulary

5 Write *Phrasal verb* on the board. Ask students to give you an example of a phrasal verb and elicit explanations of what a phrasal verb is. Then read through the explore vocabulary box with the class to check their ideas. Ask for more examples of phrasal verbs that students already know. Write them on the board and elicit their meanings from the rest of the class.

Possible answers

take on, turn out, come across

6 Ask students if they have been to an art gallery exhibition recently. Ask: *What it was about? Did you enjoy it?* Ask for suggestions of how art galleries could improve the experience for people. Write the words *smell / sound / touch* on the board and ask the question again. Ask students to read the article individually, ignoring the highlighted words, to answer the questions in Ex 6. Conduct class feedback.

Multisensory art exhibitions are exhibitions that try to stimulate all of our senses (touch, sight, hearing, taste and smell). The idea came from a desire to encourage more people, who would normally not go to art galleries, to come and enjoy art.

7 Read through the phrasal verbs in the box. Then ask students to replace the highlighted phrases in the article with the correct form of the phrasal verbs. Weaker students can do this in pairs. Conduct class feedback.

1 are put off **2** have missed out **3** have been trying out **4** add to **5** get across **6** is taking off

8 Ask students to complete the questions individually and then compare with a partner. Monitor and check weaker pairs. Students then continue and discuss the questions. Encourage students to give examples or reasons rather than give short answers. When all pairs have had the opportunity to discuss the questions, conduct class feedback to find out the most interesting or unusual answers.

1 add to **2** have missed out **3** put, off **4** are, taking off **5** get, across

Speak up

9 Check understanding of *sympathetic* (being understanding when someone is upset) and elicit some phrases we can use when we want to be sympathetic: *I'm so sorry. You must feel terrible. It's OK to be upset.* Read through the two questions with the class and ask students to discuss them in small groups. Conduct class feedback to find the most sympathetic people in the class.

Possible answers

1 I usually talk with friends. I find that talking about problems is the best way to deal with them.
2 I'm usually sympathetic, and I definitely try to understand what other people are thinking or feeling. The only times I don't feel sympathetic are when I think someone is in trouble because they've been selfish or lazy.

To finish

Put students into pairs. Ask them individually to choose what they think are the most useful or important five vocabulary items from this lesson. They then tell these items to their partner who has to write a sentence using each one to show the meanings clearly. Nominate a few students to tell the rest of the class what they thought the most useful or important items were.

extra: fast finishers

Ask students to write a short text or dialogue using as many phrasal verbs from the lesson as possible. You could make this a competition to see who can use the most items.

Presentation tool:	Unit 1, Vocabulary
Workbook / Online Practice:	p7
Photocopiable activity:	1B
Extend vocabulary:	SB p160
Audioscript:	SB p175
Extra Practice App	

LISTENING SB p12

To start

Organise students into small groups. Tell them they are going to talk about things they can sense or feel. Write these categories on the board: *Smell, Touch, See, Hear, Taste.*

Ask students to discuss things they like in each category, and things they dislike. They should say why. Give your own example first, for example, *I love the smell of freshly cut grass because it reminds me of summer.*

Power up

1 Read the activities with the class. Then ask students to discuss which senses might belong to each one. Ask for reasons and examples. Conduct class feedback and write their ideas on the board in the right columns.

Suggested answers

	smell	touch	sight	hearing	taste
learning to windsurf	sea salt	hard board / wet water	birds / blue sky	birds / waves	salt
talking to a friend	–	a friend's hand	a friend's face	a friend's voice	–
playing the guitar	–	strings, hard guitar	musical notes	music	–
going shopping	cleaning products, food, etc.	soft clothes, money, etc.	people, crowds, things to buy	people talking, music in shops	coffee when having a break

2 Focus students on the image of the boy wearing headphones. Elicit what the coloured shapes are, to the right of his head (musical notes). Write the word *synaesthesia* on the board. Ask students what they think it means. Encourage them to make guesses in relation to the subject of senses.

Listen up

3 1.4 Tell students that they will listen to a girl talking about her experiences of having a problem with one of her senses. Then play the recording and ask them for their ideas. Read them the definition below.

Synaesthesia is a medical condition which makes people experience a mixture of feelings from two of their five senses at the same time, for example seeing numbers as colours or experiencing colours as a smell.

exam tip

4 Read through the exam tip with the class. Look at gap 1 in Ex 5 together, and elicit the part of speech that is missing, and why.

Put students into pairs, to decide what kind of word should go in gaps 2–10. They should try explain their reasons to each other. Conduct feedback with the class and write their suggested answers on the board.

1 It's a noun or a noun phrase, because *the* comes before the gap.
2 noun or noun phrase – There is an indefinite article before the gap.
3 adjective – It's a word that tells you more about the type of music.
4 plural noun – It's talking about experiencing something and it must be plural because of the word 'different' before the gap.
5 plural noun – It must be a noun, probably connected with people, and it must be plural because of 'them'.
6 noun – It must be a period of time because of 'during'.
7 adjective – It's a word describing the type of subject.
8 adjective – It's an adjective describing types of painters and composers.
9 adjective – It's an adjective describing how she feels.
10 noun or noun phrase – It's an example of something that causes Rachel to lose concentration.

exam task: sentence completion

5 e 1.5 Play the recording and ask students to fill in the missing words individually. Then they should compare their answers in pairs, giving their reasons. They should also check one another's spelling, as the missing words should be spelt correctly. When they have finished checking, nominate one student to write the answers on the board. If students disagree, they should discuss why. Remind them that they must write the exact word they hear on the recording, and not a synonym, and that it must be grammatically correct in the sentence. Don't tell them if they are right or wrong at this point. Finally, play the recording a second time for them to confirm their answers.

1 name (frustratingly, I've only recently found out there's a name for my condition.)
2 magazine article (I was thrilled when I found a magazine article that summed up my own situation exactly.)
3 jazz (I often see bright red and yellow colours when I listen to rock music, but darker colours such as purple when I'm listening to Jazz.)
4 tastes (there are some people who experience different tastes when they hear certain sounds, which must be incredible.)
5 visitors (I used to make visitors laugh when I was younger – I used to enjoy telling them what colour their name was)
6 (early) childhood (experts believe that the condition begins in early childhood)
7 creative (people with synaesthesia are often not as good as our peers at subjects such as maths or science and our sense of direction is often worse too, but we're very creative.)
8 famous (What I wasn't aware of was the number of famous artists and musicians such as Van Gogh and Franz Liszt who had the condition)
9 stressed (If I'm feeling relaxed it's a nice experience, but if I feel very stressed, the sounds and colours feel much stronger.)

10 traffic	(Then it's hard to concentrate when I'm seeing the equivalent of fireworks produced by all the sounds of traffic around me.)

6 Tell students that the sentences come from the recording. Put them into small groups to decide what the highlighted words mean. Conduct class feedback. If they find it difficult to explain the meaning, ask them to think of other words with similar meanings.

1 *seminars* – a seminar is a meeting in which a group of people discuss a subject (I attended my first university seminar this morning.)
2 *approved* – to think that someone or something is good, right or suitable (My father never approved of me spending all my time playing football.)
3 *have concluded* – decide that something is true after doing some research (Scientists have concluded that bilingual children have an advantage over monolingual children.)
4 *Apparently* – used to say that you have heard that something seems to be true, although you do not have direct knowledge of it (Apparently, listening to classical music can make you more intelligent.)
5 *is affected by* – to cause a change in someone or something, or to change the situation they are in (My mood is affected by the weather.)
6 *gift* – a special ability or talent (My sister has a gift for languages.)

Speak up

7 Put students into pairs to discuss the two questions. Monitor their discussions and collect any useful vocabulary they use to share with the whole class later. Don't correct any minor grammatical errors you hear, as this is a fluency activity, but make a note of them to tell the whole class at the end of the activity along with the useful vocabulary. If there are recurring grammatical mistakes then leave them for a future class so that you can focus on them in more detail. When most pairs have finished, conduct class feedback and ask students to comment on other students' ideas.

Possible answers
1 I think sight is my most important sense. I would find it most difficult to live without it. I wouldn't be able to read, or watch anything. Perhaps smell is the least important. There aren't many situations where it's really necessary to smell something.
2 I would like to be able to strengthen my sight, so that I could see in the dark! Then I could read books without turning the light on!

extra

If appropriate for your class, ask: *Which of the five senses would be most difficult to live without?* Encourage them to give reasons, and to imagine how life would be without it.

For extra discussion practice, you could ask students to think of jobs in which the five senses might be important, and why. Suggestions include: chef (taste/smell); a wine taster (smell, taste, touch); a physiotherapist (touch), etc.

Fun footer

Read through the footer with the class and ask students whether they think the statistic is true. Ask them to give reasons to support their ideas.

To finish

Write the following sounds on the board: *a car horn, a door opening, a bird singing, fireworks exploding*. Then ask students to think about each sound, and try to decide what colour they think each sound is. Put them into pairs to discuss whether or not they have similar ideas.

You could also do the same by writing days of the week on the board and asking students which colour each day is.

Finally, ask students: *Do you believe synaesthesia is a common condition? Have you ever experienced it?*

Presentation tool:	Unit 1, Listening
Workbook / Online Practice:	p8
Audioscript:	SB p175
Extra Practice App	

USE OF ENGLISH 1 SB p13

To start

Give students an example of something you are better at than a member of your family. For example,

I can run much further and faster than my younger sister.

Then ask: *What can you do better than one of your family members?* Nominate a couple of students to answer the question.

1 Put students into pairs. Explain that they are going to use comparative forms. Focus their attention on the explore grammar box, and the examples. Point out that they all use different comparative structures, which are shown in bold. Ask them to do Ex 1. Conduct class feedback, and discuss any wrong answers.

1 better **2** most efficiently **3** too difficult **4** as fast **5** more relaxed **6** the funniest

explore **grammar** → SB p142

The Grammar file covers comparative adjectives and adverbs. Get students to read the explanations and complete Exs 4–6. Organise fast finishers into pairs. Ask them to check each other's spelling of the comparative adjectives and adverbs carefully, as students often make mistakes with this.

2 Ask students to discuss the questions in pairs. Write some follow-up questions on the board, and encourage them to extend their discussions: *Why is that? Can you explain why? How does that help you? Tell me more about it. Can you give me an example?* Point out that extending their discussions will help them to conduct conversations in the Speaking paper.

Possible answers

1 I can speak English better than my father, who doesn't speak any English. But my mother is an English teacher, so I'm nowhere near as good as her!
2 I study most efficiently in the evenings, because it's quiet and there's no-one around to disturb me.
3 I usually talk to other people in my class. Often, they're having the same problems as I am.
4 I'm not a very fast runner, so I think I'm the slowest out of all my friends.
5 Usually, listening to music, or just going to sleep is the best way to make me feel less stressed.
6 Marco is the funniest in our class, but sometimes the teacher asks him to be quiet!

3 Tell students they are going to read an article about sense. Read the title to them and ask: *What do you think the article will actually be about? Why?*

Ask students to read the article quickly to see whether they were right. Ask: *Do you agree with the article?* Tell them to work in pairs to complete the gaps in the article using comparative phrases from the box.

1 more upset **2** more accurately **3** not as good as **4** finer **5** the most debated **6** as well as **7** better **8** too

exam task: key word transformation

In the Cambridge exam the first item in the Key Word Transformation task is always an example. The equivalent tasks in this unit and others do not give an example as the teacher is present to advise.

The focus of this task is on comparative structures as this is looked at in the lesson. In the Cambridge exam a variety of structures is tested.

4 e Tell students that in the exam, they will have to rewrite sentences so that they have a similar meaning to each other, using a given word. They must not change this word, and should only use between two and five words. If they find that they are using more than five words, then their answer is incorrect.

Explain that it is also a useful skill to be able to say things in different ways in English. It helps students to use a range of structures and vocabulary in their writing and in their speaking.

Put students into pairs and ask them to finish the exercise. They should then compare their answers with another pair. Go through all the answers together, and discuss any that students got wrong or are not sure about. Remind students that contractions (*I've*, etc.) count as two words.

1 loudly enough for me to (*not* + adverb + *enough*)
2 was not as strong as (*not as* + adjective + *as*)
3 thinks more deeply than (*more* + two syllable adverb)
4 not interesting enough (*not* + adjective + *enough*)
5 can cook better than anyone/everyone (irregular comparative *better* + *than*)
6 strangest feeling I have/I've ever (regular one syllable adjective superlative + *than*)

alternative: mixed-ability classes 

Before doing the exercise, write this example on the board.

I play the guitar much better than my sister.

LESS

My sister .... than I do.

Ask students to suggest possible answers to complete the second sentence. Write all their suggestions on the board, then complete the second sentence correctly.

My sister plays the guitar less well than I do.

Point out the changes that have been made: *play* to *plays*, *better* to *well*.

Then go through the first example in Ex 4 with the class. Write up all their suggestions, then give them the correct answer. Remind them that if they can think of an answer that is more than five words, then it is not correct.

Speak up

5 Tell students about something you have tasted in the last 24 hours, like a meal, a snack, or a special cake. Then put students into pairs. Give each pair a sense to talk about. They should discuss what they think they have tasted, smelled, seen or heard. Nominate a few students to share their ideas with the rest of the class.

Possible answers

In the last 24 hours, I've been to the market. It was very busy and I heard all the people talking, and stallholders calling. We bought some meat and my parents cooked it at home. The smell filled the whole house. My brothers came home in the evening, and we chatted and laughed. When we ate the meal, it was delicious. We had the meat with vegetables and then had a sweet chocolate ice cream afterwards.

To finish

Remind students of the five senses, and ask students to think about which one is the most important. Then ask them to put the other senses in order, according to their importance. If they think some senses are equally important, then this is fine.

Put students into small groups to discuss which senses are more important than others, and to give reasons. Encourage them to use comparative adjectives and adverbs in their discussion.

Finally, find out which sense most students in the class think is most important.

Presentation tool:	Unit 1, Use of English 1
Workbook / Online Practice:	p9
Grammar reference and practice:	SB p142
Extra Practice App	

USE OF ENGLISH 2 SB p14

To start

Ask students to discuss the following questions in small groups: *Have you ever danced? What kind of dancing did you do? Do you still dance? Why did you stop? Would you like to dance? Do you think you would be good at dancing?*

1 1.6 Write the following expressions on the board. Ask students whether they think they are positive or negative (they are all negative).

- *I look a bit childish.*
- *I've got two left feet.*
- *I'm really dreadful.*

Point out that *to have two left* feet means that someone is clumsy, or bad at dancing. If something is *dreadful*, then it is very bad. Play the recording and ask them which student has a positive attitude and thinks they can dance well.

Speaker 2

explore **vocabulary 1**

2 Tell students that they're going to focus on word formation. Write the word *differ* on the board. Ask them if this is a verb, a noun or an adjective (a verb). Ask them what the noun form of this word is (*difference*). Point out that *-ence* is a suffix that we can add to some verbs to create a noun.

Go through the explore vocabulary box with the class. Then ask them to do Ex 2 in pairs. Conduct class feedback.

1 achievement **2** athletic **3** painful/painless **4** laziness
5 comfortable **6** excitement

watch out for

Students may have problems with spelling. For example, a *y* at the end of a word may change to an *i* when we add a suffix. In the exam all words need to be spelt correctly, so encourage students to pay attention to their spelling. Suggest that they keep a record of words they often spell incorrectly.

3 1.7 Organise the class into three groups. They should all listen to all three speakers, but give each group only one of the speakers to concentrate on. Play the recording again, and ask students to tick the words in the box that they hear for their speaker. They should check their answers in their groups before you conduct class feedback. Point out that *confident, difference, painful* and *painless* are not used.

Speaker 1: confidence, childish, competitive
Speaker 2: fitness, comfortable, movement
Speaker 3: hopeless, dreadful, visible

USE OF ENGLISH 2 (Continued)

extra

As a follow-up activity, ask the three groups to think of other forms of their three words.

- *confidence* – *confident* (noun – adjective), *childish* – *child* (adjective – noun), *competitive* – *compete* (adjective – verb)
- *fitness* – *fit* (noun – adjective), *comfortable* – *comfort* (adjective – noun), *movement* – *move* (noun – verb)
- *hopeless* – *hope* (adjective – noun/verb), *dreadful* – *dread* (adjective – noun/verb), *visible* – *visibility* (adjective – noun)

4 Read the title of the article with the class. Elicit reasons why some people can't dance. Ask: *Are you interested in dancing? Do you think it's possible to teach someone how to dance well?* Then put students into pairs to discuss the questions in Ex 4.

Possible answers

My sister is a good dancer. She's been learning since she was four years old, and she's already won some competitions. I can't dance at all. I've got no sense of rhythm. I prefer just watching other people.

exam task: word formation

In the Cambridge exam the first item in the Word Formation is always an example. The equivalent tasks in this unit and others do not give an example as the teacher is present to advise.

The word forms tested here all involve suffixes, as this is the focus of the lesson. In the Cambridge exam there would be a greater variety of word forms.

5 **e** Go through the exam tip with the class, and remind students of the importance of reading the whole sentence and not just looking at the gap before they decide on the form of the word. Focus students' attention on the first gap in the article, and ask what type of word might be missing, and why.

A noun, because it is preceded by *the*.

Do the first gap as a class. Then ask students to finish the task in pairs. Conduct class feedback and discuss any answers they are unsure of. Check that students know all the vocabulary in the text and point out some useful collocations: *sense of rhythm, tap your feet, clap your hands.*

1 enthusiasm (adjective to noun)
2 impressive (verb to adjective)
3 deafness (adjective to noun)
4 ability (adjective to noun)
5 difficulty/difficulties (adjective to noun)
6 scientific (noun to adjective)
7 foolish (noun to adjective)
8 fashionable (noun to adjective)

explore vocabulary 2

6 Go through the explore vocabulary box and point out that *sense of achievement, sense of adventure*, etc. are all common collocations with the word *sense*. Ask students to discuss the question in pairs. Conduct class feedback and identify the sense that is most important to most people in the class, and why.

Possible answer

A sense of humour is the most important to me. It's important to be able to laugh at things, and make other people laugh. It's also important to be able to laugh at yourself. People shouldn't be so serious all the time.

Speak up

7 Put students into pairs to discuss the questions. Conduct class feedback.

Possible answers

1 Someone with a sense of adventure probably loves travelling, or doing exciting sports like sailing or mountaineering – something which is fun but a little bit dangerous.
2 My father has a great sense of humour. Not everyone thinks he's funny, but I do. He's always telling jokes, and finding the funny side of things.
3 I usually get a sense of achievement when I've set myself a goal, and then worked hard to reach it. I feel proud that I've managed to plan for something, and then get there in the end.
4 My sense of direction is pretty good. I don't usually get lost, but maybe that's because I know how to use a map. I wouldn't like to try getting anywhere without one.

Fun footer

It's not clear what the origin of this expression is, but it comes from the theatre. Actors think they shouldn't wish one another good luck because it could mean they think they might have bad luck. The expression *break a leg* also has the meaning 'try hard'. Elicit other ways that we can wish each other good luck in English (for example, *Good luck! I hope it goes well! I wish you all the best!*).

To finish

Focus students' attention on the collocations in Ex 6. Ask them to think of one sense that they have. Then put them into pairs to talk about this sense, and to give reasons or examples of why they think they have it.

Direct students to the section on Part 2, Long turn in the Speaking file on page 163 of the Student's Book and ask them to read the information at home, in preparation for the next lesson.

Presentation tool:	Unit 1, Use of English 2
Workbook / Online Practice:	p10
Audioscript:	SB p175
Switch on videoscript	p171
Extra Practice App	

SPEAKING SB p15

To start

Ask students about the things they like to celebrate with family or friends. Suggestions might include *birthdays*, *passing exams* or *anniversaries*. Nominate a few students to say how they think most of their classmates would celebrate special occasions. Write their answers on the board.

Power up

1 Put students into small groups to discuss the questions. You could also put these questions on the board for students to discuss: *What kind of celebrations do you enjoy with family or with friends?*

What do you think is the best way to celebrate something special? Why?

Possible answer

We usually go round to each other's houses and watch films or play games together. If we want to celebrate something, we go to a pizza restaurant in the city centre. We went there last month for my friend's birthday, and the waiters even came to our table and sang *Happy birthday* to him!

2 Focus students' attention on the two photos. Elicit ideas from the class and write appropriate suggestions on the board.

Possible answers

A They're enjoying music, dancing, spending time together in the evening.

B They're enjoying being outside, perhaps at a fair, spending time together on a day out.

exam tip

3 Go through the exam tip with the class. Tell students that they will have a minute to talk about the photographs, and that if they simply describe each photograph separately, then will not use a range of appropriate language, and will not be answering the question.

Ask students in pairs to list three things that are similar and three things that are different in the photos. Conduct class feedback.

Possible answers

Similar: young people, happy atmosphere, everyone is enjoying themselves in their free time

Different: location (indoors and outdoors), time of day (evening and daytime), activities (dancing, walking, talking)

useful language: comparing photos

4 1.8 Tell students they are going to listen to a student talking about the two photographs.

Go though the useful language box with the class, and encourage students to give a reason for their ideas where possible, when speaking. Explain that the student in the recording uses some of this useful language, and that students should listen out for and tick the phrases they hear.

In both photos, …
The photos are similar because …
One of the main differences is that …
In the first photo …, whereas in the second …

5 1.9 Ask students where they think the photos were taken. Then play the recording for them to compare their ideas. Nominate a few students to say if they agree or not.

Photo 1: in a club or at a party
Photo 2: at a fun fair, in front of a fairground ride

Speak up

exam task: long turn SB p163

The exam task has no question for the listening candidate to answer as in the Cambridge exam, because the focus here is on the long turn.

6 **e** Ask students to work in pairs to do the tasks. Monitor them while they are speaking and offer them encouragement to extend their conversations and speak as fully as possible.

You could ask students to record themselves on their phones while they are speaking. They should then listen to their individual long turns and decide on one or two things they could improve upon (for example, whether they successfully spoke without pausing for a full minute). They should then repeat the long turns, and try to address the issues they have identified.

Possible answer

In both photos, we can see people spending time outdoors, being active. The photos are similar because there are two people in each one, and the people are all doing some form of exercise. One of the main differences is that in the first photo, the people are together, but they are focused on running. They both look serious, like they're concentrating on their own performance, and one is wearing headphones, so they aren't really communicating with each other. In the second photo, the people are actually playing. They are having a snowball fight, and the boy is just about to throw one at the girl. They're clearly having fun. Another difference is the time of the year. The first photo was probably taken in the autumn, whereas the second one was taken in the winter.

Speaking extra

7 Put students into pairs or small groups. Ask them to choose a photo, and to plan a conversation by making brief notes. Monitor them and help with any ideas as they do this. After students have acted out their conversations, the class could vote on the most interesting one.

Possible answer

(The bottom right photo of people playing in the snow.)

A: It's cold! Let's go home!
B: Just another ten minutes! It's so nice to play in the snow. It hardly ever snows here.
A: I know, but it's OK for you. You've got a better coat than I have.
B: Here comes a snowball!
A: Hey! OK, I'll get you for that!

SPEAKING (Continued)

To finish

If students have photos of themselves on their phones, having a good time with friends or celebrating something, ask them to share these photos in pairs or small groups. Encourage them to say what is happening in the photos, who the people are, etc.

Speaking file

Direct students to the section on Part 2, Long turn in the Speaking file on page 163 of the Student's Book for further information if you didn't ask them to read it in preparation for this lesson.

Presentation tool:	Unit 1, Speaking
Workbook / Online Practice:	p11
Photocopiable activity:	1C
Speaking file:	SB p163
Audioscript:	SB p175

WRITING

To start

Write these topics on the board: *Films, Concerts, Books, TV programmes, Video games, Computers, Places to visit.*

Organise students into pairs. Ask them to discuss whether they have ever read or written reviews of these things (in newspapers, magazines or online), and how much influence a negative review might have on them. Conduct class feedback and identify the thing most students would read reviews about, and which would have the greatest influence.

Power up

1 Ask students to discuss the questions in pairs.

Possible answer

I've been playing the guitar a lot recently – or trying to. I found an old guitar in my house, which used to be my dad's when he was in his 20s. He said I could have it, because he hasn't used it in a very long time. It's not in great condition, but it's fun to practise on. I think the guitar is a cool instrument to learn, so I'd like to get a good one, one day.

2 Read the questions with the class and elicit ideas. Write appropriate activities on the board, and then ask students to say which activities depend on the season (time of year).

Possible answer

There is a ski centre near where I live, so people can practise skiing or snowboarding. There's also a very large indoor swimming pool with an amazing slide. Those things are good at any time of the year. When it's warm, there's a large park which people can go cycling in, or play football. It's not possible to do that in the winter, because it gets too dark and there aren't any lights there.

Plan on

3 Tell students that they are going to write their own review of an activity they like. Ask them to read the task and underline the things they need to do. Ask: *How many words should you write?*

reviews of leisure activities that young visitors can do in your area

an activity you have tried

describe your experience … of trying the activity

say whether or not you would recommend it to other people your age

140–190 words

4 Go through the questions with the class, so that they understand exactly what a review should consist of.

1 The target reader is the person who the writer expects to read the review. This will affect the kind of language used and how the review is written. In this case the target readers are people who read the tourist website, and young people interested in doing activities in your area.

2 A review should always give information so that the reader can make a choice, but should also be interesting and engaging to read, and the writer should give their own opinion. In this case, the purpose is to inform other young people about an activity so they can decide whether to do it or not.

3 A review should always be interesting and engaging to read. In this case, the style should be chatty, and informal because it is for a website.
4 A title is a good way to engage the reader's interest. It should be followed by paragraphs, which would include an introduction, some information, some assessment of the activity and your own opinion or recommendation.
5 Some basic facts about what is being reviewed, plus quite a lot of description and opinion.
6 You should always give your own opinion at the end, and say whether or not you would recommend the activity.

5 **Ask students to read the review and discuss the questions in pairs. Conduct class feedback and ask: *Did you enjoy this review? Why/Why not?***

1 Yes, because it is written in a chatty, informal style.
2 The writer uses opening rhetorical questions and addresses the reader directly as *you*. (A rhetorical question is useful for engaging the reader as it makes them think but doesn't expect them to think of an answer.)
3 Yes (*atmosphere, suitable, levels, abilities, instructor, extremely patient, fantastic, memorable, artistic*, etc.).

extra

Point out that adjectives are useful for reviews. Ask: *Which adjectives did the writer use in the review? Are they generally positive or negative?*

Answers include: *cool, local, patient, creative, informal, fantastic, memorable*. They are generally positive.

explore **vocabulary**

6 **Point out that a good way of extending language is to use compound adjectives. Go through the explore vocabulary box, then ask them to find examples from the review. Ask: *How has each compound adjective been formed?***

Point out that in the compound adjective *26-year-old*, the word *year* is singular.

middle-aged (adjective + verb)
old-fashioned (adjective + verb)
18-year (number + noun)
one-day (number + noun)
laid-back (verb + preposition)
brightly-lit (adverb + verb)
26-year-old (number + noun)
well-known (adverb + adjective)

extra

Play a game. Put students into groups. Tell them they're going to make compound adjectives. Write the second part of the compound adjectives below as a list on the board (*aged, fashioned, important, quality, confident, known, used*).

Call out the first part of the compound adjectives one at a time, in any order you like (e.g. *middle, old, high, self, well, low*). Students race to write the word you call out next to one of the words on the board. If it's correct, they get a point, and the chance to make a sentence with it for another point. The group with the most points wins.

Possible answers are: *middle-aged, old-fashioned, high-quality, low-quality, self-confident, well-known, well-used, self-satisfied, self-important.*

7 **Remind students that they should give their own opinion at the end of a review, and a recommendation so that readers can make up their own mind.**

Students complete the sentences individually, then compare their answers with a partner. Encourage them to use expressions like these in their own reviews.

1 worth trying **2** wouldn't recommend **3** thoroughly
4 not really worth **5** perfect **6** won't regret

Write on

8 **Students read the review task again. They decide which activity they want to write about, and whether they are going to recommend it or not.**

Before they start, ask students if they can think of any ways of <u>not</u> recommending something. For example, *I wouldn't recommend … , I regret … , It's not worth … , I wouldn't try … .*

exam tip

9 **Read through the tip with the students, to remind them of the structure of a review. Offer help and encouragement as they plan their reviews.**

exam task: review

➥ SB p168

The review task in the Cambridge exam more usually focuses on films, products, websites, holidays, etc. However, it is quite possible to find a review task like this about an activity.

10 **e** **Students write their review. It might be helpful to give them a time limit of 20 minutes. Alternatively, students can write the review for homework and Exs 11 and 12 can be done at the beginning of the next lesson. Students can swap essays and provide feedback on their partner's writing, using the ideas in Exs 11 and 12 as a guide.**

Model answer

Why not try ice skating?

If you're looking for a new way to keep fit, and to hang out with friends at the same time, then how about learning to ice skate? And if you think that this is only something you can do in the winter, think again! The new Skate World Ice Rink is the perfect place for beginners or even advanced skaters to have fun.

First of all, Skate World is large, with room for about 400 people. So, there's no need to worry about bumping into other people. If you're a complete beginner like I was, it's easy enough to practise without disturbing other people or worrying about anyone else watching you.

There's a real social element to Skate World. If you go as a group, with friends or family, you get a discount. There's also a great café where you can sit and relax, or watch the really good skaters and examine their technique.

Learning to skate is a great way to improve your balance and confidence, and it's well worth trying, even if you've never considered it before.

WRITING (Continued)

Improve it

11 Encourage students to use the tips in Ex 9 as a checklist every time they write a review, to make sure that they have covered all the relevant points. If students wrote their reviews in class, you could set Exs 11 and 12 for homework. Collect the reviews and provide feedback on how well they are structured, and how clearly they express an opinion or recommendation.

12 Make sure that students always check their writing for grammar, vocabulary and spelling mistakes before submitting it.

To finish

Ask students to think of some activities they like, and have tried. Put them into pairs to recommend these activities, saying why they would recommend them or not. They should try to use the expressions from Ex 7.

Presentation tool:	Unit 1, Writing
Workbook / Online Practice:	p12
Writing file:	SB p168

SWITCH ON

Chef tests

1 Put students into pairs to do Ex 1. Read through the task with the class. Monitor and assist any weaker students. Conduct class feedback and write any interesting or useful adjectives or comparisons that students used on the board.

Possible answer

The best food I've eaten recently was something my grandfather made. He makes the best version of this dish I've ever tasted. It's soft, fluffy and savoury. It's great on its own or to go on top of something else. It looks like clouds and you can eat it really quietly, as there's no crunch at all. (mashed potato)

2 Write the name *Gordon Ramsay* on the board and ask students if they have heard of him and what they know.

background 

Gordon Ramsay is a British chef who was born in Scotland in 1966. He has many restaurants which have received awards, including 16 Michelin stars, but he is most well-known for his TV shows in the UK about cooking. These, like *Hell's Kitchen* and *Ramsay's Kitchen Nightmares* are popular all over the world. Gordon himself is famous for having a very bad temper and his high expectations of other chefs. Many of his TV shows involve competitions.

Tell students that they are going to watch a video clip about Gordon Ramsay and some other chefs. Ask: *What is the situation*? Play the video clip and conduct feedback (Gordon Ramsay wants a new head chef. He's giving six young chefs a competition for him to choose one. The competition involves sense tests.)

Then ask: *Which sense does he think is the most important?*

The sense of taste.

3 Ask: *Can you remember the names of any of the contestants?* (Mary and Cyndi). *What foods did Gordon Ramsay test them on?* (egg yolks, polenta, turkey, cauliflower, pistachio).

Play the video clip again. Check understanding of *palate* as used in the video (a person's ability to distinguish between and appreciate different flavours).

1 cold, shiny
2 She says that turkey and egg yolk 'don't even have the same texture'.

4 Students work in pairs to discuss the question. Conduct class feedback. You could extend the discussion with further questions: *Would you like to be a chef? Would you like to work for Gordon Ramsay? Do you enjoy cookery programmes like this on TV? Why/Why not?*

Possible answers

Even experienced chefs need more than their sense of taste alone. Cooking involves all of our senses, so only using one of them makes cooking more difficult. Although we prioritise taste in this context, the food's appearance and other factors contribute to the eating experience.

extra 

Ask students to write a short review of the clip they've watched, summarising what happened, saying what was interesting about it and whether it would make them want to watch the series of programmes.

Project

5 Elicit the names of any popular food festivals where students live. Ask them to describe what happens.

Explain the project to the class. They need to present an interesting food festival from any country. Put students into small groups and read through the different stages of the project. For Step 1, they should conduct research on different festivals, then share their ideas in the group and select one to focus on. Encourage students to search for interesting photos or videos of the festivals, which they could use in their presentations later. This step could be done for homework.

Each person in the group should be allocated a different task related to the project. This could be drafting notes, writing the notes up, finding images or video clips to accompany the presentation, delivering the presentation, etc.

alternative 

Students present their favourite dish. They should: describe all the ingredients and the recipe for making it; describe the taste, texture and appearance of the food; explain where they first ate it, how old they were, whether it's a family recipe, etc. They could go online to research the history of the dish, as well as finding images to support their presentation.

Presentation tool: Unit 1, Switch on
Switch on videoscript: TB p171

INDEPENDENT LEARNING SB p18

Self-assessment

It is important for students to become independent learners, and self-assessment and peer assessment are both skills they need to develop. However, some students may find it difficult to talk about their strengths and weaknesses in front of others, so be sensitive about how you deal with this section. You could give Ex 4 to students to complete at home.

1 Write *self-assessment* on the board and elicit what it means. Elicit definitions and then read through options A–C to check if their ideas are among them. Put students into pairs to discuss these questions and give reasons: *How do you assess your progress and performance? Is it important to do this yourself rather than rely on the teacher?*

B

2 Write *peer assessment* on the board and ask for the meaning. Ask: *How is it different from self-assessment?* Conduct class feedback.

Peer assessment involves students looking at and assessing each other's work, rather than just their own.

3 Read through the list of words and phrases and ask students to complete the sentences individually, before comparing answers with a partner. Conduct class feedback.

1 independent learners **2** reflect **3** responsible **4** critical **5** strengths and weaknesses **6** each others' **7** feedback **8** learn more

4 Give students time to check back through the unit and note down their ideas. Whether you decide to do Ex 4 in class or give it for homework, it is always a good idea to finish a unit on a positive note focusing on what the students have learned. Ask students to close their books and work in pairs or small groups. They should note down what they learned in terms of grammar and vocabulary that they hadn't known before, and also what they found most interesting about the topics and what new information they acquired. Conduct class feedback, and elicit their ideas.

Possible answers

Things I have done well are:

1 I have used present tenses well, and accurately.
2 I have been able to describe my experiences and feelings well.

Things I should focus on are:

1 listening for specific information.
2 organising a review, and making my opinion clear in a recommendation.

UNIT CHECK SB p19

extra: using the wordlist 

- Encourage students to refer to the wordlist when they do their homework.
- Ask students to work in pairs and to test each other's spelling.
- Challenge students to write a short story using as many of the phrasal verbs and collocations as possible.

Practice

Note on core language: The Unit check tests present tenses, comparative adjectives and adverbs, and word formation.

1 **1** sense of **2** put off **3** dreadful **4** energetic **5** strong-willed **6** visible **7** confidence **8** accessible

2 **3** 1.10 and 11 **1** approve **2** cosy **3** willing **4** dull **5** Apparently **6** gift

4 **Possible answers**

It has a similar meaning to *boring* and can also describe grey, unpleasant weather. (dull)

It's a talent that someone has, for example, being musical or athletic. (gift)

It's a warm feeling, and we often use it to talk about rooms or homes which have a nice, welcoming atmosphere. (cosy)

Review

1
1 goes
2 Has, persuaded
3 's (is) thinking
4 've (have) been planning
5 's (has), seen
6 Is, burning

2 **1** C **2** E **3** A **4** D **5** F **6** B

3
1 haven't seen Sam for
2 early enough to see
3 weren't as cheap as
4 has been playing
5 much better than
6 a more confident performer than

4
1 the (a definite article before a superlative adjective)
2 been (past participle to complete the present perfect form – indicating indefinite period in past)
3 than (to complete a comparison)
4 has (to complete the present perfect)
5 more (to make a comparison)
6 since (indicating the start of a period in the past)
7 have (to complete the present perfect)
8 much (an emphasis of degree of comparison)

5 1.12 She's trying to persuade Joe to go to her dance club with her. Yes, he agrees to go.

6 1.13 **1** has been going **2** has **3** better **4** 's wearing **5** as good as

7 Hi John,

How are you? I hope you're OK.

My brother and I are going zorbing on the weekend. Do you know what zorbing is? Basically, you get inside a large, clear plastic ball, and roll down a hill inside it! It sounds crazy, but it's completely safe, and it's a lot of fun.

Would you like to come? My dad's going to drive us there. And if three of us go, we get a discount, so it won't be very expensive.

Let me know by this evening, if you want to try it out!

See you soon,

Katya.

GRAMMAR FILE SB p143

1 **1** hasn't finished **2** have been **3** Does it look **4** cancel **5** 's saving up **6** cycle

2
1 has been looking forward
2 is, borrowing
3 have, been doing
4 've (have), woken up
5 're (are) standing
6 've (have) been celebrating

3
1 've (have) tried
2 've (have) been
3 recommend
4 am, enjoying
5 've (have), wanted
6 have, waited
7 feel
8 haven't regretted
9 has shown
10 've (have) been looking forward

4 **1** most amazing **2** stronger **3** best **4** more powerful **5** further/farther

5
1 too scary for
2 writes more slowly than
3 isn't warm enough to
4 is as old as
5 can dance better than anyone/everyone
6 further/farther from school than

6 **1** taller than **2** darker **3** better than **4** worse **5** higher **6** harder than **7** as strong as **8** too sweet **9** the older **10** the better

Presentation tool:	Unit 1, Unit check
Workbook / Online Practice:	p13
Audioscript:	SB p175

On the bucket list 2

READING
topic: inspiration for travel
skill: finding specific information
task: multiple matching

GRAMMAR
past tenses
articles

VOCABULARY
travel anecdotes and apps
idiomatic phrases and expressions
collocations; linkers

LISTENING
topic: travel-writing
skill: listening for specific information and opinion
task: multiple choice

USE OF ENGLISH
multiple-choice cloze
open cloze

SPEAKING
topic: summer holidays, photo bombing
skill: giving concise answers
task: interview

WRITING
topic: best and worst holiday experiences
skill: describing, narrating and expressing contrast
task: article

SWITCH ON
video: Sidi Driss
project: film location map

Lead-in SB p21

Refer students to the title of the unit *On the bucket list* and ask if they can guess what the meaning of this phrase is (things you want to do in your lifetime). Put students into pairs and give them two minutes to list what might be on their 'bucket lists'.

Focus students' attention on the photograph and ask: *What's the photo of? Where do you think it is? How do you think she's feeling?* You may need to provide the verb *balance* to help students describe what the person is doing.

Read the quote with the class, *Whenever I leave, I want to come back.* Ask students what they think it means and if they have felt the same way.

Put student into small groups to discuss the three questions. They may give geographical names in their own language. If so, write up the English equivalents and check pronunciation.

Possible answers

1 I'd love to visit this place, because I like to spend time near the sea, even if it's windy or cold.
2 There is a river near my school, and I often go there with friends. I like it because it feels far from the city, even though it isn't. It's relaxing and a good place to have fun.
3 I'd like to visit Australia, because they have very nice beaches there and lots of wildlife. I'd like to visit any country where you can easily see animals in the wild.

READING SB pp22–23

To start

Tell students about the last place you went to on holiday and the reason you went there, for example, *Last year my sister and I went to Ibiza for a week. Our friend had gone there the year before and loved it. Her stories and descriptions made us want to go.* Put students into pairs to discuss different reasons people might choose a particular holiday. Conduct class feedback and find the most common suggestions.

Power up

1 Refer the students to the photos and ask if they recognise any of the places or can guess where they might be. Conduct class feedback and list new words on the board.

Possible answers

1 St. Basil's Cathedral in Moscow: imposing, colourful, domes.
2 A road in Northern Ireland, going through a forest: gnarled, tunnel, ancient trees, dark.
3 The Northern Lights (or Aurora Borealis) in Iceland: vibrant, magical, luminous, icy.
4 A waterfall near a forest in North Carolina: serene, peaceful, natural.

alternative

Organise students into small groups and assign each group one of the photographs. They should discuss vocabulary that can be used to describe the photo and find at least three new words in a dictionary. They can write a short description of their photograph to read to the class.

extra

In pairs students share favourite photos of landscapes or views on their phones that they have taken or have been sent. They tell each other where the photo was taken and any other interesting details. Students report back to the class on their partner's favourite photo, describing it in as much detail as possible.

Read on

2 Read through the title of the forum posts on page 23 with the class. Ask them whether they can now guess which book, film or TV series might have inspired someone to visit the places in the photos. At this stage, do not confirm or reject any suggestions. Students read the posts quickly to match the photos. Remind students that they are reading quickly to find the places mentioned and that they should not worry about unfamiliar vocabulary at this stage. Conduct class feedback.

1 C – Alexandra has been reading a book by a Russian author.
2 A – Trish was interested in locations from a TV series.
3 B – Rich had seen a documentary about volcanoes and the Aurora Borealis.
4 D – Sam had won a competition.

background

Game of Thrones is American fantasy TV series which started in 2011 and is based on *A Song of Ice and Fire* by George Martin. The series concerns the struggles of several families to gain the Iron Throne and other families' fight to become independent from it. The series is extremely popular internationally and has won many awards. The series has the appearance of a historical drama and the focus is more on battles and war than on magic. One of the primary film locations is near Belfast, Northern Ireland with other locations in the UK, Canada and many other countries across the globe.

Anna Karenina is a 1,000-page book by the Russian author Leo Tolstoy which is considered by many to be one of the greatest books ever written. It was first published in 1878 and follows the tragic story of a young, married aristocrat who falls in love with a count. The story deals with many political and moral issues of the time and has been filmed and televised many times.

The Hunger Games is a trilogy of young adult novels by Suzanne Collins which have been made into four very popular films, the first in 2012. The books are set in a future time where children from 12 districts are forced to compete in a televised death match. The books have been an international success, with more than 60 million sold around the world.

exam tip

Point out that in the multiple matching part of the Reading exam, students need to find different information in separate parts of a text or short texts. There are ten questions and students identify which part of the text or text gives the answers. Some sections might answer part of a question, but only one will have the complete answer.

Read through the exam tip box with the class. Students then scan the texts to find which contains the answer.

D: Sam hadn't expected to win the first prize of a trip to the USA; he had planned to travel to Greece but went to the USA instead.

exam task: multiple matching

In the Cambridge exam the reading texts do not usually have engaging lead-ins, used here to interest the reader, but shorter introductory titles.

3 **e** Read through the task with the class. Students complete the exam task individually and then compare answers. Monitor weaker students and help where necessary by indicating two (as opposed to four) of the texts to choose a particularly difficult answer from. Conduct class feedback and ask students to justify their answers.

1 D (*I was due to go off on holiday to Greece just then, but I ended up going to the US instead!*)
2 C (*It was just like being on a movie set!*)
3 A (*… the recent boom in visitors to parts of Ireland …*)
4 B (*The volcanic landscape doesn't appeal to everyone, …*)
5 C (*This year, since I am studying Tolstoy's* Anna Karenina *at school, my mother decided the time was right to go back.*)
6 A (*I live in Northern Ireland, where several scenes from the* Game of Thrones *TV series were filmed. I hadn't realised that until …*)

7 D (*... but as a city boy not used to such awe-inspiring nature, I was freaking out!*)
8 C (*Russian is really difficult to learn. I was going to give it up but then I thought, No, I can do this!*)
9 B (*Mum wanted to go somewhere different for her birthday ...*)
10 D (*... North Carolina, an area I recognised from pictures ... I recognised the Triple Falls and Bridal Veil Falls that had featured in the first film ...*)

extra: fast finishers 

Fast finishers can think of one more question (or more depending on time) to ask about the texts. Allow fast finishers to ask their questions to the group after you have conducted class feedback.

4 Put students into groups of three or four and ask them to find the words in the texts that mean the same as those in the task. This can be a competition to see which group can finish first. Conduct class feedback. Ask personalised questions to practise the vocabulary:

What has there been a boom in recently?

What has not lived up to your expectations recently?

Name an exotic place for a holiday.

Can you name a vast area of forest in your country?

Has someone you know freaked out recently? Why?

1 medieval
2 boom
3 live up to sb's expectations
4 appeal to
5 exotic
6 have access to
7 vast
8 superb, awe-inspiring, incredible
9 feature
10 freaking out

extra 

Organise students into four small groups (or pairs depending on class size). Ask each group to look again at a different text on page 23. They should try to find three or four words or phrases they think the other groups may not know, and check the meanings in a dictionary or online. Monitor and help where necessary. Bring groups together and let them take turns to offer a word or phrase to the class. If no one knows the meaning, they gain a point. Students should explain the meaning by paraphrasing and giving examples.

Sum up

5 Students answer the question, justifying their answers in full group. Encourage them to say why they would identify with one, or all, of the people.

Possible answer

I identify most with Alexandra. My grandmother was from Hungary, so that means I'm a quarter Hungarian. I've never been there, but I know a lot about it, and I've read some books by Hungarian authors. I also like quite a lot of traditional Hungarian dance music, and I would like to go there one day, and practise it for real.

Speak up

6 Students discuss the questions in pairs. Monitor and contribute to the discussions to encourage students to extend their answers. Pairs could then join another pair to exchange ideas.

Possible answers

1 I liked the Harry Potter films when I was younger, and I know that a lot of the places in the films and the books are not real, but there is a place near London where you can see the studios where they made the films. There is a street inside the studio, which you can visit. It's full of magical shops, and you can actually go inside and walk around. I think you can go there on a guided tour, and I'd like to do that one day.
2 It would be great if a film was shot in my home town, although I can't imagine it happening because my town isn't very interesting. It would be funny to see famous film stars walking around near the supermarket!

extra 

Students think about locations they have seen in films. Ask them to look online to find out where these places really were, and then to describe these places to each other.

To finish

Ask students to think of an interesting place near where they live (or where you are now studying) for tourists to visit. Put them in pairs to advertise the place to their partner using words from the page but without naming the place. Their partners guess the place. Give an example: *You must visit this place because it's very old with a lot of ancient woodland ...*

Fun footer

Nominate a student to read the footer aloud. Ask students if they have similar phrases in their own language, and if so, ask them to translate the phrases into English.

In preparation for the next lesson, ask students to complete Ex 1 on page 24, read the Grammar reference on past tenses on page 144 and complete Grammar practice Ex 1. Check the answers in class after the 'To start' activity.

Presentation tool:	Unit 2, Reading
Workbook / Online Practice:	pp14–15
Extra Practice App	

GRAMMAR SB p24

To start

Use the start of this lesson to assess students' existing knowledge of the target grammar point. Explain to students that you're going to tell them about a journey you went on. They need to listen carefully, as you'll be asking questions afterwards. Then describe what happened using a range of past tenses. For example, *Last month we went to the airport. We'd planned to get up at 6.00 and drive to the airport. Unfortunately, we overslept and finally left the house at 7.30! Then, we were getting into the car when we noticed that one of the tyres was flat. We were always having problems with that car! So, we phoned for a taxi but it didn't arrive. I was going to call them again, but then the taxi arrived. Apparently, the driver had been sitting outside the wrong house for ten minutes! By now it was 8.15! There had been an accident on the motorway so were delayed for another 20 minutes. When we got to the airport, our flight was boarding. We were just in time!*

Ask questions, using appropriate past tenses: *What had we planned to do? Why didn't we do as planned? What happened when they left the house? Why did I complain about the car? What went wrong with the taxi? Why were we even later at the airport? Did we catch the plane?*

explore **grammar**

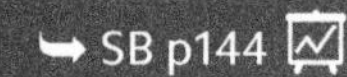

1 Organise students into pairs and ask them to match the sentences with the rules in the explore grammar box. Conduct class feedback. Ask questions to check students understand each example:

1. *Which action was interrupted by another?* (*waiting* is interrupted by *realising*)
2. *Did he leave early?* (No, he didn't.)
3. *Did Paul leave his shoes there on one occasion or many?* (many)
4. *Was making a list a regular activity, and does it still happen?* (It was a regular activity, but it no longer happens.)
5. *When did the inspiration happen*? (while looking on the internet)
6. *Did they visit friends in France?* (No, they didn't.)

1 F (*I'd been waiting*), A (*I realised*)
2 D (*I was hoping*), A (*I didn't manage*)
3 C (*Paul was always leaving*)
4 G (*I used to make*), A (*I wanted*)
5 B (*I was looking*), A (*I got*)
6 D (*We were going to visit*), A (*my sister was sick; we had to*)

The Grammar reference covers past tenses with time expressions and *used to / would*. Get students to read the explanations if you haven't already, and complete Exs 1–4 on page 145. Ask fast finishers to write things they *used to* or *would* do in the past, and to compare their sentences in pairs. They can ask each other follow-up questions to find out more.

extra

Give students the beginning of sentences and ask them to complete them individually so that some are true for them and some are not true. They compare sentences in pairs and then guess which of their partner's sentences are true or false.

1. *Last night I was planning to … but …*
2. *When I started primary school I used to …*
3. *I annoyed my parents a lot when I was younger. I was always …*
4. *Last weekend I was watching … when …*
5. *My friend was late at the weekend because she'd been …*

2 2.1 Tell students they are going to listen to an account of something that happened while someone was on holiday. They need to answer the question in the rubric. Play the recording and then conduct class feedback.

A dog had fallen down a hole in the road which some workmen had dug and then left uncovered.

3 2.2 Students individually complete the sentences with the correct forms and then compare with a partner. Play the recording for them to check.

1 was walking, saw
2 was going to meet, stopped, was going
3 had been digging, had finished, (had) gone
4 had fallen
5 called, came

4 Ask students if they or anyone they know has ever complained about a holiday. Ask for details if they have. Ask what people usually complain about after a holiday (for example, the accommodation, loud noise, delays to flights, illness, cancellation of excursions, etc.). Then students read the customer complaint to see if it includes any of their ideas.

Ask: *How does the customer feel? Why?* Elicit ideas about whether students feel this was a reasonable complaint and what sort of action should be taken next.

Students read the complaint again and choose the correct verb forms.

The customer feels angry because the website directions to the hotel were wrong. She wasn't able to have a proper meal upon arrival and there was no medication or cream available to treat her sunburn.

1 booked **2** happened **3** 'd arrived **4** had been **5** was **6** 'd given **7** got **8** arrived **9** 'm not used **10** got **11** was sitting **12** managed

extra: fast finishers

Fast finishers should think of reasons for their choices. Conduct class feedback. and ask the fast finishers for reasons for the choices.

5 Explain the task to students and elicit an example from a strong student, for example, *I was going to do my homework last night, but I decided to watch a good film instead.* Students complete the sentences individually and then share in pairs or small groups.

Possible answers

1 ... there was an important football match on TV.
2 ... had been waiting for 20 minutes in the rain.
3 ... was writing him an email.

Speak up

6 Tell students to choose one of the ideas, not both. Give them a few minutes to think about the situation and make notes if necessary. Put them into pairs to tell their partners about the complaint or the funny event. Remind them to try to use a range of past tenses. Conduct class feedback and ask students to report on anything interesting that their partners talked about.

Possible answers

1 I usually catch the 3:45 bus when I go home, but yesterday, it didn't turn up. I'd been waiting there for more than 20 minutes. And when it finally arrived, the driver was so rude with everyone.
2 My friend David went to live in Australia with his family about a year ago. I'd been thinking about writing to him, when suddenly I got an email. It was from David. It turned out that he'd been thinking about me at the same time. But he'd written an email first!

To finish

Read through this question with the class: *Some people say that it's not worth complaining because nothing ever happens. It's better to never go back to the place or use the service again. What's your opinion?*

Put students into groups to brainstorm ideas about the topic. Then have a full group discussion, and find out what the most common opinion is.

Presentation tool:	Unit 2, Grammar
Workbook / Online Practice:	p16
Photocopiable activity:	2A
Grammar reference and practice:	SB p144
Audioscript:	SB p175

VOCABULARY SB p25

travel anecdotes and apps

To start

Write the word *anecdote* on the board and elicit the meaning (a short account of a personal experience, often amusing). Then tell students an anecdote about something that happened once while you were on holiday. Use past tenses. For example, *When I was a child my family went rafting down a river in the USA. I was sitting at the back and I leaned over the boat to look into the water. Unfortunately, I leaned too far and fell out. Luckily the water wasn't too fast or deep and I was picked up by the raft behind us! They were very kind but I felt a bit silly!* Ask students if they have a similar anecdote of their own. Encourage a stronger student to tell it to the class.

1 Read through the phrasal verbs in the box with the class. Ask students to work in pairs to complete the sentences. Conduct class feedback.

1 dressed up **2** lived up to **3** think up **4** conjured up **5** ended up **6** gave up

alternative

With a weaker group, before students complete the sentences, write these definitions on the board in random order, and ask students which phrasal verbs in the box have a similar meaning.

imagine (conjure up)
put special clothes on (dress up)
do something eventually (end up)
no longer want to do something (give up)
be as good as you'd expected (live up to)
invent (think up)

extra

To practise the phrasal verbs more, put students into pairs to talk about the following topics (write them on the board for the class to refer to).

1 *Something they have dressed up for recently.*
2 *Something they ended up doing last weekend.*
3 *A good excuse they once thought up.*
4 *Something that didn't live up to their expectations.*
5 *What a holiday in Iceland or the Caribbean conjures up.*
6 *An idea they gave up because of the weather or lack of time recently.*

explore **vocabulary 1**

2 Write this idiom on the board: *pull your socks up.* Ask students what it means. Then say: *My friend is very lazy and she doesn't work very hard. She has an exam next week and she needs to pull her socks up if she wants to pass.* Elicit that *pull your socks up* is an idiom, and its meaning is *work harder.* Explain (or remind students) that an idiom is a fixed group of words, and you cannot always guess the meaning from the individual words. Read through the explore vocabulary box with the class. Remind them that when recording idioms, they need to give a clear situation that shows the meaning and how the idiom works – not just a translation. Check through the meanings of the idioms in the box.

VOCABULARY (Continued)

alternative

Give examples to show the meanings of each idiom. Elicit the meaning of each one.

blown away – The view was incredible. I was blown away by it. (extremely impressed/surprised)

down in the dumps – All my friends were off on holiday apart from me and I was down in the dumps for a few days. (feeling low/depressed)

high on the list – Tidying my house isn't high on my list of things to do for this weekend. (my priority)

over the moon – When I passed my driving test, I was over the moon! (very happy)

fall in love – In the film, the woman falls in love with a millionaire. (starts to have strong romantic feelings)

get into the swing/spirit of – I wasn't used to working in an office but I soon got into the swing of things. (start to understand/enjoy)

Students complete the blog. Conduct class feedback. Ask: *Why is the word 'interesting' in line 2 in quote marks?* (It's what we say when we weren't that impressed by something but don't want to be negative). Give an example of something you found 'interesting' recently and elicit examples. For example, *The restaurant we went to was 'interesting' – everything was painted black, but I don't think we'll be going back again.*

1 high on my list
2 blown away
3 get into the swing of things
4 down in the dumps
5 over the moon

watch out for

Students need to be aware that when learning or using idioms, they must be careful not to try to change individual words, as this can sound very strange. For example, *You need to pull your socks up your legs* doesn't work!

Also, advise students not to overuse idioms, as their language will sound unnatural.

explore vocabulary 2

3 2.3 Say to students: *I usually travel light when I go on holiday.* Write *travel light* on the board. Elicit that it means *don't take a lot of things with you.* Tell students that this is an example of a collocation: words that go together, and sound natural. We cannot say *I usually travel heavy* because the words do not collocate. Read through the explore vocabulary box with the class.

Read out the title *Great travel apps!* and the first sentence in the notes. Elicit that the answer to 1 is *experience* because it is a collocation. The words *travel* and *habits* do not go together naturally.

Elicit the type of collocation that *travel experience* is (a noun + noun collocation).

Students work individually to choose the correct alternatives and then compare answers with a partner. Conduct class feedback.

1 experience **2** everyday **3** enter **4** book **5** record **6** make **7** take

extra

Ask: *Which of these apps do you think would be useful? Would you use them on holiday? Why/Why not?*

Students work in small groups to think up a new travel app that they think most people would find useful. They should think about how it would work and write a short description so that other people can understand it. They read their descriptions to the class. Ask the class to vote on the most useful-sounding apps.

Speak up

4 Discuss the meaning of *digital suitcase* (apps you may need on holiday or while travelling) with the whole class. Organise students into pairs to explain what would be in theirs. Compare ideas in class feedback and see whose 'digital suitcase' would be the fullest.

Possible answer

A 'digital suitcase' includes all the apps you may need on holiday or while travelling.

My digital suitcase would include maps, so I would know where I was going. It would also include all my friends' contact details. It would probably also have lots of music on it, so I wouldn't get bored while I was travelling.

extra: whole class

Say: *Some people think it might be good for us to switch off our smart phones when we're on holiday. What do you think?* Ask half the class to come up with ideas why this might be a good idea and the other half why it might not be a good idea. Give them time to make notes. Then ask the whole class to debate the question.

To finish

Put students into pairs. Elicit the idioms and collocations from the lesson and write them on the board. Ask students to choose two which they could include in an anecdote. Organise them into small groups to take turns telling their anecdotes.

Fun footer

Ask students to read the fun footer and elicit what they think the joke is.

background

The name of the town is *Accident* and the road sign is famous. The origin of the name is still a mystery but it is thought to have got the name because two surveyors in 1774 selected the same section of land 'by accident'. They were friends, so one agreed to let the other have the land to develop. The town was called *Accident* because of this.

Presentation tool:	Unit 2, Vocabulary
Workbook / Online Practice:	p17
Photocopiable activity:	2B
Audioscript:	SB p176
Extra Practice App	

LISTENING SB p26

To start

Organise students into small groups. Tell them they are going to talk about the kind of places they like travelling to or visiting, and why. Write some suggestions on the board: *mountains, beaches, hot places, cold places, cities.*

Give an example of your own to get students started, for example, *I love going to mountains because the air is always so fresh and clean and it makes me feel relaxed.*

Bring the class together and ask students to share their results. Identify the most popular type of place in the class for students to travel to, and why.

Power up

1 Read through the words and phrases with the class and explain any that students don't know. Put them into pairs to discuss the questions.

Possible answer

I've been to New York City. It's a really impressive place, with some amazingly tall buildings. On my first day there, I was completely awestruck by how high they were. And everywhere in the city is easily accessible by subway. You can get from one end to the other in about 30 minutes.

2 Tell students they are going to listen to an interview with a travel writer. Put them into pairs to discuss the two questions. Conduct class feedback and write their ideas on the board so they can compare them with what they hear.

Possible answers

The job might involve travelling to interesting places, interviewing people, writing articles for online websites.

The attractions might be that you get to travel and see interesting places, and meet different people.

The difficulties could be that it gets tiring, you have to meet deadlines for submitting articles, you might even get bored waiting around at airports, or sitting on planes, etc.

Listen up

3 2.4 Tell students that the travel writer they will listen to has had several jobs, and that they should listen to identify them. Play the recording and then conduct class feedback.

He's worked in a travel agency, as a research scientist, for an online magazine. Now he is a full-time travel writer.

exam task: multiple choice: longer text

4 2.5 Go through the exam tip with the class. Explain that in this part of the exam, all the options contain information that they may hear on the recording, but only one of the options will answer the question exactly. Tell students that it's easier to listen for the right answer if they have already identified what the question is actually asking and the key information they need to listen for. Ask them to look at question 1 and all the options, and to underline what they think are the key words.

Ask students to work in pairs and to underline key words in questions 2–7. Play the recording so students can identify the right answers. Ask: *Did the underlined words help you focus on what you had to listen for?*

Suggested underlining

1 *first* (This question is asking to identify the content of first articles he wrote.)
 A *inspired, history lessons*
 B *combination, travel and research*
 C *published, almost immediately*

2 *feel, first break* (This question is asking about feelings.)
 A *relieved, different ideas*
 B *disappointed, took so long*
 C *surprised, hadn't expected*

3 *start job, travel agency* (This question is asking for the reason he started the job.)
 A *learn, demanding clients*
 B *a way, meet more travel writers*
 C *work, other people*

4 *worried* (This question is asking for the reason he felt worried.)
 A *lack, formal training*
 B *certain kinds of writing, more difficult*
 C *too much time, social media*

5 *decide, subject* (This question is asking for how he decides what to write about.)
 A *any job, pay well*
 B *destinations, interest him*
 C *works with his colleagues, exotic places*

6 *subject, award-winning article* (This question is asking about his feelings about his article.)
 A *frustrated, difficulties, location*
 B *reluctant, place, secret*
 C *irritated, attitude, publisher*

7 *most important quality* (This question is comparing qualities but only one is most important for travel writers.)
 A *love, what they do*
 B *desire, best*
 C *belief, themselves*

1 B (*I went on a couple of school trips. I realised that visiting new places gave me a real buzz. So I started reading up about the places I'd seen – the history and culture, you know – and then I wrote up my impressions. I didn't know how to get the articles published, so I kept them on my computer for over a year.*)

2 C (*Then finally I sent an article to a local newspaper – and to my amazement it was accepted!*)

3 C (*... but I'm a sociable type of guy and missed having others to bounce ideas off. So during the university vacation, I got a job at a travel agency.*)

4 A (*I found that writing about scientific matters bored me! I realised I'd made a mistake, but on the other hand, I had no qualifications in travel writing.*)

5 B (*The places that inspire me are largely undiscovered parts of the country. I spend my weekends exploring those, rather than more glamorous venues abroad as my colleagues do! It's a good idea to become an expert in a certain 'niche' area ...*)

6 B (*The beach I chose is in a fantastic cove but there are some very steep steps going down to it. Not a place for the faint-hearted! I'd like to have kept it for myself ...*)

LISTENING (Continued)

7 A (*Top of the list, though, is that you need to have passion for the craft of writing. If you are half-hearted, it won't get you anywhere.*)

5 Tell students that the words and expressions in Ex 5 are from the recording, and are quite useful to remember.

After they have discussed what they think these words mean, conduct class feedback. They should keep a note of useful words like these so that they can use them in their writing or speaking.

1 an idea or opinion of what something or someone is like
2 to tell someone an idea to find out what they think of it
3 a particular type of something
4 to be able to change easily according to the situation
5 the best or most exciting
6 (people) lacking courage or strength

Speak up

6 Organise students into pairs and give them time to conduct some online research. They can do this in the class on their phones. Students then work in pairs to discuss the questions. Make sure that they justify their answers and give reasons for their opinions.

Possible answer

A good place to go, if you like stunning landscapes, is the north of Scotland. Parts of it are mountainous and quite remote. You can see lots of wild animals, and unspoilt lakes and forests. It's not easily accessible by public transport, but if you like being alone in nature and breathing fresh air, it's really worth going.

To finish

Once students have talked in pairs and discussed their answers to the questions in Ex 6, run a short class debate. Students (or pairs of students) each have a minute to explain to the rest of the class why their chosen place is the best one for other people to visit. The class then votes on the most persuasive talk. As this is a fluency activity, don't correct mistakes while students talk, but make a note of any recurring mistakes for future lessons.

In preparation for the Use of English lesson, ask students to read the Grammar file section on articles on page 144 and to revise the basic rules.

Presentation tool:	Unit 2, Listening
Workbook / Online Practice:	p18
Audioscript:	SB p176
Extra Practice App	

USE OF ENGLISH 1 SB p27

To start

Focus students' attention on the two photos on page 27. Ask them to suggest two similarities and two differences that they can see.

Write their ideas on the board, and highlight any articles that are used. For example, *The first picture has a …, whereas the second picture has a … ; The … in the first picture is very remote, but there are … in the second picture.*

explore grammar SB p144

1 The Grammar reference covers articles (*a, an, the*) and the zero article. If you didn't follow the flipped classroom suggestion at the end of the last lesson, go through the Grammar reference section on articles on page 144. Get students to read the explanations and complete Exs 5 and 6 on page 145.

Put students into small groups. Assign each group a type of article (A, B or C) and ask them to look at this type in the explore grammar box and read the examples. Ask each group to then think of more examples of their particular use of the article and then present their rules and examples to the rest of the class.

Possible answers

A *the Spanish, the middle classes, the elderly, the police, the military*
B *creativity, music, art, history*
C *a piece of cake, the real thing, on the whole, as an example*

2 Tell the class about your own ideal kind of holiday. Then ask students whether they have the same opinion, and if not, to suggest their own ideal holiday.

exam task: open cloze

In the Cambridge exam the first item in the Open Cloze task is always an example. The equivalent tasks in this unit and others do not give an example as the teacher is present to advise.

The task here tests articles and allows for a - response as this is the lesson focus, unlike the Cambridge exam task which tests a variety of structures and does not allow a - for an answer.

3 **e** Put students into pairs. Ask them to read the article and choose the correct options to complete it. Conduct class feedback.

1 – (No article is needed in front of plural nouns.)
2 – (No article is needed in front of plural nouns.)
3 – (No article is needed in front of uncountable nouns.)
4 the (*the* is needed in front of particular groups of people.)
5 – (No article is needed in front of uncountable nouns.)
6 – (No article is needed in front of uncountable nouns.)
7 the (*the* is needed in front of a specific case – *the beauty of historical architecture*)
8 – (No article is needed in front of plural nouns.)

9 the (*the* is needed in front of a specific case – *the … craziness of New York*)
10 a (We use *a* to talk about one non-specific thing.)
11 a (We use *a* to talk about one non-specific thing.)
12 an (We use *an* to talk about one non-specific thing.)
13 – (No article is needed in front of uncountable nouns.)
14 a (We use *a* to talk about one non-specific thing.)
15 a / the (We could use *a* or *the* here, depending on whether we are talking about beaches in general, or a specific beach.)

extra: fast finishers 

Organise fast finishers into pairs to say whether they agree or disagree with the views expressed in the magazine article.

4 Tell students that they're going to play a game. Tell them to read the quiz and complete the gaps with the correct article.

Students should then answer the questions for themselves, but should not show anyone else their answers. In pairs they should ask one another the questions, and try to guess their partner's chosen destination. They should make a note of the destination.

Ask students to move around the class, forming different pairs. They should ask and answer the questions, and write down each new destination.

After a while stop them and conduct feedback. Ask: *Which places did people suggest? Why?*

1 the/– **2** the **3** the **4** – **5** – **6** – **7** a **8** – **9** the **10** –

Speak up

5 This could be done as a speaking activity without preparation, or you could ask students to do this for homework. Ask them to search online for information about a place of their choice. They could make a short two-minute presentation to the class at the start of the next lesson.

Fun footer

Ask students what they think the quote means. Give them time to discuss their ideas in small groups. Then conduct feedback.

Possible answers

You can't find out about other countries from other people's opinions. It's better to find things out for yourself than to rely on others.

background 

Aldous Huxley was an English writer (1894–1963). He wrote nearly 50 books, including *Brave New World* and was a respected intellectual.

To finish

Write the names of some countries on the board (not the students'), for example, England, Japan, Italy, France, the USA, etc. Ask students: *What comes to your mind when you think of these countries?* Suggest that they focus on people, history, food, weather, etc.

Elicit students' views. They might suggest things like *It always rains in the UK. People in Italy eat a lot of pasta. Japanese people are very healthy and live a long time. The food in France is excellent.*

Ask students how true they think each view really is.

Organise students into pairs and ask them to list some things that other people might believe about their country. Then they work in groups to compare their ideas and discuss how far each of these ideas is true.

Presentation tool:	Unit 2, Use of English 1
Workbook / Online Practice:	p19
Grammar reference and practice:	SB p144
Extra Practice App	

USE OF ENGLISH 2 SB p28

To start

Ask students the following questions:

Where is Mount Everest? (It's in the Himalayas. It sits on the border of China and Nepal.)

Why is it famous? (It's the tallest mountain in the world.)

What do you know about it? (Students' own answers.)

1 Ask students to skim the article quickly to find the answer to the two questions.

1 natural disasters
2 overcrowding, damage to the ecology

explore vocabulary

2 Write the word *collocation* on the board. Ask if they can remember what this means (words that are commonly used together). Go through the explore vocabulary box with the class.

watch out for

Remind students to make sure they use the right words in a collocation. For example, we say *take risks*, not *make risks*. Say the nouns below and ask students to call out the right verb.

harm (do) *an impact* (have) *jobs* (provide)

alternative

Before asking students to complete the newspaper article, check that they understand the collocations in the explore vocabulary box. Ask the following questions.

Which collocation means to have a very big effect (huge impact).

What sort of things do you do if you 'take risks'? (do dangerous activities like climbing)

What are some of the signs of 'global warming'? (rising sea levels, more extreme weather)

Which collocation means to do damage? (do a lot of harm)

Ask students to read the article again and in pairs, choose the correct collocation. Conduct feedback, and elicit the full collocation for each answer. This will help them to remember it.

1 run into 2 natural 3 goal 4 attempt 5 use 6 risks
7 sign 8 mass 9 having 10 cause 11 cope 12 twice

3 Tell students that they are going to read about Venice. Ask: *Do you know anything about the problems Venice faces?* Ask them to read the text to identify the problems.

There are too many tourists. The city is often flooded. This leads to the erosion of buildings.

exam task: multiple-choice cloze

In the Cambridge exam the first item in the Multiple-choice Cloze task is always an example. The equivalent tasks in this unit and others do not give an example as the teacher is present to advise.

The items tested here are all collocations, which is the focus of the lesson, unlike the equivalent task in the Cambridge exam which tests a wider variety of types of items.

4 **e** Go through the exam tip, and remind students of the importance of reading a text first so that they understand the topic and the general point it makes. As with the open cloze task, they should always read the whole sentence and not just look at the gap before they read the options. They often need to identify the option that completes a collocation. If they don't actually know the collocation, they could try saying each option quietly to see which one sounds best.

The answer for question 2 in Ex 4 is A, *cope*. The words *handle, manage and accept* are not followed by the preposition *with*. They all take an object (e.g. *handle a situation*).

Ask students to work in pairs to choose the best answers. Go round and monitor how they are approaching the task. When you conduct feedback, make sure that they can tell you why they think the other options are not possible.

1 B – *tourist season* is a collocation; *time* doesn't collocation with *tourist*. The words *group* and *attraction* are collocations with *tourist* but don't make sense in the sentence.
2 A – *handle, manage* and *accept* are not followed by *with*.
3 D – *tourism* is a noun. *Mass tourism* is a fixed phrase. Although *enormous, huge* and *large* have a similar meaning, they don't collocate with *tourism*.
4 B – the meaning is 'earn enough money' and the collocation with this meaning is *make a living; win, take* and *work* don't create a collocation with *a living*.
5 C – the meaning is 'having a bad effect'. The word that completes the collocation is *impact*.
6 A – the meaning is similar to 'a good standard of life'. Although *value* and *worth* have this idea, they don't collocate with *of life*; *importance* has the wrong meaning.
7 D – the collocation is *cause damage*. *Give* and *produce* don't collocate, and *prevent* has the opposite meaning.
8 C – *fail, destroy* and *finish* all need to have direct objects. They also don't have the right meaning.

To finish

Tell students to close their books. Say the word *tourist* and ask students what collocation this word was part of in the text (*season*). Then check that they have understood the meaning of this collocation by asking: *When is the tourist season in your country?* Go through the other collocations from Ex 4 in this way.

cope with (What do you find hard to cope with when learning vocabulary?)
mass tourism (Is this a lot of tourists or a few?)
make a living (How would you like to make a living in future?)
negative impact (What has a negative impact on your studies?)
quality of life (Does a lot of free time improve your quality of life or not? Why?)
cause damage (Is this something good or bad? Why?)

Presentation tool: Unit 2, Use of English 2
Workbook / Online Practice: p20
Extra Practice App

SPEAKING SB p29

To start

Tell students some kinds of holidays you enjoy, and why you enjoy them. For example, *I love walking holidays because I find them relaxing.* Ask one or two students what kind of holiday they enjoy most. Write reasons for choosing holidays on the board. Ask: *Have you ever had a holiday you didn't enjoy? What happened?*

Power up

1 Put students into pairs and ask them to discuss the photo.

Possible answers

It shows a beach holiday, perhaps in a sunny country like Italy, with several beach umbrellas and sunbeds. People who like this kind of holiday enjoy relaxing near the sea for most of the day, and doing little else except reading or sleeping.

2 2.6 Tell students they are going to listen to three people talking about their holidays. Play the recording and ask students to write down the questions the people are asked and any important vocabulary they use.

1 Where do you like spending your holidays?
(staying in my home town, I can do what I like, lots of things on in the summer, music festivals)
2 What do you like doing during your holidays?
(activity, learning a new sport, a language course, met students from all over the world)
3 Where did you go during your last summer holidays?
(family holiday to Croatia, fantastic weather, interesting historical sites, beaches were rather crowded)

useful **language: explaining/giving reasons; giving examples**

3 2.7 Go though the useful language box, and point out that when answering questions, students should give a reason for their ideas where possible. Play the recording again and ask students to identify the words and phrases in bold that the students use.

I like staying in my home town during the holidays. <u>Because</u> I don't have school, I can do what I like every day.
There are also lots of things on in the summer, <u>such as</u> music festivals and things like that, <u>so</u> I don't mind not going away.
I prefer to do some sort of activity when I'm on holiday, <u>like</u> learning a new sport ...
Last year, <u>for example</u>, I did a language course ...
It was great, <u>as</u> we had fantastic weather ...

extra

Put students into pairs. Tell them to imagine that they have both just returned from different holidays. One holiday was good and the other one was not so enjoyable. Tell them to ask one another questions about their holiday. In their answers, they should give reasons and examples of things that were good or bad, and why they did or didn't enjoy the holiday.

Speak up

exam task: **interview**

➥ SB p162

In the Interview section of the Cambridge Speaking test the questions are not related to each other and are all stand alone questions, unlike questions 2, 3 and 5 in this task

4 e Go through the exam tip box. Remind students that in the first part of the Speaking test, they are asked personal questions. They should give interesting answers, and always give a reason or explanation for what they say.

Possible answer

For example, we might go to the cinema or go to someone's house and watch a film, and sometimes we go to the shopping mall and hang out.

Tell students they are going to work in pairs and ask each other the questions in the Questionnaire. As they work, go round and monitor each pair. Assess how well they are doing the task so that you can give feedback. Focus on the following points. Is the student engaged in the conversation or giving rehearsed answers? Does the student achieve the task? How well? If students are struggling with the task, organise them into different pairs and ask them to repeat the task. After a few minutes, stop them and ask for any answers that were particularly surprising or interesting.

Model answers

1 I spent last summer visiting my relatives who live near a beach. I went swimming nearly every day, or playing on the beach.
2 I was with my uncle, aunt, and my three cousins.
3 I didn't take many photos, because I was too busy having fun. I don't usually share photos online.
4 I didn't have time to read any books, unfortunately! I usually read when I have to spend time indoors, and the weather is bad.
5 I took a few selfies with my cousins. There is one of us standing on a big rock in the sea. It's really funny because it looks like we're far out at sea.
6 One of my cousins plays guitar, and in the evening, when the sun went down, he often played it. I'll remember that more than any other kind of music,
7 It's always good to meet up with people who know a place well, because they can show you secret places that only locals know about.
8 The worst souvenir I've ever received was from my uncle. He bought me a T-shirt that said 'My uncle went to London, and all he bought me was this T-shirt!' He thought it was really funny, but I didn't. I've never worn it.

SPEAKING (Continued)

Speaking extra

5 Put students in groups to tell an anecdote based on the photo. Monitor the groups, but don't correct the language, as it is a fluency activity. Ask the group with the most interesting story to tell the rest of the class.

Model answer

I was walking on the beach one day, having a sandwich I'd bought in a shop. I'd finished most of it when suddenly, a huge shape appeared in front of my eyes, and grabbed a piece of bread in my hand. It was an enormous seagull! It made a loud noise and disappeared.

Then, about 10 more seagulls flew down around me. I still had one last piece of bread in my hand, and all the seagulls knew about it. I tried shouting to make them go away, but they didn't. The same seagull which had taken my bread dived at me again, and tried to take my last piece. I quickly ate it before it had another chance.

Next time I go to the beach, I won't take food with me!

Fun footer

Read through the fact with the class. Ask students to use their phones to find similar facts on the internet about a road, train line, mountain, etc. in their own country. Then ask them to share their facts in small groups.

To finish

Ask students to write their own question, similar to the ones in the Questionnaire, and go around the class asking as many other students as they can. Students can report their findings in small groups.

Presentation tool:	Unit 2, Speaking
Workbook / Online Practice:	p21
Speaking file:	SB p162
Audioscript:	SB p176

WRITING SB pp30–31

To start

Ask students to look at the photo on page 30, and discuss the following questions: *What is she doing? How does she feel? How do you know? How would you feel in the same situation?*

Power up

1 Put students into small groups to discuss the questions. If necessary, tell them that the girl in the photo is water-skiing. Give them some more examples of water sports: surfing, sailing, diving, canoeing, fishing, etc.

Possible answer

I like swimming, but I'm not very good at it yet. I'd love to try surfing one day. I've seen people surfing in the sea and it always looks so cool. I think I'd need some special equipment or clothes, and of course, I'd need to take lessons. First though, I need to become a stronger swimmer, and learn how to swim in the open water.

2 Elicit suggestions for what can make a holiday enjoyable or can spoil it. Write the three main ideas on the board, and ask students to explain their ideas. Ask them if they have any particular examples of their own to support their ideas. If necessary, help them by giving your own example, for example: *I once went on a beach holiday and it rained every day.*

Possible answers

good: being with friends, having good weather, having lots of things to do and see

bad: bad weather, not having enough money, becoming ill

Plan on

3 Tell students they are going to write their own article about a holiday. Ask them to read the task and underline what they need to do (write an article and the best and worst things that happened on a trip or holiday). Ask students to read the article and ask: *Have you experienced anything similar?* Ask them to briefly write their own answer to this question, and give their writing to another student to read.

Possible answer

I had an experience once when something went wrong on holiday. We were driving from our hometown to the beach on a long five-hour journey. It was the first day of our two-week holiday and I was having a sandwich in the car. Suddenly, I felt something bad happen to my tooth. I'd broken it!

It was too late to go back home, so I had to spend the next two weeks with a broken tooth. I felt terrible, and I couldn't eat anything on holiday except soup or soft food. I couldn't even eat ice cream, because the cold hurt me too much.

4 Tell students that this is a good article. Ask: *Can you find four good things about it?* Point out that the article has a good title, it gives examples and details to explain why the trip was good or bad, the language is interesting and informal, and it is easy to follow, with a good introduction and conclusion and clear paragraphs. Ask students to underline phrases that could help them when writing an article.

Possible answers

My most enjoyable holiday experience was when ...
Of course, I ...
By the end of the holiday, I ...
It was ... that ...
We were ... when ...
Luckily, I ...
I think it's better to ...

5 Tell students they're going to read another article written about the same task. There are four things wrong with it. Ask students to read it in pairs and identify the four things.

There is no title.
The ideas are all mixed up,
It is not separated into paragraphs and there is no introduction or conclusion.
It's too short.

extra 

Ask students whether there are any good things about the article. Point out that the language is interesting and informal: *a disaster, rained steadily, scared of heights*, etc. There are also examples to explain what went wrong and what was good about the holiday.

6 Remind students of the interesting language used in the first article. Point out that in the Cambridge First exam, marks are given for following the conventions of the genre. An article should hold the reader's attention, as well as inform the reader. This means using interesting language appropriately. Ask students to find the phrases from the box in the articles. Then put them into pairs to practise saying a sentence using each of the phrases.

Possible answers

I can't wait for school to finish and the summer holidays to begin.
I feel sorry for people who pay a lot of money for a holiday, and then something goes wrong.
If you want to gain confidence in speaking English, it's a good idea to find some friends to practise with.
I hope nothing goes wrong with our car while we're travelling.
My friend says he's going to Japan for a holiday. I can't believe it!
I'm looking forward to starting my water-skiing lessons next week.
Sunny weather usually makes people feel better.
I'm scared of heights, so I would never try anything like bungee jumping.
I hope it doesn't rain tomorrow. It will really spoil the day.

explore **language**

7 Write these examples of linkers on the board, and ask students what type of linker it is.

We were on holiday in the UK, and even though the water was cold, I went out every day. (concession/contrast)

I was horrified because I hadn't had the phone long. (cause/result)

Go through the explore language box and ask students to complete the sentences using linkers from the box. There may be more than one possible answer, and there is one linker they don't need to use.

1 Since/Because **2** Although/Even though
3 though/however **4** However **5** so

extra: fast finishers 

Ask students to write one or two more sentences using a linker they didn't use from the explore language box. They then swap their sentences with a partner to check.

Write on

exam tip

8 Go through the exam tip. Conduct class feedback.

Possible answers

enjoyable, cold, I didn't give up, I can't wait, horrified, I'm afraid that spoilt, disasters, good times

Students read the task in Ex 3 again. Ask them to decide which holiday or trip they want to write about, and discuss what they can say about the good and bad aspects of it. Ask: *What title will you give to your article?*

9 Read through the points in the checklist with the class, to remind them of what they should think about when they write an article. Offer help and encouragement as they plan and write their articles.

WRITING (Continued)

exam task: **article** ➥ SB p169

10 **e** Students write their article. Alternatively, you can ask them to do this for homework, and Exs 11–13 can be completed at the beginning of the next lesson.

Model answer

Family times together

Holidays are times for relaxing and enjoying yourself. Sometimes, though, things don't work out as planned.

Last year we stayed in the UK and my parents had booked a week in Devon. I had really been looking forward to this after working hard for my exams. Unfortunately, it was a disaster! It rained steadily for six days. I couldn't believe it. My only views of the sea were through the car windows. I also actually felt sorry for my parents since they had paid to hire a cottage and we didn't see much of Devon at all. However, we played lots of board games inside, and I won every time!

My best trip away was on a day trip to Paris. Even though I'm a bit scared of heights, we went up the Eiffel Tower! Then we had a boat trip down the River Seine through the centre of Paris. I even managed to practise my French with some French students. It was really an experience I'll never forget.

In the end, memories of family times together are good to have, even if things weren't quite perfect at the time!

Improve it

11 Remind students that in the exam, they should always read their final answer through before handing it in, so this is a good habit to develop now. Encourage students to use the checklist every time they write an article to make sure that they have covered all the relevant points. Make sure they check their answers for grammar, vocabulary and spelling mistakes, and that they organise their writing into paragraphs with an introduction and a conclusion.

12 Encourage students to support each other in a positive way as they do this exercise.

13 When you check students' work, rather than commenting on every aspect of the article, concentrate on the items in the checklist. Focus especially on whether students used a range of past tenses accurately, as well as collocations. Remember to praise good language as well. Choose a strong essay to display on the IWB if you have one and ask the class to read it. Alternatively, read the essay out to the class. Ask students to explain why it is a successful article and how well it addressed the points in the checklist.

To finish

Focus students' attention back on Ex 3, and point out that the winning article could see students go on the 'trip of their dreams'. Ask students to imagine what the trip of their dreams would be like. Put them into pairs to explain their ideas.

Presentation tool:	Unit 2, Writing
Workbook / Online Practice:	p22
Photocopiable activity:	2C
Writing file:	SB p169

SWITCH ON SB p32

Sidi Driss

1 Draw a location that students will know on the board, for example, the interior of a restaurant or a square in a town. Ask students to guess where it is. Elicit some sensory information, for example, what you can see, smell or hear there, or what the temperature is like. Then ask students to do the same in pairs. Tell them that, if they wish, they can choose a fictional place from a film, book or TV series, but it should be one that other student are likely to know. Monitor and give help, especially regarding the sensory information. Ask: *What sounds are there? What can you see? Is there a special smell?* Conduct class feedback and ask students to vote on which of the places described would be the most popular to visit and why.

Possible answer

I'm going to describe Matteo's, the Italian restaurant. It's usually quite noisy inside because there are lots of people. It's a really popular place. It's nice inside because all the walls are covered with shelves, and on the shelves are displays of different types of pasta, bottles of sauces, and so on. You can see the kitchen, and the chefs busy making things. It's great to order a pizza and see them making it, throwing the bread in the air, covering it with sauce and cheese and then putting it inside the hot oven. If you sit at a table near the kitchen, it makes you really hungry when you're waiting and you smell all that food!

2 Ask students if they have seen the first *Star Wars* movie from 1977, or the 2002 film *Attack of the Clones*. If they have, elicit anything they can remember about the character Luke Skywalker, or his home planet. Tell students that they are going to see a video clip of a location used in these films. Play the video clip and ask the class why Sidi Driss attracts so many tourists.

It is the film location of the planet Tatooine in the *Star Wars* films.

background 

Matmata is a small town in southern Tunisia where many traditional underground homes can still be found. These homes were built from deep pits, with caves leading from them to serve as rooms linked by passages. People lived here (and some still do) as protection against enemies. Heavy rains in 1967 caused the structures to collapse. However, many families refused to live in the town and repaired the caves and continued to live there. The Hotel Sidi Driss is adapted from one of these homes and is a tourist destination. In 1977 and later in 2002, it was used in the *Star Wars* films to represent the interior of Luke Skywalker's home on the planet Tatooine.

3 Read through the questions with the class. With a strong group, ask if they can remember the answers and play the video clip again to check. With a weaker group, play the clip again and then ask for their answers.

Possible answers

Visitors felt amazed, happy, nostalgic, relieved or connected. They felt compelled to touch and smell the place. They thought it was still in surprisingly good condition.

4 Ask students if all the visitors to Sidi Driss have been *Star Wars* fans (no, one woman has never seen the movies). Ask: *Why might she have visited the place?*

Possible answer

She went with someone who was a fan. She heard it was a tourist attraction, so went along to see what it was like. She was intrigued and wanted to learn more. We hear from another visitor that Tunisian architecture is unique.

5 Students discuss the question in pairs.

Possible answers

It felt like the culmination of years of dreaming. It was satisfying to achieve a goal. Sometimes the things you want to do the most feel like they will never happen, so it must have been emotional for them when it did. It was a reward at the end of a long journey. It can be hard to know quite what to expect when you are about to do something you're really excited about, and it must have been amazing to find that it lived up to expectations. It was an opportunity to meet up with other fans.

Project

6 Ask students to read the steps for the project. If your class is large, this project may be a little unwieldy to do, so split the class into smaller groups. It may be more practical to copy and enlarge outlines of a world map rather than ask students as a group to draw one. It may be that each group (or the class) has a relatively good artist who can do this as his/her part of the project. The map should be poster sized.

Step 3 can be done as homework, with students researching locations online. Advise groups (or nominate different students in a class group) to delegate responsibility for writing cards about different films to members of the group. Students should consider and present the advantages and disadvantages of filming in these different locations. Ask them to think about the practicalities of shooting in a particular location, how it affects the crew, the actors, the directors, etc. Finally, each pair or group of students presents their findings to the rest of the class. Follow up with a discussion about the most interesting locations.

alternative

Organise students into smaller groups and allocate a continent to each group. Then follow the steps for the original project. This time, however, students should research film locations on their given continent. When students present the location from their continent, allocate a wall (or part of a wall) in the classroom as a different continent. Students place their pictures or cards on the relevant walls and they can walk round to view the different results.

Presentation tool: Unit 2, Switch on
Switch on videoscript: TB p171

INDEPENDENT LEARNING SB p32

Feedback

1 Feedback is a potentially sensitive topic. It is very useful for students to be able to comment and learn from others' comments, but some students may take it personally and it has the potential to create friction within a group. Bear this in mind when deciding whether it is appropriate for your students. Say the words *peer feedback* and ask students what they think it means (when you comment on another students' work, or strengths and weaknesses). Ask them to suggest when it can be helpful and when it can be unhelpful. Ask them what the person giving feedback can do to make it helpful and also how the person receiving the feedback should react. Note any interesting suggestions on the board. Then ask students to do the task individually. Conduct class feedback and compare with any ideas you noted on the board.

2 Put students into pairs to share the articles they wrote. Ask them to assess their own work by finding good points and mistakes they will try to avoid in the future. Ask them to also comment on their partner's. Monitor and make sure students are making positive comments, and using phrases from the *When giving feedback* box to make comments which are less positive.

3 You could ask students to reflect on this task and complete it for homework. Students note down two things they will try to do better next time they write an article. At the beginning of the next class, conduct class feedback about some of the main things that students would like to improve in future.

Possible answers

1 I will try to pay more attention to using linkers, so that I can make longer, clearer sentences.

2 I will try to include a variety of language, like adjectives and idiomatic expressions, to make my articles more interesting.

UNIT CHECK SB p33

Note on core language: The Unit check tests idioms and collocations, past tenses and articles.

Practice

1
1 was blown away
2 was high on my list
3 fell in love
4 was over the moon
5 got into the spirit of things

2 **Model answer**
There is a place I've been to which is a high hill. You can get there by car, or by public transport. In the winter, there is a large slope, and if it has been snowing, it's a popular place for sledging. From the top of the hill, in one direction, you can see nothing but other hills and forests stretching all the way into the distance. In the other direction, you get an amazing view of the city. You can see for miles, and it's probably one of the best places I know to come for a picnic.

3 2.8 **1** summit **2** couldn't believe **3** scared of heights **4** achieving my goal **5** gain confidence **6** can't wait **7** 'm looking forward **8** spoil the day

Review

1 **1** arrived, had been **2** have texted **3** had been working **4** were going **5** had eaten **6** was running, tripped **7** used to

2 2.9 **1** had been planning
2 organised
3 felt
4 would normally visit/normally visit/normally visited
5 has been
6 had been having/had had

3 **1** an **2** – **3** a **4** the **5** – **6** The **7** a **8** the **9** a **10** the **11** – **12** – **13** – **14** –

4 **1** best **2** had **3** was **4** so **5** by **6** although/though **7** am **8** more

5 This Sentence Transformation type task only has five items instead of six and they test past tenses, which has been the focus of the unit.

1 has been travelling abroad for
2 used to tell
3 we were having
4 was thinking of taking
5 have had this tablet since

6 Students' own answers.

GRAMMAR FILE SB p145

1 **1** A **2** C **3** C **4** B **5** A

2 **1** used to **2** get used to **3** isn't used to **4** didn't use to **5** used to/would **6** got used to **7** wasn't used to

3
1 had been waiting
2 was always taking
3 had already finished, arrived
4 was going to ring
5 was going to arrive
6 was raining, was blowing

4 **1** had been following **2** asked **3** rushed **4** were watching **5** announced **6** nodded **7** thought up **8** had happened

5 **1** – **2** a **3** the **4** –, the **5** a **6** an

6 **1** a **2** – **3** a **4** the **5** – **6** the **7** the/– **8** the **9** the **10** the/– **11** – **12** the **13** – **14** the **15** –

Presentation tool: Unit 1, Unit check
Workbook / Online Practice: p23
Audioscript: SB p176

All in a day's work 3

READING
topic: virtual school
skill: understanding detail and opinion
task: multiple choice

GRAMMAR
future forms
determiners with countable/ uncountable nouns

VOCABULARY
education and work
phrasal verbs
verbs + prepositions

LISTENING
topic: job shadowing
skill: understanding different speakers
task: multiple matching

USE OF ENGLISH
multiple-choice cloze

SPEAKING
topic: part-time jobs
skill: justifying an opinion
task: collaborative task

WRITING
topic: intergenerational schools
skill: including your own idea
task: essay

SWITCH ON
video: 16-year-old boss
project: research a business

Lead-in SB p35

Focus students' attention on the opening photograph and elicit what the people are doing. Read through the quote *Practice makes perfect* and ask for examples from the class of what they've practised in recent weeks and what the results were. Put students into pairs to discuss questions 1–3. Conduct class feedback.

Possible answers

1 You can do research with a friend, and practice doing some kinds of sport.
2 It's good to do homework with a friend, because then you can help each other when you get stuck, and bounce ideas off each other. The problem is though, when you have to produce your own work, like in a test or an essay. Then, it's important that your work is all your own, otherwise you might be accused of cheating or copying someone else's ideas.
3 I usually need to be alone if I want to concentrate, and if I can't, I put on headphones and listen to music.

extra 

Ask students to work in pairs and discuss the following questions: *What distracts you when you're trying to work? Do you prefer noisy or quiet environments? Does music or chewing gum help you focus?* Give examples of how you work and focus to interest and motivate the class.

READING SB pp36–37

To start

Tell the class one difference between schools you attended when you were a student and schools now, for example, *Students don't just listen in class, they talk and discuss things*. In pairs, students think of different ways schools have changed since they started education. Ask them to consider class size, activities, homework, technology and student–teacher relationships. Conduct class feedback and compare students' ideas. Ask: *Have these changes been positive or negative? Why?*

Power up

1 Focus students' attention on the sign and ask what the reason might be for the school closure. Ask for examples of occasions when their schools have closed for a day in the past and list reasons on the board. Ask: *How might students feel about these closures? How might teachers feel? What problems can these closures lead to?*

Possible answers

The school is probably closed because of heavy snowfall. Other reasons a school might close include a heat wave, special training days, an outbreak of a contagious disease, water leaks in classrooms, etc.

Read on

2 Focus students' attention on the title of the article. Ask when a teacher might say: *Hands up!* to a class (when asking for answers to a question) and what the title might mean.

Cyber school days are occasions when students don't go to school, but learn online or remotely.

3 Ask students to read the article quickly to find the answer. Give them a time limit of one or two minutes, depending on the level of your class. Remind them not to worry about unfamiliar vocabulary at this point.

alternative

With a weaker group, ask the following questions, and allow students more time to become familiar with the article they are going to read.

How will Anna's day tomorrow be different to her usual school day?
Will she have a set order of lessons or can she choose?
What can she do if she has problems?
Why did this idea start?
Why do some people think this is a good thing for the future?
Why do some people think it is a bad thing?
What might be difficult to study in this way? Why?
What problems might students have?

exam tip

4 Explain the exam task to the class. Point out that there will be questions about the text and each question will have four possible options (A, B, C and D), only one of which will be correct. The questions will come in the form of direct questions with four possible answers or question stems with four possible endings. Focus students' attention on question 1 in Ex 5 as an example. Ask students: *How will you go about the task? Will you read the questions and options first or will you read the text?* Then read through the exam tip box with the class. Ask students to read the first paragraph of the article and think about the answer to question 1. Conduct feedback and ask students why they chose a particular option. Elicit why the other options were wrong.

1 B The main point that comes across in the opening paragraph is the newness of the experience.
There are no details given about virtual schooling itself, her school or the way she gets ready, even though these exact words come up in the text.

exam task: multiple choice

The title and lead-in to the reading texts in the Cambridge exam are not usually as engaging as this is with a direct question.

5 **e** Students complete the task individually. Allow stronger students to work through the questions without help, but monitor and give guidance to any weaker students. Conduct class feedback, ensuring students justify their answers.

2 B (*... she'll log on, check her timetable and get going on the day's lessons. Maybe she'll start with maths. Who knows? For one day, the choice will be hers.*)
She clearly has a timetable of what needs to be studied, but can choose what order to do it in.

3 A (*So, is this paving the way for full-time cyber school? Not at all! ... a small number of planned virtual study days ... following the success of a trial at a neighbouring school ... When one neighbouring school offered its students the chance to study at home the results were surprising, with a 90% online attendance.*)
The cyber school days were surprisingly successful, not stressful. The disruption caused by the snow was stressful.

4 B (*The results caught the attention of other head teachers on the look-out for suggestions on how to motivate teachers and students alike and, ultimately, improve grades.*)
The focus is on motivation, not the fact that students work better from home. The creativity of the teachers would be in the planning, and it wouldn't be holiday time.

5 C (*... some teachers worry that the scheme is likely to put them under increasing pressure to plan even more than they already do.*)
There is no reference to getting better grades or benefits. The focus is on the teachers being under pressure.

6 D (*Possibly the biggest drawback for students like Anna is that her younger brothers will probably be a bit of a pain when she's trying to concentrate ...*) Anna has some ideas for doing sport and she is still in regular contact with her friends. There is no reference to helping her siblings.

alternative

If your class is generally weak, they could do the task in pairs. Alternatively, you could give the correct answers and ask students to find out why they are correct by looking closely at the article.

6 Students work in pairs to find the vocabulary items in the text.

1 gearing up **2** siblings **3** support **4** pilot (scheme) **5** win-win situation **6** collaboration **7** distractions **8** drawback

extra: fast finishers

Ask fast finishers to choose one or two words or phrases and then write sentences using them, with the words or phrases gapped. Later, they can take turns to write the gapped sentences on the board for other students in the class to complete.

Sum up

7 Ask students to cover the article and answer the questions in small groups. You could extend the discussion by asking: *How would you personally react to the idea of cyber school days and, ultimately, cyber schools?*

Possible answers

Advantages: more freedom, choosing what to study when, exciting change, extra motivation, teachers can be more creative, online collaboration (which is good preparation for life)

Disadvantages: teachers need to do more planning, they'll be on call all day, less sport or physical exercise, being near family members, which could be a distraction, students may miss their friends

extra

To help with article writing, ask students: *Would you find this article in a serious newspaper or a more light-hearted magazine or website? Why?* Elicit students' suggestions and point out that this article is quite light-hearted, uses some colloquialisms (e.g. *a bit of a pain*) and also poses questions to the reader (*Is this paving the way for full-time cyber school?*). It also uses exclamation marks (*Not at all!*).

Speak up

8 Put students into small groups to discuss the questions. Go round and contribute to the discussions. Remember that this is a fluency activity – try to note down any common errors to deal with later, rather than interrupt students' flow. Corrections can be done with the whole class. Conduct feedback as a class and elicit students' thoughts on how they would organise their cyber days.

Possible answers

1 I'd enjoy learning to code, or make my own computer games. That kind of thing is probably better done online than in a traditional kind of classroom.

2 I would probably be less motivated if I was only in a virtual school environment. There would be so many other things to do, like check other websites, or watch TV. I think I need someone to make sure I'm really doing the work.

3 I study best in the mornings, so I would try to do most of my work then. I might not study at all in the afternoons, but go and do some exercise instead. I also enjoy working at night – I often go to bed late. So, if I could study in the evenings before going to bed, I would.

To finish

Remind students of the disadvantages they discussed in Ex 7. Elicit these ideas and write them on the board. Put students into small groups and ask them to discuss possible solutions for each of these disadvantages, in order to make cyber-schools a productive and positive experience. Conduct class feedback and find out which were the easiest disadvantages to solve, and which were the hardest.

Fun footer

Read through the footer with the class. Point out that *virtual* means something that we can experience, but does not physically exist. Ask students what they think it means and how important it is to divide home and school life.

Explain to students that the next lesson will focus on future forms. Ask them to complete the exercises on page 26 in the Workbook in preparation for this.

Presentation tool:	Unit 3, Reading
Workbook / Online Practice:	pp24–25
Extra Practice App	

GRAMMAR SB p38

To start

Tell students about your plans for the rest of the day (trying to include as many future forms as you can). For example, *I'm meeting another teacher for lunch. We're going to try the new Italian restaurant. I think I'll have ... My first class this afternoon starts at ...* , etc. Use forms that students will probably be familiar with. Ask students: *What are your future plans?* and ask them to note them down in as much detail as they can, and then compare with a partner to find how similar or different their plans are. Conduct class feedback and on the board, write some of the students' examples of *will, going to*, the present continuous or the present simple to talk about the future.

Underline the future forms in the examples on the board and elicit why students think the different forms are used. Point out that *will* can be used when giving an opinion or making a prediction and when we make a decision at the time of speaking. Remind them that *going to* is used for intentions and when something is very likely to happen.

1 Ask students what the time is and write the day and time on the board. Ask: *What are we doing?* and elicit *We're studying English.* Write up the time and date of next week's lesson and tell them: *This time next week, we'll be studying English.* Next, ask: *How many pages of the unit have we done so far?* Elicit: *We've done three pages.* Point at next week's time and date and say: *By this time next week, we'll have done four pages of the unit.* Finally, ask: *How long have we been working?* Elicit: *We've been working for 20 minutes.* Point at next week's time and date and say: *By this time next week we'll have been working for 20 minutes.* Focus students on Ex 1 and sentences 1–4. Ask them to underline the future forms. Then ask them to identify the time expressions used and write them on the board.

1 will have had (This time tomorrow)
2 'll have been collaborating (By the time they get to university; for a few years)
3 is likely to
4 won't be including (for the time being)

explore grammar

➥ SB p146

2 Read through the explore grammar box with the class. Then ask students to complete the examples. They can do this individually or in pairs depending how strong they are. Conduct class feedback.

1 will be revising
2 'll have finished
3 'll have been studying
4 to be

3 3.1 Read through the topics in the box with the class and ask students to listen to the six people and choose the topics each one mentions. Play the recording once. With a weaker group, pause the recording after each speaker to give them time to make their decisions. Conduct class feedback. Play the recording again so that the students can see if they were right or wrong.

1 university studies, career plans
2 career plans
3 travelling
4 socialising, travelling
5 travelling, hobbies, socialising
6 university studies, career plans

4 3.2 Students complete the sentences from the recordings with the correct verb forms. Stronger students could do this first without listening, and then listen to check. Weaker students will need to hear the recording again first. Depending on your students' abilities you may need to pause the recording after each speaker.

1 would've graduated
2 'll be able to
3 'm gonna (going to) be hanging around, 'm travelling
4 'll wake up, 'll go
5 'm packing
6 won't, have changed

5 Tell students to look at the photo at the bottom of the page and ask: *What is Ed's hobby?* They then read the blog, ignoring the gaps, to check.

Ed is young and goes to school (he takes classes), but he has also been asked to act in a film.

6 Students work in pairs to complete the blog with the items in the box. Conduct class feedback.

1 about to **2** not going to **3** is due to **4** will **5** won't
6 is providing **7** won't **8** to be

Speak up

7 Tell students some of your plans, both short-term (tomorrow or the weekend) and more long-term (in five months or a year's time). Organise students into pairs to tell each other about their plans. Monitor and check appropriate use of future forms. Conduct class feedback and see how many similarities there are among students.

Possible answers

At the weekend, I will wake up late, and then I'm going to find out what my friends are doing. If the weather is OK, we'll go cycling somewhere. If it's not OK, we'll go to the swimming pool. We enjoy doing sporty stuff, even if the weather's bad.

alternative

Students write down five plans they have, three true and two false. Put them into pairs and ask them to share their plans. Students have to identify which of their partner's plans are true and which are false.

game on

In pairs students write predictions for their partner (or alternatively, another student in the class). They then share the predictions with their partner and see how many were correct.

To finish

Ask students to imagine themselves aged 18 (or older/ younger depending on the age of your students). In pairs, they discuss the plans they might have at that age. You could extend this by asking them to imagine they are their parents' ages or their grandparents'. Ask them to think about how their plans might change as they become older.

Fun footer

Read through the footer with the class. Ask students why this is funny. Tell them: *Some people say continual learning is one of the most important things we should do in life. Do you agree? Why/Why not?*

Presentation tool:	Unit 3, Grammar
Workbook / Online Practice:	p26
Photocopiable activity:	3A
Grammar reference and practice:	SB p146
Audioscript:	SB p176

VOCABULARY SB p39

education and work

To start

Put students into small groups to discuss what they like most about school life and what they like least. Circulate to encourage and offer examples of your own. Bring students together and share their ideas. Nominate a stronger or more confident student to tell the class the best and worst thing that happened at school yesterday (or today if class is in the afternoon) and why it was good or bad.

1 3.3 Tell students that they are going to hear two students talking about the topics in the box, but they won't use the same words. Play the recording for students to listen and put the topics in the order they are mentioned. Conduct class feedback.

1 discipline **2** grade(s) **3** timetable **4** syllabus
5 experiment **6** handout **7** attendance

2 3.4 Students complete the sentences using words from Ex 1.

1 discipline **2** grade(s) **3** timetable **4** syllabus
5 experiment **6** handout **7** attendance

3 Explain to students that they are going to look at collocations with three verbs, *be*, *have* and *work* in relation to education and work. Organise students into pairs to add the words and phrases from the box to the correct lines.

be: creative, self-employed, your own boss, responsible
have: a good salary, control over your own time, a lot of pressure, time off
work: independently, shifts, part/full-time, as a team

extra: fast finishers 

Ask fast finishers to add two more items to each line (also connected with the topic of school and jobs). Elicit their ideas when you conduct feedback with the class.

extra 

In pairs, students choose a job that one of their family or friends has. They tell their partners about the job using items from Ex 3, without giving the job title. For example, *My cousin has a full-time job. She earns a good salary. She and her colleagues work as a team and they save people's lives. Her job is very responsible and dangerous too. There's a lot of pressure when there's an emergency. She works shifts and doesn't get a lot of time off.* (a firefighter)

VOCABULARY (Continued)

4 Focus students' attention on the title of the article and ask: *What do you think 'Unschool' means?* Students skim the article quickly, ignoring the gaps, to check. (See the background box below.) Ask: *Do you know anyone who is unschooled? If yes, what do you think about their education?* In pairs students complete the article with the correct words from Ex 3. Conduct class feedback.

1 control **2** their own boss **3** responsible **4** independently **5** a lot of pressure **6** full-time **7** time off

background

Unschooling is different from home-schooling in that home-schooling usually has a timetable and syllabus that the parents follow with their children at home. This is less strict than a school curriculum, but should ultimately follow the same paths, leading to qualifications, etc. Unschooling is a system in which children follow their own interests and learn that way, guided by their parents. It's based on the idea that all children are curious and natural learners, therefore they will end up with as good an education, if not better, than those who go through the mainstream schooling system.

extra: fast finishers

Ask fast finishers to find the verbs which collocate with *lessons* (*have*), *a syllabus* (*follow*), *homework* (*do*), *experience* (*gain*), *a chance* (*get*). Then, when everyone has finished Ex 4, ask the fast finishers to present these collocations to the rest of the class. Remind students that it is always a good idea to look out for collocations when they read texts.

explore **vocabulary**

5 Quickly revise some phrasal verbs students have learned in previous units and remind them that a phrasal verb consists of a verb + particle/preposition. Write examples on the board: *My uncle recently gave up his job because he became ill.* and *I came across an old school book in my cupboard.* Remind students that with some phrasal verbs (e.g. *give up*) the object can come after the particle or between the verb and particle. However, a pronoun such as *it* can only be placed after the particle. With other verbs (e.g. *come across*), objects must come after the particle. Tell students that you *get on with* most people in your family well and ask who they get on best with. Explain that some phrasal verbs (e.g. *get on with*) have two particles.

Read through the explore vocabulary box with the class and the examples. Students read the story quickly. Ask: *Why are Luke and Megan unschooled*? (Their mum got a new job abroad.) *Do they enjoy it?* (Yes, they do.) Students match the highlighted phrasal verbs with definitions A–F. They can do this individually and check in pairs. Conduct class feedback.

1 F **2** C **3** B **4** D **5** A **6** E

extra

Put students into pairs. Ask one student in each pair to start writing a sentence, but to finish after writing half a phrasal verb (e.g. *Yesterday, my mum came up …*). The other student has to complete it (e.g. *with an idea for our next holiday.*) They continue until they have written sentences including each of the phrasal verbs in Ex 5.

Speak up

6 Put students into pairs to discuss the questions. While students are discussing the questions, monitor, contribute, give help and note down any errors you may wish to address later. Also note any interesting ideas and mention these in class feedback.

Possible answers

1. The topics in Ex 1 are usually controlled by teachers. An unschooler would need to have a lot of self-discipline. Systems like a syllabus, detention or timetables would not exist.
2. Unschooling is an interesting idea, but it wouldn't suit everyone. You would need a lot of self-discipline and curiosity. You would still need the support of your parents, and you might miss a lot of things that other people your age are learning.
3. You can learn 'real world' skills, like how to develop your own curiosity, set your own goals, and how to explore your own interests.

To finish

Ask students to list as many advantages and disadvantages of unschooling as they can. Go through the lists with the whole class, and then take a vote on whether unschooling is a good or not such a good idea for young people.

Presentation tool:	Unit 3, Vocabulary
Workbook / Online Practice:	p27
Photocopiable activity:	3B
Audioscript:	SB p176
Extra Practice App	

LISTENING SB p40

To start

Organise students into groups. Tell them they are going to talk about the kind of jobs they would like to have in the future. They should say why these jobs appeal to them. Start them off by writing *doctor* on the board, and eliciting ideas about what would be good or bad about this job (e.g. good pay, helping people, long hours, a lot of training, etc.). They should share their ideas for their preferred job with their group, and then discuss the advantages and disadvantages of each one. When the groups have finished their discussions, bring the class together and ask students to share their results. Identify the most popular type of job in the class and the least popular, and why.

Power up

1 3.5 **Tell students they are going to listen to some sounds from three different workplaces. Put them into pairs to listen and identify the workplaces. Conduct class feedback and write their ideas for the three questions on the board. Discuss any vocabulary they might have had problems with, or things they didn't know how to say. Using evidence from the recording and their own ideas, ask them to think of the advantages and disadvantages of working in these places.**

Suggested answers

1 1 a hotel reception
2 receptionists, porters, waiters
3 communication skills, organisation skills

2 1 a supermarket
2 shop assistants, managers
3 communication skills, finance skills

3 1 a train station
2 engineers, train staff, ticket inspectors
3 communication skills, organisation skills

2 Ask the class to describe the workplace in the photos, and to suggest who the people might be and what they might be doing. Confirm that they understand the meaning of *job shadowing* and ask them to suggest the advantages of doing this. Ask: *Can you suggest any other jobs that it might be a good idea to shadow? Are there any that would be impossible to shadow?* Make sure that students justify their ideas.

Job shadowing is when a junior employee, student or trainee follows and observes a more experience person doing a particular job. This usually happens over a period of time.

The advantages of job shadowing are to see what the job involves, to experience the reality of difficult jobs and to confirm whether it's really what they want to do. It could mean that they don't waste time studying to do a job that they end up hating.

3 Students work in pairs to discuss the questions.

1 F – The person shadowing is learning the job.
2 T – Teamwork is considered a very positive aspect of the workplace.
3 F – Shadowing is often unpaid as the people doing it may be students. However, some companies run a shadowing scheme for new employees, in which case they would be paid.
4 T – The goal of the person shadowing is to learn what the job involves.
5 T – They learn by watching not by doing.
6 T – They are not doing the job and taking responsibility for it, they are just learning about it

Listen up

4 3.6 **Tell students they are going to listen to five students talking about job shadowing. Ask them to read the five jobs, then to listen and match the speakers to the jobs. Conduct feedback and ask what vocabulary gave them the answer.**

Speaker 1 D – design process / dream homes
Speaker 2 C – famous celebrities / programme
Speaker 3 A – constructing buildings / outdoors / hard in winter
Speaker 4 E – burning cakes / kitchen / local restaurant / cooking
Speaker 5 B – fresh air / farm / animals

exam tip

5 3.7 **Go through the exam tip with the class. Explain that they will not hear the actual words written in the options, but may hear paraphrases of the same ideas. Ask them to read all the options in Ex 5 and to think of things the speaker might say to express each idea.**

Possible answers

A People tell me what they think.
B I love something that is difficult to do.
C It helped me understand what I want to do.
D I meet loads of different people.
E I have to make my own decisions.
F I found out about something completely different.
G There are great chances for promotion.
H It made me really fit and healthy.

Tell students they will listen to the first speaker, and choose the correct option for the question: what does the speaker enjoy most about shadowing? After playing the recording, conduct class feedback and ask them which word or words gave them the answer.

1 D The speaker talks about visiting clients and says *what was especially cool was meeting loads of interesting customers and hearing them talk about their dream homes.*

exam task: multiple matching

6 e 3.8 **Tell students to listen to the other four speakers and to identify the correct option for each one. This time, they should compare their answers in pairs before you conduct class feedback. Remind them that they must choose the option that tells them what each speaker enjoyed most about the experience. Explain that they may hear things that the speakers enjoyed in general, but only one will be the thing they enjoyed most. Play the recording and then ask them to compare answers.**

LISTENING (Continued)

2 A The speaker says that the positive comments were *so worthwhile*.
3 G Here, the speaker mentions the colleagues doing college courses to *get a promotion* and having *their own company one day. That made me realise what potential there is for a good career in the future.*
4 E The speaker mentions being given more *interesting stuff to do* and said that it was *brilliant to know that somebody wanted to put [you] in charge of something* (i.e. to give you responsibility).
5 C The experience only made this speaker more convinced about a future career. *I'm even more determined now.*

Speak up

7 You could run this as a formal debate, with a vote at the end of the discussion. Give the groups time to discuss their ideas first, and to consider what to say for their side of the debate. Then run the debate with the whole class. A spokesperson for each group should make a brief statement giving the views of the group, and then the debate can be open to everyone.

Possible answers

Arguments for: students are more likely to get higher qualifications without money worries; students are the future and we should invest in them.

Arguments against: if students are not doing a job, they shouldn't get paid; they are too young to get paid; schools and universities might attract people who want money, and don't only want to study.

extra

For homework, ask students to write a short essay (up to 190 words), giving their opinion on the statement: *Students should be paid to study.*

Fun footer

Nominate a student to read out the quote to the class. Elicit explanations of the joke from the class, and also the serious meaning behind it.

background

Donald Kendall is a successful businessman. The quote basically means that it's impossible to be successful without doing a lot of hard work first, and nothing comes easily. The serious message is that you should expect to work hard in order to do well in life.

To finish

Ask students to write their own definition of 'success' and what it means to them. They share their ideas with the class and vote on the definition that most people like best. Direct students to the Workbook exercises on countable/uncountable nouns in preparation for the next lesson.

Presentation tool: Unit 3, Listening
Workbook / Online Practice: p28
Audioscript: SB p177
Extra Practice App

USE OF ENGLISH 1 SB p41

To start

Write the word *advice* on the board. Ask students what form of word this is (it's a noun). Elicit the verb form of this word (*advise*). Next, write the word *course* on the board. Again, elicit the type of word this is (noun). Elicit the plural form of this word (*courses*). Ask students: *Is there any difference between the two nouns, and the way they are used?* Elicit that *advice* is uncountable. The word *course* is countable, and can be made plural. To revise what students already know, tell them that they should say *countable* or *uncountable* as you read out some nouns. Call out the nouns below in any order you like.

(countable) *books, desk, schedule, challenge, risk, group, job*

(uncountable) *stuff, information, health, enjoyment, work, money, respect*

explore **grammar** SB p146

1 Refer students to the explore grammar box, and to the Grammar file on page 146. Point out that it's important to be able to use countable and uncountable nouns correctly and that these might be tested in the exam, often as part of a phrase. Ask students to do Ex 1 in pairs. Conduct class feedback. Point out that not all plural nouns have an *-s* at the end (for example, *people*).

A single countable nouns: boss, role, task
B uncountable nouns: information, stuff, advice
C plural countable nouns: people, courses, colleagues

2 Ask students to work in pairs and identify the nouns in each sentence. They should decide whether each noun is countable or uncountable, and then complete the sentences. Conduct class feedback and refer them back to the explore grammar box if necessary. There is also a useful table of examples on page 146.

1 much **2** a large amount of **3** many **4** less **5** several **6** a few

3 Tell students they're going to read an article with examples of the phrases they've been studying. Focus their attention on the title. Ask: *What do you think it is about?*

Possible answer

Jobs that aren't glamorous or cool can also have benefits and are worth doing.

4 Ask students to read the article in more detail and choose the correct answers.

1 a bit of **2** some **3** few **4** several **5** a great deal of **6** little

exam task: **key word transformations**

The sentence transformations are all linked to the unit topic of work and jobs which doesn't happen in the Cambridge exam.

The items tested here are all related to determiners and countable/uncountable nouns, whereas in the Cambridge exam there would be a variety of structures tested.

5 **e** Tell students that this exercise concentrates on phrases with countable and uncountable nouns. Remind them that when they do this task they must only use 2–5 words to complete each sentence, and they must not change the word given in any way. Remind them that contractions (e.g. *don't* are counted as two words).

1 only a few teenagers
2 earn little/only earn a little
3 few teenagers
4 have been plenty of changes
5 a great deal of
6 don't/do not need much

Speak up

6 You could do this as a whole class discussion. Alternatively, organise the class into three groups. Ask each group to discuss one question. After a few minutes, stop the discussion and ask each group to report back to the whole class on their question.

Possible answers

1 I know a waiter who works very hard. He takes pride in giving customers what they want, and likes it when customers return to the restaurant.
2 A waiter has to deal with rude or unhappy customers, even if the waiter hasn't done anything wrong.
3 It must be interesting to work in a busy restaurant and learn about different foods. I'd like to do it once, maybe as a part-time job.

To finish

Ask students: *Which is most important, job satisfaction or a high salary? Why? Which would you choose, if you could only have one?* Take a class vote.

Presentation tool:	Unit 3, Use of English 1
Workbook / Online Practice:	p29
Grammar reference and practice:	SB p146
Extra Practice App	

USE OF ENGLISH 2 SB p42

To start

Ask students to think about what skills might be important for getting a job in the future. Conduct feedback, and write the skills they suggest on the board. Then ask the class to vote on what they all think will be the top three skills. Computer skills will probably be high on the list and this will link to the next section.

1 Write these words on the board: *computer, programming, instructions*. Ask: *What links these ideas?* Then write *coding* on the board. Elicit students' ideas.

2 3.9 Play the recording so that students can check their ideas.

Coding is the skill of telling a computer what you want it to do through a series of typed step-by-step instructions for the computer to follow.

extra 

Ask: *Would you like to do, or have you ever done a coding course. Why/Why not? What do you think would be good or bad about becoming a computer programmer?*

explore **vocabulary**

3 3.10 Go through the explore vocabulary box. Ask students if they can think of any other examples of verbs followed by a preposition (e.g. *believe in, go through, benefit from, listen to, speak to, depend on*). Students listen and complete the sentences.

1 depends on **2** referred to **3** cope with **4** benefit from

4 Ask students to read the article quickly without worrying about the gaps, and decide whether statements 1–4 are true or false.

1 F (That's what people thought in the past.)
2 F (It's likely that all jobs will benefit from basic coding skills.)
3 T
4 T

exam task: **multiple-choice cloze**

The items tested here are all related to the lesson focus of verbs + prepositions.

5 **e** Go through the exam tip with the class. Remind students that reading the words before and after each gap is a good way of looking for prepositions and collocations in general. Ask them what the answer to question 2 is.

The preposition that goes after the gap is *in*. The only collocation that matches this preposition is *believe* (option C).

Students should work together to complete the whole task. Conduct class feedback, and make sure that they read out aloud both the verb and the preposition, and explain their answer. Suggest that they record the correct verbs + prepositions, and try to remember them.

USE OF ENGLISH 2 (Continued)

1 B (preposition *on* collocates with *rely*) **2** C (verb *believe* collocates with *in*) **3** D (preposition *in* collocates with *specialise*) **4** A (*benefit from* is a collocation)
5 A (preposition *in* collocates with *succeed*)
6 B (verb *apply* collocates with preposition *for*)
7 C (preposition *on* collocates with *depend*) **8** D (verb *appeals* collocates with preposition *to*)

extra

You could play pelmanism. Prepare several sets of cards, with verbs on one half and prepositions on the other. Organise the class into groups, give each group a set of cards and tell them to lay the cards face down on the table. They should take it in turns to turn over a verb card and then a preposition card. If they think the cards go together, they should use them in a sentence. The others should decide if it is correct or not. If the cards don't match, then they should be replaced, face down, on the table and the next student turns over another two cards. The person in the group that makes the most matches wins.

Speak up

6 These questions are quite complex, and worth spending time thinking about as a class. Ask students to think about them for homework and spend the start of the next lesson discussing them in pairs.

Possible answers

1 As technology is developing, it is become more important to keep up with it. More and more jobs are becoming automated and there might come a time in the future when people who don't know how to code are at a disadvantage when it comes to finding a job.
2 Schools could teach students by giving them 'hands-on' access to technology, such as tablets or phones. Students learn best by doing things for themselves.
3 I would like to learn how to make my own apps. I often have ideas for apps I'd like to download, but I have no idea how to go about making one.

Fun footer

Read through the footer with the class. Ask students: *Why do you think people are sometimes afraid of new technology and new ideas?* Allow them to discuss this in pairs or small groups.

To finish

Tell students to close their books. Call out the following verbs one by one and ask students to call out the dependent preposition which goes with each one: *agree* (on), *apologise* (for/to), *believe* (in), *choose* (between), *result* (in), *insist* (on), *lead* (to), *rely* (on), *specialise* (in), *succeed* (in).

Presentation tool:	Unit 3, Use of English 2
Workbook / Online Practice:	p30
Photocopiable activity:	3C
Audioscript:	SB p177
Extra Practice App	

SPEAKING SB p43

To start

Ask students to think about the kind of jobs people often do part-time (e.g. waiter, receptionist). Ask: *What do you think the advantages and disadvantages of doing these jobs part-time might be?*

Power up

1 Focus students' attention on the two photos at the bottom of page 43. Once students have discussed the questions in pairs, conduct class feedback. Find out which of the two jobs is most popular with the whole class and why.

Possible answers

1 The person on the left is working in a café, possibly as a barista. The person on the right is a primary school teacher or assistant.
2 A barista needs to know how to make good coffee, in a variety of styles. A teacher needs to be patient, and have empathy with the children she is teaching.
3 I would prefer to be a primary school teacher, because I like being around young children.

2 Focus students on the task. Put them into pairs to think about the benefits of part-time jobs in general. They should make notes on the points in the diagram.

Possible answers

They can learn about managing their own time – juggling the job with other duties.
They can learn how to solve problems that arise in the workplace.
They can earn money, and either save it or use it to pay for college, etc.
They can make new friends, or come into contact with a range of people they wouldn't otherwise.
They can learn that having a job means having different kinds of duties or responsibilities.

3 Explain that the points in the boxes are there to give them ideas to start their discussion, and that in the exam they don't need to discuss them all. It's more important that they interact well, so they should give a reason for their ideas where possible and ask their partner to explain their reasons for their opinions. Ask them to match the phrases to the points. There may be several possible answers, so allow students time to think about their ideas.

Possible answers

time management: cope with pressure, be punctual, organise your time
problem solving skills: become more independent, become more self-confident, make judgements about situations, find solutions, take decisions
financial independence: learn the value of money, become more independent
meeting people: become more self-confident, improve communication skills, learn teamwork
sense of responsibility: become more independent, take decisions, earn trust

4 3.11 Ask students to read the two questions, then play the recording. Students compare their answers in pairs, and explain their opinion to each other.

1 time management and financial independence
2 be punctual, organise your time, (learn) the value of money

5 3.12 Students complete the task. Ask: *Do the speakers provide reasons and evidence for their opinions?* (Yes, they do.)

1 Shall we start with
2 how do you think
3 What do you think
4 How about
5 Don't you agree
6 what about

Speak up

exam tip

6 Go though the exam tip. Remind students that in the exam, they are marked on their language not their ideas, so they should say as much as they can about each point without worrying whether it is 'right' or 'wrong'. It is also important that they interact with each other, as this is one of the aspects they are marked on in the exam.

Possible answer

A possible response should be something that adds to the point being made, so that it is interactive, for example, *I think it would be useful because ..., Well, have you thought about ...?, Actually, I think it could help because you have to work within definite hours and finish your work.*

Organise students into pairs. Remind them that in this part of the exam, it is important to have a genuine discussion and that they should explain and justify their ideas. They have to talk for two minutes, but they don't need to discuss all the prompts in this time. Ask them to do the task in pairs within a two-minute time limit.

Go round and monitor during the two minutes. After two minutes, ask them how many points from Ex 2 they managed to discuss. Explain that it's more important to have a detailed discussion about a couple of prompts than to say a little about them all.

Model answer

A: OK, so why might it be a good idea for students to have part-time jobs? What do you think?
B: Well, let's think about financial independence first. It's important for people to have their own money, and learn how to use it, don't you think?
A: Yes, and nothing teaches you the value of money more than when you earn it for yourself. And what about meeting people? Do you think students can meet a lot of people when they do a part-time job?
B: It depends on what the job is. If you work in a café, you'll just meet customers all day. I'm not sure how useful that really is.
A: It does teach you people skills, and how to communicate with different kinds of people, I think.
B: Yes, I agree. And what about time management? I mean, if you have a part-time job, you're probably doing other things as well, like studying.
A: So actually, doing part-time work makes you think more carefully about how much time you have, and how you can fit everything into a day. So that's valuable, I think.
B: And that relates to problem-solving skills. If your life is busy, and you're juggling lots of different tasks then that's definitely a problem.
A: Also, different jobs have different problems. For example, a primary school teacher might have to deal with a difficult child or an angry parent. How about 'sense of responsibility'? Part-time jobs don't usually have a lot of responsibility, do they? You don't have to take important decisions or anything.
B: Maybe not, but you still have to be punctual and work as part of a team.

extra

Ask students to record their discussions using their phones. They could then listen back to what they said, and consider how well they interacted with each other.

7 Tell students that in the exam, they have another minute to make a decision about the topic they have discussed. Ask: *Which benefit of having a part-time job do you think is most important?* Time them again as they discuss this in the same pairs as in Ex 6. Explain that in the exam they don't have to agree, as long as they have good reasons for their opinion.

Model answer

A: For me, having financial independence is important.
B: Yes, I agree. And when young people have a part-time job, it's usually their first experience of earning and having their own money.
A: And this can help students become more self-confident, and more independent, too.
B: So, yes. Financial independence is the most important benefit here.

exam task: collaborative task ➥ SB p164

8 **e** Direct students to page 171 and go through the task. Remind them that they should interact with each other and not just give their own opinions. Monitor students while they do the task, and give feedback on how well the students responded to what their partner said. For example, comment if one student dominated the discussion, or whether they really listened to each other and responded to different ideas. Also give feedback on how well (if at all) they used the phrases for agreeing and disagreeing from Ex 5.

SPEAKING (Continued)

Possible answers

teach language skills: many employers look for people who can speak more than one language, or can work abroad

provide IT courses: as more jobs become automated and technology increases, it becomes more important to learn about IT

encourage critical thinking: students who can think for themselves, make their own independent decisions and think objectively make better life choices later on

have meditation classes: helps students relax and concentrate on their own emotions and well-being

run interview/CV workshops: helps students understand what employers are looking for, and how to apply for jobs

Speaking extra

9 **Point out that in the exam, students will have to discuss further questions related to the task they have been discussing. Focus students' attention on questions 1–3. Ask them to talk about these questions in pairs. Conduct class feedback and see what ideas the whole class can agree on.**

Possible answers

1 I'd like to become a journalist, because I've always liked writing, and I think I've got a gift for it.

2 I think it's important to have an idea of what you want to do, because this helps you choose what to study, or whether or not to study.

3 It might be better to follow one profession that you are really interested in, and try to develop your career in this area as far as possible.

To finish

Ask students: ***Where do you see yourself in five years' time?*** **Explain that this is a typical question asked in job interviews. Give students one or two minutes to think and make notes on this question. Then organise them into pairs. Students should take turns to talk for one or two minutes about the question.**

Presentation tool:	Unit 3, Speaking
Workbook / Online Practice:	p31
Speaking file:	SB p164
Speaking tasks:	SB p171
Audioscript:	SB p177

WRITING SB pp44–45

To start

Write the following words on the board: ***Teacher, Elderly person, Parent, Friend.*** **Ask:** ***What kind of help can each of these people give other people, especially young people?*** **Suggestions can include: a teacher can share knowledge or give career advice; an elderly person can share wisdom or experience; a parent can offer support or advice; and a friend can give advice or help someone have fun.**

Power up

1 **Ask students to look at the photo, and discuss the following questions.** ***What is the woman doing? What kind of help is she giving? How does the girl feel? How do you know? How would you feel in the same situation?***

Suggested answers

The older woman is teaching the girl calligraphy (the art of writing letters in a very decorative way).

2 **Focus students' attention on the article and the questions. Put students into pairs to discuss the questions.**

1 A mentor is generally an experienced person who advises another person who is less experienced. This is often at work or school.

2 Pensioners who are energetic, experienced, interested in young people, keen to learn about young people, kind, helpful, etc.

3 Teenagers can talk to them, share their knowledge about what they're learning at school, help them with computer problems and other technical skills.

4 Reasons why it might be a good idea include the possibility that younger and older people can learn from each other, it gives them both a different perspective on life, and encourages them to try different things. Reasons why it might be a bad idea include the possibility that young and older people tend not to have much in common, and might become frustrated with each other.

explore **language** ➥ SB p146

3 **Ask students to read through the explore language box on possession. Then go through Ex 3 together with the class, so that they understand the point of each one and why the apostrophe is used in this way.**

1 Pensioners' (The words *pensioners* is plural. This means 'the advice of the pensioners'.)

2 Both (This means 'the mentor and the student'.)

3 person's (The word *person* is a singular noun. This means 'the confidence of one particular person'.)

4 Neither (This means that discussing the problems is not possible for pensioners or students.)

5 or (This means that there are two possible outcomes, but only one will happen)

4 Organise the class into two groups. Tell them to read the essay task, and to suggest a possible third point.

Possible answers

health benefits, a better social life, why it's good for the community

5 Ask students to read the essay. Students try to find what points the writer makes about ideas 1 and 2 from the task in Ex 4, and what third point was made.

1 For points 1 and 2, the writer mentions that teens and pensioners experience similar challenges, they both struggle to socialise, and experience loneliness and low self-confidence. Also, pensioners can help teens by being patient and understanding. Parents are often too busy to do so.

2 Teens can motivate older people by introducing them to new experiences, technology, sport, etc.

6 Remind students of the importance of a conclusion in an essay, because it sums up the argument and states the writer's point of view very clearly. Focus students' attention on the different endings, A and B and put them into pairs to discuss the questions.

A: This works and balances the argument. It is more cautious in its summing up than the essay in Ex 5, which gives definite opinions. That's why the writer uses *but* to express doubt or concern. It could be a good alternative conclusion.

B: This disagrees with the statement in the original task. It doesn't work with this essay as the main part of the essay talks about how teens and pensioners can learn from each other.

Plan on

7 Tell students that an essay must be well-organised and present a logical argument. This means that they should always plan what they are going to write. The essay in Ex 5 is well-organised, and uses linking words well to make the argument easy to follow. Ask students to match the functions to the paragraphs in the essay.
They should identify key phrases that helped them identify the functions.

1 B (This makes a general statement that introduces the topic.)

2 D (*It is often said that* … introduces the first idea.)

3 A (*Another important point is that* … introduces a second idea.)

4 E (*From my own experience* … introduces the writer's own idea.)

5 C (*To sum up* … concludes the argument and the essay.)

8 Ask students to decide why the highlighted items are important. Put them into pairs to decide what function each word or phrase has.

They all link the text and give it structure and cohesion.
Despite contrasts two different ideas.
It is often said that introduces an idea.
Likewise gives similar information.
Another important point is/Moreover both give additional information.
From my experience introduces the writer's own opinion.
To sum up starts a conclusion.

Write on

9 Put students into pairs and ask them to read the task. They should decide what they could say about each point, and what they can add as their own idea. As they discuss their ideas, monitor and make suggestions if they can't think of anything or their ideas are not relevant.

Possible answers

academic knowledge: it's important to have qualifications; it helps to get a job, but experience is also good; schools should help students get practical experience.

money management: schools teach maths, but actually saving and managing money is an important life skill.

your own idea: schools could also teach careers advice, social skills or technology skills.

exam task: essay

SB p165

The essay tasks on this spread do not have the full lead-in as in the Cambridge exam task, as this is the first essay task in the book and the focus is on the question.

10 **e** Go through the exam tip to remind students of the importance of planning their essay. Point out that in the exam, they won't have time to write two versions of their essay, so it's very important to make a plan. Spending just 10 minutes planning can make a big difference. This plan can simply be notes under headings, but it will help them with paragraphing and with including everything required in the task.

Write this plan outline on the board, and ask students to use it every time they plan an essay.

1 introduction
2 first idea
3 second idea
4 third idea
5 conclusion

Tell students to write their essay using their notes or ideas from Ex 9. When they have finished, they should exchange their essay with a partner.

Model answer

Although schools teach students a range of subjects and skills, some people believe that students need to learn more in order to be successful adults.

It is often said that academic knowledge isn't always useful. For example, people rarely need to know historical dates, or how to solve mathematical problems in their day-to-day lives. However, that is not to say that academic information is useless. It does develop students' ability to think and read and write. The problem is that there is much more that students should learn.

As an example, students do not learn about money management in schools. This might lead to them becoming adults who do not know how to save, or manage debt.

Similarly, many schools do not spend enough time teaching social skills, such as how to work in a team, to solve problems together, or understand other people's feelings. These skills are undoubtedly important in later life.

To sum up, I agree that schools need to teach more than academic knowledge to students. Moreover, teaching young children a wider variety of skills would help create a better society.

WRITING (Continued)

Improve it

11 Give time for students to revise their essay according to the checklist. When you assess their work, focus on the following issues.

- Is there a clear introduction stating the general topic?
- Is there a clear point in each paragraph?
- Are the ideas linked with good linking words?
- Is there a conclusion and is it logical?

If you feel students need more help in writing essays, refer them to the Writing file on page 165 for homework, to remind them of the format and organisation of an essay.

To finish

Ask students to work in new pairs to summarise and explain their conclusions from their essays. Their partner can ask questions about why they have arrived at this conclusion.

Presentation tool:	Unit 3, Writing
Workbook / Online Practice:	p32
Writing file:	SB p165

SWITCH ON SB p46

16-year-old boss

1 Read the task through with the class and then organise students into pairs to discuss the points. If necessary, give them examples of your own. Circulate and contribute to discussions. Conduct class feedback and ask students to tell the rest of the class interesting things they learned from their partners.

Possible answers

I'm naturally good with numbers. I've always been able to do sums in my head, without needing a calculator.

I'd really love to learn how to play a musical instrument. I'm envious of anyone who can just pick up an instrument and start playing.

I know that I'll never learn how to code, or build a website, or anything like that. It's just not something that interests me.

2 Tell students they are going to watch a video about a young person called Philip. Refer them to the picture and elicit what his job may be. Explain that Philip is from Yorkshire, a part of the UK, and he has a fairly strong accent. Read the task with your class and play the recording. Allow students to share their ideas with a partner before checking answers around the class.

He plans to train sheepdogs and sell them to farmers.

extra

Depending on the strength of your class, you may need to check understanding of some vocabulary items. Put students into groups and give them different words and phrases. Ask them to research their meanings online. Then ask them to explain their words to the whole class.

a dairy farm (a farm with cows for milk)
a flock of sheep (a group of sheep)
to shear (to cut wool from sheep)
a tricky start (a difficult start)
to convert (to change one thing into another)
a kennel (where a dog lives and sleeps)
to do something for a living (a profession/job)
to get your teeth into something (to do something with energy and enthusiasm)
to have something under your belt (to have a useful experience)
to live the dream (to do what you've always wanted)

3 Put students into pairs to complete the task. Explain that they need to identify the different skills that Philip shows and give examples from the video. Play the video clip again and give them some time to discuss the answers. Conduct class feedback.

Possible answers

Philip can negotiate. He can successfully make deals to secure the materials for his new dog kennels.

He can train sheep dogs. He starts a business that depends upon it.

He can shear sheep, and shears some of his own flock.

He is practical. He builds the kennels himself after clearing out the cow shed.

He has the ability to spot good-quality sheep dogs. He bids for and wins the dog he wants at an auction.

4 Elicit answers to this question from the whole class. Encourage students to answer it in their own words.

Possible answer

She's pleased with the way Philip is approaching a difficult venture. She is positive about the future and is glad that he is interested and working hard to find answers. She is letting him make his own decisions because it will be his future job.

extra 

For homework, ask students to write a short summary of the documentary and what Philip talks about in no more than 100 words. Give them this to start with: *Philip is a young boy who has grown up on a farm. He has just left school and is planning …*

To finish

Ask students to discuss these questions in pairs, based on evidence from the video and their own ideas.

1 *Do you admire Philip? Why?*
2 *What do you think Philip's life will be like in five years' time?*
3 *Would you like to have Philip's job? Why/Why not?*
4 *What does 'living the dream' mean to most people*
5 *Some people turn their hobby into a career. Is this always a good thing?*

Project

5 Explain the project to the class and put them into small groups. Suggest that all members of the group do some research and collate their ideas before deciding on whose idea to follow through. This can be at home if time is short, or in class time if you have internet access and students have smart phones, tablets, etc. Students may find it helpful to research the local area for businesses that might have an unusual back story. Perhaps they heard of a strange story once from a family member. If so, they could try and verify it. Each group should discuss their research and choose the best ideas to include in the presentation. After each group has presented their findings, the class votes on the best original story.

alternative 

Students do this as an individual project, rather than as a group. They should do the research and planning stages for homework. Then, allocate class time at the beginning of the next lesson for each student to present their projects in small groups. Each group then decides on their favourite presentation to be given to the whole class.

extra 

In pairs, students discuss their own hobbies and ways in which they might turn them into a career. They take turns to interview each other about their hobbies and whether they could ever imagine turning these hobbies into a job in the future. They then share their ideas with the rest of the class and discuss how viable these might be as businesses or jobs.

Presentation tool: Unit 3, Switch on
Switch on videoscript: TB p172

INDEPENDENT LEARNING SB p46

Skill assessment

1 Tell students that you will be discussing *skill assessment*, which means thinking about which skills they are strong at and which may be weaker. Ask why this type of assessment might be useful. Ask students to tell you as many things they studied in this unit as they can remember. List them on the board. Include grammar points, vocabulary, exam tips, etc. Then put students into pairs to look back through the unit and tell each other which tasks they found interesting and quite easy and which they found more difficult. Then they should think about what they have learnt which could help them in the future with their Reading, Listening, Grammar, Vocabulary, Speaking and Writing. Be careful not to be too critical of students' work at this point, but to be encouraging, praising and helping them come to their own assessments. Bring students together in full group and compare their ideas. It is important here to foster an atmosphere in which weaker students do not feel threatened about discussing their weaknesses, and you should not ask students to contribute if it would be uncomfortable for them.

2 In pairs students compare their essays and discuss what they wrote. Ask them to focus on content, organisation, grammar, spelling, punctuation and vocabulary. Encourage them to make at least one positive point about each topic (e.g. *That's a great sentence, and you've used a good linker here* …). They should try to give each other tips for the next essay. Again, remind them to be polite and to make suggestions rather than give instructions (e.g. *You could* … , *If I were you, I'd* …).

Possible answers

Try to use more linkers, to make your writing clearer, and to write longer sentences.

Make sure you include paragraphs, and that each paragraph is on a different point.

Check your spelling and grammar carefully after you have written your essay.

3 Students identify what is most important for them to think about in the next unit. Ideas could range from *extending my vocabulary* to *trying to speak more in class* or *checking my writing before I hand it in*. It is important that students come to their own conclusions here, and make their own plans. Give them time to note down three things to work on and ask them to check them at the end of the next unit.

Possible answers

1 When speaking, I should try to interact more with my partner by asking them questions, rather than just saying what I think.
2 I should try to focus on using future forms accurately, and to use a variety of forms.
3 Before listening, I should try to read through the options more carefully, and make sure I know what I'm going to be listening for.

UNIT CHECK SB p47

Note on core language: This Unit check covers education and employment vocabulary, future forms, countable/uncountable nouns and phrasal verbs.

Practice

1 **1** grades **2** a lot of pressure **3** gets on with **4** drawback **5** rely on **6** detention

2 3.13 **1** attendance **2** have a good salary **3** run out of **4** benefit from **5** choose between **6** become self-confident **7** distraction **8** pocket money

3 **1** organise my time **2** specialises in **3** discipline **4** apologised for **5** led to **6** works **7** keep up with **8** being self-employed

Review

1 **1** D **2** H **3** A **4** G **5** C **6** B **7** F **8** E

2 3.14 **1** number **2** plenty **3** Most **4** few **5** every **6** lot **7** little **8** some

3 3.15 **1** came up with **2** keep up with **3** gets on with **4** catch up on **5** make up for **6** run out of

4 **1** be/start/begin **2** up **3** few **4** plenty/lots/loads **5** is **6** have **7** unlikely **8** the/any

5 Hi Sara,

I hope you're OK. I'm just writing to say that I've had an email from the organiser of the local food festival. Guess what! They have asked me to help out. I've always wanted a part-time job at a festival, and this sounds like fun!

The organisers says it's going to be busy and I might feel under pressure sometimes, but I'll be working as part of a team, and the actual work seems like it's going to be easy.

So, if you want to come along to the food festival next week, you might see me there! I'll be helping out at the ticket office!

See you soon,

Mark.

GRAMMAR FILE SB p147

1 **1** 'll (will) explain
2 Are you doing, 're (are) having
3 's going to be
4 'll (will) be celebrating
5 'll (will) have been working
6 starts, 'll (will) go
7 is about to

2 **1** will begin **2** 'm doing **3** starts **4** is going to **5** 'll be learning **6** won't be **7** will be **8** 'll have gained **9** will have been studying **10** won't have earned

3 **1** D **2** F **3** E **4** C **5** A **6** B

4 **1** a lot **2** much **3** a few **4** number **5** little **6** a great, lots of

5 **1** school's **2** twins' **3** both **4** Harry's **5** either **6** neither

Presentation tool:	Unit 3, Unit check
Workbook / Online Practice:	p33
Audioscript:	SB p177
Extra Practice App	

The heart of the city 4

READING
topic: real or fake cities
skill: scanning a text to find information
task: multiple matching

GRAMMAR
conditionals
alternative conditional forms

VOCABULARY
town and country
compound nouns
as or *like*
prepositional phrases

LISTENING
topic: public spaces for teens
skill: recognising distractors
task: multiple choice

USE OF ENGLISH
open cloze
multiple-choice cloze

SPEAKING
topic: visiting cities
skill: giving an opinion
task: discussion

WRITING
topic: a day in the city
skill: giving the right information
task: informal letter or email

SWITCH ON
video: design gone wrong
project: analyse a building

Lead-in SB p49

Ask students to look at the photo and ask where it might have been taken and what is happening. Refer to the unit title, *The heart of the city* and ask students to guess what it refers to (literally, the centre of the city, but also what gives a city its identity). Nominate a student to read the quote and elicit students' reactions. Ask: *Do you feel the same? Why/Why not?* Discuss the first two questions as a class. Then put students into pairs to discuss question 3. Conduct class feedback and see whether the majority of the class are country or city lovers.

Possible answers

1 I live in a big city, so during the early part of the day you mostly see people rushing to work, or older people going to the markets. In the daytime, you see a lot of shoppers and workers. But in the night time, everything changes and people are happier and more relaxed. You can see a lot of people enjoying restaurants and cinemas.
2 I like it most in the evenings, because a lot of beautiful buildings are lit up and it can look very beautiful.
3 The city! There are so many things to do, and all my friends live here. It's also much easier to get around because there are lots of public transport options.

extra 

Ask students to name as many capital cities in the world as they can. You could do this as a class competition. Each student gives the name of a city in turn. If a student can't name a different city, they drop out. Continue until the last student.

READING SB pp50–51

To start

Describe one of your own favourite places in a city or town where you live. Say something like: *My favourite place in my city is on the hill, overlooking the river. I like seeing all the bridges, especially when they are lit up at night. It's nice that I can see all the boats travelling on the river. I like it because my parents used to take me there when I was younger.* Ask students to think of a favourite place in their town or city. They should describe it to their partner in as much detail as possible and they should tell their partner why it's their favourite. Ask students to report back on their partners' answers.

Power up

1 Ask students to look at the adjectives and say which one they would automatically use to describe city life. They then look at the words more carefully and try to explain why.

Possible answer

I think the words *lively* and *busy* best describe city life. I wouldn't choose *crowded* or *stressful*, because these sound too negative. I like the energy of living in a city, so I would choose more positive words.

extra

Ask students to imagine a tourist visiting the students' capital city for the first time. Elicit examples of the following:

1 three items the tourist should bring
2 two pieces of advice for tourists
3 adjectives that might describe the tourist's first impression of the city.

Read on

2 Ask students if they know of any unusual cities in the world. If you have time you could ask students to research these online. They might give *Venice* as an answer (because it's sinking). Refer students to the photos in the article on pages 51 and 52 and the title, and ask them to predict what the article might be about. Read the introduction with the class to check their ideas. Then ask them to look at the individual section titles. Ask: *Which of these cities do you think really exist?*

See the answer for Ex 3.

3 Students read the article quickly. Give them a time limit of one or two minutes, depending on their level, to check their ideas. Conduct class feedback.

They all exist, but the only city people actually live in now is the Underground city (D).

extra

With a weaker class, ask the following comprehension questions before they do the exam task. This will help focus their attention on the general ideas of the article.

1 *Why was Mcity created?* (To test driverless cars.)
2 *Why is Lion City under water?* (It was flooded to create a dam.)
3 *Why might floating cities be a good thing?* (They use greener energy, helping solve climate-change problems; there is space for more people; and it might be cleaner.)
4 *What are advantages of the underground city?* (It is warmer and uses space better.)

exam tip

4 Remind students of the format of the multiple-matching task. Point out that they will need to read four or more sections of a text and match questions to the correct sections. Tell them that this could be one long text divided into paragraphs, or a text with different sections, like the article on page 51. Read through the exam tip box and explain to students that when doing the matching task, the phrasing in the question and the text will not always be exactly the same, so they need to look for different ways of explaining something. They should read the texts through first, then read through the questions and underline the important words that will help them identify the correct texts. Look at question 1 in Ex 5 with the class. Say that *flood* or *flooding* is mentioned in more than one section of the article but *deliberate* only relates to one section. Ask students to scan for *flood* or *flooding* and then decide which section relates to *deliberate*, and why. Point out that section C mentions rising sea levels and flood risks but section B says the city was flooded on purpose. Explain that *on purpose* means *deliberately.*

1 B (*But in 1959 a massive dam was built, and the city <u>was flooded</u> <u>on purpose</u>.*)

exam task: multiple matching

The introduction to the text is more detailed than in the Cambridge exam.

5 **e** Ask students to read through the questions and underline the words they think are important. You may wish to explain the following words: *mishaps* (accidents or problems), *redefined* (reshaped), *expanding* (growing), *concerns* (worries). Students complete the task individually and then compare answers. Monitor to help weaker students.

2 D (*But if town planners knew about the benefits, they decided to ignore them.*)
3 A (*… many accidents in previous tests involved pedestrians.*)
4 B (*… if it hadn't been for a decision to build a new hydro-electric power station, it would have stayed that way.*)
5 D (*… cities have sprawled, leaving little space for any more building.*)
6 C (*Sceptics are bound to ask if such an innovation can solve some of the issues facing cities today such as over-population, pollution and rising sea levels.*)

7 A (*Take a closer look and you'll see that behind the shop fronts there's nothing on sale at all.*)
8 B (*... inhabitants had to be relocated, with many of them leaving their ancestral homes.*)
9 D (*... in order to create extra space and maintain a low rise skyline.*)
10 C (*... if they had paid more attention to these concerns years ago, they might have prevented the current housing crisis and flood risks.*)

6 Elicit the synonym for *not real* in text A. Students should produce *simulated* quite easily. Students work in pairs to complete the task. Check answers around the class. Get students to note down any new words so that they remember them.

1 simulated **2** defaced **3** imposing **4** ancestral
5 amenities **6** issues **7** increasingly **8** insulated

extra

Deal with other potentially unfamiliar words by writing the following on the board and asking students in pairs to find them in the article, look at the context, and try to work out the meanings.

pedestrian (text A) a person walking in a street
deteriorating (text A) getting worse
massive (text B) very large
thriving (text B) healthy, working well
in high demand (text C) popular, wanted
boasts (text C) includes, is proud of
sprawled (text D) grown untidily
chilly (text D) cool

Sum up

7 Students discuss the two questions in pairs. Encourage them to use their own words as far as possible.

Possible answers

1 These cities show interesting ways of dealing with our modern problems of over-crowding. It's possible that in the future, we will consider building cities which float on water, or are deep underground. As we develop new technology, such as driverless cars, we will have to explore different styles of living. We know that some cities don't last forever, such as the sunken city of Shicheng. Perhaps the cities we now live in will one day disappear, and be replaced with something completely different.
2 For me, the most interesting city is Shicheng, or Lion City. I love the idea of exploring an old city which is perfectly preserved, and finding out how people used to live in the past.

alternative

This could be a written summary for homework. Tell students that they have to write a short description, in their own words, of one of the cities for a webpage. Show a selection of summaries on the IWB, if you have one, and ask the class to read them and vote on which should be included.

Speak up

8 Ask students to discuss the first question in small groups. You could also ask: *How likely do you think it is that new types of city will be built in the future?* Encourage students to think about cost, levels of interest, disruption, traditions, etc. Put students in pairs to talk about question 2, in order to give each student more talking time. If your class is monolingual, they could also discuss how their own city or area could be improved.

Fun Footer

Read through the fun footer and ask: *Would you like to visit a very hot or very cold place? Why/Why not?*

To finish

Ask students to go online and research an unusual city, town or place. They could search for pictures and make notes about the city in order to prepare a short profile. Ask them to present their city to the class in the next lesson.

Suggested searches could include: Coober Pedy in Australia (an underground town); Neft Daslari, in Azerbaijan (a floating city); Songjiang in China (which is modelled on an English town); and Mawsynram in India (supposedly the world's rainiest place). Refer students to Workbook page 38 to complete the exercises on conditionals in preparation for the Grammar lesson.

Presentation tool:	Unit 4, Reading
Workbook / Online Practice:	pp36–37
Extra Practice App	

GRAMMAR SB p52

To start

Tell students about a place you'd like to live in. Try to use some conditional sentences, for example: *There's a fishing village on the south coast. It's lovely. If you go there in the winter the weather is changeable and you sometimes get a lot of storms but if you go in the summer, it's usually really warm with fabulous sunsets. If I lived there, I wouldn't want to leave. It would be a very peaceful life!* Ask students to think of a place they'd like to live in, and to tell their partners what it would be like if they lived there. Conduct class feedback and if possible, elicit some examples of conditional language to put on the board.

Consider flipping the classroom by asking to students to complete Ex 1, read the Grammar file on SB p148 and complete grammar practice activities 1 and 2 on page 149 before class. This allows more time for discussion and questions during class.

explore **grammar** → SB p148

1 Read through the explore grammar box with the class. Refer students to the sentences and identify the conditional clauses together. Point out that the conditional clause often starts with *if* and can go at the beginning or the end of a sentence. Then ask students to match the sentences to the examples and explanations in the grammar box.

1 C If you went shopping in Mcity,
2 A If the roads are empty,
3 D If it hadn't been for a decision to build a new hydro-electric power station,
4 B If water levels continue to rise,
5 E If they had paid more attention to these concerns years ago,

2 4.1 Tell students they are going to hear two people talking about a magazine article. Play the recording and ask: *What idea are they talking about?* (Moving from the city to live on a farm.) Ask further questions: *Have either of them ever lived on a farm?* (No, but the boy spent a holiday on one.) *Would they both like to live on a farm?* (The boy would because of the nature. The girl wouldn't because she would feel isolated.) Students complete the sentences with the correct form of the verbs in brackets. Then check answers around the class.

1 would have got, had moved
2 could have been, had grown up
3 is, will be
4 saw, would love
5 would hate, left

extra

Write this sentence on the board. Then play the recording again.

If my parents had moved us to a farm, I'd have got upset.

Ask: *How is 'have' pronounced?* Point out that in third conditional sentences, *have* and *had* often have a very weak sound.

3 Ask students to write down in 30 seconds three things they would do this weekend if they had more money. Compare answers in full group and see how many would spend it on entertainment. Read the title of the article and elicit what it might be about. Students skim the article quickly, ignoring the gaps, to check their ideas. Students complete the article with the phrases in the box. Remind them to think about the meaning and look at the text around each gap. Check answers around the class.

1 'd go **2** 'll get **3** could have seen **4** wouldn't have gone **5** hadn't given **6** had been

4 Read through the first sentence starter with the class and elicit some ideas to complete it. For example, *I could have gone shopping with my mum. I would have been told off by my teacher.* Organise students into pairs. They complete the sentences individually and then compare their answers with their partner. Conduct class feedback and find the most interesting or funniest sentences.

extra: fast finishers

Ask fast finishers to write some more sentence starters, then swap them with another student to complete.

extra

Write these phrases on the board:

more time *a friend in the USA*
drive a car *good at languages*

In pairs students, write a different type of conditional sentence for each phrase. Give them an example: *If I'd had more time last night I would have marked all of your essays.*

Suggested answers could include: *If I'd had a friend in the USA when I was younger I might have spent a holiday there. If I could drive a car I wouldn't have to cycle to college every day. If I were good at languages I'd travel more often to other countries.*

Speak up

5 Ask students to discuss the question in pairs. Monitor and encourage and contribute. Give quick corrections if they make errors with the conditional verb forms, but do not interrupt the conversations. Make notes of common errors to deal with later. Conduct class feedback and find the most original suggestion.

game on

Explain the game and read through the examples given. Organise students into small groups to take turns to add a link to the chain. Circulate to help with ideas if necessary. When students have finished, nominate a few students to share their stories with the class. Ask: *How did the stories end and how did they get there?*

To finish

Write these questions on the board.

If I don't give you any homework for tonight, what will you do?

If we had more time in this lesson, what would you like to learn?

If I'd cancelled this lesson earlier today, what would you have done?

Students write their answers individually. Then conduct feedback and find the most interesting ideas.

Presentation tool:	Unit 4, Grammar
Workbook / Online Practice:	p38
Photocopiable activity:	4A
Grammar reference and practice:	SB p148
Audioscript:	SB p177

VOCABULARY SB p53

town and country

To start

Choose a place in your local area and describe the view. For example, *I'm looking down and I can see people sitting at tables and drinking coffee. On the right there's some grass and a river – there are some people sitting on the grass and having a picnic. On the other side of the river there's a tall building and I can see ten floors.* Students should try to guess where you are. Put students into pairs and ask them to think of a place and do the same. Conduct class feedback and elicit any words they used to describe places (e.g. *traffic signs, bus stop*, etc.).

1 Focus students' attention on the word box. Ask the following questions and elicit the word you are describing.

Which word is an adjective to describe somewhere that is away from a lot of other houses? (remote)
Which is an adjective to describe a place where there are too many people? (overcrowded)
Which is a very fast train? (express)
Which is an adjective to describe something that is very safe? (secure)
Which is a road that turns a lot? (winding)
Which is very useful because it is close? (handy)
Which is a place that has a good transport system linking it to many other places? (well-connected)
Which is the centre of a city? (inner-city)

Students then complete the task in pairs. Conduct feedback.

1 remote **2** handy **3** express **4** Inner-city **5** winding **6** overcrowded **7** secure **8** well-connected

2 4.2 Tell students that they are going to listen to two young people talking about where they live. Play the recording and ask students to say what type of places the people live in. At this point, they should not go into too much detail.

The first speaker lives in the middle of a city.
The second speaker lives in the countryside, near mountains.

3 4.3 Play the recording again (stronger students can probably do the task without listening again) to match the places and things described with the words from Ex 1. Ask students: *Do you live (or know anyone who lives) in a similar location to either of the speakers?*

Speaker 1:
The flat is handy for shops and local amenities
Some people would say the flats are overcrowded.
The flat is well-connected with public transport.
There's an express train.
Speaker 2:
The cottage is remote.
The speaker feels secure.
The roads to the house are winding.
The cottage is handy for skiing in the mountains

VOCABULARY (Continued)

explore **vocabulary**

4 Write the word *traffic sign* on the board and ask if they know what type of word this is (a compound noun). Ask for other examples of compound nouns made from two nouns (e.g. *car park*, *department store*, *shopping mall*, *window shopping*). Read through the explore vocabulary box with the class and focus on the plural forms, as students sometimes make errors with this. Read through the nouns in boxes A and B and elicit one compound noun using a word from each box (e.g. *apartment block*). Put students in pairs to find more compound nouns. Conduct class feedback.

apartment block/complex
country cottage
market square/hall
play area
public space/square
shopping/leisure complex
tourist spot/area
town square/hall
traffic jam

watch out for

You might be asked about whether to use hyphens or not with compound nouns. Explain that compound nouns made from two nouns can be found in three different forms:

1 separate words without a hyphen (e.g. *car park*)
2 hyphenated words (e.g. *ice-skating*)
3 made of one word (e.g. *website*).

The only way to be completely sure about what form a compound noun should be is to check in a dictionary.

extra

Write these compound nouns on the board:

public transport *power station* *water levels*
window shopping *housing crisis*

Ask students to say the words and to try to identify which is the odd one out and why. (It's *public transport*. The stress is on the second noun. Usually, compound nouns are pronounced with a stress on the first noun.)

5 Students work individually to complete the article with compound nouns. Check answers around the class.

1 housing crisis
2 apartment block/complex
3 traffic jams
4 town planners
5 public space
6 weather conditions
7 play area

Speak up

6 Put students into pairs to discuss the questions and ask them to make some notes about each other's ideas. They should then join another pair to continue the discussion. Conduct class feedback.

To finish

Write all the compound nouns from this lesson on the board. Students study the board for 30 seconds and then close their eyes. Rub off one compound noun. Students open their eyes and try to remember which compound you have rubbed off. Continue until the board is clear.

Fun footer

Read the fact with the class and ask if it surprises them. Then ask: *Is putting rubbish underground a good idea? Why/Why not?*

background

Tourists to Disney World may not know about these tunnels but fans do. There are an incredible number of tunnels which cover 392,040 square feet of space and are called 'Utilidors'. This is a network for all sorts of things. They are used for transport of rubbish, money, cast members, food, etc. and also contain kitchens, cast cafes, hair salons, security offices and all sorts of electronic systems. Because the tunnels can be very confusing (especially for new cast members) many of the walls are colour coded! It is possible to go on an organised tour of the tunnels but this is quite expensive.

Presentation tool:	Unit 4, Vocabulary
Workbook / Online Practice:	p39
Photocopiable activity:	4B
Extend vocabulary:	SB p160
Audioscript:	SB p178
Extra Practice App	

LISTENING SB p54

To start

Ask students: *What is the most important thing to you about where you live?* Take feedback. Give them an example of your own if necessary. You could say something like, *The most important thing for me about where I live is the local park because I love green spaces and I think we all need them.*

Power up

1 Ask students to work in pairs. They should consider each of the things in the box, and choose their top three in order of importance. Collect the most important thing from each pair and write them on the board to find out generally which is the most important aspect of living in a city.

Possible answers

Public transport is very important to me. I don't have a car, so I need to be able to get around quickly and easily. Places to meet friends is another very important thing. I like to be able to meet people after school, without needing to meet them in their homes. The other thing I'd like to mention is entertainment. I love going out, especially to the cinema, but also to the theatre. I don't think I could live somewhere where there weren't many entertainment options.

2 4.4 Tell students they are going to listen to eight people talking about some of the topics in Ex 1. Play the recording all through without stopping and then conduct class feedback about which topics were mentioned.

1 moving to a remote village and not being able to sleep because of noises (noise pollution)
2 plans for a new skate park (places to meet friends)
3 competition to find ways to improve a town square (local facilities)
4 lack of buses in the evening (public transport)
5 museum exhibition (entertainment)
6 traffic chaos due to bad weather (traffic)
7 aunt can't sell house because it's too remote (neighbours)
8 using the gym to meet people (places to meet friends/ local facilities)

Listen up

exam tip

3 4.5 Go through the exam tip with the class. Remind students that they have time to read through the questions before they listen, and that they should use this time to identify exactly what they are listening for. Focus students' attention on question 1 and ask them to underline the main words. Then play the recording for them to choose an option (A, B or C).

The main words are *move to the country* and *How does she feel*.

The question is focusing on the speaker's feelings.

C (*It's especially irritating when the dogs start barking … Eventually I managed to adjust and now it doesn't really bother me.*)

exam task: multiple choice: short texts

4 e 4.6 Give students time to read questions 2–8 and identify the focus of each one. Then play the recording. Students can check their answers in pairs. Then conduct class feedback.

2 B (*There's nowhere to skateboard at the moment.*)
3 A (*In case you've forgotten … As long as we get them by midnight on Friday we'll enter them in the prize draw.*)
4 B (*But you know there aren't any other buses. There's one at nine and then nothing until eleven. The basketball match doesn't finish until nine-thirty.*)
5 C (*… unless you book soon, you might miss this opportunity. Unfortunately the exhibition is moving to another museum in just a few weeks.*)
6 A (*Queues of traffic have started to form in other areas of the city and unhappy commuters are reporting severe delays of up to two hours.*)
7 B (*It's a cute house but really remote. There aren't any neighbours at all and that puts people off.*)
8 C (*I like seeing other friends from school and the gym is the perfect place for that.*)

Speak up

5 Remind students that giving and justifying opinions is a key part of the Speaking test. You could run this as a formal debate, with a vote at the end of the discussion. First explain what *amenities* are so that students know what they are going to talk about (they could include things like skate parks, tennis courts, football pitches, etc.). Give students time to discuss their ideas first, and to plan what to say for their side of the debate. After this preparation, run the debate as a whole class. A spokesperson for each side should first make a statement giving the views of the group, and then the debate can be open to everyone. Chair the debate and make sure that both sides have equal time. Set a time limit, and take a vote at the end. As a homework activity, ask students to give a brief report about the debate, explaining what happened and what the result of the debate was.

Possible answers

The town council: We put a lot of money into facilities that aren't used. We could use the money better in other ways. Older people need facilities more than teenagers. We have a responsibility to use the council's money wisely.

Local teenagers: We need to do school work so can't use the facilities all the time. The weather sometimes stops us using outdoor facilities. It's important for us to have places where we can spend time with other teenagers. We're the future, so you should invest in us!

To finish

Tell students: *Some people like the idea of living 'in the middle of nowhere' with few amenities like public transport or shops.*

Then ask this question: *What would the pros and cons be? Is it better to live somewhere with lots of amenities? Why/Why not?*

Presentation tool:	Unit 4, Listening
Workbook / Online Practice:	p40
Audioscript:	SB p178
Extra Practice App	

USE OF ENGLISH 1 SB p55

To start

Write this sentence on the board: *I can't sleep unless it's quiet.* Ask: *Is it quiet or not? What happens when it isn't?* (It may be quiet sometimes, but when it isn't the speaker can't sleep.)

Follow on with this statement on the board: *I wish we'd stayed in our old house.* Ask: *Did the speaker stay in the old house? How does the speaker feel about it?* (No, the speaker moved, but doesn't feel happy about it.)

Finally, write this on the board: *If you'd told me earlier, I could have changed the time of my meeting.* Ask: *Did the speaker change the time of the meeting? Why/Why not?* (No, because he wasn't told in time.)

explore **grammar** ➥ SB p148

1 Refer students to the explore grammar box. Go through the box, and ask students which tense is used after the words in bold. Explain that the tense is not necessarily the same as the time it refers to, but they are all conditional forms. If necessary, remind students of the basic forms of the conditionals and refer to the Grammar reference on page 148 for more information.

A present simple or *can* to talk about a hypothetical state/past simple (a hypothetical second conditional)
B present simple, to refer to present or future time and repeated situations
C present simple, but the time referred to is a hypothetical future
D present simple (a hypothetical first conditional)
E past simple, to talk about a present wish
F past tense (or *could*) for a present or future ability
G past perfect (or *would*) to talk about a present situation that we can't change
H past perfect, to talk about a past situation you regret

2 Ask students to work in pairs and complete the sentences. Conduct class feedback.

1 had taken **2** would go **3** came **4** hadn't chosen
5 finds

3 Do this as a speaking activity with students in pairs. Students should complete the sentences with their own ideas, and then explain them to their partner. They should check each other to make sure they are using the right form of the verb. Monitor and be prepared to correct, as the focus here is not on fluency but on accuracy.

Possible answers
1 + present tense (e.g. *I have to work*)
2 + past perfect (e.g. *had been*)
3 + present tense (e.g. *you need it*)
4 + present tense (e.g. *the sales are still on*)
5 + present tense (e.g. *you don't damage it*)
6 + present tense (e.g. *go to Australia*)

exam task: **open cloze**

Items tested here are all related to conditional structures, unlike the Cambridge exam task which tests a variety.

4 **e** Remind students that when they do this kind of gap fill, they should always read the words before and after the gap. For example, the missing word might be part of a collocation, or its form might depend on a previous word. Ask: *What is the answer to gap 1?*

1 could (You need the past form of the verb after *wish* to talk about a present situation.)

Ask students to read the title of the article and look at the picture. Ask: *What do you think a 'tree house' is? Why might they be important for teenagers?* They read the article quickly to find out. Tell them that all the gaps are related to conditional forms, although this would not be the case in the exam. They should read the article and complete the rest of the gaps with one word only. Students who finish quickly should go back and check that all their missing words are grammatically correct, make sense and are spelt correctly.

2 unless (We need something here that means 'if not'.)
3 provided (We need something here that means 'only if' and goes before *that*.)
4 if / when (The start of a simple conditional clause.)
5 case (part of the phrase *in case*)
6 condition (part of the phrase *on condition that*)
7 had (using the past perfect form to talk about past regrets)
8 only (part of the phrase *if only*)

Speak up

5 Students could discuss and plan their ideas in small groups, then formally present their plans to the class. They should use hypothetical expressions where possible.

Fun footer

Ask students if they have heard the expression *a walk in the park* to mean that something is easy to do, and usually enjoyable. Give them the example in a sentence: *I was nervous about writing the essay but in the end it was a walk in the park.* Ask: Do you know any other expressions with a similar meaning? You may like to teach these expressions: *It's a piece of cake. It's a doddle. It's child's play. It's not rocket science.*

Presentation tool:	Unit 4, Use of English 1
Workbook / Online Practice:	p41
Photocopiable activity:	4C
Grammar reference and practice:	SB p148
Extra Practice App	

USE OF ENGLISH 2 SB p56

To start

Ask students to work in pairs and to discuss these questions:

Talk about a person in your family who is the same as you. What is the same?

Talk about a person in your family that you look like. How are you the same?

1 4.7 Tell students that they are going to listen to a conversation. They should listen and identify what the friends are talking about. Play the recording and then conduct class feedback.

They're talking about a fancy dress zombie party that one of them went to.

extra 

Ask students some comprehension questions.

Who went to the party – the girl or the boy? (The boy.) *What problems did the girl have?* (Problems with transport.)

Then ask: *Have you ever been to a party like this? If not, would you like to?* Encourage students to give reasons.

explore **vocabulary 1**

2 4.8 Go through the explore vocabulary box with the class. Play the recording again so that students can listen and identify the examples of *like* and *as*. Conduct class feedback and elicit the use for each example.

1 *What was the party like?* (Asking for a description of something.)
2 *We all dressed up as zombies.* (Describing an appearance or a role.)
3 *… villages like mine are rubbish for public transport.* (Giving an example.)
4 *The party was in the same road as my house* (Part of an expression with *the same …*)
5 *You looked like a zombie in a horror film!* (To say that something is similar to something else.)

3 Ask students to do the exercise in pairs. When they have completed the sentences, they should discuss the questions.

1 like, like **2** as **3** like

explore **vocabulary 2**

4 Remind students that they have already studied verbs followed by prepositions. Elicit some examples from Unit 3, for example *believe in*, *rely on* and *depend on*. Tell students: *Now you're going to study phrases which start with prepositions.* Explain that these are fixed phrases, and may be tested in the Use of English parts of the exam. Go through the explore vocabulary box. Check that they understand the meaning of the phrases. Explain that because these are fixed phrases, it is useful to learn them by heart.

extra 

Put students into pairs. Each student writes three sentences, each one using a phrase from the explore vocabulary box. They then read their sentences to their partner without the preposition. Their partner should say the missing preposition.

5 Point out that the article students are going to read focuses on prepositional phrases. Refer them to the photo and the title. Ask: *Can you guess what you're going to read about?* They should then read the whole article quickly without filling in any gaps to get an idea of what it is about.

Possible answer

I've never seen this kind of bus before. It's good that people are thinking of how to improve public transport, but I can't imagine it working in my city. It looks like it might slow down traffic, and create even more problems.

exam task: multiple-choice cloze

This task tests prepositional phrases, the focus of the lesson, rather than a range of item types as in the Cambridge exam.

6 **e** Go through the exam tip with the class. Remind students that they should always read the whole sentence before choosing the missing word. When they look at the first sentence, they should be able to see that it is a fixed phrase: *to look out of place*. Ask students to complete the article in pairs. Make sure that when you conduct feedback, students give the whole phrase and not just the missing word, so they get used to using the whole phrase.

1 B *took many by surprise* (This is a fixed phrase meaning that something was unexpected.)
2 A *at first sight* (This means the first time you see something.)
3 A *in fact* (This means 'actually'.)
4 C *at least* (This means 'a minimum'.)
5 B *used as a space* (We use *as* here to describe the role of the upper level.)
6 D *on the move* (This is a fixed phrase meaning that something is physically moving.)
7 B *for real* (This means 'in reality'.)
8 D *in danger* (In the text, this is used as an example of a potential problem with the bus.)

USE OF ENGLISH 2 (Continued)

Speak up

7 This discussion could be done in groups, and each group could present their plan. Once all the plans have been presented, the class could vote on the best one. Students could also suggest disadvantages of the other ideas that they didn't choose.

For homework, students could write a short report on their discussion, and the plan that was chosen.

Possible answers

Possible solutions include: a car-sharing scheme, in which families with cars share rides with families who don't; a bike club, in which people with bikes agree to travel to and from school together at the same time; a 'study-from-home' scheme, in which students are able to come to school less, and have online lessons or receive more homework.

Fun footer

Ask students to go online and research some facts that interest them about new forms of transport, and share the information with other students in small groups. You could conduct feedback and find out which facts the class finds most interesting.

To finish

Organise students into small groups. Say to students: *Imagine the 'straddling bus' in your city. Would it be a realistic solution to public transport problems? Why/Why not?* Encourage students not to give their instant opinion, or to say whether they personally like the bus or not, but to fully explore the possible advantages and disadvantages of the bus, as objectively as possible, before coming to a conclusion. Conduct class feedback and find out what students have concluded.

Presentation tool:	Unit 4, Use of English 2
Workbook / Online Practice:	p42
Photocopiable activity:	4C
Audioscript:	SB p178
Extra Practice App	

SPEAKING SB p57

To start

Ask students: *What kind of transport do you like using most?* You could suggest things to think about such as impact on the environment, speed, cost and so on.

Power up

1 Ask students to discuss the three questions in pairs.

Possible answers

The bottom left photo shows people riding Segways. These can be useful because they're slow and can go along little streets in a city.

The bottom right photo shows peoples using a cycle rickshaw (or bike taxi). These are useful because the cyclist can take you anywhere and can also explain about the places you are seeing.

Other ways to see a city include walking on foot on a guided walking tour or taking an open-top bus.

2 Ask students to discuss the question in pairs. Conduct feedback.

Your opinion and why you have that opinion.

3 Students work in the same pairs. Conduct class feedback and write their ideas on the board.

Possible answers

Pros: fun, relaxing, interesting, healthier, you see more, you can see and smell things, get the atmosphere, you can visit smaller areas that transport can't get to, also doesn't pollute the environment

Cons: tiring, can be boring if you're somewhere you don't like, dangerous (if there's a lot of traffic), unhealthy (air pollution)

4 4.9 Play the recording and ask students to compare their ideas with those on the board.

Cons:
It can be boring and your legs ache.
It's very tiring.
Pros:
You can enjoy the atmosphere in the streets.
It gives you more time to stop and look at things.

useful **language: giving your opinion**

5 Go though the phrases in the useful language box. Ask: *Which phrases do you think express a strong opinion?*

I'd definitely say that …
Frankly, I think that, …
To be honest, I don't understand (why/how) …
I'm absolutely convinced that …

6 4.10 Ask students to read the dialogue and complete it with possible phrases from the useful language box. Play the recording again so that they can compare their ideas with what the students actually said. Tell them that one student gave a better answer than the others. Ask: *Which one? Why?*

1 ... this is just my opinion but
2 I'm absolutely convinced that
3 To be honest, I don't understand
4 Frankly, I think that
5 I imagine

Speaker B gives the best answer, using more than one expression and including several ideas.

Speaker A is also good and does back up ideas with personal experience. It would be nice to have a second expression from the box here because the speaker does feel quite strongly about it.

Speaker C gives a short answer and doesn't demonstrate enough language. As the student begins with *I imagine...* a second sentence could have started with *I haven't got much experience of this but ...*.

Tell students that there are other phrases for giving opinions and reasons in the Speaking file on p164. They should make a note of these as well as the ones from the useful language box, and try to use them in discussions.

Speak up

exam task: discussion

➥ SB p164

7 e Remind students of the importance of expanding their answers, and that this is what Speaker C didn't do. Say: ***In the exam you need to show that you can speak fluently and express your ideas. If you give brief answers this could look as though you are not interested in talking, or have nothing to say. The examiner needs to hear what you can do.*** **Remind students that it is also a good thing in general not to give monosyllabic answers in response to questions. Ask students to work in pairs and read the exam tip. They then discuss question 2 using some of the phrases in the useful language box. Remind students that there is no 'right' answer to any of the questions in this part of the exam, and that the important thing is that they give their opinion using a range of language. Put students into groups of three. They should take it in turns to ask a question to the other two students, who should answer it between them. The students who asked the question should listen and make suggestions about improving the answers the other students give. Remind students that in this part of the exam, it's important to give an opinion and then give reasons for that opinion.**

Possible answers

1 Yes, because it exposes you to other cultures
2 With family because you can feel comfortable with them. With friends because you can have a good time.
3 Some people prefer the peace and quiet of the countryside and find cities too busy.
4 Sightseeing, visiting cultural places like museums, photographing famous landmarks.
5 Yes, because otherwise you waste time, especially in a big city. It's good to plan what you can do.
6 You can find out for yourself, but it's quicker if local people introduce you to the interesting places that tourists don't find.

Speaking extra

8 Tell students that they are going to use the ideas they've already discussed in a formal debate. Go through the steps in the task, and give students time to consider their arguments before you start the debate.

Possible answers

For: cities usually have many things like museums and theatres, which offer educational opportunities; students can learn more than simply by sitting in a classroom; students have the experience of travelling as part of a group and seeing a new environment.

Against: many exhibitions or landmarks can be seen or experienced online; it often costs a lot of money; it takes away valuable time from learning traditional school subjects.

alternative

Alternatively, put students into small groups and assign each group a side of the debate which they have to present and defend. Tell students that it can be challenging to present an opinion you do not necessarily agree with, but this is good practise for objectively discussing a topic. Remind them to state their arguments clearly by introducing them with appropriate phrases. They should also give reasons for their arguments.

To finish

Put students into groups. Ask them to tell each other about a school trip they have been on, explain where they went, what they learned and whether they thought it was a useful experience or not. They should give reasons for their opinions.

Presentation tool:	Unit 4, Speaking
Workbook / Online Practice:	p43
Speaking file:	SB p164
Audioscript:	SB p178

WRITING SB pp58–59

To start

Ask students to think about a visit they've made a to a city. Ask: *How did you feel? What made the biggest impression on you?* If any students have not visited a big city, get them to ask others questions about it. Ask: *Is there a particular city you'd like to visit. What attracts you to this city?*

Power up

1 Ask students to look at the photos, and discuss the questions.

Possible answers

You will hear lots of people, possibly speaking different languages. You might hear buskers, playing music on the street, or the noise of different vehicles. You might see and be able to taste or smell different food than you are used to. The weather might also be different. It may feel much colder, wetter or warmer than you are used to.

2 4.11 Students listen to four people discussing a day in the city. Ask: *Do they mention any of your ideas? What other things do they mention?*

Speaker 1: the crowds of people
Speaker 2: the food stalls
Speaker 3: a fountain and the heat
Speaker 4: the noise from mopeds and car horns

3 Students should read the email and decide what the relationship is. Ask: *Is the language formal or informal? What questions does Sophia ask?*

Liam and Sophia are good friends. They met up at the weekend.
Sophia wants to know:
1 what is Liam's favourite city.
2 what he did there.
3 was there anything he wishes he had had more time for.

4 Ask students to read Liam's reply to Sophia, and in pairs to answer the questions.

1 Hi Sophia, Bye for now!
2 It refers to the last time he saw her, and introduces the email in a sociable way.
3 Yes, he describes Segovia and where it is (north of Madrid). He says it's ancient, beautiful (*took my breath away, winding streets, stunning views over the countryside*). He wishes he'd had the time to eat there.

extra

Ask students to look online for photos of Segovia. Then put them into pairs to share and describe the photos they have found, and to say whether they would like to visit this city or not.

5 Ask students if they can remember any words that collocate with the verb *make*. Write their ideas on the board (e.g. make a decision, a noise, friends, a complaint.)

Ask: *Can you find any collocations with 'make' in Liam's emails?* They should find *make the most of.*

Go through the collocations and ask them to underline the ones Liam used.

caught a high-speed train
took my breath away
make the most of it
lost track (of time)
To tell you the truth

extra

Check that students understand the meaning of the collocations in Ex 5. Ask the following questions.

Which collocation means … ?
to reflect the sun (catch the light)
to cause trouble (make a fuss)
to be untidy (make a mess)
give someone a good time (make someone's day)
surprise you in a good way (take your breath away)
take over as a leader (take charge/control)
get maximum enjoyment from something (make the most of)
not be sure of the time (lose track of time)

6 Ask students to work in pairs and complete the gaps using collocations.

1 the light	**4** touch
2 any difference	**5** my day
3 charge	**6** track

Plan on

exam tip

7 Tell students that whenever they write a letter or email, it's important to know what kind of language to use, and this depends on the relationship they have with the person they are writing to. In the exam, they may have to write a formal or an informal letter or email. In the exam, it's important not only to use the correct style of language, but to include all the information required by the task. Read the exam tip with the whole class, and ask them which words they should underline in the task and what information they have to include.

a city or town
spent a day in with friends or family
Where is it?
What is it like?
What would you have done if you'd had more time there?

8 Students should work in pairs to brainstorm ideas for their email. Go round and monitor their ideas, making suggestions if necessary.

explore language

9 Remind students of the conventions for starting and ending an email. Go through the explore language box with the class and discuss which ones might be appropriate for this email.

Possible answers

Hi or Dear Dan

I've just read about …

All the best./Hope that helps.

Write on

exam task: an informal letter or email

➥ SB p166

The email extract in the task here has more detail than candidates will find in the Cambridge exam task, This is to help students write their response email.

10 **e** Students write their email. If they write it in class, they should exchange their work with a partner who can check it for grammar and spelling. If they do it for homework then remind students of the importance of checking their work before they hand it in.

Model answer

Hi Dan,

I've just read your letter, asking for people to tell you about cities we have visited, and I would be delighted to tell you about my experiences.

The city I visited was Vienna, which is the capital of Austria. The reason I went there was because I have a relative who was getting married to an Austrian man, so I went there with lots of family members. Luckily, I had the opportunity to see the city, too, and make the most of my time there.

It really took my breath away. Vienna has a huge number of amazing buildings, and it's difficult to stop taking photos of everything! In the centre, you can walk in small streets and it doesn't feel crowded, because there aren't many cars, and it's easy to suddenly find yourself in a quiet little square.

The only thing I wish I'd done was to go to a café. Vienna is famous for having some of the best cakes in the world, and I can't believe I didn't have any!

All the best,

Vanessa

Improve it

11 Get students to read their own emails and identify areas of improvement. Refer them to the series of questions, and encourage them to honestly think about whether they can answer 'yes' for each one.

12 Organise students into pairs. Ask them to swap emails with each other and discuss how they can make improvements. Ask students to submit their work for it to be checked. When giving feedback, focus on the style of language used to make sure that it's appropriate, and that all the required information has been included. If necessary, ask students to read the Writing file on page 166 again for homework, to remind them of the format and organisation of an informal letter or email.

Possible answers

Students should make sure that they have used a greeting and ending, in an appropriate style.

Their emails should also introduce the topic in the first paragraph.

Every paragraph should have its own separate, new point.

Finally, students should make sure that the email includes all the information that the task asked for.

Fun footer

Nominate a student to read out the joke in the footer. Explain that the convention of using capital letters in texts or emails is that you are shouting. The writer has written in capitals here to his grandmother because she can't hear, so he is shouting. Ask students: *Do you generally use the same language when you speak or write to friends, and when you speak or write to older relatives. Why?*

To finish

Ask students: What would you change in your email if it had to be a more formal email (for example, the greeting or ending)? Put students into pairs to discuss their ideas.

Presentation tool:	Unit 4, Writing
Workbook / Online Practice:	p44
Writing file:	SB p166
Audioscript:	SB p178

SWITCH ON SB p60

Design gone wrong

1 Ask students if they (or their parents) have recently had to fix (mend/repair) something in a hurry. Put them into pairs to discuss their experiences. Conduct feedback.

Possible answers

The zip on my jacket snapped while I was putting it on. I pinned the fabric together using safety pins, as I was late for the bus. It worked, but I think it looked a bit weird!

2 Write *Walkie Talkie skyscraper* on the board and ask students to search for images of it online. Then they should describe the skyscraper and say why it has been given this name. If necessary explain what a *Walkie Talkie* is (a small portable radio, invented in 1937, that allows two people with the device to talk to each other). Play the video and ask students to say what the building's design flaw was.

The curved shape (the parabolic curve) of the Walkie Talkie building combined with its reflective surface and directed sunlight and extreme heat into one concentrated area. This meant excessive heat caused smoke and fires in a particular area.

3 Play the video again. Students watch and make notes on the various problems that the building's design created.

A bicycle saddle caught fire; tiles cracked because of the heat; furniture started smoking; people couldn't stand in the space where the heat was being directed without discomfort; the light reflected from the building was dazzling.

4 Discuss with the class the solutions the physicist suggests and what was actually done to solve the problem. Play the recording again to check answers. Elicit that *deflect* means to cause something to change direction.

The solar physicist suggested that the building could be covered in a surface that scatters the light or that the windows could be re-orientated (or re-positioned). In the end, the developers fitted the building with shades to deflect the sunlight.

5 Students discuss other possibilities in pairs. Conduct class feedback.

Possible answer

The developers could have draped a giant piece of material over one side of the Walkie Talkie building. However, I don't think that would look very appealing. The curved face of the building could be re-built to make it straight, but this would probably be very expensive!

extra

Having gone through all the activities, play the recording again and stop at various points to ask for specific information or summaries. Ask: *What is happening here? What is the person talking about?*

For example, stop where the man is showing the bike saddle (he's talking about when a bike saddle caught fire), or stop when the man is frying an egg (he's doing this to show how hot the pavement is.)

Project

6 Explain the project to the students. In groups, they will choose an interesting building to find out about and present to the class. This building can be interesting for any reasons: it could be tall, short, narrow, old, in a strange place, or be unusual in any way. However, there should be some reason why the building could be considered controversial. You could suggest some interesting buildings or structures for the students to choose from. For example, Prague's Dancing House, Dubai's Burj Khalifa, Malmö's Turning Torso, Birmingham Library in the UK, the Millennium Bridge in London, or the Falcon II Headquarters in Mexico City. Once students have chosen the building, they should split into two teams to do the research, one focusing on the positive points of the building, the other on the negative ones. Then they come together to discuss their findings and where improvements could or should be made.

alternative

1 Students research a building in their own town/city. They ask local people for their opinions about it. These opinions should be categorised as either positive or negative. Students use this research to report back to the class objectively on what other people think about the building.
2 Students research a local building and find images of it to show to other class members. They then conduct interviews to find out opinions of the building. This can be done as a mingling activity with students again reporting back objectively after the interviews.

Presentation tool: Unit 4, Switch on
Switch on videoscript: TB p172

INDEPENDENT LEARNING SB p60

Reading and writing

Remind students that although learning grammar and vocabulary is fundamental to language learning, it is also important to develop good reading and writing skills, as these are two of the basic things we need language for.

1 **Put students into pairs to look back at the reading task on page 50. Ask students to discuss which things they did well, and what they could do to improve the other areas.**

Possible answers

I could find specific information, but I had some trouble with understanding detail and ignoring ideas that looked similar. One thing I could do is to practise reading the question more carefully, underlining key words and really understanding what it is I'm reading for, before I look in detail at a text.

2 **Keep students in the same pairs to discuss the writing task on page 59.**

Possible answers

I think this tip is useful. I'd give it 4. It sounds obvious, but it's very important to know why I'm writing before I start. This really helps me plan things, and organise my ideas. I think it's very important to spend at least 10 minutes planning before writing anything. It saves time later on.

3 **Encourage students to think back on their writing tasks in this unit and answer the questions. Ask:** ***Do you think you approached and completed these tasks better than in previous units? If yes, what improved? If not, what can you do to improve?***

Possible answers

1 I did quite well, but I didn't always answer the questions in the task.
2 I would like to organise my ideas more clearly, because this makes it easier for the reader to understand what I want to say.
3 I found the email most difficult to write, because I didn't spend enough time planning each paragraph.
4 I checked with my teacher, and in the Writing file at the back of the book.

4 **Students complete the sentences with their own goals for Reading and Writing. You might at this point remind students of the value of extensive reading (websites, magazines, newspapers, etc.) in English. To improve writing skills, they can write a daily blog in English, or exchange English emails and texts with classmates on a regular basis. Basically, the more they practise on an informal scale, the better their skills will become.**

Possible answers

One thing I will do to improve my reading skills is read a greater variety of texts in English: websites, newspapers and magazine articles on subjects that interest me.

One thing I will do to improve my writing skills is to make sure I spend time planning before I write anything.

UNIT CHECK SB p61

Practice

1 **1** overcrowded **2** traffic signs **3** weather conditions **4** express **5** leisure centre/complex **6** secure **7** tourist spot **8** handy

2 **3** 4.12 and 4.13 **1** sight **2** real **3** far **4** first sight **5** your mind **6** tears

4 **1** lose your temper **2** pedestrian **3** subterranean **4** make an excuse **5** province **6** make up your mind

Review

1
1 wouldn't have gone
2 'd (would)/could stay
3 could have shown
4 'd (had) found, might not have moved
5 could live
6 'd (had) seen

2
1 have (as part of the third conditional)
2 as (meaning 'the role that something plays')
3 on (part of the phrase *on condition that*)
4 unless (meaning 'if not')
5 like (meaning 'similar to')
6 provided (part of the phrase *provided that*)
7 'd (had) (used after *if only* to express a regret)
8 wish (used to express a regret)

3 4.14 They didn't like the cold.
They liked the second-hand clothes stall, the atmosphere and the music.

4 4.15 **1** it hadn't been so cold
2 she'd seen it first
3 she doesn't ruin it
4 they could have sold them
5 it might sell well
6 it's freezing cold again

5 In the equivalent Cambridge exam task there would be 6 not 8 questions. These test conditional structures and *as / like* because these have been the grammatical focus of the unit.
1 (them) unless they arrive soon
2 'd (had) been able to take the
3 (that) everybody tidies
4 only I hadn't given you
5 in case it rains
6 tell me what it's/it was
7 on condition that you go
8 is (very) like

6 There is a food festival in the town near where I live. It happens every year, and it takes place in the gardens near a large castle.

I went with my younger sister who really enjoyed it. She's not very interested in food, but she loved exploring the castle, which was free to enter. Luckily, there were lots of fairground rides at the festival, as well as lots of great places to try out food, so she could enjoy those while I explored all the delicious cakes and chocolate!

The only problem was the weather. It was unusually cold for the time of year, and it even started to rain. I wish I'd gone the day before, because then I would have experienced beautiful sunshine.

UNIT CHECK REVIEW (Continued)

GRAMMAR FILE SB p149

1 **1** needs **2** hadn't been **3** hadn't found out
4 could save **5** weren't **6** might have taken

2 **1** moved **2** would have chosen **3** 'll (will) have
4 might have known **5** doesn't work out **6** could **7** find
8 leave

3 **1** F **2** A **3** C **4** E **5** D **6** B

4 **1** provided that **2** don't mind **3** took
4 hadn't pulled down **5** won't tell **6** could

5 **1** would have invited you
2 wish I hadn't rented/wish I wasn't renting
3 in case it's/the train is
4 if you hadn't given
5 unless the residents complain

Presentation tool:	Unit 4, Unit check
Workbook / Online Practice:	p45
Audioscript:	SB p178

A good sport 5

READING
topic: sports fans
skill: understanding attitude and opinions
task: multiple choice

GRAMMAR
infinitive and verb + *-ing*
verb patterns

VOCABULARY
sport
phrasal verbs
noun suffixes; prefixes

LISTENING
topic: drone racing
skill: understanding interviews
task: multiple choice: longer text

USE OF ENGLISH
word formation

SPEAKING
topic: ways to relax
skill: speculating
task: long turn

WRITING
topic: health and fitness
skill: using paragraphs
task: article

SWITCH ON
video: cycling star
project: research a sport or discipline

Lead-in SB p63

Focus students on the title of the unit and ask them to explain what it means. Elicit that a *good sport* is someone who is fair, and plays according to the rules. Explain that it doesn't only refer to sport, but it can also be used more generally.

Read through the quote with the class, *It's not the winning, it's the taking part*. Put students into pairs to discuss whether they think this is true or not. Ask: *Is it always important to you to win things?*

Read through the questions with the class. For question 2, give students the full phrase, *push yourself to the limit* and elicit the meaning (to try to go as fast, as high or for as long as is possible for you).

In pairs, students discuss the questions. Conduct class feedback.

Ask: *Can you give an example of when you pushed yourself recently?* Also, elicit further motivations for why people do sports that have nothing to do with wanting to compete with other people, or to win anything (e.g. to lose weight or become healthier).

Possible answers

1 I don't enjoy competitive sports very much, but I like to exercise. That's why I enjoy cycling and running. The only person I'm competing with is myself, and these sports keep me fit.
2 When I'm running, I like to push myself to go a little bit further or faster each time. I think this is good, because it trains my body to become stronger or faster, and motivates me to keep on doing it.
3 My main motivation is to keep fit. I'm not interested in winning races, or trophies. I just want to be as healthy as I can.

extra 

Tell students about the last sports event you watched live and the last one you watched on TV. Ask them to tell you about their recent experiences. Encourage students to give some details by explaining what happened, why they watched the event, what the atmosphere was like and what the result was.

READING SB pp64–65

To start

Put students into pairs and ask them to think of a famous national or international sporting event (e.g. a football cup final, an athletics championship, the most recent Olympics, etc.). Tell them to make sure they think of an event that their partner is likely to have heard of! Their partner must ask *yes/ no* questions to discover which event they are thinking of. Suggest they ask questions like *Is it an international event? Does it take place this country? Is it related to football?* etc. Circulate and help where necessary. Suggest clues if the partner needs them.

Power up

1 Refer students to the photos and put them into pairs to describe what is happening.

Possible answers

1 The photo at the top shows a game being watched on a tablet. It's possible now to watch sports live, or on catch-up as long as you have a device with an internet connection.

2 The photo at the bottom shows a crowd of spectators watching a live game. The fact that they are wearing similar colours indicates that they are all fans or supporters of a particular team.

Read on

2 Write the word *fan* on the board and elicit the meaning (someone who likes a particular sport, player or team very much). Tell students what or who you are a fan of and then nominate a few students to give their ideas. Ask: *Do you support a particular sports team? If yes, how long for? Why do you think people choose a particular team to support?* Tell students they are going to read an article with the title *Sports fans*. They should read it quickly, so allow one to two minutes, and decide what the article is about. Then in pairs, they choose the most appropriate alternative title (A, B or C) and see if it matches their original idea. Conduct feedback with the class. Students should justify their choices with reference to the article.

B

exam tip

3 Remind students of the format for the multiple choice task. Tell them that sometimes they might see a particular word in one of the options and in the section of text they are looking at. They must not assume that this option is correct because of the match – it could be a distraction. They should look for a paraphrase in the text (the same idea written using different words) and check that the whole option is the same as in the text. Read though the exam tip box to reinforce this and then ask students to read question 1 in Ex 4, but not options A–D at this point.

With a strong group, elicit ideas from what they remember from the first reading, then ask them to read the first paragraph again to check their ideas. Read through options A–D and see if their ideas match any of these. With a weaker group, read the question, then ask students to read paragraph 1. Then read through options A–D and ask them to choose the correct one.

Ask students why they chose this option and why the others didn't match completely. Point out that the following words or phrases appeared in options A, C and D, as well as the paragraph: *sports fans, influenced, eight or nine*. These are examples of 'word spots'.

1 B The part of the paragraph that should help students arrive at the correct option is: *the sport or team a person decides to follow is largely influenced by their social circle rather than their personal participation in a sport.*

exam task: multiple choice

4 **e** Students complete the whole task individually and then compare answers and reasons for their choices in pairs. Conduct class feedback.

2 A (*Clearlythe fan was not personally involved in achieving either success, yet they choose to use the pronoun 'we' to report their team's performance. Fans' use of 'us' and 'we' to talk about their favourite team is common behaviour. It demonstrates the strong sense of identity fans feel with their club …*)
Options B, C and D are incorrect because *it* is followed by the word *demonstrates*, and a reference to teams, odd behaviour and sense of identity would not make sense.

3 C (*However, research shows that this is not the case with fiercely loyal or 'true' fans. They will carry on wearing their team scarf even when their team performs badly and will say with genuine sadness, 'They beat us three nil'.*)
For option A, the reference to something 'genuine' is a distraction as it implies 'real' feelings, but is only an example. For options B and D, there is no reference to mood being affected or to criticism of others.

4 D (*Someone who is usually shy and quiet can be seen shouting, screaming and jumping up and down while watching their favourite team play. The effect of being in a crowd of spectators enjoying the same activity allows people to become less self-conscious and more confident.*)
Option A is incorrect because there is no direct comparison in the text. B is incorrect because there is no indication that their behaviour is considered bad. C is incorrect because the fans' behaviour is not an indicator of stress, but a way of relieving it.

5 A (*It's a well-known fact that people define themselves in terms of social groupings. In psychology, this is known as the 'in group' and 'out group' principle, and sports fans are no different.*)
Option B is incorrect because it is the writer who realises this, not the fans. C is incorrect because the text says the opposite: that sport is no different from other activities. D is incorrect because the text doesn't say whether fans are aware of any differences or similarities.

6 B (*Of course in reality it makes no difference what kind of hat you wear or whether you have your lucky coin, but superstitions are taken very seriously by sports fans and I for one would not like to try and persuade them otherwise!*)
Option A is incorrect because 'in reality it makes no difference' and he does not comment on the potential benefits. C is incorrect because there is no indication of mockery in the text. D is incorrect because there is no implied criticism – just statements of fact.

extra: fast finishers

Fast finishers should prepare to say why the other answers are not correct. When you conduct class feedback, make sure to check with fast finishers about their reasons for right and wrong answers.

5 With a strong class, you could read through the vocabulary task and see how many items they know already, then ask them to check through the article to find the remaining ones. With a weaker group, ask them to work in pairs to complete the task. Conduct class feedback. Ask them to choose the five items they find most useful and to write sentences using the items to show meaning and use. Students share some examples in full class.

1 yelling **2** boasting **3** nil **4** rival **5** relieve **6** superior **7** rooting for **8** jinxing

extra

Students work in small groups to check or explain to each other the meaning of the following additional items. Write the items on the board.

cheer (para 1) (to shout loudly to support someone or when someone wins)

victory (para 1) (a success or winning at something)

suffer a defeat (para 3) (to be beaten by someone)

lucky charm (para 6) (something you carry to bring you luck)

Sum up

6 Students work in pairs to discuss five key points they remember from the article. Stronger students can work with the text covered. Allow weaker students to scan the article again before covering and discussing.

alternative

Ask students to cover the article. Elicit four key points they remember from it and put them on the board. Then, they work in pairs to remember or find one more key point in the article. They discuss and decide which point they found most interesting and why. Conduct class feedback and see which point most students selected.

Possible answers

Key points from the article include:

Fans develop an attachment to a particular sport or team when they are about eight or nine years old.

They talk about their team using words like 'we', and can even feel part of a team's success.

When the team loses, fans often use words like 'they', distancing themselves from a lack of success.

Usually shy and quiet fans can become much more outgoing when they watch their team play, especially when they do so as part of a crowd.

People who are fans of one team might feel superior to fans of a rival team.

Fans might even wear special clothing, in the hope that it brings their team luck.

Speak up

7 Put students into small groups to discuss the questions. Check understanding of *take advantage of*. Circulate and contribute to the discussions, taking care not to overcorrect but supplying words or ideas when and if students need them. Note down any interesting ideas and bring them into full group discussion during feedback. You could extend by asking, e.g. *How important do you think fans are to the success of a team or player? How far would you travel to support a team or friend?*

Possible answers

1 A friend took me to see Inter Milan play A.C. Milan in the San Siro stadium in Milan. Both these teams are big rivals of each other, and they were playing in one of the most famous stadiums in Italy. I'm not a fan of either team, and the actual football match was quite slow and boring, but it was amazing just to be there and watch the fans get excited and cheer whenever their team did something right.
2 My friend Matthew is a big rugby fan. Whenever there's a big match on, he always dresses up in his favourite team's clothes, or makes sure he wears their colours. For important events, he even puts up a flag in his window at home!
3 I don't think it's true that the sports industry takes advantage of fans. Most fans are very happy to spend money on tickets, clothes, and so on, and they get a lot of enjoyment from watching their favourite teams play. For fans like these, supporting their team is an important part of their life.

To finish

Students write a short summary of the article for a website. They could start: *I read an interesting article today. It was about ….* Write the following phrases on the board for them to use, if they wish: *The writer points out that … She/He adds that … She/He concludes that … .*

Fun footer

Read through the footer with students and ask if they know of any other famous stadiums in the world. Ask students to choose a famous national or international team, or a famous place in which a sport is played. They should research any interesting facts online and prepare a short presentation to deliver to the rest of the class in the next lesson.

Direct students to the Workbook. Ask them to complete the exercises on the infinitive and verb + *ing*, in preparation for the Grammar lesson. You can also ask students to prepare for the lesson by completing Exs 1 and 2 on page 66 for homework, and carefully reading though the Grammar reference on page 150. Encourage them to note down any questions about the grammar that they want to ask in class.

Presentation tool:	Unit 5, Reading
Workbook / Online Practice:	pp46–47
Extra Practice App	

GRAMMAR SB p66

To start

Write the word *superstition* on the board and elicit examples of general superstitions in students' country/countries. If you have a multilingual group, compare superstitions between different countries. For example, say *A black cat can mean bad luck in one country and good luck in another.* Elicit the adjective *superstitious*. Then tell students about a superstition or lucky routine you or someone you know has and ask: *Are you superstitious? Do you carry a lucky charm at certain times, like before exams?* If you asked students to complete Ex 1 and 2 for homework, ask them to now share with their partner what they learned and any questions to see if their partner can answer them. Encourage students to ask you any questions. Then, work through Exs 3–7 as suggested below.

1 Read through the sentences with the group and elicit the different verb patterns that follow the verbs in bold.

1 the *to* infinitive (*to develop*)
2 object + infinitive without *to* (*their team play*)
3 object + *to* infinitive (*people to become*)
4 the *-ing* form (*achieving*)

explore grammar

SB p150

2 Read through the explore grammar box with the class. Then ask students to complete it with the words in the box.

The grammar reference covers how certain verbs are followed by the infinitive, or a verb + *-ing*. Get students to read the explanations on page 150 and complete Exs 1 and 2 on page 151.

1 decide **2** advise **3** in order **4** interesting **5** enjoy

3 5.1 Ask the class: *Do you enjoy playing team sports? Do you think it's important for people to play them? Which ones do you think are important?* Tell them that they are going to listen to some people saying why they think team sports are important. Then play the recording. Students note down any reasons they hear. Play the recording again and stop after each reason. Ask students to summarise the different reasons in their own words. Conduct class feedback and ask students if they agree with the speakers.

Speaker 1: It's a great way to develop social skills and leadership. It helps people feel confident working with other people.
Speaker 2: It's important to build new friendship groups. We can learn to get on with people we might not necessarily get on with in other contexts.
Speaker 3 talks about how cricket and Rugby League are very important in Australia.
Speaker 4: Team sports are good and help people make new friends, learn to communicate and have fun.
Speaker 5: Team sports help people become more confident. They help people work better in a team.

4 5.2 Students choose the correct alternatives individually or in pairs and then listen to check.

1 taking **2** to have **3** watching, playing **4** to make **5** to help

5 Ask students to match the patterns in Ex 4 with the rules in the grammar box. Conduct class feedback.

1 F **2** D **3** H **4** C **5** A

6 Refer students to the picture of the socks and ask them to discuss what they think the picture means and what the text might be about. Students read the text and choose the correct alternatives to complete it. After they compare answers in pairs, conduct class feedback. Ask: *Which ritual do you find most surprising?*

1 training **2** winning **3** heading **4** to point **5** wearing **6** to have

7 Students read the next section of text to check their ideas. Students complete the text with the correct form of the verbs in brackets and then compare answers with their partner. Conduct class feedback.

1 having **2** to focus **3** to get **4** to prepare **5** feel **6** Gaining

Speak up

8 Students discuss the questions in groups. Monitor and quickly correct any mistakes in using the verb patterns taught in the lesson. Elicit any interesting ideas for the whole class to hear, and if students are not particularly interested in sports, focus on how students can relax before a nerve-racking event such as an exam.

Possible answers

1 Before taking an exam, there are lots of sensible things I do, like making sure I get enough sleep and revising as much as possible. But I do some things which maybe aren't sensible, too. I always have a bar of chocolate before I go into the exam room. I think it makes my brain work more quickly.
2 If I think about it seriously, then most superstitions and rituals are probably a waste of time. But the other way of looking at is that if having a ritual helps you feel more relaxed and confident, then why not do it? It probably won't cause any harm.

Fun footer

Draw students' attention to the fun footer. Ask them to tell you whether they agree with it or not and why/why not. Get students to give examples of how experiencing a defeat isn't always a bad thing.

To finish

Put students into pairs to test each other on verbs that take different patterns. Ask them to use verbs from the explore grammar box. Give an example. Say *advise* and elicit *advise someone to do* from students. They take turns in pairs to test each other.

Presentation tool:	Unit 5, Grammar
Workbook / Online Practice:	p48
Grammar reference and practice:	SB p150
Audioscript:	SB p178

VOCABULARY SB p67

sport

To start

Put students into pairs to write down as many different sports as they can in two minutes. Then ask each pair in turn to name a different sport that they noted down. As the sports are named, write them on the board. Ask: *Which sports have you tried? Which ones do you love? Which are you not interested in?* Ask students to discuss the sports on the board, giving reasons for their ideas where appropriate.

1 5.3 Refer the students to the photo of the gaming tournament and ask: What can you see? Do you know what's happening? Tell them they are going to hear a sports presenter commenting on a sport. They should listen to say what she is talking about.

an esports (electronic sports) tournament

extra

Ask questions to check understanding in more detail and play the recording again.

1 *Where is the woman?*
2 *What is she watching?*
3 *How many people are there?*
4 *What does she compare the number with?*
5 *Why are esports controversial?*
6 *What examples of real sports skills does she give?*
7 *What examples of esports skills does she give?*
8 *What is happening at the end of the recording?*

2 5.4 Play the recording and stop after the information has been given to allow students time to write the words. Students check in pairs and then conduct class feedback.

1 spectators **2** coordination **3** teamwork **4** championship **5** teammate **6** opponents **7** title **8** trophy

alternative

With a strong class, ask them to read and complete the sentences and guess what the words might be, or what type of word will fit. Play the recording for them to check or complete.

3 Remind students what a collocation is (words that go together naturally) and that there are several types. Here, they are going to look at verb + noun collocations. Students work in pairs to complete the gaps in the table with words from Ex 2. Conduct class feedback.

1 prepare for **2** attract **3** involve **4** coordination **5** compete for **6** trophy **7** defeat

extra

Ask students to choose two or three collocations and make example sentences from them. You could give some examples before they start.

I'm preparing for a marathon in May. I run every morning.
Exciting sports attract a lot of viewers on TV.
Succeeding in tennis involves a lot of intensive training.
Four teams are still competing for the local football trophy.
My friend defeated the boxing champion to win the title.

4 Ask: *How many words describe people who watch or who do sports?* Conduct class feedback and write the list on the board.

spectator, opponent, teammate, fan, viewers, teams, rival team

5 Ask students to read the post, ignoring the alternatives at the moment. Ask: *What is the poster's point?* (She believes that although gamers don't necessarily need to be very fit, as esport doesn't demand significant physical exertion, they still need to have other physical skills like coordination and fast reactions.) Students then choose the correct alternatives to complete the text. Conduct class feedback, and ask for reasons why one alternative seems better than the other.

1 athletes **2** qualify **3** involves **4** opponent's **5** win

extra

Ask: *In what way are gamers like traditional athletes? What do they have to work on?*

Elicit that gamers need to be on top of their game – at their peak – and that means a lot of training. Also elicit that like other sportspeople, gamers have to work on their technique and be aware of their opponent's strengths and weaknesses.

6 Point out that Amy supports the idea of an esport being a real sport. Tell students that they are going to read a post from someone who disagrees. Ask: *Why might someone disagree that esport is a real sport?* Elicit ideas, and then ask students to check their ideas by reading Joe's post. Nominate a volunteer to summarise Joe's opinion. Then in pairs, students match the highlighted phrasal verbs with the definitions. Conduct class feedback.

1 C **2** E **3** A **4** D **5** B

explore vocabulary

7 Ask students to read the information in the explore vocabulary box and discuss the questions as a class.

1 B **2** C **3** B **4** B **5** A

VOCABULARY (Continued)

Speak up

8 Students can discuss the questions in pairs or in full group.

Possible answers

I play video games, and I enjoy them. I think it's a good hobby. I agree that it takes a lot of skill to do esports, and you can learn a lot from doing them. I also agree that it's fun to play esports against other people, and you can probably get a real feeling of excitement. However, the problem for me is that playing esports doesn't encourage you to use your whole body in the way that traditional sports do. I'm also not sure that sitting for hours in a chair, looking at a screen is very healthy for people's bodies. Lastly, I'd argue that traditional sports can encourage people to play as part of a team, which I'm not sure is the case with esports.

extra

Extend the discussion by asking students to discuss the following questions.

Some people say that because we have less time for leisure these days, practising physical sports will become rarer and rarer. Do you agree?

Do you think esports are only for young people? Why?

Can you think of any disadvantages associated with being passionate about esports?

To finish

Conduct a short class debate. Write the debate topic on the board: *Are esports 'real' sports or not?* Organise students into groups, and give each group a viewpoint (Amy's or Joe's). Tell students that they should try to think of arguments to support the viewpoint they have been assigned.

Give them two or three minutes to prepare their arguments before conducting the debate with the whole class. Explain to students that the aim is not for them to give their own opinions, but to present both sides of the argument objectively.

Presentation tool:	Unit 5, Vocabulary
Workbook / Online Practice:	p49
Photocopiable activity:	5A
Audioscript:	SB p179
Extra Practice App	

LISTENING SB p68

To start

Write the word *drone* on the board. Ask students: *What is a drone?* Elicit answers and refer to the photo on page 68 to show students what a drone look like. Ask: *Would you like one as a present? What would you use it for?*

Power up

1 Ask students: *Have you ever heard about drone racing?* If they have they should explain what they know to the rest of the class. Write the following gapped sentence on the board. Ask students to complete it using the words from the box.

Drone racers wear a .... which is made up of .... and a .... The racers operate drones (often small radio-controlled aircraft) by .... and race these around a ....

Drone racers wear a headset which is made up of goggles and a camera. The racers operate drones (often small radio-controlled aircraft) by remote control and race these around a track.

Point out that drone racing began as an amateur sport in Australia in 2014.

Listen up

2 5.5 Tell students that they're going to listen to an interview with a drone racer. Play the recording and ask them how he started. Ask: *What was unusual about this?*

He got into it by chance as his dad bought him a remote controlled plane for his birthday instead of the skateboard he'd asked for.

exam tip

3 5.6 Go through the exam tip with the class. Tell students that they obviously can't guess an answer until they have heard the recording, but that trying to predict possible answers will help them to identify the focus of each question. It helps them to establish exactly what the question means, and to listen for the right thing. Remind students that they have time to read through all the questions and the options before they listen, and that they should use this time to identify exactly what they are listening for. Play the recording. Ask the whole class: *What is the focus of the question?* (Marc's feelings) *What is the correct option?*

1 C *... from that point on I was hooked.*
Option A is wrong. Marc says, *When I opened the parcel it was a bit of let-down, but I thought I'd better look enthusiastic.* Option B is also wrong. He says, *Although I thought it would be tricky to get the hang of, I was a natural.*

extra

Ask students to read through all the questions. Ask them to decide on the focus of each question. Elicit the following ideas with the whole class.

Question 2 focuses on detail. It answers the question 'because'.

Question 3 focuses on opinion, specifically Marc's opinion of other people breaking rules.

Question 4 focuses on Marc's feelings.

Question 5 focuses on detail, something from Marc's experiences.

Question 6 focuses on detail, something that happened to Marc.

Question 7 focuses on Marc's opinion of what new drone racers should do.

exam task: multiple choice: longer text

4 5.7 **Play the whole recording and ask students to find the answers to the questions. They should check their ideas in pairs after the first listening. Play the recording again for them to confirm their answers. Don't conduct class feedback until they have heard the recording twice.**

2 B (*The goggles are linked up to a camera on the front of the drone … so cameras on the drones are essential in order to see where you're flying.*)
A Incorrect. Marc says they look as though they're playing a video game.
C Incorrect. He says they give you a bird's-eye view.

3 C (*… there are always a few who don't, … I'm sure they impressed their friends …*)
A Incorrect. Marc says most people do respect the rules.
B Incorrect. He says that people impressed their school friends, not that they had nowhere to practise.

4 A (*I'd like to say I've got less nervous as time has gone on, but unfortunately the opposite is true.*)
B Incorrect. He says he tries to find distractions to stop him worrying about the race.
C Incorrect. He says that his teammates listen to music but that he is still looking for a good technique.

5 A (*The only thing to beat that was when I met the world champion drone racer when I was in Dubai.*)
B Incorrect. He says that it was made more special because his grandparents had flown in to watch him, but that this was bettered by meeting the world champion.
C Incorrect. He says he won't forget picking up the trophy but that feeling was beaten by meeting the world champion.

6 B (*I … took my drone out despite it being very windy. Of course drones are pretty light and one strong gust blew it into a tree trunk and it smashed … It was a good lesson to learn!*)
A Incorrect. He says he ignored the advice he was given.
C Incorrect. He says he smashed his drone into a tree, but doesn't advise against flying them near trees.

7 C (*I think it's a good idea to be part of some kind of group – like a club or an online racing community.*)
A Incorrect. He says it's not necessary to spend a fortune at the beginning.
B Incorrect. He says that it doesn't take ages to become competent.

5 **Point out that the phrases all come from the recording. If necessary, let students look at the script on page 179 to read the expressions in context, or play the recording again. Point out that they are informal phrases.**

it was a bit of let-down – It was disappointing.
I was a natural – I was good at it straight away with little effort.
I was hooked – I was obsessed, I didn't want to stop.
the stakes are higher – There is more to win or lose.
it is addictive! – You can't stop doing it. The more you do it, the more you want to do it.
to get the hang of it – To learn how to do something or become good at it

Speak up

6 **Organise students into groups and explain the task. As each group makes their presentation, ask the other groups to listen and to decide how persuasive they are. Tell them to consider the ideas they have, the language they use and the style of talking. After every group has finished, ask the class to vote on the most persuasive presentation.**

Possible answers

Unusual sports could include parkour, futsal, archery, fencing, or circus arts.

Reasons why someone might want to take up an unusual sport might include that it offers an adrenalin rush, not many other people do it, it's creative, or it helps to keep old traditions alive.

extra

As a follow-up or for homework, ask students to write a short email to a friend telling them about the unusual sport that the class voted for and explaining why they would or wouldn't like to try it.

Fun footer

Nominate a student to read out the footer. Ask: *What advantages might there be to this? Would there be any disadvantages? Should there be laws to control the use of drones?* Ask students to discuss these questions in pairs. Encourage them to justify their answers.

Presentation tool:	Unit 5, Listening
Workbook / Online Practice:	p50
Audioscript:	SB p179
Extra Practice App	

USE OF ENGLISH 1 SB p69

To start

Write these two questions on the board: *Is there anything you must remember to do in the near future? Can you remember doing anything interesting last week?* Put students into pairs to discuss the questions. Then, underline *remember to do* and *remember doing* on the board. Elicit the two different verb patterns. Then ask students: *Is there a difference in meaning between the two uses of 'remember'?*

explore grammar ➥ SB p150

1 Refer students to the explore grammar box. Go through the box with the class, explaining the difference in meaning in each sentence. If necessary, refer students to the grammar reference explanations, *verb patterns with a change in meaning*, on page 150 for more information. Ask comprehension questions for the examples where there is no explanation in the box.

regret to inform (= I'm sorry to tell you.)
Did we tell you something before? (No, I'm telling you now in a formal way.)
regret telling him (= I wish I hadn't told him.)
Did you tell him? (Yes.) How do you feel about it? (I'm sorry I told him.)
tried to tell (= I couldn't tell him.)
Did you tell him? (No.) Did you succeed in telling him? (No.)
tried using (= I was able to use the key but it didn't work.)
Could you use the key? (Yes.) Did it open the door? (No.)
forgot to tell (= I didn't remember.)
Did I tell you? (No.) Why not? (I didn't remember to tell you.)
forgot winning (= I always remembered)
Did you win the cup? (Yes.) Do you remember winning it now? (Yes – I'll always remember it.)
go on to become (= will become in the future)
Is the footballer a coach now? (No.) What will he do next? (He'll become a coach.)
go on playing (= continue playing)
Do I play football now? (Yes.) Will I continue? (Yes, for as long as possible.)

Refer students to Ex 4 on page 151 for quick practice of these structures. Do it in class if you want to check that they have understood the meaning, otherwise set it for homework.

extra: fast finishers

Put fast finishers into pairs and give them a verb pattern each (e.g. *remember to do* or *try using*, etc.). They write a sentence using each form, then exchange their sentences with another pair to check that the grammar is correct, and the sentences make sense.

2 Ask students to skim the text quickly and find out what sport Liv does, and when she started doing it.

She does freestyle football. She got into it after watching a video clip of Ronaldinho doing it. Also she was getting injured playing football so needed a new sport.

3 Students then work in pairs and complete the gaps in the text. Conduct class feedback. If they are having problems choosing the correct form, refer them to the explore grammar box again.

1 to find **2** playing **3** watching **4** changing
5 to become **6** practise **7** think

explore language ➥ SB p150

4 Tell students that there are other words and expressions that take specific structures which change their meaning. Write these two sentences on the board and ask comprehension questions.

1 *I'd rather play tennis than hockey.*
Ask: *Is this sentence talking about the past?* (No.) *Who is it about?* (I – the speaker) *Is it talking about a preference, or something the speaker should or must do?* (a preference)

2 *I would rather you didn't play music so loudly.*
Ask: *Is this sentence referring to the past?* (No.) *Is it talking about a preference, or something the other person must do?* (a strong preference)

Explain that in the second sentence, the preference expressed is for another person, not the speaker. Go through the explore language box with the class. Explain that the phrases *it's time* and *it's high time* are always followed by either the past tense, or the infinitive but in both cases they have a future meaning. Ask students to match verb patterns A–C with uses 1–3. Point out that the phrase *I'd better* is followed by the present tense, and can also have a future meaning.

Ask students to do Ex 3 on page 151 for homework.

1 A **2** C **3** B

exam task: **key word transformation**

All the sentence transformations here check verb patterns as this is the focus of the lesson.

5 e Tell students that these types of verb patterns are often tested in the exam. Do the first question together. Remind students that their answer must be between 2–5 words, and that if they think of an answer which is more than five words, then it's wrong. Contractions such as *I'd* or *it's* count as two words. Put students into pairs and ask them to do the remaining questions. Monitor them and make a note of any questions that students find difficult. Conduct feedback, and discuss any alternative answers students thought of. Explain any that are wrong.

1 time we left (*It's time* can be followed by the infinitive or simple past, but the past form *left* is given here, so must be used.)
2 'd/would rather play sports than (*would rather* + infinitive without *to* + *than* is used to express a preference between two choices.)
3 'd/had better wear (*had better* + infinitive *wear* is used to give advice.)
4 regretted missing the training (session) (*Regret* + *-ing* form is used as the sentence is expressing regret about something which has already happened.)
5 stopped playing for the team (*stop* + *-ing* form means stop an activity.)
6 must not/mustn't/should not/shouldn't forget to bring (*Forget* + *to* infinitive is used as the sentence is about a reminder to do something, not about recalling a memory.)

Speak up

6 Tell students to imagine that they have just met and they want to find out about one another's interests. Put them into groups of three. They should ask and answer the questions, and make a note of anything particularly interesting or surprising about their group members.

Possible answers

1 I remember playing football when I was very young. I was probably about six or seven, and it was in school. It wasn't real football, of course. There were only about five people on each team, and we had to play in a big room inside the school. It was only later that we used to play outside. I'd rather play in a big field, on a big team, because it's much more exciting.
2 I used to cycle a lot, and I had a really nice bike. Unfortunately, I left it in the street outside my house, and when I returned, someone had stolen it. Since then, I haven't been cycling. I hope I can get another bike in the future, because I really miss it. If I get a new bike, I'd better buy a good lock too, because I'd rather not lose it again!

Presentation tool:	Unit 5, Use of English 1
Workbook / Online Practice:	p51
Photocopiable activity:	5B
Grammar reference and practice:	SB p150
Extra Practice App	

USE OF ENGLISH 2 SB p70

To start

Tell students that a school wants to encourage its students to do more exercise, and these are some things they are considering doing. Write these ideas on the board.

- *Starting a competitive sports team to play against other schools.*
- *Opening a running club for all ages of student.*
- *Giving information to students about the importance of fitness in a school magazine.*

Ask: *Which ideas do you think would be most effective in your school?*

1 Put students into pairs and ask them to consider the ideas in the box. Conduct class feedback and write the most and least motivating ideas on the board.

2 5.8 Students listen to identify what motivates the three speakers. Ask: *Which things from the box do they mention?* If necessary, play the recording again.

The speakers mention: doing an exercise class, working out with friends, using a fitness gadget, looking at fitness magazines, watching fitness DVDs

Speaker 1 is motivated by exercising with other people.

Speaker 2 is motivated by seeing improvements in his fitness.

Speaker 3 is motivated by trying different things.

explore **vocabulary 1**

3 5.9 Write these words on the board: *connect, entertain, perform, discover.* Ask students what form of the word they are: verb, noun or adjective? (They're all verbs.) Remind students that they can change the form of a word by adding a suffix, and unlike a prefix, it doesn't usually change the meaning.Elicit the noun form of the words on the board. Underline the suffix in each one (connect<u>ion</u>, entertain<u>ment</u>, perform<u>ance</u>, discover<u>y</u>). Go through the explore vocabulary box with the class. Then play the recording again so that students can complete the sentences, using noun suffixes from the box. In feedback, highlight that *improvements* is a plural noun.

1 motivation **2** embarrassment **3** guidance
4 improvements **5** commitment **6** concentration

4 Ask students to identify the verb and spelling changes in each sentence.

1 -ion (motivate) **2** -ment (embarrass) **3** -ance (guide)
4 -ment (improve) **5** –ment (commit) **6** -ion (concentrate)

5 Model the pronunciation for students, or play recording 5.9 again.

USE OF ENGLISH 2 (Continued)

The common sound is the schwa /ə/
motivation /ˌməʊtɪˈveɪʃən/
embarrassment /ɪmˈbærəsmənt/
guidance /ˈgaɪdəns/
improvement /ɪmˈpruːvmənt/
commitment /kəˈmɪtmənt/
concentration /kɒnsənˈtreɪʃən/
All the nouns in the explore vocabulary box contain the schwa /ə/ apart from *design* and *trade*.

explore **vocabulary 2**

exam tip

6 **Remind students that in this exam task, they have to use the base form of a word in its correct form in a text. This is much easier to do if they have skimmed the text first. Tell students to quickly look at *Need help getting off the sofa?* and ask: *What is this text about?* Elicit that it is about fitness gadgets and whether they can be motivating. Explain to students that this time, they are focusing on prefixes, and that these can sometimes change the meaning of a word by making it negative. Go through the explore vocabulary box, and point out that all these prefixes have a negative meaning. Point out that the prefix *re-* means 'again', and does not have a negative meaning. Go through the exam tip and ask them to answer the questions about gap 2 in Exercise 7.**

We know it's an adjective because the gap comes before a noun. We know that it needs to be negative because of the words *you've been disappointed by*. You wouldn't be disappointed by successful attempts to get fit.

exam task: **word formation**

7 **e** **Tell students they're going to work in pairs to complete the text using prefixes. As always they should read the whole sentence before they decide on the form of the missing word. Students should complete the rest of the text. Then, they compare answers in pairs, explaining their decisions.**

1 unmotivated – the clue that a negative is needed is in the word *but*
2 unsuccessful
3 unbelievably – the meaning of the word is 'difficult to believe' so it's negative
4 undoubtedly – the meaning of the word is 'without doubt', so it needs a negative prefix. There is a possible answer using a suffix (doubtless) with the same meaning.
5 misleading – the clue is that advertising can give the wrong information, so it's negative
6 impatient – the meaning is negative – we can't wait to see improvement in fitness
7 unrealistic – we need a negative adjective because of *not only*
8 discourage – it has to be negative because the sentence is saying that although the writer wouldn't stop anyone from using gadgets they would advise them to be careful

extra

Ask students to close their books. Tell them that you will call out an prefix and they will have 30 seconds to write as many words with that prefix as they can before you call out another one. Call out one prefix (e.g. *re-* or *un-*) at a time. Give 30 seconds for students to write, and then call out another prefix. Stop after a few examples, and ask students to compare their lists in pairs.

Fun footer

Read the fun footer with the class. Elicit the meaning of *burns calories* (the way that the body uses up energy created by the food we eat). Ask: *What's the best exercise for keeping fit and losing weight?* Elicit the most popular answers from the class.

Presentation tool:	Unit 5, Use of English 2
Workbook / Online Practice:	p52
Photocopiable activity:	5C
Audioscript:	SB p179
Extra Practice App	

SPEAKING SB p71

To start

Write the phrase *switch off and relax* on the board. Ask students: *What do you do when you want to do this?* Write their suggestions on the board, and the class can vote on the most popular and/or useful idea.

Power up

1 Read through the question and elicit student's ideas. Find out the most popular places that students like to go to.

Suggested answers

Anywhere outdoors, in nature, for example a lake or a forest or a mountain.

Other ideas could include the cinema or a theatre, a sports hall, or simply the students' own bedroom at home.

2 Ask students to match the phrases in the box to the pictures. Conduct feedback, and see if they can add any ideas of their own. Write their ideas on the board.

Suggested answers

both pictures: physical exercise, energetic, athletic, reduce stress, equipment

picture A: fresh air, be outdoors, lonely, peaceful, calm and content, nice scenery

picture B: competitive, sociable, be indoors, social skills, friendships

3 5.10 Play the recording and elicit the answers. When students have given their answers, remind them of the importance of completing both parts of the task: comparing the photos and answering the question.

B, D

4 5.11 Play the recording and ask students to tick the words and phrases used.

physical exercise, fresh air, be indoors, reduce stress, nice scenery, calm, competitive, sociable, social skills, energetic

useful language: speculating

5 5.12 Remind students that the task asks them to speculate about the photographs, so they need to use language of speculating and giving opinions. Check that they understand the meaning of *speculate* (to make a guess about what is happening). Go though the useful language box, then ask students to look at the sentences. Ask: *Can you guess which phrases from the box might fit the sentences?* Play the recording again so that they can write in the phrases that the speaker uses.

1 maybe, looks like
2 probably
3 it seems
4 looks
5 may not
6 might

exam tip

6 Read through the information in the exam tip box. Stress the words in bold, and point out that these are the key words in each sentence. Explain that these words carry the main meaning, and if students stress them naturally, it will help them become better communicators. When they work through the sentences in Ex 5, make sure that they read the sentences aloud so that they practise stressing the key words.

1 ... the second photo shows a group of people playing volleyball maybe, in what looks like a school hall.
2 ... the girl is doing her sport outside in the fresh air which is probably healthier than being indoors.
3 ... I think her sport is good for reducing stress as it seems very relaxing.
4 She has nice scenery around her and she looks very calm and content.
5 As they're playing a game and want to win, they may not feel as relaxed as the girl in the first photo.
6 It's very sociable and might improve their social skills as you need to work as part of a team.

Point out that we can stress words like *looks like, probably, seems* when we are speculating. If we do so, this emphasises to the listener that what we are saying is only speculation.

Speak up

exam task: long turn ➥ SB p163

There is no question for the listening candidate as there is in the Cambridge Speaking test because the lesson focus is on the long turn.

7 e Put students into pairs and refer them to the photos on pages 172 and 174. You may prefer students to work with a partner they don't normally work with for this exam task.Students can record themselves using their phones. When they listen back, they can identify whether or not they were using language for speculating, rather than just describing the pictures.

Possible answers

Student A: The first photo shows people using exercise bikes. They are probably in a gym, and they might be taking some kind of class. The second photo shows people playing a video game. They're holding games consoles, and they seem to be looking and pointing at a screen. Both photos show people doing something indoors. The people in the first photo are definitely more energetic, and they are probably healthier because they are exercising their bodies more, whereas in the second photo, the people are sitting down, but it looks like they are having more fun.

Student B: Both of these photos show people having fun, and they are all outdoors in the fresh air. Whereas the first photo shows two friends just walking in what looks like a park, the second photo shows people in a much more athletic situation. They might be taking part in some kind of competition. In the first photo, the two people look relaxed. They're probably talking and laughing about something, and they don't look like they are in a hurry to get anywhere. In the second photo, the people are white-water rafting. They might be on a dangerous river, and it might be important that they work together as a team. They don't look relaxed, but they look excited. They are probably using all their energy to try and beat another team.

SPEAKING (Continued)

Speaking extra

8 As students do this task, time them so that they get used to speaking about the photographs for one minute.

Possible answer

(For picture A)

I like being alone in the fresh air. I often come here for some peace and quiet. It's nice to be outdoors on the river. There is some great scenery here. Some people might feel lonely doing this, but I don't, because I can often see lots of wildlife. It's nice to be away from cars and people, and I get some physical exercise, too. I don't do this sport because I want to be competitive. I just do it to switch off and reduce stress.

To finish

Ask students to show their partner a photograph they have with them on their phones. They should speculate about where their partner's photo was taken, and what was happening. Their partner can confirm if these ideas were correct or not.

Presentation tool:	Unit 5, Speaking
Workbook / Online Practice:	p53
Speaking file:	SB p163
Audioscript:	SB p179

WRITING SB pp72–73

To start

Give students an example of what health and fitness means to you. This is to prepare them for thinking about the relationship between the health of the mind and the health of the body. For example, say something like: *I always feel much happier when I've done some exercise. Running makes me feel relaxed. Surprisingly, when I exercise it gives me energy, and doesn't make me tired.*

Ask students: Do you agree that a healthy body leads to a healthy mind? Elicit ideas and examples.

Power up

1 Put students into small groups to discuss the question.

Suggested answers

Health and fitness means doing some regular exercise and eating well so that you don't get ill, and you have enough strength and energy to do things like run, ride a bike, climb hills, etc.

If you have a healthy body, it can reduce stress and make you think more clearly. Doing exercise can also help you think more creatively, and work out problems faster.

2 Do Ex 2 quickly with the whole class, to prepare them for what they are going to listen to.

Suggested answers

The photos show: someone listening to music; a range of fresh fruit and vegetables; people checking something on social media; someone sleeping or having a nap.

Listening to music can improve your mood, and can sometimes help you concentrate on work or studies.

Eating fresh fruit and vegetables helps you get the vitamins and nutrients you need to stay healthy.

Having friendships online can help you feel less lonely, and can also be fun.

Making sure you have naps, or have enough sleep, keeps your brain fresh and alert, and allows your body to repair itself every day.

3 5.13 Tell students that they are going to hear four people talking about the photos. Ask: *What activities do they mention? What benefits do they identify?* If necessary, play the recording twice, allowing students to compare their answers between each listening.

Speaker 1: Listening to loud music and dancing makes him feel good, makes her feel more positive and happy.

Speaker 2: Laughter makes her feel less stressed, increases blood flow, exercises muscles, improves creativity and memory.

Speaker 3: Eating fruit and vegetables is good for skin and hair, makes you look and feel great.

Speaker 4: Getting enough sleep makes her feel less grumpy and healthier, improves memory.

4 Ask: *Can you add any ideas or activities to what the speakers said?*

Possible answers

Other suggestions could include drinking lots of water, doing sports, walking to school, using stairs instead of lifts, stretching or yoga/Pilates, fresh air, walking in the countryside, in forests or on the beach, etc.

Plan on

5 **Tell students that they are going to write an article. Ask: *What do you they think is the main purpose of an article?* Elicit their ideas and write them on the board. Ideas could include: to interest and inform the reader; to entertain the reader; to use interesting and colourful language. Remind students that it's always a good idea to underline the things they have to include in their answer so that they don't forget anything. Ask: *What do you need to include in this task?* Ask them to underline the relevant parts of the task.**

What kind of things you do
make you feel fit and healthy
why they make you feel good

6 **Students work in pairs to read Tom's article and answer the questions. Go through their answers and make the points below.**

1 He starts the article with a rhetorical question in order to get the reader's attention. Point out that this is a useful technique for an article.
2 The style is chatty and informal, which is interesting and engaging for the reader. It involves the reader in Tom's own experiences.
3 He didn't use paragraphs, which makes his article look badly organised and more difficult for the reader to pick out the different points.

7 **Students work in pairs to divide Tom's article into paragraphs. Remind them that they should look for typical words or phrases that start paragraphs by introducing a new idea or topic, or a different example or point of view. They should underline these words in Tom's article as they decide on the paragraphing.**

The article should be divided up as follows. The underlined words should have helped students identify paragraph breaks as well as a shift in focus/subject.

So what does health and fitness mean to me? Well, first of all let me get something straight, I'm not one of those sporty types that's always at the gym. So for me feeling good is not about being athletic and super fit, but about a combination of things.

First of all, I love being outdoors, in fact I need it. It really gets me down if I'm stuck inside all day. So fresh air makes me feel healthy and more alive. When I'm studying hard, I often need to get up and move about a bit. I love going for walks in the park near our house, it really clears my head.

Another thing is meeting up with friends. I often get together with friends and we'll kick a ball around or go to the beach and have a swim. We're not into competitive sports, just having fun together. It always puts me in a good mood.

All in all, I think being fit and healthy is not just about doing exercise, but also having a laugh with friends and spending time outdoors.

explore **vocabulary**

8 **Remind students that because an article should be engaging and the language interesting, it should include informal, personal language such as phrasal verbs, so that it seems as though you are communicating directly with the reader. Ask students to underline any other phrasal verbs in Tom's article.**

let me get something straight
It really gets me down if I'm stuck inside all day.
When I'm studying hard, I often need to get up and move about a bit.
I love going for walks in the park near our house, it really clears my head.
Another thing is meeting up with friends.
I often get together with friends and we'll kick a ball around
We're not into competitive sports, It always puts me in a good mood.

9 **Students may know the phrasal verbs already. Let them discuss them with their partner before using their dictionaries, and see if they can complete the sentences without help. They can often use the context to help them, and in the exam they may not know all the words, so this is good practice for them.**

1 get through **2** get together **3** gets down
4 get round to **5** get back to **6** get up

Write on

exam tip

10 **Read through the exam tip with the class. This tip highlights the importance of paragraphing, which Tom failed to do in his article. It also points out the importance of the title, because an article should get the reader's attention and make you want to read the article to find out what the title really means. Ask: *What do you think of Tom's title? Can you think of any other titles he could have used?***

The title *The feel-good factor* works well as it gets your attention. It's an interesting and short phrase. The fact that it doesn't explain exactly what the article is going to be about is good, as it makes the reader want to read on and find out.
Suggestions for other titles: *What makes me feel good / Why I exercise / What exercise means to me*

Ask students to work together and make notes in preparation for their own article.

Suggested answers
going to the gym, being outdoors, having fresh air, going for walks, meeting friends, going to the beach, having a swim, listening to music, eating fresh food, getting enough sleep

11 **Read through the tips with the class. When they plan their article, they should work through the checklist. Make sure that they make a clear plan before they start to write, adding the ideas they want to include in each paragraph, so that they don't forget to use paragraphs clearly.**

If students want to see a model before they start to write, refer them to the sample answer on page 169. There is a useful checklist there that they could also use to help them.

exam task: article

➥ SB p169

12 **e** **As students write their article, go round and monitor. Make sure that they are writing in an informal, chatty style, and are using paragraphs in their article.**

WRITING (Continued)

Model answer

What makes me feel good

There are many things that we can do to make ourselves feel fit. Everyone's different, of course, but here are some of the things that I do to try to keep healthy. Maybe you have the same ideas, too!

The first thing that I think is important is to make sure I eat lots of fresh fruit and vegetables. They're not always my favourite food. I love chocolate, for example! But I've noticed how bad I feel when I don't get enough vitamins – especially in the winter, when it's also freezing and there isn't much sunlight.

Another thing I do which never fails to put me in a good mood is to hang out with friends. It doesn't matter what we do, as long as we're together. We can be hanging around in a park or going bowling – the important thing is that we're together and having fun. Spending time by myself just isn't as good.

So, all in all, eating well, and hanging out with friends are the two main things that keep both my body and my mind feeling good.

Improve it

13 Read through the instructions and put students in pairs. Ask them to swap articles and check them carefully. They should not only look for mistakes but also check whether they have included the correct information, used appropriate language and written in the appropriate style, and whether the article was interesting to read.

14 Ask students to discuss how each other's articles could be made more interesting. Encourage them to make notes on the feedback they get. Conduct class feedback on any important areas for improvement that students discussed.

Possible answers

Things students could improve are including personal information, making a few jokes, including more idioms and informal language and communicating directly to the reader.

15 Ask students to complete this for homework, if there is no time in class, and hand the articles in to you in the next lesson. Check, especially, that they have used clear paragraphing, and an appropriate style.

Fun footer

Nominate a student to read out the footer. Ask students: *Why is it important to drink enough water? Do you drink this much every day?* Elicit their answers and find out whether the class is generally following the advice in the footer.

To finish

Ask students to talk in pairs. They should summarise the ideas they included in their articles, and explain why they included them.

Presentation tool:	Unit 5, Writing
Workbook / Online Practice:	p54
Writing file:	SB p169
Audioscript:	SB p179

SWITCH ON SB p74

Cycling star

1 Tell students about a physical risk you've taken at some point in the past. Describe the event, the outcome and how you feel about it now. Was it a silly, unnecessary risk? Put students into pairs to tell each other about the greatest physical risk they've taken. The anecdote could be from any area of the students' lives: in a sport, in a game, as part of a performance, etc. Read through the ideas of what they should include. Ask them to also say whether it was a planned risk or whether it happened out of the blue.

Suggested answers

I decided once that I would try climbing a mountain alone. It wasn't a very high mountain, and it was popular with other walkers. The problem was that I did it alone, and I didn't even tell anyone I was going to do it.

At the start, there were lots of other walkers, who were also trying to get to the top, so I didn't feel alone. But, at one point, I saw a choice of paths. One looked quite easy, but the other looked like it would get to the top more quickly and directly. So, I thought that I'd rather take the short route.

Unfortunately, the path I had taken got steeper and rockier. Worse, the weather suddenly changed, as it often does in the mountains, because it's so unpredictable. Clouds rolled in, and I quickly became unable to see anything in front of me. The path I was on also became extremely wet and slippery.

I was terrified, because I didn't know where I was, and couldn't see anything. Luckily, the weather changed again, and I decided to go back down as carefully as I could, on the treacherous rocks.

I think I made a stupid decision, especially because I didn't tell anyone where I was going. Anything could have happened to me, and I'll never do anything like that again.

2 Ask students to join another pair and swap stories. They should compare to see whose stories are the most dangerous, exciting, etc. They should then decide what they would have done in the other's situation. Conduct class feedback for students to tell each other any interesting points that came up.

3 Tell students they are going to watch a video clip of a young person taking on a difficult and risky challenge. Read through the questions and then play the video. Point out the meaning of *notorious* (famous for being difficult, or horrible in some way, e.g. a notorious event/a notorious criminal), *treacherous* (when there are hidden dangers), *slippery* (easy to slip on) and *unpredictable* (impossible to know what will happen).

Possible answers

1 It's longer, harder, with more technical and physical challenges than he's had before. He doesn't have experience in a race of this difficulty. He is more anxious about it.

2 Bad weather, rain, wet weather. It's not easy to see. The surfaces on and off road will be wet and dangerous.

4 Go through the questions and elicit the answers. With weaker students, you may need to play the video a second time.

She isn't sure if he should continue but follows along to look out for him. Obviously, she doesn't want him to suffer, but also doesn't want him to feel disappointed in not finishing the race.

5 Play the video again. Conduct class feedback. If necessary play the video through again and focus on the parts that give the answers.

The race was one of the hardest things he's done and he's exhausted, but he's pleased to have done well and feels proud. Although he thought he would never do it again, he might come back and give it another go.

Project

6 Students could conduct the research in class, then create their slideshow for homework. Or alternatively, students could conduct the research at home and then create their slideshow in class. Organise students into groups and explain the project to them. Write some example sports on the board and ask groups to choose one to research. Brainstorm ways they can find out about the risks and rewards, for example, searching websites for online articles about sports stars or interviews, watching clips from documentaries, etc. Also discuss ways of presenting the information. They could create a slideshow presentation with pictures they have found online, by using for example, PowerPoint or Google slideshow, or they could present their research from notes. Students decide who will research what in their group.

When the research stage has been completed, ask each group in turn to present their findings to the rest of the class. The whole class then ranks the sports in terms of how dangerous or rewarding they are. Students use the results to create a graph. This is probably best done using tools such as Excel or Google Charts. Each group could create their own graph, and these could be shown to the rest of the class on the IWB, if you have one. Ask students to discuss the correlation between risk and reward amongst the sports, as well as their own reactions to their findings.

Project extension

1 Students can create a poster for their chosen sport using the information they have researched. The poster could either be aimed at attracting people to the sport or warning them about the health risks involved. Circulate or display the posters around the class, and if appropriate, have a class vote on the best.

2 Ask students to describe a sport that they take part in. They should describe the sport and give examples of any possible health risks that might happen (or have happened). Ask: *Do you feel that the rewards of doing the sport outweigh the disadvantages?*

Presentation tool: Unit 5, Switch on

Switch on videoscript: TB p173

INDEPENDENT LEARNING SB p74

Listening and speaking

1 Students discuss their performance in listening and speaking skills work in this unit. If students are happy to talk about their weaknesses together, make this a full group discussion.

2 Students work individually to rank their listening and speaking skills. Circulate and help if appropriate, but remember that the focus is on students assessing themselves here, rather than getting an assessment from a teacher.

3 Students can work in pairs to talk about their individual rankings and give advice, make suggestions on how their partner might improve. If your students are wary of discussing this with a partner (or if there is a great difference in level between students' ability) skip this stage and deal with the advice on a one-to-one basis, if possible.

4 Encourage students to note down any advice they find useful.

Ask the whole class: *What aspects of the unit have you found particularly interesting or helpful?*

Possible answers

In the Listening tasks, check the questions before listening, and decide what you have to listen out for. Underline key words, if possible.

Decide what the speaker is going to focus on before you listen. Is it going to be feelings, opinions, or factual detail?

When speaking, try repeating the same task with a different partner. This will help you focus on fluency, rather than thinking about what to say.

Try to plan what you say before you say it, by writing down any useful vocabulary or phrases you'd like to use.

UNIT CHECK SB p75

Practice

The Unit check focuses on: verb patterns and vocabulary related to sports.

1 2 5.14 and 5.15 **1** irresponsible **2** impolite **3** dishonest **4** inexpensive **5** rearranged **6** nonverbal **7** unexpectedly **8** illogical

3 **1** get through **2** got round to **3** count on **4** is getting, down **5** get together **6** knocked out **7** got up **8** get back to

Review

1 **1** to improve **2** playing **3** to have **4** telling **5** missing **6** practising

2 5.16 One boy is from the USA and the other is from the UK. The American boy is surprised that the British boy has never been to a baseball game before.

3 **1** *-ing* **2** *-ing* **3** infinitive with *to* **4** infinitive without *to* **5** infinitive with *to* **6** *-ing* **7** *-ing* **8** infinitive with *to*

4 5.17 **1** watching **2** playing **3** to find out **4** leave **5** to know **6** reading **7** throwing, hitting, running **8** to cheer

5 This open cloze type task has an item that tests a collocation (7) which is unlikely to appear in the Cambridge exam task, as open cloze items usually have a grammatical focus.
1 being **2** by **3** Playing **4** on **5** how **6** let **7** paying **8** as

3 **1** did something else
2 went swimming
3 we tidied up/to tidy up
4 bought a new one
5 hurry up
6 asked me first

7 **Possible answer**
The Fast Finishers Running Club is great for anyone who wants to try running, but gets bored with running alone. It's a great way to get fit, practice running, and meet new people all at the same time.
Running is a great sport, which helps you build speed, stamina and discipline. It doesn't need any special equipment, and it's a great way to stay healthy. It's also something you can do in almost any weather, and it gives you a good reason to get outdoors!
Come along, and make sure you're wearing a good pair of running shoes. Wear anything you feel comfortable with, such as shorts, a tracksuit, or a t-shirt.

GRAMMAR FILE SB p151

1 **1** A **2** C **3** C **4** A **5** C **6** A

2 **1** coming **2** to get **3** watching **4** playing **5** being **6** have **7** to give **8** not to ask

3 **1** B go **2** D to finish **3** A wear **4** F moved **5** C didn't bring **6** E enter

4 **1** getting **2** to have **3** to wear **4** giving up **5** meeting **6** to receive

Presentation tool:	Unit 5, Unit check
Workbook / Online Practice:	p55
Audioscript:	SB p180

6 Viewpoints

READING
topic: filming small creatures
skill: understanding text cohesion
task: gapped text

GRAMMAR
the passive
have/get something done

VOCABULARY
time and place
prepositions of place, time phrases
word formation: suffixes, irregular changes

LISTENING
topic: map exhibition
skill: listening for detail
task: sentence completion

USE OF ENGLISH
key word transformations
word formation

SPEAKING
topic: useful items
skill: making a decision
task: collaborative task

WRITING
topic: differing opinions
skill: linking ideas
task: essay

SWITCH ON
video: eyeborg
project: plan a film or documentary idea

Lead-in SB p77

Write the word *view* on the board and ask students to work in pairs to make different sentences using the word, showing different meanings. Conduct feedback and write some examples on the board, for example, *I have a great view from my bedroom window. My friend and I have different views about how to improve our English vocabulary!*

Write the word *viewpoint* on the board and elicit its meaning (a particular way of thinking about a topic). Then write *it's the way you look at things*. Point out that the same thing can look very different, depending on who is viewing it, and how they are viewing it.

Refer students to the photo and ask them to describe it to each other. Ask: How would this photo look from another viewpoint?

Discuss questions 1–3 with the whole class and be prepared to contribute your own opinions. If your class is reticent, let them discuss in pairs first and then bring into open group.

Possible answers

1 I'd like to think that I'm good at understanding people, and trying to imagine what their life is like. I visited my grandfather last week, and he's really old and can't walk very well. I tried to imagine how difficult it is for him to do simple things like go to the shops, or go up the stairs. Simple things like that are easy for me, but hard for someone who can't walk very well.
2 I usually only ask for people's opinions when I'm in a very bad situation, and I can't make a decision. Sometimes, it's better to get other people's opinions, because they might be able to think of something that I can't.
3 My friends and I don't disagree very often, but when we do, it's usually about sport. We don't support the same teams, and I can't understand why my friends are so passionate about a team that I think are terrible.

READING SB pp78–79

To start

Tell students about an interesting wildlife documentary you have seen recently. Say why it was special and what you learned from it. In pairs, students choose a wildlife documentary or film they have both seen and discuss why they might recommend it to others. Conduct class feedback, and nominate pairs to recommend their choice of documentary, presenting the reasons for watching it. The class can then vote on the film or documentary that sounds most interesting.

Power up

1 Put students into pairs and ask them to compare the two photos, saying what different views of the world they show and how they think each photo might have been taken. Conduct class feedback. Ask: *What challenges might there be for a cameraman in filming these animals?*

Possible answers

The photo on page 78 shows a hawk (or bird of prey). These birds can fly at great speeds, and have extremely good eyesight, which enables them to spot and then hunt small animals far beneath them. Therefore, they are good at looking across huge distances.

The photo on page 79 shows a dormouse. These small mammals live in high grass, or fields of wheat, and eats small berries, nuts and insects. Their view of the world is from the ground, seeing everything around them in close detail, and never having a wide view of anything.

Read on

2 Tell students that they are going to read an article about a TV wildlife series. Refer them to the title and introduction of the article and ask what they think they might learn from it.

Suggested answer

How very small animals cope with life and the dangers from large predators, and the particular skills that small animals have.

3 Students read the whole article quickly, ignoring the gaps, to find out the name of the series and what it was about.

It was called *Hidden Kingdoms*, and it was about the life of small creatures and their daily struggle for survival.

exam tip

4 Remind students about the requirements of the gapped text task and how important it is to focus on referencing and linking words to help choose the right sentences to complete a gap. Write *it* on the board and brainstorm other referencing words (*he, they, there*, etc.). Then write *However* on the board and elicit other words or phrases that can link back to a previous sentence (*so, because of this, as a result, in spite of this, as well as this, also*, etc.). Also remind students that in addition to looking for structural links, they should look for content links as the text must make sense. Read through the exam tip and if necessary add additional words and phrases from it to the list on the board. Ask students to read the second part of the exam box and to find the sentence for gap 1.

Check the answer in full group asking for what they have underlined. Also ask how the sentence fits the content of the paragraph.

alternative

With a weaker group, ask students to read the paragraph carefully. Check understanding of the situation. Ask: *What is the mouse's problem? How is it feeling? Why? Why are Harris Hawks dangerous?* Then read the task with the class and point out that when scanning sentences A–G, they should look for a possible contrast, a reference pronoun and a synonymous phrase. When they have found the correct sentence, students should underline the points mentioned.

1 F *By the evening, however,* (this contrasts with previous sections about being out in the daytime) *it is back in control. In the darkness,* (this is a synonymous phrase for *By the evening*)

exam task: gapped text

In the Cambridge exam the reading text doesn't have a detailed lead-in as there is here.

5 **e** Students complete the task individually. Ask them to underline any words and phrases that helped them.

2 D The sentence before the gap points out that the elephant shrew cannot burrow to hide from danger. Sentence D (*Instead, it creates trails or pathways through the grass …*) describes the alternative that exists for this mouse to stay hidden from danger. In the sentence after the gap, *These need to be kept clear at all times* refers back to the *trails or pathways* mentioned in D.

3 A The sentences before gap 3 mention the challenge presented by trying to show the animals' point of view while filming. Sentence A describes what was done to meet that challenge: *a certain amount of forward thinking and planning*. The sentence begins with *So*, showing that this is a result of the challenge. The sentence in place after the gap describes the first step of this forward planning: *Firstly the behaviour and life history of each individual animal had to be researched.*

4 E The sentence before the gap introduces the fact that the next step was to create storyboards. In E, *These* refers to the storyboards and describes what they consisted of (*a series of step-by-step pictures showing a breakdown of each animal's behavioural habits*). The sentence after the gap describes the result of having these storyboards, (*The correct shots could then be filmed …*).

5 G The sentence before the gap describes various filming techniques used to convey the action in the TV series. Sentence G introduces another method (*Another method used was high-speed filming shown in slow* motion) and explains what that is and how it is done. In the sentence after the gap (*This meant that an 'action scene' of a few seconds could be shown in much greater detail*) refers to the use of high-speed filming shown in slow motion and shows its effects.

6 B The sentence before gap 6 summarises the result of the various filming techniques in producing *an amazing series*, portraying *the intense and pressured lifestyle of smaller animals*. In sentence B, *these tiny creatures* refers back to *smaller animals*, and *while watching* refers to the *amazing series*. The sentence goes on to describe what we generally learn from watching this series. The sentence after the gap continues talking about what else we generally learn from watching it (*we are also forced to consider…*).

extra: fast finishers 

Fast finishers can work individually or in pairs to write another sentence as a distractor, making sure that it can not be used in any of the existing gaps. This will help raise awareness of the structural and content links between sentences. Nominate a few fast finishers to say their sentences and ask the rest of the class to check that they do not fit in gaps 1–6.

6 In pairs students match the words from the text with their meanings. Conduct class feedback.

1 C **2** J **3** H **4** A **5** E **6** I **7** B **8** F **9** G **10** D

background 

The grasshopper mouse is very aggressive compared with other types of mice and is found in the US and Mexico. It is not very sociable and lives alone or in pairs. It is well known for being able to kill poisonous centipedes as well as scorpions. It is small, with a body length of up to 13 cm and a tail of up to 6 cm long.

Sum up

7 Students cover the article. In pairs, they discuss the film-makers' methods in making the programme more dramatic and what they found interesting about their approach. Conduct class feedback.

Suggested answers

The film-makers made the programme more dramatic by filming scenes through the eyes of the small animals. They used different filming techniques, e.g. tracking cameras, storyboards, and special effects to make detailed action sequences.

extra 

Students write a short email to a friend summarising and recommending the programme based on the introduction that they have just read. Encourage them to write the email using their own words and writing a maximum of 190 words, so that they focus on the important information. Summarising is an important skill which focuses on the gist and eliminates unnecessary detail.

Speak up

8 Students discuss the questions in pairs or small groups. Conduct class feedback and nominate a few students to share their ideas with the class.

Possible answers

1 Humans have a lot in common with certain animals. For example, humans often use other animals for food. Like all animals, humans have a need to survive. This means that humans will do what is necessary to find food and shelter and will also feel the need to escape or hide when there is danger.
2 Answers could include: fierceness, forward planning, and the belief that everyone and everything has special abilities.

extra 

Ask students to discuss wildlife in their local areas. Ask: *What kinds of animals are common? What animals are rare, and what are people doing to protect them?*

To finish

In pairs students choose an animal that they find interesting or admire and plan and research what they would include in a documentary about it. They should consider its habitat, the challenges the animals face, how to film the animal in a dramatic way (and the challenges the film crew might also have) and how they would advertise the programme. Students describe their plans for the programme in open group and the class votes on what they think would be the most interesting documentary.

Give them some examples of animals (the great white shark, the snow leopard, the blue whale, the orangutan, etc.).

Fun footer

Read the footer aloud. Ask students to research an interesting fact about another animal. They can do this by searching for information online. Conduct class feedback and elicit some of the facts that students found.

In preparation for the Grammar lesson, ask students to complete Ex 1 on page 80 for homework, and to read the Grammar reference section on the passive on page 152. Encourage them to note down any questions they have.

Presentation tool:	Unit 6, Reading
Workbook / Online Practice:	pp56–57
Extra Practice App	

GRAMMAR SB p80

To start

Tell students about a film you love. Choose something that is well-known. Describe the film without naming it, and ask students to guess what film was being described. Then in pairs, they do the same. Nominate a few students to say what films they talked about. Ask extra questions using passive forms: *When was it made? Who was it directed by?*

Ask students the following questions. Elicit some answers.

Can you name a film that:
is being made at this moment?
has been nominated for an Oscar this year?
was made in your country?
will be released next month?
is believed to be one of the most expensive movies ever made?

Write the questions on the board, and underline the passive forms. Elicit that we form the passive by using a form of the verb *to be* + the past participle. Ask students: *In these examples, do we know who did the actions?* (No.) *Which do these questions focus on more – the action or the person who did the action?* (the action).

explore grammar ➥ SB p152

1 Read through the explore grammar box with the class. Then ask students to complete sentences 1–4 with the correct forms. They can either do this individually, or in pairs. Conduct class feedback. If you didn't take up the flipped classroom suggestion at the end of the previous lesson, refer students to the Grammar file on page 152. Set Grammar practice Exs 1–3 on page 153 for homework or for fast finishers to complete in class.

1 be successfully shown **2** is captured **3** are said **4** being filmed

2 6.1 Focus students on the photo on page 80 and elicit the sport (surfing). Elicit some more water-sports, for example *water-skiing*. Tell them they are going to hear two friends discussing some photos. Play the recording for them to say whether the boy enjoyed the activity or not and to give reasons. Elicit the answers.

No, because water-skiing was difficult, he kept on falling in.

3 6.2 Students complete the sentences with the correct verb forms. Students do the task individually. Conduct class feedback.

1 were they taken (passive)
2 tried (active)
3 was being picked (passive)
4 'd (had) never been made (passive)
5 be helped (passive)
6 get (active)

alternative

Before you play the recording, focus students on the gaps and ask: *Which sentences need an active form? Which ones need a passive form?* Then play the recording for them to check their answers and complete the gaps.

4 Ask students: *Do you enjoy taking photographs? If so, of what and when?* Students read the text and choose the correct alternatives. Students compare answers. Conduct class feedback.

1 has never been done **2** had been given **3** had immediately started **4** be taken **5** could see

Speak up

5 In pairs, students choose two or three favourite photos (on their phones, tablets or laptops) and describe them to their partner. They should say when and where they were taken and why they like them. They could also say what led up to the photo being taken and what happened next.

Possible answer

This is a photo of me at my cousin's wedding about two months ago. I'm with my cousin here, and of course she's wearing her wedding dress. The other people who can be seen in the photo are my other cousins, my uncles and aunts, and my grandparents. The photo was taken in a garden, which is why there are so many flowers in the background. It was taken by me – it's a selfie. I like this photo because it was a really happy day. All my family were there, and it's really rare that we all get together like this.

alternative

If students have no photos to show, or are unwilling to share photos with each other, ask them to tell their partner about the best or most unusual photo they have ever seen.

game on

Read through the instructions, explaining that the statements should be in the passive and they should be true. Make sure that each student has a piece of paper to write on, and they don't write their name anywhere. Give an example: *I was given a guitar for my tenth birthday.* Then ask students to write their own sentences. Distribute the statements to other students, who then guess who originally wrote them.

To finish

Ask students: *Do you like to do things with their photos, for example, edit them or add filters? How long do you like to keep your photos before deleting them?*

Fun footer

Read out the footer and discuss the question with the class. Elicit some ideas. Ask: *Is it ever appropriate for a magazine or newspaper to airbrush a photo? What effect might this have on people who see the airbrushed photos?* Explain that if a photo has been airbrushed, it means that the photo has been changed, usually digitally, to make it look better, or to remove something that someone doesn't want to be there.

Presentation tool:	Unit 6, Grammar
Workbook / Online Practice:	p58
Grammar reference and practice:	SB p152
Audioscript:	SB p180

VOCABULARY SB p81

time and place

To start

Write the word *selfie* on the board. Ask: *What is a selfie? Do you like taking them? Where was the last selfie that you took?* Elicit answers for the last question (e.g. *at a party*). Write these answers on the board, and underline any prepositions of place (e.g. *at*). Elicit that these small words are used when we say where an action took place.

explore **vocabulary 1**

1 Students read through the explore vocabulary box, and then complete the selfie quiz individually. Conduct class feedback before asking them to add two more questions of their own. You may need to help weaker students with ideas for their questions. In pairs, they ask and answer the questions.

1 A at	B in	C in
2 A on	B at	C in
3 A on	B (up) on	
4 A on	B at	C in/by/near/beside

Suggested questions

What expression do you usually use in your selfies?
Do you usually take selfies with other people?

2 6.3 Write *time-lapse video* on the board and elicit the meaning (a series of photos taken at certain time intervals, which are then put together to be shown as if normal time has speeded up).Tell students that they are going to hear a conversation about a selfie time-lapse video. Play the recording for students to answer the questions.

A record of seven years' of a boy's life shown in selfies.
Over 2,550 photos were taken.

extra

For extra comprehension practice, ask these questions. You might need to play the recording again.

1 *How long is the video?* (90 seconds)
2 *What age period does it show?* (the boy from 12–19 years old)
3 *What is interesting about a time-lapse video such as this?* (You can see all the changes more clearly.)
4 *What is the only thing that doesn't change?* (the boy's expression)

3 6.4 Tell students that they are going to listen again, this time to find synonyms for the phrases listed. Read through the list with the class so that they are aware of what they need to listen for. You may need to pause the recording occasionally, to give them time to note down the phrases. Conduct class feedback, and if necessary, play the recording again for students to hear the phrases in context again.

1 on a daily basis **2** stick at, keep up the momentum
3 speeded up, accelerated **4** occasionally
5 throughout

4 Students discuss the question as a whole class. You could extend it by asking: *If yes, where would you take the selfies? What expression would you use? How often would you take each individual photo?*

Possible answers

I'd love to take a time-lapse video. I'd like to make one with my brothers and my parents. I think it would be a really interesting thing, to show how people change over time. I'd love to watch it when I'm older, and see how I changed from being young, to being old.

explore **vocabulary 2**

5 Tell students that there are many expressions they can use when speaking or writing to talk about time. Read through the time phrases in the box. Then ask students to explain the differences between the alternatives in the sentences.

1 in the middle of doing something = be busy doing something; on the point of doing something = be about to do something very soon
2 on time = at the correct time or the time that was arranged; in time = do something earlier than necessary; in good time = much earlier than necessary; running late = later than expected
3 at the last minute = just before it is too late; sooner or later = when something is certain to happen but it is not sure when; in no time at all = very quickly or soon

6 Students complete the posts with the correct phrases and then compare with a partner. Conduct class feedback.

1 on **2** by the **3** running **4** at the last minute
5 on the point of **6** in good time/on time

Speak up

7 Put students into pairs to discuss the questions. Monitor and encourage them to give examples.

Possible answers

1 I try to write down important dates and times in a diary, so I know what I need to do. I'm usually on time for things, because I don't like to run late.
2 I don't like arriving late for things, because it makes me feel stressed, and it can be rude. If possible, I try to turn up in good time, usually much earlier than anyone else.
3 I think it's rude to keep people waiting, especially if they don't tell anyone that they are going to be late.

To finish

Ask students to write a post of their own to add to the teen forum in the Ex 6 thread. Students then read out their posts to the rest of the class and find out which students are the best at planning their time.

Presentation tool:	Unit 6, Vocabulary
Workbook / Online Practice:	p59
Photocopiable activity:	6A
Audioscript:	SB p180
Extra Practice App	

LISTENING SB p82

To start

Ask students to discuss in pairs: *Do you have a good sense of direction? Have you ever been lost? What did you do?*

Power up

1 **Ask students about the way they use maps, and when. Collect the most common experiences of using them.**

Possible answers

I use the map on my phone all the time. It's great for searching for things like shops or cafés. I just type in something I want to find, and the map shows me where it is.

2 **Ask students to work in small groups and discuss the different types of map. If they don't know any they should look them up, and then discuss their uses.**

atlas: a book containing maps, especially of the whole world. Used mainly to learn about the geographical position of other countries.

globe: a round object with the map of the Earth drawn on it. Use: as above. However, it gives a more true-to-life view of the Earth as a spherical object.

Google Earth: an online resource whereby you can find places anywhere in the world through the help of GPS and satellite navigation.

navigational charts: maps that are especially drawn for sailors and people who are using the sea for trading purposes.

road/metro (underground) map: map of the road system or the underground system that helps people to find their way from A to B.

topographical map: a map that shows features of the natural landscape such as hills, rivers, cliffs, etc. Useful for walkers and other people who need to know more details about the environment.

digital map / Google maps: maps that are available on the internet which you can access from your smartphone or other electronic devices.

Listen up

3 6.5 **Tell students that they're going to listen to a girl talking about an exhibition she visited, and that the exhibition was about maps. Tell students they should listen and identify the types of maps from Ex 2 she mentions. Play the recording once and let students compare their answers.**

globe, digital map, Google Earth

exam task: sentence completion

The sentence completion task in the Cambridge exam is a set of different sentences rather than a combination of sentences in the form of a text as in this task.

4 e 6.6 **Go through the exam tip. Remind students that when they read through the sentences, they should think about the form of the missing word. Is it plural? Is it a noun or an adjective? Ask them to think about question 1.**

It's likely to be *borders*, since the sentence has already talked about *maps* and *countries*.

Play the recording once for students to complete the sentences. Students should then compare their answers. Play the recording again for them to confirm their ideas. Remind them of the importance of checking the form of the word, and also the spelling. Check that they have not written more than one or two words for each gap.

1 borders: *He also produced maps that had no borders between countries.*
2 pictures: *people used to draw pictures of things they thought were in a particular spot*
3 sea monsters: *the so-called mythical maps, had … sea monsters for things … that might cause accidents.*
4 flat: *I thought it was funny that some of them showed the world which they thought was flat.*
5 globe: *a globe … I wasn't expecting to see something like that in the map exhibition*
6 oceans: *the oceans were lit up … which showed very clearly just how much of our planet is taken up by them!*
7 fantasy: *Tolkien spent hours developing his maps in detail and they really brought his fantasy alive …*
8 town: *My plan is to create an interactive map of my home town …*
9 explorers: *map-makers in the past … were dependent on explorers for most of their data.*
10 information: *Maps are particularly useful because they can communicate a huge amount of information …*

5 **Students can do the matching exercise in pairs. If they want to hear the words used in context, play the recording again or refer them to the Audioscript on page 180.**

1 C **2** D **3** E **4** A **5** F **6** B

Speak up

6 **Discuss questions 1–3 as a whole class. Set question 4 for homework, and ask students to make presentations at the start of the next lesson. Alternatively ask them to write a short report on what they have found out.**

Possible answers

1 It's probably not very important these days for most people to be able to read a traditional paper map. But it's very important for people to be able to use digital maps, and find out the information they need.
2 If you're going somewhere where there isn't much internet access, for example a mountain or a forest, then it's definitely useful to have a paper map.
3 Satellite mapping has made maps seem more 'real'. We can now see individual streets and buildings in great detail. For example, if someone wants to check how to get to a place, they can look online and see what the place really looks like, and not only how they can get there.

Fun footer

Some students may have a genuine interest in planets. If so, they could talk to the other students about it.

In preparation for the next lesson ask students to read the Grammar file on *have/get something done* on page 152.

Presentation tool:	Unit 6, Listening
Workbook / Online Practice:	p60
Audioscript:	SB p180
Extra Practice App	

USE OF ENGLISH 1 SB p83

To start

Write these two sentences on the board:

A I had my house painted.
B I painted my house.

Ask the class: *Which action did I do myself?* (B) *Which did someone else do for me?* (A). Point out that A is a form of the passive. Then ask students to discuss these questions: *Do you have these things done for you, or do you do them yourself? Why?*

- *cut your hair*
- *do your homework*
- *make breakfast, lunch or dinner*
- *tidy your room*

explore **grammar** ➥ SB p152

1 Refer students to the explore grammar box. Go through it with the class, explaining the difference in meaning in each sentence. If you haven't already asked students to do so, refer them to the grammar reference on page 152 for more information. Ask students to look at the example, then decide which sentences (2–5) are passive and which use *have/get something done.*

Refer students to Ex 4 on page 153 for quick practice of these structures. Do it in class if you want to check that they have understood the meaning, otherwise set it for homework.

2 passive **3** have something done
4 get something done **5** passive (with modal)

2 6.7 Before they listen, ask students to predict which things Tom might still need to have done, or might already have got done. Then play the recording for students to check their ideas.

✓ do the posters, Musicians from school
✗ Radio station advertising, Other musicians, Chairs, etc. in school hall, Sell tickets

3 Students complete the questions. Then they discuss them in pairs.

2 has had tattoos done
3 getting/having your hair dyed
4 needs to be done/needs doing
5 got someone to look after

extra

Once students have checked their answers, ask them to write an extra two questions to ask their partner using *have/get something done.* If necessary give them an example: *Have you ever had your nails painted?*

exam tip

4 Go through the exam tip with the class.

are having the books delivered

exam task: key word transformations

The sentence transformations here target *have/get something done* and passives, as opposed to the Cambridge exam task which tests a variety of grammatical forms.

5 **e** Ask students to look at the questions in Ex 5. Ask: *What structure is being tested in each sentence?* Once they have identified that each sentence needs either a passive structure or *have/get something done,* ask them to write in the answers to each question. Remind them to check that the verbs are in the correct form, that they haven't changed the form of the given word and that all the words they have used are spelt correctly.

1 must get the concert (*get something done*)
2 ought to be booked (passive)
3 were being supported financially/funded (passive)
4 were advised to have/get (passive)
5 the team do (*have somebody do something*)
6 is included in the (passive)

To finish

Put students into small groups. Ask them to tell the others an anecdote of something bad that has happened to them (which could be true or false), but they should use the passive form. The rest of the group should listen and guess whether it was true or not.

You could give an example: *Once, I had my bike stolen from outside a coffee shop. I had only popped in for a minute to buy something for my lunch.*

Presentation tool:	Unit 6, Use of English 1
Workbook / Online Practice:	p61
Photocopiable activity:	6B
Grammar reference and practice:	SB p152
Audioscript:	SB p180
Extra Practice App	

USE OF ENGLISH 2 SB p84

To start

Tell students that they are going to match some suffixes to their form. Draw a table on the board, with three columns, headed *noun, adverb* and *adjective*. Then write the following words in the table, under the correct heading, each on a separate line: *industry, accurately, occasion, high, enthusiastic, education.*

Divide the class into two groups, A and B. Group A then nominates a person from Group B to go up to the board and complete the table with another word. Group A decides whether the answer is correct or not. Then Group B nominates someone from Group A to write in one of the other words. Carry on until the table is completely filled. The team with the most right answers wins. The completed table should look as follows:

noun	adverb	adjective
industry	industrially	industrial
accuracy	accurately	accurate
occasion	occasionally	occasional
height	highly	high
enthusiasm	enthusiastically	enthusiastic
education	educationally	educational

explore vocabulary 1

1 Go through the explore vocabulary box. Tell students that certain suffixes can be learned, because they always make the same change of form. Give the example that *-al* makes an adjective. Also, *-ly* usually (but not always) makes an adverb. Give the example of *environment* (noun) → *environmental* (adjective) → *environmentally* (adverb).

Remind students that some nouns are uncountable and can't be made plural. Ask students to read *The secret life of your cat* quickly for gist. Ask: *What was Yollo doing every night?* (He was going to a neighbours' house to get food.) Then ask students to work in pairs to decide the form of the word that completes each gap. Once they have decided on this, they should write the word in.

1 verb to noun = variety
2 noun to adjective = mysterious
3 noun to adjective = behavioural
4 noun to adjective = suspicious
5 adjective to adverb = enthusiastically
6 noun to adjective = tracking
7 noun to adjective = passionate
8 verb to plural noun = inhabitants

2 Students complete the questions in pairs. Conduct class feedback.

1 confident **2** passionate **3** environmental
4 accidentally **5** dramatically

watch out for

Make sure students spell words correctly when they change the form. Point out the double letters in the adverbs.

exam task: word formation

explore vocabulary 2

The word formation task here tests suffixes because of the focus of the lesson.

3 e Tell students that there are some irregular changes which don't follow these suffix patterns. Ask: *Can you think of any words where the adjective and adverb are the same?* Give some examples, such as *hard, tough* and *fast*. Go through the explore vocabulary box with the class. Then ask them to read the text quickly. Ask: *What is an albatross?* (a bird) *What problems did the albatross face?* (They were being killed by fishing lines.) Tell students to decide on the form of the word that is needed in each gap and then to write the word. Encourage them to think about the spelling as they do this. Conduct class feedback.

1 verb to adjective = fascinating
2 adjective to noun = height
3 adjective to noun = length
4 noun to adverb = accidentally
5 noun to noun = environmentalist
6 adjective to adverb = happily
7 verb to noun = failure
8 noun to adverb = optimistically

Speak up

4 Before they discuss the question, students may first need to think about what types of animals can be tagged. Suggestions can include: dogs, cats, cows, sheep or birds.

Possible answers

What we can learn: where the animals are, how to retrieve them if lost, how to identify who they belong to

Possible disadvantages: owners might think it hurts the animals; the tagging could be expensive

Fun footer

Read the footer aloud. If they don't know the answer, ask them to research the question online. Then ask students: *What about your country?* Ask them to research the popularity of pets in their country online, and report back to the class.

The most popular pets in the UK are:
1 dogs **2** cats **3** indoor fish.

To finish

Put students into pairs. Write the following gapped questions on the board. Ask students to complete the questions with the correct form of the words in brackets (1 optimistic, 2 happiness, 3 environmentally). Then discuss their answers and give reasons for their ideas.

1 *Do you think you are an .... person? (optimism)*
2 *What do you think is the secret to .... ? (happy)*
3 *Are you an .... friendly person? (environment)*

Presentation tool: Unit 6, Use of English 2
Workbook / Online Practice: p62
Photocopiable activity: 6C
Extra Practice App

SPEAKING SB p85

To start

Ask students: *Have you visited a new city recently? How did you find out the most interesting places to visit? How did you travel round?* If they haven't visited a new city, ask: *What do you think would be the best way to find out about a new city?*

Power up

1 Ask students to identify the things in the photos. Elicit that they show a public transport (metro) map, a selection of guidebooks and a Sat-Nav device or smartphone with a digital map. Then students should discuss the questions in pairs. Conduct class feedback.

Possible answers

All the things would be useful for finding out directions, or where to go. The map and the Sat-Nav/smartphone are especially useful for finding out how to get somewhere. The guidebooks are especially useful for researching a holiday destination before arriving there. All are useful if you find yourself lost in a new place, although the guidebooks might have limited information in the form of detailed maps.

2 Students discuss the question in pairs. Remind them to discuss each of the prompts in detail, and to think of advantages and any disadvantages of each one.

Possible answers

a city guide: gives useful information about restaurants, etc., can get out of date quickly, can be annoying to carry around

a smartphone: easy to carry, very practical, difficult to use when there is no internet, may be expensive to use mobile internet abroad

a globe: gives a good idea of the world, not useful for details about a city, impractical to carry around

a history book: interesting to provide context and background information, not very practical for modern cities, can be impractical to carry around

Google Earth: very up-to-date, useful for finding out about places before you go there, difficult to use when there is no internet

3 6.8 Remind students that once they have spoken about the task for two minutes, they have to discuss another question for a minute, and that this involves making a decision. Explain that they are going to listen to two students doing this. Ask: *What do they decide?*

They decide the smartphone and the city guide are the most helpful.

4 Put students in pairs to decide what they think the most helpful items are. Elicit ideas from the class about the most popular items.

useful language: evaluating options; coming to an agreement

5 6.9 Go through the useful language box with students. Ask them to write short dialogues in pairs, using one phrase from the evaluating options, followed by an agreement phrase of their own and then one from coming to an agreement. Give an example:

A: In my opinion, a smartphone is more important than a globe because it's easier to carry around.

B: I totally agree. So let's make a decision on this.

A: OK, so we'll go with the smartphone.

Nominate a few students to read their dialogues to the class.

Play the recording again. Students decide on the phrases they hear being used.

a) I don't think X is so useful, do you?
I think Y is definitely less useful than X because …
I wouldn't really use Z when …

b) So, let's make up our minds about this.
What do you think?
OK, so we'll go with X and Y.

Speak up

exam tip

6 Go through the exam tip. Tell them that although the timing is important and they should practise doing the task in the correct time, in the exam, the examiner will time them. Tell students that in the exam, they should always give reasons and explanations for their choices and decisions, but that this is also a good thing to do in 'real life'. Put students into groups of three. Two students should discuss the task and the third should time them and check that they are using phrases from the useful language box. After two minutes the students could swap round. Go round and monitor the groups and make sure that they are timing themselves accurately.

Possible answer

A: So, let's think about which ones are useful in everyday life, and why. Mobile phones – in my opinion, these are useful for just about everything, from sending texts to checking maps or taking photos.

B: You're right. They're definitely useful. I don't think reference books are so useful, do you? I mean, most of the information I get is online. I wouldn't really use reference books.

A: You might be right. But I have a lot of reference books at home, and I use them all the time. What do you think about laptops, though? We need them for work, for studying.

B: Yes, they're more useful than television, I think.

A: You're right. And how about cameras? Are they actually useful?

B: They are, but you can find cameras on mobile phones. Having an actual, expensive camera as a separate piece of equipment isn't so useful, I don't think.

exam task: collaborative task ➥ p164

7 **e** Students discuss this question in the same groups. This time, the third student times them talking for a minute. Monitor students again, and check that they are justifying their choices and explaining why the others options are not so good. When you give feedback, remind students that they have to talk about their decision for a minute, so they should not make their decision too quickly. They can also choose an option that they did not have time to discuss in the first part of the task if they like, and this can be a productive way of extending the range of language they use and avoiding repetition of ideas or language.

SPEAKING (Continued)

Possible answer

A: So then, which do you think are the most useful? Which two items?

B: In my opinion, mobile phones are the most useful. We can do so many things with them, as long as we have an internet connection. What do you think?

A: I agree with you on that. How about the other thing? I actually think reference books are useful.

B: OK, but laptops are more useful because we can't type, or create files without laptops. We can't find information online, or watch TV, for example.

A: I can see what you're saying. OK, so let's make a decision on this. Which are more useful – reference books or laptops?

B: I would say laptops. So, we'll go with mobile phones and laptops.

Speaking extra

8 Before you run the debate, give students time to discuss their ideas in their teams. It would be a good idea to encourage them to brainstorm ideas first, and then select the three or four ideas that best suit their argument. This will help them to develop their ability to analyse and think about the topic critically. This is especially important in an activity like this, where they may not actually agree with the opinions they have been given, but they still need to justify them. Allow each team two minutes to present their ideas, and then allow time for open class debate.

Possible answer

supporting the statement: people are addicted to checking their emails or texts; we spend too much time looking at screens; we use our phones for everything – from taking photos to waking us up in the morning

opposing the statement: smartphones are just tools, and it's up to us how we use them; they help us to achieve goals and find information; they improve our lives by making it easier to contact other people and stay up-to-date with what's happening

To finish

As a follow-up, students could write an essay arguing their real view about whether smartphones are taking over our lives. As part of this, and in preparation for the Writing lesson, ask students to revise the Exam file essay section on page 165.

Presentation tool:	Unit 6, Speaking
Workbook / Online Practice:	p63
Speaking file:	SB p164
Audioscript:	SB p180

WRITING SB pp86–87

To start

Write these phrasal verbs on the board: *get on with, fall out with, make up with, work it out, break up with, talk things through.* Tell students that these phrasal verbs are all connected with relationships. Elicit what each phrasal verb means.

get on with = have a good relationship with someone
fall out with = have a disagreement with someone
make up with = re-establish a relationship with someone after an argument
work it out = find a way to resolve an argument
break up with = stop a relationship with a friend
talk things through = discuss problems or issues to find a solution

Organise students into small groups. Write these questions on the board and ask them to discuss their ideas.

Is it possible to fall out with someone and still be friends with them later on?
Is it easy to make up after an argument? What's the best way to do this?
What kinds of things cause the most arguments between friends?

Power up

1 **Put students into small groups to discuss the two questions. Elicit some ideas.**

Possible answers

1 I normally try to understand someone's point of view and reach an agreement. Sometimes, it's impossible though, and I end up trying to argue with them.
2 Social media makes it easy for people to post things online. Sometimes, these things have a particular viewpoint about a subject, and show what a person thinks about it. If I disagree with what someone has posted, I usually just ignore it. But if I strongly disagree with someone's viewpoints, then I can block them.

2 **Ask students to read the comments. In pairs, they should come up with a good reason for their choice, which they should explain to the class.**

Possible answers

I like the first one best. The good thing about the internet is that it really is possible to connect with people from all around the world, and then, you find out how similar we all are, and how much we can learn from each other.

Plan on

3 **Tell students that they're going to read an essay about arguments and relationships. First, they should read the task. Ask: *What extra point could you include in this essay, based on your previous discussions?* Elicit some answers.**

Possible answers

family relationships, generation difficulties, social media, ways of making up with someone

4 **Students read the essay. Ask: *What third point is included? Did it match your ideas?* Ask students to check the opinions expressed in the essay. Ask: *Do you agree with any of them? Which ones?* If they disagree, they should explain why.**

The third point is on the subject of family relationships, specifically parents objecting to what their children wear.

explore **language**

5 **Remind students that good linking words or phrases are very important in an essay because they make it easier to read and the argument easier to follow. (In the marking scheme, exam candidates are marked for this under coherence and cohesion). Ask students to read the explore language box, and try to find examples in the essay they have just read.**

staging: *Firstly, Secondly, Finally, In conclusion*
expressing opinion: *in my opinion*
giving examples: *For example*
referring to sub-topics: *with reference to*

6 **Tell students they are going to analyse the essay in detail. They should work through the questions in pairs. Monitor their discussions and help if necessary. Conduct class feedback on each question.**

1 Present tenses are mainly used, along with modals (*can, may, will*) because it's a discussion about a general situation. One passive form (*trust is built up*) is used.
2 Phrasal verbs: *come across, talk things through, work it out*
Collocations: *basic issues, bad habits, learning process, positive outcome, family life, differences of opinion*
3 The sentence structure is mainly complex: *Whatever the problem, whether it is about your attitude or your bad habits, it's a good idea to talk things through in person rather than sending a text message*. For variety, some shorter sentences are used, e.g. *Sometimes, they may even be right.*
4 There is a nice introduction. There is a clear paragraph for each point and a conclusion.

Write on

7 **Prepare students for writing their own essay, using all the ideas they've thought about in this section. Read through the task with them, to make sure they understand exactly what they have to write about. Then they could discuss the plan in pairs, or if you feel they need support, then go through the five points together as a class. It's very important that they decide on the third point at the beginning of the planning process, and also that they decide on what their conclusion will be. This will help them to write a logical and well-organised essay.**

Possible third points include: art, politics, films, books or sport. Students should be encouraged to choose a topic that they feel comfortable discussing.

exam task: **essay** ➥ p165

The essay question in the Cambridge exam is unlikely to have a slashed option as there is here.

8 **e** **Go through the exam tip with the class. As students write, monitor and check they are using semi-formal language, and organising their three points into separate paragraphs.**

Model answer

Most of us encounter different opinions, and this is a good thing. If we didn't come across viewpoints other than our own, not only would the world be a more boring place, but we'd also risk never learning new things.

Firstly, it would be dull if we all had the same tastes in fashion. It's nice to walk down a street and see so many people wearing different things. In my view, when people wear uniforms, for example in the army, they cannot express their own identity.

Secondly, it's good that people have different tastes in music. Generally speaking, I don't like a lot of music that my friends do, but that's fine. It makes it more special when I find someone who likes the same bands as me.

Finally, the world would be more boring if we all liked the same sports. We would never be able to try anything new, or develop different skills if there were only a few to choose from.

In conclusion, if everyone had the same views, we wouldn't be individuals. Moreover, we would never be tempted to experience new things.

Improve it

9 **Put students into pairs to read each other's work. If they see any grammar or spelling mistakes, ask students to underline them. If they see any other problems, ask students to write short notes in the margins.**

Possible answers

The word order in this sentence might be wrong.
Try to use more linking phrases.
I don't understand this idea.
Start a new paragraph here.

10 **You could ask students to make corrections to their essay for homework.**

Remind students that there is a sample answer on page 165, and they should look at this when correcting their essay. Encourage students to make sure their argument is coherent and leads clearly to their conclusion. Their points should not be difficult to follow, and all their ideas should be relevant.

Fun footer

Nominate a student to read out the footer. Elicit that it means that you have to back up your ideas and opinions (what you say) with actions.

Ask students if they can think of any expressions in English or in their own language with a similar meaning. Other expressions in English include *Put your money where your mouth is* and *Actions speak louder than words*.

To finish

Put students into pairs with partners they haven't worked with so far in this lesson. Ask them to tell each other about the ideas they wrote about in their essay and what their third point was. Ask: *Did you have the same idea? If not, which idea do you think was best?*

Presentation tool:	Unit 6, Writing
Workbook / Online Practice:	p64
Writing file:	SB p165

SWITCH ON SB p88

Eyeborg

extra

Ask students to close their books. Write the word *bionic* on the board. Tell students to look at it closely, and try to guess what it means. Elicit that the prefix *bio-* means 'life', and that the ending *-onic* comes from the word 'electronic'.

1 Elicit an example of a character from film, TV or literature with bionic body parts. Then put students into pairs to think of as many advantages as they can of having bionic body parts.

Possible answers

1 Examples include Darth Vader, Robocop and Iron Man.

2 leg: the ability to run very fast or jump very high

ear: the ability to listen to things which are very far away, or even to record sounds and play them back

hand: the ability to move your fingers extremely fast

eye: the ability to see in the dark, or to zoom in on objects which are far away

2 Elicit the meaning of *cyborg* (in science fiction stories, a creature that is part human and part machine) and ask students: *What is an 'eyeborg'?* Tell students they are going to watch a clip about a person called Rob James. Warn students that this video includes some graphic images of a man with an implant in his eye (some may not want to watch those parts). Play the video clip for them to answer the questions about Rob's occupation and the special equipment his bionic eye has. Encourage students to take notes while they are watching. Conduct class feedback.

Rob is a documentary filmmaker and he has a camera inside his eye.

3 Read through the questions. If students have internet access, ask them to look up *capture* and *perspective* in the Longman Dictionary of Contemporary English (www.ldoceonline.com).

Play the video for students, and then check their answers. You may need to explain *tracking* (following something) and *blinking* (the natural opening and shutting of the eyes).

1 The other people also have bionic body parts, such as bionic legs or arms.

2 The perspective that Rob captures is that of a human because the camera is positioned in his eye.

3 The two aspects that make this perspective very realistic are: a) the camera eye can track movement; and b) it can record blinking.

4 Check understanding and pronunciation of *puny* (small and weak, /pjuːniː/). Students discuss the question in pairs. Elicit some opinions.

Suggested answers

Yes: He can get away with increasingly discreet filming in more places because his equipment is not obvious, whereas the rest of us would be asked to put our phones or cameras away.

No: Everybody has a camera now, so our technology will improve at the same rate as his, if not faster because there's a mass market for our technology, whereas he is one individual.

extra 

Finish by asking class: *In the same situation, would you have chosen to do the same as Rob did?* Encourage students to give reasons.

Project

5 Put students into small groups to plan and pitch a film or documentary. Read through the different stages with the class. They should start in class by brainstorming ideas within the groups for a project that could use Rob's 'eyeborg' technology. Then they need to decide on the storyline of their film or documentary, the people involved, the locations and why it would be interesting for viewers. When the planning stage is complete they need to write a pitch for one or more members of the group to present to the class.Explain that a pitch is when someone is trying to persuade someone to buy or accept a new product or idea. It is shorter and more concise than a presentation. It can be less formal, and is aimed at persuading the listener of the value of the product or idea. Students choose a person from their group to pitch their idea to the class. This can be done as a series of pitches from each group to the whole class. Alternatively it can be done as a mingling activity, in which each student goes around, and tries to pitch their idea to as many other people they can within a 10-minute time limit. Finally, conduct a class vote on the best idea.

extra 

1 Students can prepare an outline for a biopic about a real person who has a bionic body part. They should research the life of the person online, then 'pitch' their documentary to the rest of the class, explaining how and why they are inspiring.

2 Students can explore the world of cybernetics. They can conduct research online and give a short presentation about the current state of play and what the latest inventions are/can do. They should focus on the particular field (i.e. sport, travel, disability, etc.) that interests them most.

Presentation tool: Unit 6, Switch on

Switch on videoscript: TB p173

INDEPENDENT LEARNING SB p88

Grammar and vocabulary

1 **Give students time in class to work through the points individually and note down ideas. Then ask them to share ideas with the rest of the class. Encourage discussion, but do not give too many ideas of your own as this section is for students' self-assessment and focuses on their own views of their learning and what they can learn from their peers.**

2 **Students discuss the points in pairs. Conduct class feedback.**

Possible answers

Extra ideas could include the following.

Arranging times to speak in English to a friend (e.g. after school, during break time, in the evenings, at coffee bars, etc.).

Trying to 'think' in English (e.g. talking to yourself in English or writing notes or a diary when you would normally write in your own language).

3 **Give students time for individual reflection on their progress. You could set this task for homework.**

Possible answers

1 If I make a mistake with grammar, I'm going to check in the Grammar file. If I can't find the answer there, I will ask the teacher.

2 When the teacher gives me feedback on my written work, I'm going to spend some time reading the feedback. I'll review the feedback before the next writing task.

3 When I write something, I'm going to check it again, and see if I keep on using the same words over and over again. If I do, I will try to find new words or phrases I could use instead.

UNIT CHECK SB p89

This Unit check covers the passive, *have/get something done*, and words connected to time and place.

Practice

1 **1** poisonous **2** survival strategies **3** blur **4** sequence **5** expand **6** combination

2 **1** on a daily basis **2** on the point of **3** Sooner or later **4** in the middle of **5** at the last minute **6** running late **7** in no time

3 **1** strengthen **2** daily **3** confidence **4** environmental **5** educator **6** height

Review

1 **1** been seen **2** have taken **3** are said **4** will be held **5** we hadn't been told **6** were being warned

2 **1** be made **2** is shown **3** to be hooked **4** are being/are filmed **5** have often been helped **6** was/was being approached **7** was/got bitten **8** are said

3 **1** needs **2** had **3** got **4** need **5** having **6** get

4 6.10

1 to blow up 20 balloons

2 make lots of little sandwiches and baby pizzas

3 made by Ben, and the house decorated by Sally

4 need buying

5 had her hair done

6 needs doing

5 **1** been **2** will **3** are **4** have **5** being **6** if **7** more **8** to

6 **Suggested answer**

I used to think we had too much homework to do and too much schoolwork generally, but my opinion was changed when I watched a programme on television about Japanese high-school students. The amount of studying they had to do was incredible! A lot of them had to get up really early, at around six or six-thirty and after school, they would go on to a private school where they would study for university entrance exams. Then, after that, they'd spend a couple of hours in the library, sometimes until really late in the evening! Well, my friends haven't heard me complaining any more since I saw that programme!

GRAMMAR FILE SB p153

1
1 were illegally released
2 has, been wiped out/has been, wiped out
3 should be completed
4 are given
5 must be visited
6 are spotted/have been spotted

2
1 her project has been
2 is said to be
3 was given to/won by
4 hasn't (has not) been heard from
5 must be completed

3 **1** were shown **2** had been seen **3** were asked to **4** was made **5** be asked/asked

4
1 needs investigating
2 get researchers to find out/have researchers find out
3 get them to identify/have them identify
4 get the research started
5 get a saliva sample taken/have a saliva sample taken
6 get all your doubts and questions solved/have all your doubts and questions solved
7 get it done/have it done

Presentation tool:	Unit 6, Unit check
Workbook / Online Practice:	p65
Audioscript:	SB p180
Extra Practice App	

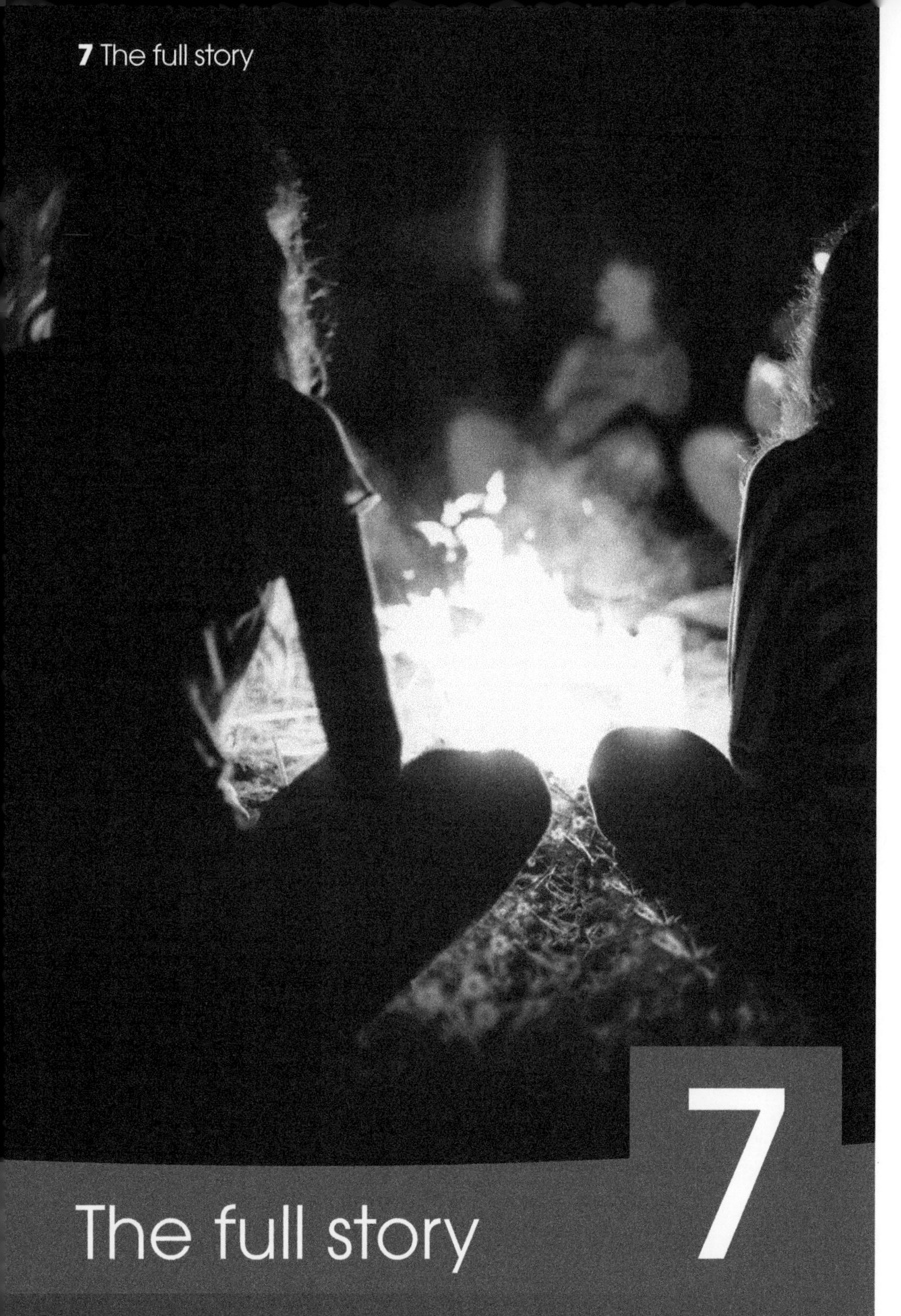

7 The full story

READING
topic: storytelling
skill: paraphrasing
task: multiple matching

GRAMMAR
reported speech
reporting verbs

VOCABULARY
storytelling in literature, film and TV
phrasal verbs
prepositional phrases
adjectives + prepositions

LISTENING
topic: film and cinema
skill: recognising speaker's point of view
task: multiple choice: short texts

USE OF ENGLISH
open cloze
multiple-choice cloze

SPEAKING
topic: social media
skill: agreeing and disagreeing
task: discussion

WRITING
topic: creative writing
skill: sequencing events
task: a story

SWITCH ON
video: museum mystery
project: create a fictional news report

Lead-in SB p91

Tell students about the last time you told a story to friends. If appropriate, tell them the story in class. Ask them if they can remember a story they told recently and ask one of the confident students to tell the class about it. Write the word *story* on the board and ask what types of story we can tell. Elicit things like anecdotes, lies, jokes, the plot of books or films, etc.

Read the title of the unit, *The Full Story*, and explain that we use the phrase when we're talking about getting an accurate story: *The news item was interesting, but I don't think we're getting the full story.*

Read through the quote and ask students: *Do you agree or disagree, and why?* Refer students to the photo and ask: *What's happening? What type of stories might the people be telling?* Put students into small groups to discuss questions 1–3.

Suggested answers

1 I enjoy telling stories when I'm with friends. I like saying what I've been doing, or what other people have been doing. And I like telling them about films I've seen.
2 Some people are definitely better than others at telling stories. They know how to hold other people's attention, and make things come alive in an interesting way.
3 New technology can include: TV, online videos, video games, social media.

extra 

Write the following questions on the board for students to discuss in pairs.

1 *What was the first book you remember reading?*
2 *Did your parents read bedtime stories to you? Do you remember any?*
3 *How important do you think it is to read to children? Why?*

READING SB pp92–93

To start

Ask students to work in pairs and note down as many fiction writers as they can in two minutes. These can be from any country, alive or dead. Check back through the names the class have given and ask if students have read any of the books by the writers, which they have enjoyed, and which they would like to read again.

Power up

1 Ask students to look at the photo on page 93. Elicit that the type of story is *horror*. Read through the list of types of story and ask students to discuss which types they enjoy most or least and why. Be ready to give your own opinion. Ask: *How do you feel when you watch or read stories like these?*

Possible answers

The photo illustrates horror or fantasy stories.

I like horror and fantasy stories, because I enjoy being scared, or reading about other worlds, or characters that can do fantastic things. I'm not really into love stories, because they're usually very predictable. They always have the same kind of story, and it's easy to work out what happens in the end.

2 Ask: *What is important for a good story?* Read through the phrases in the box and elicit how important these things are. Ask for examples from books or films. In pairs, students discuss other aspects and share these in full group.

Suggested answers

an unexpected ending, fast action, good dialogue, good description

Read on

3 Read the title of the article with the class. Ask them to predict what they think they will read about. Write some of their ideas on the board. Students read the article quickly to check their ideas. Ask students to match the people 1–4 with the sections. Conduct class feedback.

1 C **2** D **3** B **4** A

extra

Ask students how they decided on their answers. Elicit the following ideas.

The science fan relates to planets, space and facts in text C.

The drama teacher relates to the ideas of students and classes in text D.

The researcher relates to the idea of research in text B.

The recreational reader relates to the ideas of fun and switching off in text A.

exam task: multiple matching

The lead-in to the text is more detailed than in the Cambridge exam.

4 **e** Ask students how they usually approach the multiple matching exam task. Remind them that it can often be useful to read the whole text first to get the idea of each person's standpoint and then read through the questions. Also remind them that the questions will probably not use the same words as in the texts, but paraphrases. This means that they have to look for words and phrases with similar meanings in the texts. Read the first question with the class and elicit the answers to the questions.

relatives = parents, grandparents, brothers, sisters, etc.
experiences = what happened or what they did

Ask students to read through the other options and underline the key words before completing the exam task individually. Conduct class feedback and discuss the paraphrased information that helped students find the answers.

1 C (*I love hearing stories at home about what life was like in the past for my grandparents …*)
2 D (*… it's how we share events in our lives with those around us* relates to *our life experiences*)
3 A (*But for me, horror stories are not only fun* … (relates to *appreciates the entertainment value*)
4 D (*their brain is inventing stories to try* and *make sense of a situation* relates to *someone acts in a certain way*)
5 C (*I just have a different choice of reading material. Instead of a novel I would always choose books about planets or space* … relates to *more about facts than fiction*)
6 A (*Sometimes they don't even make sense but they don't have to* relates to *isn't sure all stories need to have* …)
7 B (*However, if that information is delivered in the form of a story* with *memorable facts or interesting characters, the brain can deal with it* relates to *engage with facts more easily* …)
8 D (I try to show them that we often create stories without realising … relates to *natural ability to invent stories*)
9 A (they're also the best way to switch off from my social media posts relates to *instead of spending time online*)
10 C (*I know the covers looked good* … relates to *appeared attractive*)

extra: fast finishers

Fast finishers can write another multiple-matching sentence for one section of the text, using a paraphrase. Ask fast finishers to say their sentences. Write them on the board and ask other students to match them to a particular text.

READING (Continued)

5 Students work in pairs to find the words in the text with meanings 1–8. Conduct class feedback.

1 spooky **2** make-believe **3** delivered **4** memorable **5** appeal **6** daydream **7** realising **8** genuinely

extra

To practice these words, ask:

1 *Tell me about a spooky place you've been to.*
2 *Do you know someone who had a make-believe friend when they were a child?*
3 *Which piece of information in this reading do you think is most memorable?*
4 *Do you often daydream? What about?*

Sum up

6 Students work in pairs to summarise the opinions of one of the writers. They can either choose the person themselves or you could allocate a text to get a spread of summaries. Monitor and give help where necessary. Nominate a few students to give their summaries to the class. Other students listen and discuss who they agree with and why.

Possible answers

Text A:

This person loves horror stories, although other people can't understand why. She/He suggests it's because they are fun and allow her/him to escape from the 'real world'. She/He finds them scary, even though she/he knows they are just stories. She/He ends by saying that getting lost in a story is a great way to relax.

I agree with this point of view. I often get caught up in films which are scary or very exciting, even though I know that what I'm watching isn't real at all. Stories are a good way to escape problems and forget about things, even if it's only for a few hours.

Speak up

7 Put students into small groups to discuss the questions. Circulate and contribute to the discussions.

Possible answers

1 There is so much to read online that sometimes, I've become used to just looking at things quickly, and going quickly from one webpage to the next. I've definitely noticed that it's more difficult for me to get used to reading a book, where I have to concentrate on one page at a time. Spending time online hasn't stopped me reading books, but it's made me read in a different way.
2 The last story I read was a book I read for my little sister. It was a funny children's book about some fruit which came alive in a kitchen in the middle of the night, and started a party!
3 If I see someone interesting in a café or in the street, who looks like they might be really happy or upset, then I often imagine why they might be feeling like that.

extra

You can ask extra questions to find out about students' reading habits:

- *How much time do you spend reading a book as opposed to reading things online?*
- *How important is the cover of a book when you're choosing something to read?*

To finish

Students write their own sections for the article about their attitude to reading. They can do this for homework. Give them the following task:

Write an article (140–190 words) about how important you think stories are today.

Do you think they are more or less important than they were in the past?

Give reasons and examples, explaining your opinion.

If your students need extra written practice, take these in for correction. Otherwise, students can show their writing to another student to read in the next lesson.

Fun footer

Read the footer through with the class and ask students to paraphrase it in their own words. For example, *Best friends are old friends who have been through lots of experiences with you.* Ask students if they agree with this statement or not.

In preparation for the Grammar lesson, you could ask students to complete Ex 1 on page 94, read the Grammar file on reported speech on page 154 and complete Grammar file Exs 1–4 on page 155. Check the answers in class after the 'To start' activity.

Presentation tool:	Unit 7, Reading
Workbook / Online Practice:	p68–69
Extra Practice App	

GRAMMAR SB p94

To start

Ask students to write down two or three questions they would like to ask their partner. For example, *Have you done your homework?* In pairs, they ask and answer each other's questions, noting the answers.

Conduct class feedback, and ask students to report what their partners said. Write any good examples of reported speech on the board.

explore grammar → SB p154

1 Read through the explore grammar box with the class and ask students questions 1–4.

1 A We imagined all sorts of reasons for our friend's behaviour.
B Something might catch my/our attention.
C Your brain is inventing stories to try and make sense of a situation.
2 It usually shifts back a tense. It doesn't after the past perfect or *would*, *could*, *might*. It also doesn't shift back when we are talking about facts that are still true.
3 Pronouns and time and place words, e.g. *tonight* → *that night*, *we* → *they*
4 Questions which take *yes* or *no* as answers.

2 7.1 Play the recording for students to say what the two people are discussing and where it happened. Conduct class feedback.

There's been a fire at a local book shop.

3 7.2 Put students into pairs to tell each other what they remember about the conversation. Elicit some answers. Then play the recording. Students complete sentences 1–6. You may need to pause the recording after each piece of information to allow students to write their answers. Conduct class feedback.

1 had destroyed the
2 had been
3 if he could
4 if John had seen the shop that
5 had seen/had walked past, it was/is
6 had written, was called

4 Students rewrite the interview questions in reported speech individually and then compare answers with a partner. Remind them to use pronouns where appropriate. If necessary, elicit the answer to question 1 from the class as an example. Conduct class feedback.

1 I asked (him) when he had written his first story.
2 I wanted to know if the book had been difficult to write.
3 I asked him why he liked/likes writing.
4 I wanted to know if he was going to write another bestseller.
5 I asked if he thought anybody could/can write a good story.
6 Then he asked me if I would recommend his book to my friends.

5 Students complete the blog with one word for each gap. Conduct class feedback.

1 us **2** past/previous/last **3** had **4** following **5** are/were **6** been **7** why **8** they **9** told **10** that

alternative

Before doing the task, ask students: *What do you think the title of the blog means? What will the blog mention?* Give students a minute to skim the blog, and elicit that older authors who write books for teens think they're cool because they use slang but it doesn't work. It sounds false, and they write about things that don't really happen such as falling in love at first sight.

extra: fast finishers

Ask fast finishers to write the direct speech for the sentences in the blog that the teacher originally said. Check their ideas after going through the answers to Ex 5.

watch out for

It is not always necessary to use *that* or pronouns in reported speech if the meaning is obvious.

- *When our teacher asked (us) what books we had read ...*
- *He said (that) he had found some young adult books in the library.*

Speak up

6 Put students into small groups to discuss the questions.

Possible answers

1 There are many adult writers who can write for younger people, such as J.K. Rowling. But it takes a lot of skill for adults not to sound patronising, or like they're trying to be 'cool'.
2 Examples can include books by Patrick Ness, Philip Pullman, Judy Blume and Suzanne Collins. Older books could include those written by Harper Lee, J.R.R. Tolkien or Sue Townsend.

To finish

Ask students to write two questions on a piece of paper for another student in the class. They should sign the paper. Students exchange questions with other students in the class and write answers on the papers. They should also sign the paper. Students then pass the paper to a third person who reports on what is written on his/her paper, for example, *David asked Susan when she'd met her best friend and Susan said that she'd met her when they'd both been at primary school together.*

Presentation tool:	Unit 7, Grammar
Workbook / Online Practice:	p70
Photocopiable activity:	7A
Grammar reference and practice:	SB p154
Audioscript:	SB p181

VOCABULARY SB p95

storytelling in literature, film and TV

To start

Describe the ending of a famous film or book, using the present simple, for students to guess. In pairs students do the same. Students report back in full group on the endings that their partners described. Ask: *Which books or films have you seen or read? Which ones did you like?*

1 Students complete the task individually. Elicit the answers.

1 illustrations **2** paperback **3** passage **4** publisher
5 print **6** novel **7** ending **8** series **9** e-book

extra

You may wish to extend the vocabulary by asking the following questions.

- *What is a novel divided into?* (chapters)
- *What form does a book first come out in?* (hardback)
- *What do we call the summary of a novel on the back cover?* (the blurb)

2 In pairs students discuss the questions.

Possible answers

1 I prefer paperbacks. I just prefer to touch, and even smell, the paper! And afterwards, I can put it on a shelf and remember that I've read it.
2 The last TV series I watched was *Game of Thrones*. It was also a series of books, but I haven't read them yet.

extra

Extend the discussion by asking these questions.

1 *Name a paperback you've read recently. Do you prefer reading paperbacks (to hardbacks)?*
2 *Do you prefer short stories to novels?*
3 *Do you, or does anyone you know, browse books in a bookshop rather than online? Why do you think people still enjoy going to bookshops?*
4 *Are there any disadvantages to reading e-books?*
5 *Will hardbacks and paperbacks become unavailable in the future?*

3 7.3 Refer students to the photo and elicit their ideas as to what it shows. Play the recording to check. Ask: *What sort of stories can you get? Where can you find these machines? Who uses them?*

A machine that distributes stories.

4 7.4 Play the recording and elicit students' opinions.

Possible answers

It's a nice idea, for people who love reading. And it's a great way to encourage people to read the work of new writers. I'm just a bit worried that it uses up a lot of paper. I'm sure people just throw the paper away after their journey, which is a waste.

extra 

Ask: *How important it is for you to having reading material during a journey? What other things can or do you do to pass the time?*

background 

The Poems on the Underground project started in the UK in 1986 following an idea from an American writer. It was designed to help make train journeys less boring and also to bring poetry to a wider audience. Poems include classics and modern poems, all celebrating the diversity of London. They are displayed in the carriages of underground trains, on station walls, on linked websites and recently free booklets of poems were handed to passengers. The idea has since been copied around the world.

5 Read through the phrases in the box and ask students to discuss the meanings in pairs. If students have internet access, ask them to look up words they don't know in the Longman Dictionary of Contemporary English (www.ldoceonline.com). Conduct class feedback and ask for examples. Ask: *Which phrase is not used with books?* (special effects).

Possible answers

complicated plot (a story that is difficult to understand/complex/has lots happening in it)
final scene (the last part that you see or read)
happy ending (a positive ending, or one that makes us feel happy)
main character (the most important person in a story)
rave reviews (very good comments from the public or critics)
special effects (an unusual image or sound that has been produced artificially for a film)
unexpected twist (a sudden event in a story that surprises us)
weak storyline (a story that doesn't work well or hold our interest)

6 Students complete the sentences individually and then compare their ideas with a partner.

Possible answers

1 … is one where the hero learns something, and becomes a better person.
2 … someone we can identify with and look up to.
3 … a problem because film-makers use them too much instead of focusing on storytelling.
4 … I like not knowing what's going to happen next.

extra 

Ask students to report what their partner said. Encourage correct use of reported speech.

explore **vocabulary**

7 Ask students: *How do you record and try to remember phrasal verbs?* Read through the explore vocabulary box, then check how many students record phrasal verbs according to the preposition. Students match the phrasal verbs with the definitions. Check answers together. Elicit other phrasal verbs students know with the same prepositions (e.g. *take up, work out, stand in, look for,* etc.).

1 figure out **2** cheer up **3** leave out **4** go for **5** fall for **6** give in **7** look up **8** take in

8 Read through the title of the text and ask: *What do you think it means?* Elicit that *Hollywood Happy Ending* means making every film a 'feel-good' film with a happy ending. Students complete the text with the correct phrasal verbs from Ex 7. Point out that not all of them will need to be used. Conduct class feedback.

1 figure out **2** leave out **3** cheer up **4** take in/figure out **5** fall for **6** give in

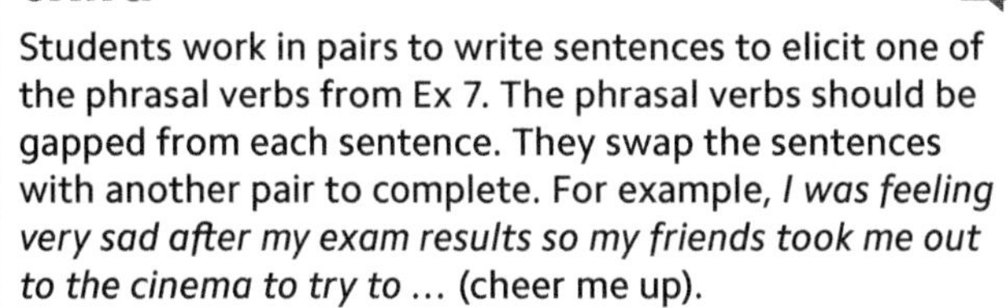

extra

Students work in pairs to write sentences to elicit one of the phrasal verbs from Ex 7. The phrasal verbs should be gapped from each sentence. They swap the sentences with another pair to complete. For example, *I was feeling very sad after my exam results so my friends took me out to the cinema to try to …* (cheer me up).

Speak up

9 Students discuss the questions in pairs. Monitor and give help where necessary. Conduct class feedback.

Possible answers

1. I'd probably go for a love story. I don't like violence in films. I like films which cheer me up, and have a happy ending.
2. I'll usually talk to my teacher if I need help figuring something out.
3. If my friends want to go out somewhere, and I'm feeling tired or I have too much homework to do, then I'll usually give in. The main reason is because I don't want to be left out, and be the only one sitting at home while everyone else is having fun.

To finish

If your class is interested in poetry, ask them to research some of the current London Underground poetry online. They could choose a poet, find out some information about him or her and copy an example of a short poem to read to the class in the next lesson.

Fun footer

Read through the footer with the class. Ask students if they have ever heard a *tall story*. If they can remember it, they should tell it to the rest of the class. Ask the class how believable the tall story is.

Presentation tool:	Unit 7, Vocabulary
Workbook / Online Practice:	p71
Audioscript:	SB p181
Extra Practice App	

LISTENING SB p96

To start

Ask: *Do you know much about Hollywood?* Then read out the following statements. Students should call out if they think they are true or false.

1. *Hollywood was established in California in 1853 as a farming community.*
2. *Hollywood only became part of the city of Los Angeles in 1910*
3. *The first ever films were made in Hollywood.*
4. *The name 'Oscar' for the statues given in the annual film awards came from the artist who designed the statue.*

1–2 True
3 False. The first films were made in Paris by the Lumière brothers at the end of the 19th century.
4 False. A woman called Margaret Herrick called it 'Oscar' because she thought the statue looked like her uncle Oscar.

Power up

1 Ask students to work in small groups and discuss the questions. You could take a class vote on the most popular type of films.

Possible answers

Types of film: drama, thriller, cartoon, romance, horror, blockbuster, action, mystery, fantasy, sci-fi

Possible feelings: tense, nervous, amused, cheerful, scared, excited, confused, sad, bored

2 Ask: *How do you decide what kind of film to watch? How much influence does each of the ideas in the box have?* Conduct class feedback and establish which is the most influential thing for students.

Possible answers

I usually pay more attention to friends' opinions than online reviews, because my friends know what kind of film I like, and we share similar tastes. I don't care so much about special effects, or who is in the film, because I'm more interested in the story and what happens.

Listen up

3 7.5 Ask students to read the options, then play the recording once. Ask students to explain how they decided on the answers, but don't let them look at the audio script yet.

A 2 (*I was a bit apprehensive about watching the film version of the book …*)
B 5 (*Having spent some time on visual elements of a film, we'll be studying audio, …*)
C 1 (*A: And the lead actor was brilliant, he really made me laugh out loud at times.*
B: I think the whole cinema heard you!)
D 6 (*My phone company's sent me a two for one offer to go to the cinema this evening …*)
E 4 (*… but are not interested in paying extra for the special effects on a regular basis …*)
F 3 (*I never go online to read reviews …*)
G 8 (*In fact, even my drama teacher advised me to delay my acting career until after university.*)
H 7 (*To be honest, I'd have preferred that kind of film, but I went with my sister's choice just to annoy him!*)

LISTENING (Continued)

exam tip

4 **Before you play the recording for the second time, go through the exam tip. Remind students that they will have time to read the questions before they listen to the extracts. They will hear the extracts twice. If they're not sure of their answer, they shouldn't worry about it, but focus on the next extract. Ask them to look at the first question in Ex 5. Ask: *What's the situation? Who is talking and what are they talking about?* Once you have checked the answers, point out that understanding the words people use when they express their feelings or thoughts is a real-life skill.**

Situation: a conversation about a film
The speakers: two friends
Focus: what they agree about

exam task multiple choice: short texts

The conversations are all related to the topic of film in some way whereas in the Cambridge exam the situations are different.

5 **e** 7.6 **Give students one minute to look at questions 1–8. They will not have time to read all the options, but they should make sure they are clear about what each situation is in each question, and what the focus is. Play the recording.**

6 **After listening, students compare their answers in pairs. Ask: *How did you decide on the answers? Why were the other options wrong?***

1 B (*Girl: he really made me laugh out loud at times. Boy: I must admit I did think there were some great comic moments.*)
A Incorrect: The boy says that he'd guessed what would happen and it was predictable. The girl doesn't agree
C Incorrect: The girl says the main actor was brilliant and the main stars were convincing. The boy doesn't agree.

2 C (*So I guess I was ready to be disappointed. I know film adaptations of books can be a let-down. However, contrary to all my expectations, it was very true to the book.*)
A Incorrect: she was apprehensive about seeing the film after reading the book
B Incorrect: She says it took time to get used to the characters, but not that she was disappointed

3 B (*My agent then offered to go through the reviews for me. And that's what we've done ever since. I never go online to read reviews.*)
A Incorrect: He talks about the reviews of the film, not his acting skills
C Incorrect: He doesn't read any reviews

4 C (*Another criticism is that the 3D effects sometimes make it difficult to concentrate on the story itself.*)
A Incorrect: Most people will see it once, but there's no mention of whether attendance was expected
B Incorrect: People may not be interested in paying extra for 3D but it doesn't say it's too expensive

5 A (*… we'll be studying audio, in particular, how a soundtrack can bring a film alive.*)
B Incorrect: She talks about developing character, but not the advantages of exploiting different techniques
C Incorrect: She mentions a well-written script but not the positive aspects of writing scripts

6 C (*My phone company's sent me a two for one offer to go to the cinema this evening … I thought you could go with your cousin if you want.*)
A Incorrect: She's out with Sarah, not inviting him
B Incorrect: she's not recommending the film – she says it's not her thing, but he might enjoy it

7 B (*I think she wanted to watch a comedy anyway, … I went with my sister's choice just to annoy him!*)
A Incorrect: Jake suggested this but they didn't watch it
C Incorrect: Jake said he didn't want to watch a horror film – it gave him nightmares

8 A (*Thankfully, it has all turned out well. However, I do acknowledge that my success has mainly been due to being in the right place at the right time.*)
B Incorrect: He's not annoyed – he could see their point.
C Incorrect: He understood his parents' worries, but doesn't say he was concerned himself about them

Speak up

7 **Ask students to discuss the questions in small groups. Conduct class feedback.**

Possible answers

1 I'm happy to pay more to see a big blockbuster film in 3D. Usually, it makes the film come alive, and you really feel like you're there in the action.

2 I prefer watching films at home. Whenever I go to the cinema, I get annoyed by other people arriving late, or making noises and all the adverts before the film.

3 Possible ideas include:
- Films will be interactive, so you feel as though you're in the film.
- You can change the visual aspect of the scene and see it from different angles.
- You can choose a character and follow them through the film.

To finish

Write these feeling words on the board: *scary, exciting, boring, disappointing, unexpected*. In pairs, students choose a feeling and tell their partner about a film that made them feel that way and explain why.

Fun footer

Nominate a student to read out the footer. Ask students: *Have you seen any Bollywood films? Do you know any famous Bollywood actors?* If they don't, ask them what they know about Bollywood films, and if they would like to see any. Consider asking students to read the Grammar file on reporting verbs on page 154 in preparation for the Use of English lesson.

Presentation tool:	Unit 7, Listening
Workbook / Online Practice:	p72
Audioscript:	SB p181
Extra Practice App	

USE OF ENGLISH 1 SB p97

To start

Read out the following sentences, one at a time. Nominate different students to report what you said to the class after each sentence.

- *I met a famous film star last week.* (Elicit *She said she had met a famous film star last week.*)
- *I enjoy blockbuster films.* (Elicit *She said she enjoys blockbuster films.*)
- *I was watching a film at midnight last night.* (Elicit *She said she had been watching a film at midnight last night.*)

Now explain that you're going to look at reporting words other than *say* and that these have different patterns.

explore **grammar** ➥ SB p154

1 Go through the explore grammar box with students. If you feel they are happy with this concept, then ask them to do Ex 1 in pairs, referring to the explore grammar box to match the structures. If you feel they need more help, refer students to the grammar reference section on reporting verbs on page 154. Ask them to do Exs 6 and 7 on page 155 for homework.

A admit, agree, deny, persuade, promise, recommend, remind, threaten
B agree, promise, refuse, threaten
C encourage, invite, persuade, recommend, remind
D admit, deny, recommend
E agree (with someone on/about), boast (about), congratulate (someone on), insist (on)

2 Ask students to complete the exercise in pairs.

1 not to tell **2** seeing **3** to switch off **4** booking
5 to meet **6** to take up

3 Ask students to write their sentences individually. Then put them into pairs to show each other their sentences and ask follow-up questions to find out more.

Possible answers
I've agreed to help my friend with his homework tomorrow.
My brother denied breaking my smartphone.
My teacher encouraged me to learn more about reporting verbs.

alternative

Put students into pairs and give each pair three pieces of paper. They write one sentence about themselves on each piece of paper. Collect the papers and mix them up. Either hand them out at random to other pairs or read them out yourself. The class should guess who wrote each sentence.

4 Focus students on the article and the title. After they have read the title and predicted the content of the article, ask students to read it quickly without worrying about the gaps. Ask the following questions.

- *What is the text about?* (It's about a boy who won a competition.)
- *What happened when Marley arrived at school?* (He was told he had won a scriptwriting competition.)
- *What does Teen Connections do?* (It encourages teenage writers and experienced directors to work together.)
- *What will happen to Marley's script?* (It will be made into a short film.)

exam task: open cloze

5 **e** Remind students that in the exam, they will have a text like this with gaps that they must complete, and that they can only use one word. Go through the exam tip with students. Ask students to complete the article. Then ask them to compare answers in pairs.

1 that (the only word which can follow the reporting verb *suggested*)
2 him (We need an object after the reporting verb *persuaded*.)
3 about (the dependent preposition which follows *forget*)
4 on (the dependent preposition which follows the reporting verb *congratulate someone*)
5 who/that/to (This is the start of a relative clause.)
6 be (part of a passive construction)
7 into (part of the phrasal verb *turn into*)
8 his (We need a possessive pronoun here.)

Speak up

6 Students discuss questions 1–3 in small groups. Then ask them to write their own individual questions for the group to answer, using the reporting verbs.

Possible answers
1 They insist on me cleaning my room once a week, and helping to tidy up around the house at weekends.
2 I often warn my brother not to borrow my things without asking!
3 The last time I said sorry was yesterday. I was apologising to my mother for breaking something in the kitchen.
4 When was the last time you offered to help someone? Have you ever refused to do something?

To finish

Ask students to discuss these questions:

- *Have you ever heard anyone boasting? What did they say? How did you feel about it?*
- *Has anyone ever encouraged you to do something useful? What was it? Was it really useful?*
- *Has anyone ever made or broken a promise to you? What was it? What happened?*

Presentation tool:	Unit 7, Use of English 1
Workbook / Online Practice:	p73
Grammar reference and practice:	SB p154
Extra Practice App	

USE OF ENGLISH 2 SB p98

To start

Write these words and phrases on the board: *social media, phone, text, letter, email, face-to-face*.

Ask students: *How do you usually choose to communicate with friends? Why?* Take a class vote to find the most popular method of communication.

1 Put students into small groups. Give them five minutes to come up with the story behind the text messages. Ask each group to share their ideas with the class. Ask: *Which story is most convincing?*

2 7.7 Play the recording. Students listen to the conversation and compare it with their guesses.

Text 1: It's from a friend called Amy. She's sent it because she's just got a TV role.
Text 2: It's from the boy's mum reminding him not to be late for a meal at his aunt's house

explore vocabulary 1

3 7.8 Remind students of some of the verbs and prepositions they learned in the previous lesson. Call out some of the verbs and elicit the prepositions: *insist* (on), *congratulate someone* (on), *remind someone* (of), *boast* (about). Tell them that they are going to look at some more uses of prepositions, first with phrases and then with adjectives. Play the recording so that students can identify the prepositional phrases they hear.

1 at a guess **2** by email **3** in general **4** for sure **5** on our way

explore vocabulary 2

4 Go through the explore vocabulary box with the class, and given them time to check any words they don't know.

extra

Ask students in pairs to write a short dialogue using two of the adjective + preposition phrases from the box. Nominate a few pairs to read out their dialogues to the class.

exam tip

5 Focus students on the article and the title. Once students have discussed the title of the article, ask them to read the text quickly to check their ideas.

The article is about a new style of documentary in which people's digital activity (texts, photos, posts, etc.) is shown to an audience.

exam task: multiple-choice cloze

The items tested here are all related to prepositional phrases, which is the lesson focus.

6 e Remind students how important it is to know what a text is about before they try to fill in any gaps. In the exam, they should always read it through quickly first to get the gist of what it is about, as this will actually save them time when they do the task. Ask students to do the task in pairs. Point out that in the exam, there are only eight questions with an example, but here they have to do all the questions. Remind them to always read the words before and after the gap, as this will help them to identify the word needed to complete it.

1 B (*dedicated* is the only word that can be followed by *to -ing*)
2 A (*aware* is usually followed by *of*)
3 B (*involved* is followed by *in*)
4 D (*limited* is followed by *to*)
5 A (the phrase is *on screen* – none of the other prepositions can complete the phrase)
6 C (the phrase is *in person*)
7 D (*respectful* is followed by *of*)
8 B (*horrified* is followed by *at* or *by*)
9 C (*addicted* is followed by *to*)

Speak up

7 Organise students into small groups to discuss the question.

Possible answer
I wouldn't like to take part in a documentary like this. Most of my text messages and tweets aren't in any way interesting! And I really wouldn't like my pictures to be shown to everyone. I don't share my photos or posts with many people, and I wouldn't like complete strangers to comment on everything I've ever written or posted. Also, people only post things on social media when something nice has happened – they don't put bad experiences online. This makes it look as though their lives don't have any problems, but really they do. So I don't see how a documentary like this could really be 'honest'.

Fun footer

Focus students' attention on the footer. Ask: *What do you think the saying means? Do you agree that people's lives often look more interesting on social media? Why?*

To finish

Put students into groups of three. Ask two of the three students to close their books. The third student reads out a prepositional phrase or adjective without the preposition, and the other two students have to say what the missing preposition is. The first student to say the right answer gets a point. After two or three minutes, see which student in the class has the most points.

Presentation tool:	Unit 7, Use of English 2
Workbook / Online Practice:	p74
Photocopiable activity:	7B
Audioscript:	SB p181
Extra Practice App	

SPEAKING SB p99

To start

Put students into pairs to discuss these questions: *What kind of things do you like to post on social media? Is there anything you would not post? Why?*

Ask the class: *What are the advantages and disadvantages of using social media?* Elicit ideas and find out whether the class thinks there are more advantages or more disadvantages.

Power up

1 Focus students' attention on the photos and put them into pairs to discuss the questions. Conduct class feedback.

Possible answers

1 Photos like this would be found on social-networking sites such as Facebook or Instagram.

2 The comments in blue are what the person posting the photo wrote for everyone to see. The thought bubbles show what one of the people in the photo might have really been thinking.

2 7.9 Tell students that they are going to hear people discussing the question. Play the recording so that they can decide who answers better.

The girl sounds better because she is more polite and friendly and tries to include the boy in the conversation by saying 'what do you think?' She also accepts his opinion 'I have to admit you have a point'. The boy sounds a bit rude and direct. He's not really interacting with the girl and just says what he thinks in a direct manner.

3 7.10 Play the recording. Give them time to discuss their ideas in pairs, and to give some examples to support their ideas.

They both use expressions to express agreement and disagreement. The boy uses questions to show disagreement and he also includes the girl in the discussion. His intonation sounds much friendlier.

I completely agree that it's good for keeping in touch with people, but do you really think we learn what's happening … ? Wouldn't you agree that … ?

useful language: agreeing; disagreeing/ persuading someone of your opinion

4 7.11 Go through the useful language box with students. Read the *agreeing* phrases aloud and tell students to copy you, so that they can practise their intonation and sounding friendly. Before you play the recording, ask students to read through the conversation and predict what was said. Play the recording so that they can check their answers.

1 completely agree
2 do you really think
3 Wouldn't you agree that
4 have to admit, you have a point

Speak up

exam task: discussion ➥ SB p164

5 **e** Remind students that in the exam, their opinions are not marked – only the language that they use is. They should think about ways of involving their partner in the discussion, and should not dominate it. This is a good social skill as well as being a good exam technique. Put students into groups of three to discuss the questions. If you think that students might spend too long on one question and might not discuss them all, allocate specific questions to the groups. Go round and monitor their discussions, but don't correct them as this is a fluency activity. Make a note of any problems that are common to all the groups, and discuss them at the end. In your feedback, concentrate on how well the students interacted, and whether they were good at taking turns rather than dominating the conversation. Remind them of the need to focus on the question and not get side-tracked into irrelevant details.

Possible answers

1 A: I think there are more people posting online.
B: I couldn't agree more. I guess most people now think that if they're not online, then they're missing out.

2 A: I think children can start using social media as soon as they like. It's a great way to meet new friends, and find out about the world.
B: I'm not sure I agree. I think the limit should be 16. I don't think teenagers should be allowed to have their own social media profile before that.

3 A: I don't personally use social media for more than a few minutes at a time, so I don't think it's a problem for most people.
B: Yes, you're absolutely right. But don't you think that over a whole day, people spend hours checking photos and posts online?

4 A: I think it's important to get information from a lot of sources, not just social media.
B: I couldn't agree more. People can post what they like on social media, so you can't exactly trust it to be 100% accurate or honest.

5 A: I think most teenagers like watching films or TV shows. I expect a lot of teenagers like reading, too.
B: I think so, too. But also, podcasts are becoming more common. And video games are actually a good way to experience different types of story.

6 A: I liked listening to my grandparents' stories when I was younger, and I learned a lot from them about how things were in the past. I'm not sure they learned anything from me, though.
B: Maybe, but isn't it true that older people can learn a lot from younger people, too? Like about new films, fashions, or about what young people are going through these days?

SPEAKING (Continued)

Speaking extra

6 Explain the task and organise the class into three different groups. Give them time to prepare arguments and ideas for the discussion, and make sure they are aware of their roles. Point out that the aim of this discussion is not necessarily for students to give their own opinions, but to try and decide about what a particular group of people would think about a situation. Organise the class into groups of three, with one type of person in each group. Monitor the discussion and make a note of any on-going language problems. Concentrate on phrases they use for agreeing and disagreeing, and make sure that all the students in each group are involved in the discussion.

Possible answers

Group A: Some celebrities might feel that the press is too intrusive and that they have no privacy. They might also feel that stories are written about them simply to sell more newspapers, rather than to report what is honestly happening.

Group B: Journalists might feel that the public wants to hear about celebrities, and that their role is to give the public what they want. Whether or not the stories are completely accurate is besides the point. They might also feel that celebrities want the publicity, and so journalists are really doing celebrities a favour.

Group C: Members of the public might feel that celebrity stories are exciting and interesting, and make a change from more serious news topics. They might also feel that celebrities are part of a fictional world anyway, and it doesn't really matter that stories about them are true or not.

To finish

Put students into new pairs, and assign them a few questions from Ex 5. This time, students should deliberately try to disagree with their partner's opinions. This will give students more practise in turn-taking, and in politely disagreeing and responding to disagreement.

Presentation tool:	Unit 7, Speaking
Workbook / Online Practice:	p75
Speaking file:	SB p164
Audioscript:	SB p181

WRITING SB pp100–101

To start

Ask students to discuss in pairs: *Have you ever written any stories? Would you like to be a writer? What would be easy or difficult about it?*

Power up

1 Focus students' attention on the photo on page 101. Put students into pairs to discuss the questions. Point out that they need to speculate, and be creative, as there is not much detail in the photo. What they discuss here will help them with ideas for the writing task in Ex 2.

Possible answers

1 He is sitting on a bike and seems to be using his phone. He might be texting someone.
2 The boy might have been waiting for a friend to arrive, who hasn't turned up.
3 He might be feeling anxious or sad, and is now texting his friend to find out what happened.

Plan on

2 Refer students to the advert. Give them a chance to discuss possible stories in pairs.

alternative

Help students by reading out the sentences below before they start their discussions.

- *Who is Nick?*
- *Why does he think I sent the text?*
- *Did I send it?*
- *What was in the text?*
- *Who did I send it to?*
- *What might the surprise be?*
- *What might happen at the end of the story?*

These questions will help students to think of ideas. Tell them that it's a good idea to think of the end of the story as they make their plans, so that their story is logical. They should make notes of their ideas, and how the story will develop.

3 Students read the story and answer the questions. Ask: *Did the story match your ideas? What actually happened at the end? Why?*

Possible answers

The main characters are the author (the person using 'I'), Nick and Ellie. The author's name is probably Charlie.

Nick is an old friend of the author's. He's young, good-looking and people like him.

Ellie might be Nick's girlfriend and shares the same tastes.

4 Tell students that the development of a story is very important, and that a good story should interest and engage the reader. It should have a clear opening and ending, and include some excitement, tension or interest. Ask them to answer the questions in Ex 4 in pairs.

1 *That was the moment Nick asked me if I had sent the text.* A good prompt should make you wonder what has happened and what's going to happen next.

2 Tension keeps the reader interested. Without any tension, a story could be boring.
3 A climax is when a story reaches its most exciting part and usually comes at the end.

5 **Students look again at the story in Ex 3 and make notes. Then ask them to work in pairs and to retell the story by only looking at their notes. Students should check that they have both included all the main events.**

Possible answers

Nick and the author are sitting together. Nick thinks the author is hiding something from him.

The author remembers how everyone liked Nick at school, including a girl called Ellie.

He then remembers hanging out with Nick when a text arrives on Nick's phone. Nick isn't there to see it.

At the end of the story, the author reads the text, which is from Ellie. The author replies, pretending to be Nick and refusing the invitation, but suggesting that she ask Charlie (the author) instead.

exam tip

6 **Students should look at the model in Ex 3 as you go through the exam tip.**

The information in the second paragraph gives background details, so the tense used is the past perfect at the beginning.

7 **This exercise helps students relate the tenses to the storyline and the sequence of events, and gives them ideas for their own story.**

Possible answers

the past continuous: *Nick and I were hanging out* (a description of something happening over a period of time in the past)

the past perfect: *I hadn't wanted to make him angry*. (an action that happened before another action)

the past perfect continuous: *We'd been sitting in the garden* (an action in progress before another action occurred)

reported speech: *That was the moment Nick asked me if I had sent the text.* (for reporting what somebody said)

direct speech: *'I know you're hiding something', he said.* (the actual words someone said)

the past simple: *It was a stupid idea ...* (a completed past event)

explore **language**

8 **Go through the explore language box, and then ask students to do the exercise in pairs.**

Possible answers

a long difficult day; a beautiful old house; an absolutely amazing idea; an incredibly long journey; a totally unexpected letter; a really scary stranger

Write on

9 **Read through the task with students. They can use the diagram in Ex 4 to help them plan their story.**

10 **Tell students that as adjectives and adverbs can bring a story to life, it is a good idea to plan some phrases to use at this stage.**

exam task: story

→ SB p170

11 **e** **You could set the writing task for homework along with Ex 12. Encourage students to time themselves for 30 minutes. (They will have more time in the exam, but have already spent some time planning.) You could also ask them to refer to the model story and useful language on page 170.**

Model answer

The dark old house

He had warned me that it would be dangerous, but I didn't believe him. It was just a dark old empty house. How dangerous could it be to have a look inside?

I had always wanted to go inside the house. I had never seen anyone go in or out, and all the windows and doors had been locked and boarded up a long time ago. People sometimes said that they had seen mysterious lights moving inside the house, but I hadn't.

One day, I asked my friend Nick if he'd come to the house with me. I said I had found a strange little door around the back, and we could go in. 'We can't!' said Nick, 'It's dangerous!'

I ignored him, and I went to the house in the middle of a dark stormy night. As the lightning flashed above, I touched the handle and I was slowly turning it when I heard an incredibly strange noise from behind the door. It was like a voice saying 'No ...'.

I stopped in fear, and then I ran! To this day, I've never been back to the house.

Improve it

12 **You could set this reflection for homework. Collect in the essays and provide feedback on the assessment points listed. Point out that students could use this checklist every time they write a story. When you give students feedback on their stories, concentrate on whether they have used interesting language such as adjectives and adverbs, have organised their story into separate paragraphs, and have used a range of appropriate tenses.**

13 **This could be a short activity at the end of the lesson. Encourage students to find something positive in their partner's writing to comment on.**

Fun footer

Nominate a student to read out the footer. Ask students what they think it means.

Even though the actual narrative has finished, the characters or people continue to grow and develop.

To finish

Put students into different pairs, and ask them to tell each other their stories without revealing the ending. Their partner has to say what the ending might be.

Presentation tool:	Unit 7, Writing
Workbook / Online Practice:	p76
Photocopiable activity:	7C
Writing file:	SB p170
Extra Practice App	

SWITCH ON SB p102

Museum mystery

1 Refer students to the photo and elicit that it shows some ancient Egyptian statues. Explain that there are stories of ancient objects that have an unexplained power or ability and that they will soon watch a video clip about one of these. Ask them to discuss a well-known place or object that is associated with a mystery.

Possible answers

The Pyramids of Giza in Cairo are often the subject of mystery. No-one is completely clear as to when the largest of these pyramids was built, or how. Nothing has ever been found inside it, although there are many passages and chambers. Researchers have sent a small robot inside various tunnels in the pyramid, and have discovered mysterious metal gates, suggesting that there might be more rooms we don't know about. In 2017, another large, empty space was discovered inside the pyramid. As yet, no-one has found out what might be inside it.

2 Play the video clip for students to answer the question. Conduct class feedback.

A time-lapse camera was used to capture the movement of the statue.

3 Play the clip again for students to discuss answers to the questions in pairs. Elicit any answers. You might need to explain that *convex* is a word used to describe something that has a curved surface.

1 People believed that the spirit of the ancient Egyptian man it belonged to, Neb-Senu, made the statue turn around. Other people believed that it might have been the spirit of Michael Jackson making it turn.
2 The scientific explanation is that vibrations from passing traffic and visitors walking past the exhibit caused the statue to slowly turn because it had a slightly convex (or curved) base.

4 Stronger students may be able to answer the questions without watching the clip again. For weaker students, play the clip once more and then check answers.

Some people who were involved with the discovery of King Tutankhamun's tomb died shortly after. The press attributed this to a curse which protected the ancient king's resting place.

Joyce believes that because the story of Tutankhamun's curse is so popular and famous that it influences how people think about the ancient Egyptians today.

Project

5 Organise students into small groups and explain the project. They are going to produce a fictional news report about the mystery surrounding an ancient object, or an unexplained event, myth or legend. Read through the stages of the project so that the students understand clearly what they need to do. If appropriate, the group should choose an organiser/leader who allocates tasks for the project.

Students can do the research at home and then discuss which event or object to study in depth, during class time.

Each group decides who will be witnesses, experts and a reporter. Witnesses imagine what they might have seen or experienced and give details. Experts can do some additional research or use their imagination to come up with scientific explanations for the event. The reporter should think about questions to ask during the interviews.

Then in the following lesson, the reporter interviews the witnesses and experts and notes their answers. The groups discuss the news report they are going to make using the interviews.

Get students to film their news reports on their mobile phones. Play students' films on the IWB and elicit feedback and discussion from the rest of the class. Students discuss the news reports they've seen and decide whether the conclusions are convincing.

alternative

Each group chooses a mystery to research. Each member of the group then researches a different aspect of the mystery at home and then in class, the findings are discussed and compiled into a news report or a fact file. Students can download pictures to accompany the report. The finished report can be read to the class by one of the group or written up and circulated. If individual presentations would be too time consuming, the presenters could circulate to give their presentations to different groups.

extra

1 Working in small groups, students can explore the story of King Tutankhamun further. They should do some research about the discovery of the tomb, what was found there and the so-called curse of Tutankhamun. They can allocate roles of the key people involved: expert, witness, explorer, etc. to people in the group, then write a news report as it might have been written at the time of the discovery. They should present it as a short newspaper article with a headline, photo, and text.
2 Groups invent their own 'mystery'. They should think about something that has or could be mysterious: a ghost, strange noises, disappearing pictures, etc. Then film their report for the rest of the class to watch.

You could ask students to complete (and reflect on) the independent learning questions for homework in preparation for the next lesson. Then use the class time for students to discuss their ideas.

Presentation tool:	Unit 7, Switch on
Workbook / Online Practice:	p76
Switch on videoscript:	TB p174

INDEPENDENT LEARNING SB p102

Reading and writing

1 Ask students to compare how successfully they did the reading and writing tasks in this unit with how they'd done in previous units. They should identify mistakes they have stopped making and those they continue to make. It's usually rewarding for students to look back at work from an early unit and work from the latest to see how much improvement they have made. Students complete the task individually and then share their ideas with a partner or the whole class.

2 Give students time to read the questions and think about their answers individually.

3 Ask students to complete the sentences so that they are true for them. If appropriate, conduct class feedback and listen to some of the completed sentences. Although this might appear threatening for some students, it can be encouraging too, as weaker students can see that the stronger or more confident students also have things they need to improve on.

Possible answers

To improve my reading skills, I will make sure that I remember to read texts – even short ones – quickly for gist first. I will learn speed-reading strategies or try an online speed reading programme.

To improve my writing skills, I will make sure that I try to use a range of adjectives and adverbs, in order to add interest. I will also try to use a range of narrative tenses to make the sequence of events and any background information clear.

UNIT CHECK SB p103

This Unit check covers vocabulary related to storytelling, prepositional phrases and reported speech.

Practice

1 **1** main character **2** series **3** complicated plot **4** publisher **5** passage **6** unexpected twist

2 **4** a guess **2** typical **3** look **4** figure **5** short notice **6** slow

3 **4** 7.12 and 7.13 **1** went blank **2** scriptwriting **3** A-list **4** predictable **5** spooky **6** laugh out loud

Review

1
1 if I was going to watch the film the following
2 she had written her
3 to send her
4 if he could see her that
5 she hadn't enjoyed writing
6 he'd love

2 7.14 graphic novels, horror stories, sci-fi stories

3 7.15
1 Kate asked Matt what his book was about.
2 Matt's teacher suggested reading it.
3 Kate wanted to know if the book was like a comic.
4 Matt explained that the pictures had helped him.
5 Matt denied that the story was scary.
6 Matt insisted that Kate try a graphic story.

4
1 apologised for missing
2 reminded him to take
3 denied telling Becky
4 threatened to stop the film

5 **1** invited **2** agreed **3** recommended **4** warned **5** insisted **6** advised **7** admitted **8** denied **9** persuaded

6 **Possible answer**

I heard two people arguing today about where to go for lunch. It was a man and a woman. The man insisted on going somewhere cheap. He recommended having fast food. The woman said that she wanted something healthier. In the end, she persuaded him to go to a salad bar. She also advised him to try and eat more healthily, instead of only having cheap food.

GRAMMAR FILE SB p155

1 **1** had had **2** might see **3** would be studying **4** had been published, before **5** not to call, I'd read **6** was going, her

2 **1** us **2** following **3** would **4** she **5** had **6** previous

3
1 You have to leave.
2 I'm going to start my new book tomorrow.
3 You'll love the film.
4 I didn't like the weak storyline.
5 I have to read before going to sleep.
6 I watched TV last week.

4
1 he hadn't liked that TV series.
2 they might leave the following day.
3 they had been sitting there for ages.
4 she had to finish her book by the end of next/the following week.
5 could call her later if he wanted.
6 I was going to love the unexpected twist.

5
1 if I/we would be there
2 if I/we had seen his
3 who my favourite character was
4 if I was good at doing
5 when I realised I was
6 how much time I/we had for

6 **1** congratulated **2** advised **3** suggested **4** agreed **5** invited **6** promised

7
1 apologised for not being at
2 warned him not to read
3 encouraged Ana to write often
4 denied taking her father's

Presentation tool:	Unit 7, Unit check
Workbook / Online Practice:	p77
Audioscript:	SB pp181–182

8 In it together

READING
topic: life as a spy
skill: understanding attitudes
task: multiple choice

GRAMMAR
modal verbs
linking phrases
such a / so

VOCABULARY
personality
phrases with *have* and *keep*
phrasal verbs
collocations

LISTENING
topic: playing music
skill: identifying opinions
task: multiple matching

USE OF ENGLISH
key word transformations

SPEAKING
topic: inspirational speakers
skill: taking turns
task: collaborative task

WRITING
topic: extra-curricular activities
skill: making suggestions
task: email

SWITCH ON
video: recycle rush
project: design a robot

Lead-in SB p105

Focus students on the picture and ask: *What is the relationship between the people?* Write *friendship* on the board and tell students when you met your oldest friend. Ask: *When did you meet your oldest friends?* Elicit answers and find out who has known their friend for the longest time. Read through the quote with the class. Ask students to write down three things that people sometimes think about them but are not true. For example, *People think I'm very organised but in fact I'm not! I just give that impression.*

In pairs, students discuss the quote and whether it is true of them. They should give examples. Conduct feedback and see how far the students think the quote is or isn't true. Students can discuss questions 1 and 2 in pairs or as a class.

Possible answers

1 a social circle could include: family, classmates, close friends, friends on social media, etc.
2 ideas include: they help make decisions, they don't judge you, they give genuine advice.

extra 

Ask: *How many real friends would you say you have?* Elicit answers and as a class, discuss the different types of friendships. You could also ask students to think back about the different circles of friends they have. Ask: *Do you show these different circles different sides or aspects of your personality?*

READING SB pp106–107

To start

Write the word *spy* on the board. In pairs students write the names of as many famous spies (fictional or non-fictional) as they can in a minute. Take feedback. Students who gave the name of a spy who other students don't know should give some information about them, for example, *He's in a series of five films, played by Matt Damon.* (Jason Bourne)

Possible answers

advantages: you might be able to travel the world; it's exciting work; you might be carrying out important work for your country

disadvantages: you wouldn't be able to tell anyone what you do; you might be in constant danger; you wouldn't be able to form normal relationships

Power up

1 Refer students to the picture and ask if they recognise the character shown. Tell them it's Alex Rider, a fictional teenage spy. Ask: *What is happening and what is the boy about to do?* Encourage them to speculate why. In open group ask students to give possible advantages and disadvantages of being a teenage spy. Ask: *Would you like to be a spy?* Elicit how they think people are chosen or can apply to be a spy.

Ask students if they know and can recommend any other teenage spy books, giving reasons why they would recommend them.

background

Alex Rider is the main character in a series of books by British writer Anthony Horowitz. There are more than 10 books in the series and the first novel, *Stormbreaker*, has been made into a movie. Alex is a fourteen-year-old schoolboy who is forced to work for MI6 because of his many talents, including excellent athletic ability. Horowitz says that he wanted to create a teenage equivalent to James Bond, the famous spy created by Ian Fleming, whose film adventures are popular all over the world. The name Rider is said to have been chosen for the teenage spy after a Bond girl called Honeychile Rider in the film *Dr No*.

Read on

2 Tell students that they are going to read an extract from *Stormbreaker*, the first Alex Rider novel. Write *MI6, SAS* and *Official Secrets Act* on the board and ask students to scan the text to find where they are mentioned. Remind them that scanning for information like this does not involved detailed reading, it is reading quickly to find where certain things are mentioned in a text. This is useful for exam tasks like this as they can scan to find where they need to read more carefully. Give students a time limit to find and underline the items. Ask students to read the sentences the items come up in and guess what they mean from the context.

1 MI6 = Military Intelligence, Section 6; SAS = Special Air Service, a special-forces unit of the British Army.

2 People might have to sign the Official Secrets Act in order to protect official information which, if it fell into the wrong hands, could cause a lot of damage to people or national security.

extra

Extend practice of scanning skills by asking students to find the following.

- *The subjects Alex has for homework* (French and history)
- *The name of his school* (Brookland School)
- *The length of time he had been away* (2 weeks)

3 Students read more carefully to answer the questions.

Alex was an orphan and also his uncle had died recently. In other words, it seems that he had no immediate family. He had been on a mission for MI6.

extra: fast finishers

Fast finishers can write another question about the extract to ask the class during feedback. For example, in the second paragraph they could ask for details about Alex's family. Conduct class feedback and allow any fast finishers to ask their question(s).

exam tip

4 **e** Remind students that when answering multiple choice questions they will need to look for clues in the text as they will not find the exact wording in the options. Sometimes words or phrases may point them in the wrong direction so they need to read carefully. Go through the exam tip box with the class and read question 2 and its options. Give students some time to find the relevant section and underline all the information that refers to the question. They should follow the advice and eliminate each option until they are left with the correct one. Check answers in full group and ask for reasons why the other options are not correct.

2 D (*... they had nodded and smiled and secretly thought him a little bit pampered and spoiled.*)

Option A is incorrect because Alex has already had time off school and there is no reference to any future time off.

Option B is incorrect because although teachers 'had not been sympathetic' they had to 'make allowances' due to the fact that he had no parents and his uncle had died.

Option C is incorrect because the homework was not 'a punishment' but 'to catch up'.

exam task: multiple choice

The Cambridge exam reading text does not have a detailed lead-in to the story extract.

5 Students then complete the task individually and compare answers with a partner. Conduct class feedback and ask for reasons why they chose a particular option and why the other answers are wrong.

1 B (*So why did he feel so out of it, as if he were watching the last weeks of the term from the other side of a giant glass screen?*)

A It is other students who may be looking forward to relaxing, Alex has a lot of homework.

C The focus is not on a dislike of routine but a concern that he feels different.

D Mention is made of hundreds of other students around him, but not that they are Alex's friends.

READING (Continued)

3 C (*It was he who had changed*)
A His uncle's death is mentioned later and not Alex's reaction to it
B Alex is looking for a reason for why he feels strange and it is not the absence from school
D There is no reference to how his friends are treating him

4 B (*Alex smiled at the memory of it. He didn't need to sign anything. Who would have believed him anyway?*)
A What has happened to Alex is unusual but he doesn't mention that he thinks the signing is unusual.
C There is no reference to his attitude to whether what he's done should be a secret, just that he doesn't enjoy lying (and this comes in the next paragraph)
D There is no reference to this

5 A (*he'd been forced to tell them that he'd been in bed, ... he hated having to deceive his friends*)
B He hadn't hidden at home, he'd been spying
C The reference to *filing cabinet* is not to information about Alex, but the fact that he had to keep everything secret
D *Alex didn't want to boast about what he'd done*

6 D (*But at the same time – he had to admit it – part of him wanted it all to happen again. ... And at the end of the day, anything was better than double homework.*)
A Part of him wished that it had never happened, not that he was happy to be back
B The reference is that he didn't feel right in the 'safe and comfortable world of school'
C Things are back to normal as far as routine is concerned but *part of him wanted it all to happen again*

6 **Students work in pairs to complete the task. Conduct class feedback.**

1 heading **2** make allowances **3** streaming **4** dribbling **5** crash course **6** lunatic **7** slouching **8** muttered

extra

Students work in pairs to find five more unfamiliar items in the extract and deduce the meanings from context. Compare choices and guessed meanings with other students in full group. Ask the class which items they think will be most useful to them (include those in Ex 5). Vote on the most useful items. Ask students to try to use at least three of the items in conversation or written work over the next few days and check at the end of the unit which items they have used.

Sum up

7 **Students work in pairs to summarise what happened to Alex and how it affects him now. Ask for examples of their summaries in full group.**

He had been away from school involved in work for MI6. This meant he had to work in secrecy and in dangerous, high-action situations.
He wasn't allowed to talk about what he had been doing so therefore he felt isolated from his school friends.
He also quite liked the action of his secret life with MI6.

Speak up

8 **Students discuss the questions in pairs. Be aware that some points may already have been covered in the lesson so far and if so, replace them with another question, for example: *Why do you think people are attracted to becoming a spy? Do you think the life of a real spy is as glamorous as we see in films? Why/Why not?* Circulate and encourage discussion. Note any interesting points and any common errors you want to deal with later. Conduct class feedback.**

Possible answers

1 I would find it very difficult not to be able to tell family or friends what I really do. It would mean that I don't have any close friends at all, and I wouldn't be able to share my problems with anyone.

2 We often hide things from people that we think might hurt them. In a way, this is a good thing, because it means that we are trying to protect other people. But in a way, it's also a bad thing because we are actually being dishonest.

3 I wouldn't like a life where I'm constantly in danger, and I never have a chance to relax. The perfect lifestyle would be one where I could choose to be active when I want to be.

To finish

In full group brainstorm what qualities a spy needs to have. For example, *discretion, loyalty, being very fit, being able to speak different* languages, etc. Put students in pairs to add to the list. Elicit their ideas and write them on the board. Then ask students to discuss these questions in pairs: *Which qualities do you have? Do you think you would make a good spy?*

Fun footer

Read the question with the class and discuss students' answers. Ask whether they think it's ever good to keep secrets from other people, and what types of thing people are sometimes secretive about.

In preparation for the Grammar lesson, you could ask students to complete Ex 1 on page 108, read the Grammar file on modal verbs on page 156 and complete Exs 1 and 2 on page 157. Check the answers in class after the 'To start' activity.

Presentation tool: Unit 8, Reading
Workbook / Online Practice: pp78–79
Extra Practice App

GRAMMAR SB p108

To start

Write on the board: *Last night I went to bed early. In the middle of the night I heard a very loud scream! I went back to sleep.* Around this sentence, write *COULD, MIGHT, MUST, CAN'T, SHOULD, NEED.*

Ask students in pairs to make comments about the event on the board using the modals. Take feedback and write some of the comments on the board. The complexity of the comments will depend on the level of your students. Elicit that these verbs are modal verbs.

Suggested comments: *It might/could have been a cat outside. You should have got up and checked. You didn't need to get up because you knew what it was. You must have been very tired.*

explore **grammar** ➥ SB p156

1 Read through the explore grammar box with the class and ask them which modal structures refer to past situations that definitely didn't happen.

You should have explained
I ought to have been more understanding
we didn't have to stay late
He should have been told the truth

alternative

Write these sentences on the board, which use modals to show attitude to the past. Ask questions to check students' understanding.

- *Tom should have finished his homework last night.* (Ask: *Did Tom finish his homework last night? What do you think the result was?)*
- *Tom shouldn't have watched a late horror film.* (Ask: *Did Tom watch a late horror film? What do you think the result was?)*
- *The students should have been told about the test.* (Ask: *Were the students told about the test? What do you think the result was?)*
- *Jenna must have been tired this morning.* (Ask: *How sure are you that Jenna was tired this morning? Why?)*
- *Jenna can't have set her alarm clock last night.* (Ask: *How sure are you that Jenna didn't set her alarm clock last night? Why?)*

watch out for

Could have + past participle can have two meanings related to possibility and ability.

- *He could have gone to the beach.* (= He went somewhere. It's possible that he is at the beach, but I'm not sure.)
- *He could have gone to the beach.* (= He was able to go to the beach, but he didn't go for some reason.)

2 8.1 Play the recording for students to answer the questions. Pause after each speaker for students to note down answers. They compare ideas with a partner. Conduct class feedback.

Speaker 1 didn't tell her mum she'd got into drama school straight away.
Speaker 2 worried about her assignments and exams.
Speaker 3 didn't keep in touch as much with family abroad as she should have done, and she didn't call enough.
Speaker 4 worried about work.
Speaker 5 didn't call her mum enough and she didn't send enough postcards.
Speaker 6 didn't make enough time for friends, and didn't get in touch with people enough.

3 8.2 Students listen again to complete the sentences.

Speaker 1: should have told
Speaker 2: needn't have worried about
Speaker 4: needn't have worried about
Speaker 5: ought to have called

extra

Ask students to discuss the questions in Ex. 2 in pairs.

4 Ask students who they turn to for advice when they have a problem. Ask if they ever read advice sections on websites or in magazines. Students read the online advice page ignoring the gaps to say what the problems are. Then they complete the problems with one or two words. Check answers in full group.

1 couldn't/can't
2 could have/should have

extra

Ask students to discuss in pairs what advice they might give the two people. Conduct class feedback and see if students give similar advice. After doing Ex 5 they check if their advice was the same as in the book, and ask if they agree with the advice given and why/why not.

5 Students read and match the replies with the problems. Then they complete the texts with a modal verb and the correct form of the verbs in brackets. They compare answers with a partner. Conduct class feedback.

1 A **2** B
1 can't have been
2 could/should/ought to have been handled
3 ought to/should/could have approached
4 can work
5 must/may/might have felt
6 have to encourage
7 'll (will) be able to

GRAMMAR (Continued)

6 In pairs students think of another problem and reply to put on the website. Monitor and check correct use of modal verbs. Help with ideas where necessary. Conduct class feedback where students read out their problems and replies and get class reaction and/or other suggestions or advice.

Possible answers

Problem: I haven't been in touch with my old friend who moved abroad. He sent me an email, but I didn't reply to it because I was busy with other things. I find it difficult to write with my news because I don't have any. I want to stay in touch with him, but I'm not good at writing long letters. Can you give me some advice?

Advice: I think your friend would be happy to hear from you, even if you don't have any exciting news to tell him. Perhaps he thinks that you don't want to write to him, or you're not interested in staying in touch. Don't wait until you have lots of news to put in a long email. Just send him short messages or maybe try calling him occasionally.

Speak up

7 Students discuss the questions in pairs. Circulate and give advice, check use of modal verbs where necessary and then conduct class feedback.

Possible answers

1 I would have suggested talking to the parents, and making them understand how stressful the situation is. I agree with Caroline that the best thing to do is to talk to other people about it, rather than keep the problem to yourself.
2 In this kind of situation, I might ask myself if I really want someone like this as a friend. Sometimes, we tell ourselves that someone is a nice person, or a real friend, when really they aren't. Try being friends with someone who doesn't make you feel bad!

To finish

Ask students to discuss these additional questions in pairs.

Who do you think gives better advice – family or friends? Why?

Should we ask for advice when we have to make important decisions – like choosing a career – or should we think about these things on our own? Why?

Fun footer

Nominate a student to read out the footer. Elicit what the proverb means (unless you're perfect, don't criticise other people). Ask students to discuss in pairs: *Have you ever criticised someone when you shouldn't have done?*

Presentation tool:	Unit 8, Grammar
Workbook / Online Practice:	p80
Photocopiable activity:	8A
Grammar reference and practice:	SB p156
Audioscript:	SB p182

VOCABULARY SB p109

personality

To start

In pairs students note down adjectives they know can describe personality. Ask them to think of both positive and negative adjectives. They should also try to give an example of a person who has this personality trait – it could be a friend, a family member or someone well-known. Conduct feedback and write the adjectives in two columns on the board (headed *positive* and *negative*). As a student gives an adjective, add it to the correct column and ask the student, or another member of the group, to mention a person and a short description of the adjective. For example, *thoughtful – positive, my sister. My sister is very thoughtful. She always asks if she can help me with my homework.*

explore vocabulary 1

1 Write *happy* on the board, and elicit the noun *(happiness)*. Read through the explore vocabulary box with the class. Then students work in pairs to go through the box again and note whether the words are adjectives or nouns, and add an emoticon to show if they are positive, negative or neutral. With unfamiliar words, they can either check in a dictionary or join another pair to see if they can help each other. Conduct class feedback.

Adjectives: anti-social (negative/neutral), arrogant (negative), cheerful (positive), cooperative (positive), courageous (positive), courteous (positive), defensive (negative/neutral), demanding (negative), eccentric (neutral/negative), flamboyant (neutral), immature (negative), irresponsible (negative), possessive (negative), stubborn (negative/neutral), talkative (negative/neutral), thoughtful (positive)

Nouns: admiration, discipline, flexibility, honesty, loyalty, sympathy, willingness (all positive)

extra 

Ask students in pairs to make nouns where possible from the adjectives in the box and adjectives from the nouns.

Adjectives: admirable / disciplined / flexible / honest / loyal / sympathetic / willing

Nouns: arrogance / cooperation / courage / courtesy / defence / eccentricity / flamboyance / immaturity / irresponsibility / possessiveness (possession) / stubbornness / thoughtfulness

2 Read through the first description of behaviour and elicit that the adjective to describe William could be *thoughtful* or *cooperative*. Students complete the matching task in pairs. Check answers together.

1 cooperative/thoughtful **2** irresponsible **3** thoughtful **4** courteous

3 Students work in pairs to describe behaviour that illustrates another three words from the box. Circulate and give help where necessary. Conduct class feedback.

Possible answers

cheerful: Joe always has a smile on his face. He's funny and always finds the positive in any situation.

eccentric: Margaret always likes to be different, and sometimes says things which other people don't understand.

stubborn: Once Esther has made up her mind, she never changes it.

explore **vocabulary 2**

4 Write the words *have* and *keep* on the board. Say: *Let's have a look at some phrases with these words but we must keep an eye on the time.* Write *have a look* under *have* and *keep an eye on* under *keep*. Ask if students can remember any other phrases using the verbs and add if they are correct. Read through the explore vocabulary box and add the phrases to the board.

Read through the introduction to the text with the class and ask what qualities they think the text will mention. Students read to check their ideas. Ask students to read the text again and find phrases with *have* and *keep*. Check answers in full group and add to the list on the board.

have: serious doubts about, difficulty with, a lot in common with, a bad day

keep: a secret, their mouths shut, in touch with

5 Students complete the sentences in pairs and then ask and answer the questions with their partner. Circulate and note down interesting points. Conduct class feedback where the students share their ideas.

1 common **2** touch **3** tidy (clean, organised, in order) **4** difficulty (difficulties, a problem, problems, success, a hard time), secret/promise

Speak up

6 Students think about adjectives to describe their personality and then check with their partners to see if they agree with them. Conduct class feedback. If appropriate have a vote on who is the easiest person in the class to get on with.

Possible answers

I would describe myself as usually cheerful, cooperative and thoughtful. I can be stubborn, though, especially if someone wants me to do something that I don't like. I also have a sense of humour that's a little bit immature. I like playing silly jokes on people. But generally, I think I'm easy to get on with.

To finish

Students test each other on the words from the lesson with a fun spelling check. Give an example. Ask: *What's the third letter of 'admiration'?* (m) *What's the second to last letter of 'immature'?* (r). Give students some time to choose the words that they want to test their partner on and which letters they are going to ask for, then the test can be quick – the quicker the better! Find out which pair managed to get through the most words in two minutes.

Presentation tool:	Unit 8, Vocabulary
Workbook / Online Practice:	p81
Photocopiable activity:	8B
Audioscript:	SB p182
Extra Practice App	

LISTENING **SB p110**

To start

Ask students to discuss in pairs: *What is your favourite song? Why do you like it? Is it the music, the words or the singer?*

Nominate a few students to play their favourite song, if they have it on their phones. Ask the class to listen and say if they like it or not, and why.

Power up

1 Put students into small groups to discuss the words. Point out the pronunciation of *choir* /kwaɪə/ and *chords* /kɔːdz/.

Possible answers

I like music, and I can play piano and guitar. I can't read music very well, though, and I definitely can't compose it. The words that interest me most are *drummer*, *gig* and *lyrics*. I'd love to play the drums, but we don't have any drums in our house. I'd love to play in a band and do a small gig one day. Some of my friends play instruments, and maybe we should get together one day. And I like writing song lyrics. The only problem is that I can't write music, so I need someone to help me with that.

alternative

Check that students understand all the words in the box first. Go through each one and elicit the meaning.

accompaniment: piano or orchestra that plays together with a soloist such as a singer

choir: a group of people who sing together

chords: a group of notes that are played together at the same time, e.g. on the piano or guitar

drummer: person who plays the drums in a band

gig: an informal word for a live performance, not usually a classical concert

lyrics: the words to a song

percussion: instruments that are played by hitting, e.g. drums, tambourines, cymbals

youth orchestra: an orchestra made up of young people only, often developed through schools

2 Students can discuss the questions in the same groups. Take class feedback to discover the most common influence of music in the class.

Possible answers

I think music plays an important part in most people's lives, including mine. I'm a member of a choir, and when we get together to sing, it's an amazing feeling. Music has the power to bring people together, to make them feel happy or sad. It can also create powerful memories, too. Whenever I hear my favourite songs, I'm transported back to when I first heard them, even if it was many years ago.

LISTENING (Continued)

Listen up

3 8.3 **Before you play the recording, ask the class:** ***Does anyone play a musical instrument? Which one, and how did you choose it?*** **Tell them that they're going to listen to people talking in five separate situations. Play the recording through once and ask them to make a note of the musical activity each speaker is involved with.**

Speaker 1: a choir
Speaker 2: a drum circle
Speaker 3: songwriting
Speaker 4: a youth orchestra
Speaker 5: accompanying someone on piano and playing gigs

exam tip

Go through the exam tip. Remind students that each part of the listening paper is played twice, so students have two chances to hear the recording and to decide on their answers. This means that they don't have to worry about getting all the answers the first time. They should relax, listen the first time, establish the topic and the speakers and get any answers they can. Then the second time they can confirm their original ideas and get any answers they weren't sure of the first time.

Speaker 1 says something which is similar to G: *In my wildest dreams, I never thought I'd ever perform to an audience of millions!*

However, the answer is C: *They became like a second family to me and since then, I've never looked back! The choir had belief in me as a singer.*

exam task: multiple matching

4 e 8.4 **Play the recording and ask students to listen and match the speakers with A–H. They check their answers in pairs. If necessary, play the recording again for them to confirm their answers.**

1 C (*They became like a second family to me and since then, I've never looked back! The choir had belief in me as a singer*)
2 H (*There's nothing like bashing away at a drum to get rid of all your worries!*)
3 A (*a friend taught me how to play a few simple chords on the guitar. Even though I'll never be really good at it, at least I was able to play along to the words I wrote.*)
4 F (*Having friends from different cultures through a love for music really makes you appreciate and understand different lifestyles.*)
5 E (*but I was also supporting someone else rather than appearing solo in public.... That I find rather stressful!*)

5 **Explain that all the words come from the recording. After students have discussed the meanings, either play the recording again or allow them to look at the Audioscript on page 182 to read the expressions in context.**

1 had confidence that I could do well
2 obligatory, something everyone has to do without a choice
3 removes something unpleasant that isn't wanted
4 places where public events happen
5 very exciting, thrilling
6 recognise the value of something or somebody
7 two people who sing or perform together

Speak up

6 **Tell students that the first question refers back to the people they heard in the listening. They discuss their ideas in pairs. Conduct class feedback. Then discuss questions 2 and 3 as a whole class.**

Possible answers

1 I found Speaker 5's story most interesting. I'd like to find someone I can create music with, and one of my dreams is to play gigs somewhere, one day.
2 You can compare yourself with others. It can make you competitive, and can give you something to aspire to. When you see what others can achieve it can be inspiring. It's often more fun and fulfilling to do things with other people.
3 It allows you to think carefully about what you want for yourself, and you can relax. It can put things into perspective, and can remove pressure.

Fun footer

Focus students' attention on the footer and elicit the meaning of the quote. (A good friend is someone who helps me become a better person.) Ask: ***Do you agree with this quote?*** **Elicit answers and encourage students to give reasons.**

To finish

Ask students to look back at the words in bold in Ex 5. In pairs they should write their own sentences using three of the words. Each pair should exchange their sentences with another pair, who should read them and correct any mistakes. Consider asking students to read the Grammar file about linking phrases on p156 in preparation for the Use of English 1 lesson.

Presentation tool:	Unit 8, Listening
Workbook / Online Practice:	p82
Audioscript:	SB p182
Extra Practice App	

USE OF ENGLISH 1 SB p111

To start

Ask students: *Have you heard of the concept of team-building activities? What do they think they are? Who might do them?*

They're activities which involve teamwork or shared experiences that bring people together and create a bonding atmosphere. They are often done in companies to create a sense of a team among employees, or sports teams. They can also be done at the start of a new term in some schools.

1 Ask students to look at the photograph and discuss the team-building activities that might happen there. Ask: *Would you like to do them? Why/Why not? What do you think an Escape room is?*

Possible answers

Escape rooms are places where people go and play in teams. They are set a series of puzzles which they have to work out in a specific time in order to unlock a door and move into the next room and do the next challenge. There are often different genres of Escape room, for example, horror, ancient history, etc.

2 Tell students that they are going to read a text about Escape rooms. They should read it quickly to see if their own ideas about Escape rooms were right or wrong. Ask: *What do you think of Escape rooms?*

explore grammar

➥ SB p156

3 Remind students of the importance of linking words when they are writing, because they make a text easy to follow and allow them to express complex ideas more clearly. Elicit some linking words or phrases that students often use, e.g. *although, on the other hand,* etc. Ask them to read parts A, B and C in the explore grammar box, and think of one more example for each linking phrase.

Go through part D with the class, because of the complication of the inversion of the subject and verb in the first part of the sentence. Ask them to suggest other examples of *not only … but also* by reading out the following sentences and eliciting a single sentence.

- *I was wet. I was cold.* (Not only was I wet, I was also cold.)
- *It was raining. It was windy.* (Not only was it raining, it was also windy.)

Ask students to go through the text again and to choose the correct options. Conduct class feedback.

1 were we **2** also had **3** being **4** that he didn't say

Tell students to read the Grammar reference on page 156, if they have not already done so, and to do Exs 3–5 on page 157 for homework.

4 Check whether there were any words in the text that students didn't know. Then check that they understand the words in bold. Elicit students' feelings about being in an Escape room.

Possible answers

creepy = rather strange, something that makes you feel frightened

freaked out = it's a phrasal verb = frightened, scared

miracle = something unexpectedly good that happens

I would love it. It must be very exciting to be locked in a room and have to solve puzzles within a time limit. I wouldn't like to do it alone, but I imagine it's an amazing thing to do with friends.

exam task: key word transformations

A majority of the items tested here are related to *in spite of* and *not only but*, as this is the focus of the lesson.

5 **e** Remind students that in the exam they have to complete a sentence so that it means the same as another sentence using a key word. Highlight that students should not write more than five words, include unnecessary details, or change the key word. They should think carefully about the real meaning of the first sentence so that they can identify what needs changing in the second. Ask students to read questions 1–6 and underline the parts to include in the answer. Do the first question with the whole class. Then ask them to work in pairs to complete the rest of the exercise. Point out that there may be one or two possible answers, but that if they write more than five words then they have got the wrong answer.

1 should have taken (matches *It's a pity you didn't*)
2 in spite of the bad (matches *even though the weather was bad*)
3 ought to have been told (matches *No one had told*)
4 only did Maria learn (matches *Maria learnt … and also …*)
5 didn't need to ask/had no need to ask (matches *it wasn't necessary to ask*)
6 despite not liking group activities (matches *Although he didn't like group activities*)

To finish

Ask students to discuss the following questions in small groups: *Would you like to take part in an activity like the Escape room? Why/Why not? How do you think you would react to it? What would you learn about yourself?* Conduct class feedback.

alternative

Alternatively, if some students have experienced an Escape room, discuss the above questions as a whole class, and then elicit some additional comments from those students about what it was really like and what they actually learnt about themselves.

Presentation tool:	Unit 8, Use of English 1
Workbook / Online Practice:	p83
Grammar reference and practice:	SB p156
Extra Practice App	

USE OF ENGLISH 2 SB p112

To start

Ask students: *What kinds of things affect your mood? What do you do to put yourselves in a good mood? Do you always do the same thing?*

1 8.5 Play the recording of a presenter introducing the topic of his programme. Ask: What is it about? Give students time to discuss their ideas after they've listened.

His own experience of feeling low, and how to get over negative feelings.

explore **vocabulary 1**

2 8.6 Go through the explore vocabulary 1 box. Read out the following words and ask students to decide which phrasal verb in the box has a similar meaning.

- *spend time with friends* (hang out)
- *continue* (carry on)
- *recover from something* (get over)
- *support someone or something* (stand up for)
- *respect someone* (look up to)

Play the recording. Students should tick the phrasal verbs from the explore vocabulary box that the presenter uses. Then they match five phrasal verbs with meanings 1–5.

two-part verbs: clear up, come across, fill in, hang out, speak up
three-part verbs: put up with, reach out to, stand up for, take up with
1 hang out **2** put up with **3** fill in **4** reach out to **5** speak up
Remaining verbs:
carry on = continue doing something
clear up = explain something or make it easier to understand
come across = find or discover something
get along (with somebody) = have a good relationship with somebody
get over = succeed in communicating ideas to somebody
put somebody off = make you dislike something or not want to do something
look up to = admire somebody
stand up for = support or defend somebody or something
take up with = start spending time with (someone)

3 Tell students that using phrasal verbs makes their speaking more natural and informal. Put them into groups to discuss the questions, and encourage them to use phrasal verbs if possible. Monitor and help with phrasal verbs if necessary.

Possible answers
1. When someone accuses you of doing something you didn't do, then you need to stand up for yourself, and defend your version of events.
2. I get along with most people, but I mostly get on with people who have similar musical tastes to me.
3. I'm not willing to put up with people who lie or cheat, or hurt other people to get what they want.

explore **vocabulary 2**

4 8.7 Remind students that they have already done work with collocations and prepositions. Explain to students that its useful to learn collocations because using them will help their speaking and writing seem more natural. Also, collocations are often tested in the Reading and Use of English paper Part 1.

Go through the explore vocabulary 2 box. Then ask them to do Ex 4 in pairs. Play the recording so they can check their answers. When you conduct class feedback, ask students to read the whole phrase so that they hear it again. This will help them to remember it.

1 E **2** D **3** H **4** C **5** A **6** G **7** B **8** F

5 8.8 Play the recording and ask students to complete the exercise. They should check their ideas in pairs. Then take a vote in the class for the best advice. Ask students to explain the reasons for their vote.

a) Don't complain too much. Try to move on.
b) Don't set yourself huge goals that are difficult or impossible to achieve.
c) Don't spend too much time in front of your computer. Get outside and join in activities.

exam task: multiple-choice cloze

6 **e** Tell students to read the text quickly to find what advice is being offered. They then read the text again and complete the task.

1. C (*pay attention to* is a collocation)
2. A (*put up with* is a phrasal verb which means 'accept')
3. D (*have a negative effect on* is a collocational phrase)
4. A (*there's no point in continually comparing* is a set phrase)
5. B (*stand up for* is a phrasal verb
6. D (*set yourself … goals* is a collocation)
7. C (*bear in mind* is a collocation)
8. A (*don't waste any more time* is a set phrase)

extra

Tell students that there are seven main pieces of advice in the text. Elicit what they are.

1 *Surround yourself with positive people.*
2 *Don't have friends with negative outlooks.*
3 *Don't compare yourself to others.*
4 *Value yourself for your own uniqueness.*
5 *Set realistic goals.*
6 *Remember other people need you as much as you need them.*
7 *Concentrate on the good things in life not the bad things.*

Then ask: *Which of these pieces of advice do you think is the best? Which do you think most people would find it difficult to follow?*

Speak up

7 Students could discuss these questions in pairs. If any students feel uncomfortable talking about their own feelings, don't conduct full class feedback.

Possible answers

1 Listening to music or doing some exercise are good ways to get out of a bad mood. Maybe the best way is to try and talk to somebody about your feelings. This often makes things better.

2 I wouldn't believe somebody who said they never experience bad moods. It's part of life. Bad things do happen, and it's important that we are aware of them, and can try to deal with them.

Fun footer

Focus students' attention on the proverb. Elicit its meaning. Ask students: *Do you have similar expressions in your own language? Which piece of advice from the text you've just read goes with the proverb?*

It means that even if times are bad, there's always something positive to be found.

The advice it matches is to concentrate on the good things in life rather than the bad things.

To finish

Ask students to work in pairs. Each student writes down three sentences which contain some bad news. Students read their sentences to their partner, who has to respond with a 'silver lining' (in other words, something positive about the situation). To help them, give this example:

A: I've just lost my mobile phone.

B: Great! Now no-one can disturb you in the evening.

Presentation tool:	Unit 8, Use of English 2
Workbook / Online Practice:	p84
Photocopiable activity:	8C
Audioscript:	SB p182
Extra Practice App	

SPEAKING SB p113

To start

Ask students: *What kind of things inspire and motivate you?* Give an example of something that inspires you personally, for example, *I find people who achieve challenging things like climbing a mountain very inspiring although it would scare me!* Put them into small groups to discuss their ideas, and to suggest any people they find inspiring. Take class feedback and see if they can all agree on one thing they would all be inspired by, and one person they would all find inspiring.

Power up

1 Ask students to read the information on page 171. In pairs they should discuss how the stories compare with their own ideas of inspiring people they discussed at the start of the lesson. Ask: *Have you heard any other stories of similar young people? Who would you find most inspiring?*

Possible answers

Of all the people here, I find Valentina (Student E) most inspiring. She was the person who had to overcome the most serious difficulties, and still managed to achieve her goals. It would be good to hear her talking about how to keep going, and to fight for what you want in life.

useful **language:** taking turns; creating time; changing your mind / backtracking

2 8.9 Go though the useful language box. Play the recording. Once students have ticked the phrases they have heard, ask: *How did the two students keep the conversation going?* Explain that these are good techniques to use in the exam, and in any situation where you have to interact with someone for any length of time.

1 The students ask each other questions as well as checking for agreement/disagreement to move the discussion forward. Neither student is passive or dominant.

2 Phrases used:
Shall we start with … ?
What do you think?
How about … ?
Let's talk about …
I'm not quite sure …

Speak up

3 Tell students that they are going to do an exam task. Put students into groups of three. Two students should do the task and the third should listen and make a note of any useful phrases the two students use. Stop them after two minutes and move the students round so that the third student becomes one of the pair and another student listens. Stop them again after two minutes and move the students round again so that they have all had a turn at listening. After two minutes ask them to compare their notes and to share any useful expressions they used.

SPEAKING (Continued)

Possible answers

a well-known YouTuber: this person might talk about how easy it is to make the videos, how much money they make, what kind of people watch them

a local business person: this person might talk about local opportunities, local man-made goods, how to find work

a young explorer: this person might talk about any difficult situations they've faced, why they like to explore, any dangerous or exciting moments they have experienced

a successful writer: this person might talk about how they got started, any difficulties they faced, whether they ever get stuck for ideas

a charity worker: this person might talk about difficulties they face, the rewards of the job, how they started, why they do it

exam task: **collaborative task** ➥ SB p164

4 e Go through the exam tip with students. Tell them that they can ask one another for help in this part, and should talk around any vocabulary they are not sure of or can't think of. Refer them to the useful language box and ask which phrases would be useful to ask for help or talk round vocabulary.

What do you think?

It's quite difficult to decide …

I'm not quite sure …

Read out the question: *Which two speakers would be most interesting for students to listen to?* Students should then discuss the question in pairs. Give them a one-minute time limit.

Remind students of the importance of keeping their conversation going. Remind them that one of the things they are marked on is interactive communication, and that the more they interact with each other the better they will do in the Speaking test. Remind students that they don't have to reach a decision in this part of the Speaking test, as there is no right answer, although it's good if they can. Give students feedback on how well they took turns, and agreed and disagreed with each other.

Possible answers

A: It's quite difficult to decide which people to choose. What do you think?

B: Well, the YouTuber is probably interesting to talk to, and the local business person. Both of these people could talk about how you can make money.

A: Yes, you're right. I'm not quite sure about the local business person, though. He or she might not be successful in what they do.

B: Yes, maybe that choice wasn't the best one. OK, I've changed my mind. How about the well-known YouTuber and the successful writer?

A: OK, so both of these people have been successful.

B: That's right, and I think that would make them more interesting to listen to.

A: I agree. OK, let's go for those two, then.

Speaking extra

5 Ask students to work in groups to discuss the questions. Conduct class feedback. Nominate a few students to tell the class what qualities they discussed in question three. Write them on the board and ask the class: *Do you agree that these are attractive qualities?*

Possible answers

1 I would like to invite some older people, who have interesting stories to tell, and maybe had a harder life when they were young. It's sometimes good to hear how people overcame difficulties in life, or to realise that other people had a harder time than you.

2 I look up to sports stars, or any athlete who works hard. It takes a lot of discipline and self-sacrifice to be successful in sport.

3 Possible qualities include: a good sense of humour, modesty, honesty, determination, discipline, a lack of selfishness.

To finish

Put students into pairs and ask them to tell each other about a particular individual they find inspiring and why. If there is time, you could conduct class feedback and see if students have thought of the same person.

Presentation tool:	Unit 8, Speaking
Workbook / Online Practice:	p85
Speaking file:	SB p164
Audioscript:	SB p182

WRITING SB pp114–115

To start

Ask students to make a quick note of all the good things about their school. Elicit ideas and write them on the board. Ask: *Is there anything you would like to change?* Tell them that they're going to think about ways in which a school could improve its extra-curricular programme.

Power up

1 In groups, students make a note of any activities already available at their school, and whether they are optional or compulsory. If necessary, explain *optional* (there is a choice as to whether these activities can be done or not) and *compulsory* (these activities must be done).

Possible answers

Activities could include: sports lessons, like swimming or football, music lessons, dance lessons, extra language lessons.

Extra-curricular activities should probably remain optional, so students can focus on what interests them most, or what they think they would like to develop more.

2 Ask students to consider the list of possible activities for a school. They should choose three and think of reasons for their choices. Conduct class feedback and write their choices on the board. The class should vote for the three most popular activities.

Possible answers

I would choose martial arts because that's something I'd like to do. I think it's useful to learn a form of self-defence because it gives you confidence.

I'd also like to have some kind of music activities, like a band or a choir. I like music, but performing it with other people is so much better than doing it alone.

A school radio station would be a good idea, too. I'd like to work in the media in the future, and this would give me lots of useful experience.

Plan on

3 Students read the task and answer the questions.

Possible answers

1–2 Suggestions Kevin makes include: a quiz club (which would test people's brains), a radio station (which would be a lot of fun, and enable students to conduct interviews or organise talent shows) and a manga magazine (which would also be fun, and enable students to build up a comics library).

3 The radio station and the magazine seem like the most interesting ideas, because they would help students develop skills like organising things, and working together. The quiz club is a nice idea for a fun event, but doesn't sound like an activity that students could do regularly.

explore **language**

4 Go through the language box before asking students to do Ex 4 in pairs. Remind them of the importance of checking their writing for accuracy. Tell them that using different phrases like *Why don't we* or *How about …* is also a good way of widening the range of language they use to make suggestions in their writing. Point out that Kevin's email only needs to be semi-formal as it is to one of his peers, but it should still follow the conventions of an email and be well-organised.

Why don't we create a quiz club? (My friends like to test their brains a bit – or at least to show they know more than other people! Quizzes are really popular.)

How about setting up a school radio station? (It must be such fun to do and lots of students would have the opportunity to contribute.)

It might be an idea to create our own manga magazine. (I think lots of students would go for that. We could also build up a manga comics library, which would be great)

5 Remind students of the ideas they discussed in Ex 2. Go round and monitor their discussions and check the ideas they are writing down. Tell them that they can use these notes when they write their own answer to the task.

Possible answers

Why don't we start a tennis club? It would be a new sport that everyone could learn.

What about organising an English-language film club? It would be a fun way to practise English.

It might be an idea to create a website or blog that everyone can contribute to. We could use it to communicate with each other, and write articles that people find interesting.

explore **grammar** ➥ SB p156

6 Students read through the explore grammar box, and complete the sentences in pairs.

1 so little **2** so few **3** so many **4** such a lot **5** so

Write on

7 Students read the task. Ask: *How many things do you have to do?* Point out that they have only been asked to suggest places for the school trips, but they must always give reasons for their suggestions. Tell them to think of three ideas in the same way as Kevin had three ideas in his email in Ex 3.

WRITING (Continued)

8 **Remind students of the importance of planning an email. This is as important as planning an essay, as the email must be logical and coherent. To help them with this ask them to complete the plan. Suggest that they use this as a model for all the emails or letters of this kind that they write.**

Possible answers
Greeting: *Dear Tom …*
Introductory paragraph: *I was really interested to read your notice …*
Idea 1: *Why don't we consider some museum trips?*
Idea 2: *It might be an idea to visit the national park.*
Idea 3: *We could also organise visits to local farms.*
Concluding paragraph: *The main idea would be to learn about the history of our area, its environment and community.*
Appropriate sign-off: *I hope these ideas are useful. All the best, …*

9 **Point out to students that the checklist can be used both as a reminder before they start writing and as a checklist after they've finished.**

exam task: **email / letter (semi-formal)**
➥ SB p167

10 **e** **Go through the exam tip, and make sure that students understand the difference between the very informal expressions and those that would be appropriate in this kind of email. Make the additional point that they should not include irrelevant information in any writing task.**

Appropriate starting expressions: Dear …
Inappropriate starting expressions: Hi!, Hello!
Appropriate finishing expressions: Best wishes, All the best, Regards
Inappropriate finishing expressions: Cheers!, Love, Lots of love, Bye!

Set students a time limit of 30 minutes for writing their email. This will help them get used to the time constraints of the exam.

Model answer
Dear Tom,
I was interested to read your notice, asking for suggestions for school trips. I would like to share some ideas with you here, as so few students are aware of the area that they live in.
First of all, why don't we consider some museum trips? There are some excellent museums nearby which teach people about the history of the area. Many of them are interactive, and give a good insight into how people lived in the past.
It might also be an idea to visit the national park, which is just a few hours away. There are many mountains, lakes and forests to explore. Not only would this give us a chance to be outdoors, but it would also enable us to learn skills such as map reading.
We could also organise visits to farms. There are many nearby and we could use the opportunity to understand where our food comes from and that such a lot of work goes into creating it.
The main idea would be to learn about the history of our area and its environment, and to teach students valuable new skills. I hope these ideas are useful.
All the best, …

Improve it

11 **Students exchange their emails and go though the checklist, in order to give each other feedback. This is a very good way of helping them to develop the habit of editing their work. Remind them that in the exam they won't have time to write several versions, so it's good to develop this habit early so that they can edit and check as they write.**

12 **Students can make final corrections to their writing for homework. After they have handed in their final versions to you, and you have checked it, give feedback on the style of language they have used, and identify any inappropriate language. Remind students that this type of email should also be well-organised and paragraphed clearly, so give feedback on this aspect of their writing.**

Fun footer

Nominate a student to read out the joke. Elicit what the joke means.

Ask: ***Is it always important to get to the point when discussing something with another person? When might it not be a good idea to get to the point quickly?***

It's a play on words – a pencil has a point because you sharpen it to write with it. When you sharpen it the pencil goes round and round in circles in the sharpener until it has a sharp point. When you 'get to the point' in a piece of writing or speaking, you explain the most important thing you want to say, and you don't avoid the main issue.

To finish

Put students into pairs and ask them to explain their suggestions for school trips to each other. Take feedback from the students and write their ideas on the board. The class can vote for what they think would make the most interesting trip.

Presentation tool:	Unit 8, Writing
Workbook / Online Practice:	p86
Writing file:	SB p167

SWITCH ON SB p116

Recycle rush

1 Start by asking: *When do people need to work as a team to get the best results?* Ask for examples (e.g. at school, for project work, in sport, in management, etc.). Put students into small groups to think about different types of teams. This could be a team of sports people (e.g. footballers, a swimming relay team), a team of actors in a play, etc. Read through what they need to consider and give the groups a few minutes to come up with some ideas. Circulate and give help and comments where necessary. Share the ideas in full group. Extend by asking: *In general, do you like to work in teams or individually? Do you prefer to be a leader or to be led? Why?*

Possible answers

An example of a good team is the Real Madrid football team. They have a solid mix of strong players in different roles and effective management that has helped them win several international championships. An example of a bad team is in the film *The Mighty Ducks*. At the start of the film, they are very disorganised, but the raw talent is there. With management and confidence, they learn to work together effectively in roles that play to their strengths and go on to become a good team.

2 Tell students that they are going to watch a clip about a special type of teamwork. Play the video clip all the way through to answer the question.

A robot that can pick up and stack plastic containers.

background

This is an annual competition. Student teams come from all over the world. They have six weeks to design and build the robot. They have to build it from parts that they are given. On the top of the stack must be a recycling container. The winner is the team whose robot can stack the highest pile of containers in the time given.

3 Play the clip again for students to answer the questions. You might need to play the clip several times. Stronger groups will probably need to watch it once again. After students have compared notes take feedback in full group. Play the relevant section of the recording to check answers.

Possible answers

They had to design the robot, build it and create a business plan.

They had to apply science, maths, engineering and technology to make real robots.

4 In pairs, students discuss how the students felt while participating in the challenge. If necessary play the clip again. Circulate and prompt where necessary. Conduct class feedback.

Possible answers

The students were excited to be there. Some students were proud to represent their country and excited to play in big teams. Students felt proud to have achieved enough to get as far as the competition. Students enjoyed the challenge as well as using science, technology, engineering and maths in more interesting ways than usual. Students felt that using these skills could be just as much fun as sports. Students were amazed when they won. One team leader was especially proud that they were building robots as complicated as machines for space.

5 In groups, students discuss how this challenge or similar challenges might inspire students to do something with their lives.

Possible answers

It could develop people's interest in science, maths and technology. It shows young people in interesting jobs that give them goals to work towards. It could inspire groups of friends to take on creative projects together. It shows that people like me can be at the forefront of technology and engineering.

Project

6 Put students into small groups. Explain the project. They have to design and promote a robot that will perform a useful daily function.

Read through the stages of the project and clarify where necessary. First, they should discuss possible robots to design in their groups in class and choose one. The roles can be given by a chosen group leader or by volunteering. Each person has a specific role but the team should work together. For example, one student may have creative skills to plan specifically what the robot could do, another could use computer design skills to create the design, another could have ideas about how to pitch persuasively and write the pitch, another could have presenting skills and present to the class. Several students could contribute to the stages but one student would have the responsibility for each one. The development of the robot design will need to be organised by the team leader to be done outside class. Allow students time at the end of lessons to consult on the progress and contribute to the final pitch.

Groups take turns to present their pitches to the class (remembering to include all the points mentioned in the task). This could be done in full group or in team groups, with the 'pitchers' going from group to group to deliver their presentations.

The class votes on the best sales pitch and gives reasons.

extra

1 Students explore the latest developments in robot technology. They research current robots and pick one which catches their interest. They should then present it to the class and explain their reasons for choosing it.
2 Students explore the negative aspects of automation/artificial intelligence: *How will our world change for the worse if automation is taken to its logical conclusion?* They should prepare a presentation. They can refer to sci-fi films and literature to illustrate their points, but should let their imaginations run!

You could ask students to complete (and reflect on) the independent learning questions for homework in preparation for the next lesson. Then use the class time for students to discuss their ideas.

Presentation tool: Unit 8, Switch on
Switch on videoscript: TB p174

INDEPENDENT LEARNING SB p116

Listening and speaking

Take a few moments at the beginning of this section to ask students to look back at the previous Independent learning section and say if they have done what they had planned. Ask for details in full group.

1 Give students some time individually to refer back to the speaking sections of the unit, and consider how their performance in this unit compared to their performances in previous units. Ask: *How far have you progressed?* They should indicate their perceived progress on a scale of 1–5 in the different skills listed.

2 Students work in pairs to compare their self-ratings and discuss ways of scoring more highly next time.

3 Students complete the sentences about their speaking skills individually. Remind them to keep these to refer to when they reach the end of the book, to see their development.

4 Give students time to reflect on their attitude to listening tasks and their assessment of their own listening skills. If appropriate they should discuss their thoughts with a partner.

5 In pairs, students look at the list of ways to improve their listening skills over the next few weeks. They should add any more suggestions to the list. They should choose one or more things that they are going to do. In the next Independent learning section give students the opportunity to look back at their decisions and say if they have done what they had planned.

Finish by asking students what they remember most from this unit, and whether they have learned any interesting facts or been encouraged to think about interesting ideas that they hadn't considered before. Check if students have used any of the new vocabulary items that they learned in the unit and if so, in which contexts.

UNIT CHECK SB p117

This Unit check covers vocabulary related to personality, phrases with *have* and *keep*, and modals.

Practice

Possible answers

1 2 8.10 and 8.11 **1** cheerful **2** stubborn **3** courageous **4** immature **5** eccentric **6** possessive

3 **1** look **2** speak **3** have **4** got **5** keep

4 **1** C **2** A **3** C **4** B **5** C **6** B

Review

1 **1** can't **2** don't have to hand **3** shouldn't **4** ought **5** weren't **6** needn't have gone

2 8.12 **1** being **2** do they have, they also have **3** a lot of **4** of having

3 **1** such good **2** so interesting **3** such an **4** so few

4 **1** have/need/ought **2** have **3** regret **4** Unless **5** able **6** only **7** should/might/would/could **8** be

5 **1** have missed **2** need to **3** must have **4** should have been **5** can't have **6** it was

6 I missed my train this morning. I should have woken up earlier, but unfortunately I didn't. I got to the station just as the train was leaving. I could have gone home and done nothing all day, but I had an important exam at school, so I had to find another way.

I quickly called a friend of mine, who was already in school. I asked him if his father could come and pick me up and drive me to school. Luckily, it was possible, and I arrived at school just in time for the exam.

I really ought to thank my friend, and his father. I should do something special for them, but I haven't decided what yet.

GRAMMAR FILE SB p157

1 **1** C **2** F **3** A **4** G **5** D **6** B **7** E

2 **1** must have been **2** had to **3** ought to have **4** needn't have done **5** can't have been **6** shouldn't have been **7** will **8** needs

3 **1** not being **2** in spite of **3** were they **4** her lack of **5** she got **6** having **7** not having

4 **1** fact **2** did **3** being **4** had **5** having

5 **1** does Vicki have
2 of having so
3 must have been happy
4 be finished
5 not to have said

Presentation tool:	Unit 8, Unit check
Workbook / Online Practice:	p87
Audioscript:	SB p182

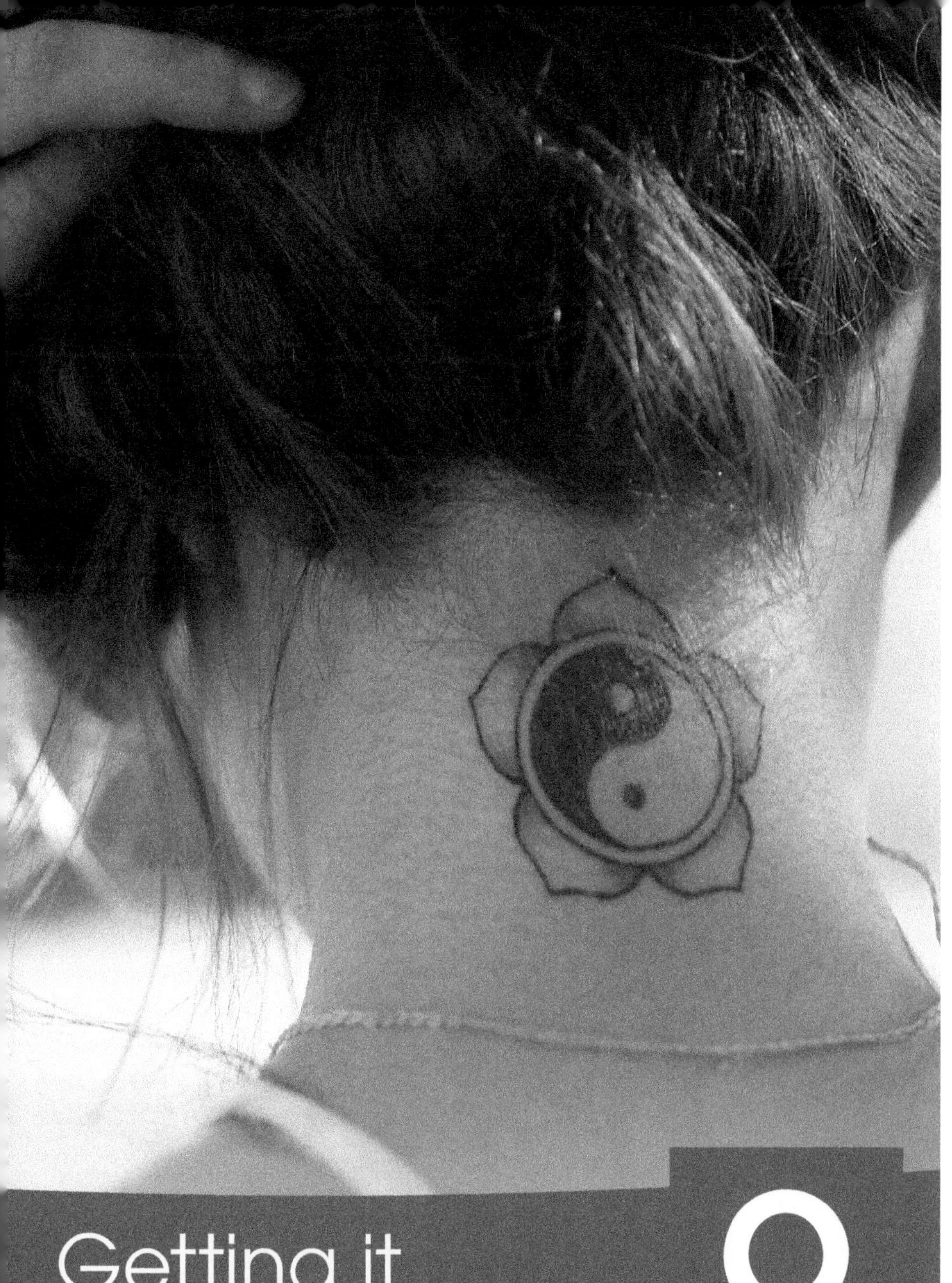

Getting it right 9

READING
topic: decision making
skill: understanding text structure
task: gapped text

GRAMMAR
relative clauses
cleft sentences

VOCABULARY
knowing, thinking and deciding
fixed phrases
word formation
collocations, nouns to adjectives

LISTENING
topic: when others decide for you
skill: recognising distractors
task: multiple choice

USE OF ENGLISH
open cloze
word formation

SPEAKING
topic: shopping
skill: talking about preferences
task: long turn

WRITING
topic: influences
skill: avoiding repetition
task: essay

SWITCH ON
videos: does smell sell?
project: create a social media campaign

Lead-in SB p119

Tell students about all the small decisions you have had to make so far today. For example, *This morning so far I've had to make a lot of decisions! I had to decide what to wear, whether to have tea or coffee, if I should take the car or walk,* etc.

Put students into pairs to find how many different decisions they have made between them. Conduct class feedback to find which pair made the most decisions or which student had the most difficult decision to make.

Refer students to the photograph and the quote. Ask them what the link is between the two. Elicit that having a tattoo is something that cannot easily be reversed, so people need to think a lot about making this decision. Ask: *What would people need to consider before making this decision?* Point out that we can say: *A decision can't be undone* as a fixed phrases. However, we cannot say *I need to undo this decision.*

Put students into pairs to discuss questions 1–3. Circulate and encourage and note down ideas. Conduct class feedback and elicit a range of decisions students have had to make recently. Ask: *Which was the most important? Which decisions did you get right?*

Possible answers

1 One thing that I've had to decide recently is what I'm going to study at college. This is such a big decision, because I know it will affect the next three or four years. It might even affect the rest of my life.

2 I trust my friends to make decisions about what films to go and see, or which cafés to go to, because we have similar tastes, and these are things that we do as a group. But I wouldn't let them decide what time I go home or what to wear, for example!

3 I'm usually quite good at making quick decisions when it only concerns myself. But I'm very bad at making decisions when they affect other people. I guess it's because I know that it can be a big responsibility when other people are involved.

READING SB pp120–121

To start

In pairs students play a game. One student should start by giving the other student a choice of two things, e.g. *Cat or dog?* The other student then has to choose one of the options very quickly: *dog*! That student then gives another choice for his or her partner, e.g. *Chocolate or crisps?*

The important aspect of this game is speed, and not to allow too much thinking time. Give an example to start and then students play the game. Conduct class feedback and find out which were the funniest or strangest choices they were given. Ask: *Are you good at making snap decisions?*

Power up

1 Refer students to the photos. Elicit what sort of decisions the people have made or are about to make.

Possible answers

The photo at the bottom of page 120 shows someone looking at a map of New York. The person might be trying to decide how to get somewhere, or where to go next.

The photo at the top of page 121 shows two people in a café. They are probably looking at a menu and deciding what type of coffee to order.

The photo at the bottom of page 121 shows two people in a sports shop, looking at a range of trainers. They are probably trying to decide which ones to buy or try on.

2 Students discuss the questions in pairs. Conduct class feedback and allow students to compare ideas.

Possible answers

Decisions involving other people are usually harder than decisions which only affect yourself.

Also, some decisions have long-lasting effects, such as deciding whether or not to accept a job, whether or not to go to university, or whether or not to get married.

extra

Write on the board:

- *choosing a holiday*
- *choosing how to celebrate a birthday*
- *choosing a career*
- *choosing how to redecorate your room*
- *choosing which smartphone to buy*
- *choosing the name of a baby*

Put students into small groups to discuss this question: *Here are some things we sometimes need to make decisions about. What do we need to consider when making these decisions?* Give students several minutes to discuss the items. Conduct class feedback and compare students' ideas.

Read on

3 Refer students to the title of the article, *Think twice!* and ask what they think it means. Give students two minutes to read the article quickly to find out. Conduct class feedback and ask: *Why should we think twice before making decisions?*

Possible answers

You should consider things carefully, take time to consider the consequences of something and not make quick decisions. If we don't think twice, we might make the wrong decision or react emotionally to something which we later regret.

exam task: gapped text

The gapped reading task in the Cambridge exam only has one gapped sentence per paragraph.

4 **e** Ask students what they need to remember when approaching a gapped text task. Elicit that they need to look for reference words and phrases, and linking words. They should also read the text first to get an overall understanding of the text. Moreover, they should read both before and after each gap carefully. Read through sentences A–G and ask students to speculate on what might have come before or after each sentence. For example, with sentence A, the following sentence might be a reaction to the received text message.

1 F (*While a child makes around 3,000 decisions a day, as you get older, you make an estimated 35,000. More than two hundred of those involve decisions that are about food.*)
2 C (*Do you know that Mark Zuckerberg, who is the founder of Facebook, always wears the same grey T-shirt? Why? Well, it means he can concentrate on important decisions and not spend ages deciding what to wear. That's a great tip from someone who, faced with huge decisions every day, can't afford to waste time.*)
3 A (*Picture this. You've just had a text from a friend that has upset you. Having thought of a reply and typed it in to your phone, you have your finger poised on the send button.*)
4 G (*You've acted without thinking it through and for a split second it feels good. However, not long afterwards the doubt creeps in. You soon realise that you've been a bit harsh and caused more upset than you really wanted to … for yourself and others.*)
5 B (*Were you influenced by a friend whose advice was short-sighted or just wrong? If that was so, learn to value your own opinion more.*)
6 E (*If you don't feel anything then beware! That could be a warning that you aren't making the correct decision.*)

extra: fast finishers

Ask fast finishers to write another distractor sentence that does **not** fit in any of the gaps. They should think about the references they could put in which would be wrong for the context. During feedback, students can say why these sentences would not fit.

exam tip

5 Read through the exam tip and remind students to always check their answers when they have filled all the gaps. Point out that they need to make sure that the text makes sense with the added sentences. Students complete the whole task individually. Elicit the answer.

D The sentence refers to children only. Although *a child* is mentioned at the beginning of the sentence before gap 1, the sentence is actually talking about decisions you make as you get older.

6 In pairs students find the words in the text. Conduct class feedback.

1 skip **2** get crammed **3** filter **4** founder **5** poised
6 a split second **7** short-sighted **8** beware

extra

To practise the words further, ask students to name:

- *something that can get crammed* (e.g. a suitcase)
- *something we can use a filter for* (e.g. cleaning water)
- *the founder of a famous organisation or company* (e.g. Mark Zuckerberg)
- *something your parents are poised to do at the moment* (e.g. buy a new car)
- *something you've done in a split second in the last five minutes* (e.g. turn a page)
- *a decision you've made recently that was short-sighted* (e.g. bought chocolate when you are on a diet)
- *a sign you've seen saying 'beware'* (e.g. for a garden with a dangerous dog)

Sum up

7 Students cover the text and try to remember the main tips, giving their opinion of the tips – with pros and cons, and saying which tips could work for them and why. This can be done in full group or in pairs.

1 Filter decisions, focus on what's important.
2 Don't act without thinking, especially when you're emotional.
3 Take time to consider the consequences.
4 Value your own judgement.
5 Think about how you feel when you make a decision.
6 Don't make a decision on an empty stomach.

Speak up

8 Put students into small groups and explain the task. Elicit some examples of decisions that were wrong, and advice that could be given. Monitor and give help where necessary.

Possible answers

An example situation could be that someone has broken up with a friend and now they regret it. They might have done this because the friend said something wrong behind the person's back.

Possible advice could be to talk through the problem with the friend, and try to reach some kind of agreement.

9 Students roleplay the situation they discussed in Ex 7. One student explains the decision and the other student(s) give sympathy and advice. Elicit some useful phrases for sympathising and giving advice. For example:

Oh no! That's terrible.
Why don't you … ?
You could always …
I think you ought to …
Have you thought about … ?
That's a great idea …
I don't think that would go down well.

Get students to film their roleplays on their mobile phones (you may wish to set this as a homework task so that students can add more detail). Play students' films on the IWB and elicit feedback and discussion from the rest of the class.

To finish

In pairs, students tell each other five decisions they have made for the future. Two should be false. Their partners have to guess which are true and which are false. Start by giving an example: *I've decided to dye my hair blonde. True or false?*

Fun Footer

Nominate a student to read the footer. Ask: *Are you usually decisive? Do you think it's good to be decisive?*

In preparation for the Grammar lesson, you could ask students to complete Ex 1 on page 122, read the Grammar reference on relative clauses on page 158 and complete Grammar practice Exs 1–4 on page 159. Encourage them to note down any questions they want to ask. Check the answers in class after the 'To start' activity.

Presentation tool: Unit 9, Reading
Workbook / Online Practice: p88–89
Extra Practice App

GRAMMAR SB p122

To start

Write the following sentences on the board and ask students to complete them with their own ideas. Students then discuss their sentences in pairs.

- *In my country, the minimum age when you can … is …*
- *The people who have to make the most difficult decisions in life are …*
- *Social media is something which …*

Underline the words *when, who* and *which* and elicit that we refer to these as relative pronouns and they start a relative clause in these sentences.

explore grammar ➥ SB p158

1 Remind students that there are two types of relative clause and read through A and B in the explore grammar box. Ask: *Which type of relative clause can be left out without the meaning of the sentence changing?* (non-defining clauses) *Which type of clause needs commas before and after it?* (non-defining clauses) *In which clause can you leave out the relative pronouns?* (defining clauses, when the pronoun is the object of the sentence).

Write on the board: *Books which are written by teenage authors are very popular at the moment.* Ask students if we can shorten this sentence in any way. Elicit that we can remove *which are*. This would then be a reduced relative clause. Write on the board: *After I had read a chapter of the book, I went to bed.* Elicit that this can also be shortened using a participle clause: *After reading a chapter of the book, I went to bed.*

Read though C and D in the explore grammar box. In pairs, students match sentences 1–4 with the types of clause, A–D.

1 B non-defining relative clause
2 C reduced relative clause
3 D participle clause
4 A defining relative clause

2 9.1 Play the recording for students to answer the questions. Conduct class feedback.

They're at a party. Lucy is surprised to see Mark because she thought he had band practice that night..

extra

Ask further questions.

Why is Mark there? (His band practice place was double-booked. He didn't have anything else planned.)
Why does Lucy know a lot of people? (They go to her street dancing club.)
Who is Clara? (A friend of Lucy's. Her dad works for a record company.)
What is Mark going to get for Lucy? (Juice and crisps.)

3 9.2 Students complete the sentences with either a relative pronoun or a present participle. Play the recording for them to check.

1 where **2** having **3** talking **4** whose

4 Refer students to the title of the text, *How old do you have to be?* Elicit some age limits where students live, for example, how old people need to be before they can drive. Ask them to read the text quickly, ignoring the gaps, to check whether the text mentions any of these limits. Elicit that it mentions riding mopeds and leaving school. Students complete the text with the correct pronouns. Elicit the answers.

1 that/which **2** that/which **3** who **4** when **5** where

5 Read the title of the article with the class and elicit the meaning of *have my say* (to have the opportunity to give an opinion). Students read the article, ignoring the gaps, to find out what point the speaker is concerned about and to summarise the writer's point of view. Then they complete the text with the correct words. Conduct class feedback.

1 that/which/– **2** where **3** Being **4** that/which **5** which **6** whose **7** Having **8** held/shared

extra

Put students into small groups. One person starts a sentence finishing with a noun or noun phrase just before the relative pronoun, e.g. *My dad is the person in the family …* .

The next person finishes the sentence, e.g. … *who always decides what we listen to in the car.*

The aim of the game is not to hesitate. The person who pauses for too long before continuing the sentence loses a point. Explain that the aim is to finish the sentences as quickly as possible. Weaker groups may need some time before starting the game in order to think of some sentence starters.

Monitor and give suggestions where necessary. Make sure students are using relative clauses correctly. Conduct class feedback and ask for funny or unusual sentences that were constructed by the groups.

Speak up

6 Students discuss the questions in pairs. You could extend this by asking: *Some people say that everyone should use their vote and people who don't use their vote should be fined. What's your opinion?*

Possible answers

1 Ideas include: when he or she can make responsible decisions alone; when he or she can start working; when he or she can get married or have children.
2 The most common voting age around the world is 18, although some countries let people vote when they are 16. Others let them vote when they are 25. Ideas include: people should be able to vote when they have reached a certain level of education; people should only vote when they start paying taxes; people shouldn't vote unless they have an understanding of politics.

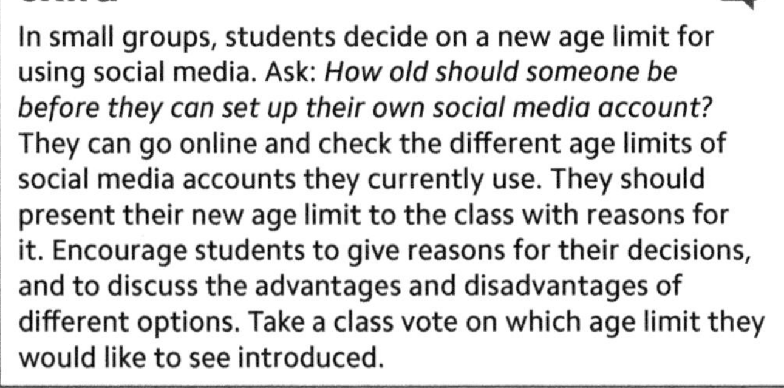

extra

In small groups, students decide on a new age limit for using social media. Ask: *How old should someone be before they can set up their own social media account?* They can go online and check the different age limits of social media accounts they currently use. They should present their new age limit to the class with reasons for it. Encourage students to give reasons for their decisions, and to discuss the advantages and disadvantages of different options. Take a class vote on which age limit they would like to see introduced.

To finish

In pairs, students show each other some photos on their phones, using relative clauses to give more information about what is in the photos. For example, *That's when I went to Paris. The girl who's standing on my left is my cousin. The book I'm reading here is the new Alex Rider one.*

Presentation tool:	Unit 9, Grammar
Workbook / Online Practice:	p90
Photocopiable activity:	9A
Grammar reference and practice:	SB p158
Audioscript:	SB p183

VOCABULARY SB p123

knowing, thinking and deciding

To start

Write *outspoken* on the board and elicit the meaning of the word (someone who speaks his or her mind without worrying about what others think). In pairs, students choose a famous person – a celebrity, a politician, etc. – who is well-known for being outspoken (they should choose someone their partner is likely to know). They have to guess which person their partner is thinking about by asking and answering *yes/no* questions: *Is it a woman? Is she an actor?*, etc. Circulate and add guesses of your own to help where necessary. Conduct class feedback and discuss what the class feels about the people they talked about.

explore vocabulary

1 Write *speak out about something* on the board. Explain that this is a fixed phrase. Using one of the celebrities chosen in the previous exercise say that this person *always speaks his/her mind.* Tell students this is another example of a fixed phrase. Read through the explore vocabulary box with the class and elicit the meanings of the fixed phrases by giving or asking for examples using the phrases. When giving examples, try to make them interesting or personalised, as this makes them more memorable for the students. In pairs, students ask and answer the questions. Monitor and note interesting points to mention in feedback. Students share their ideas in full group and tell the class two things they learned about their partner in Ex 1.

Possible answers

1 speak out about = publicly speak in protest about something
2 sleep on it = not make a decision about something important until the next day
3 be torn between = not be able to make a decision between two options
4 have second thoughts = start having doubts about a decision you made
5 have a Plan A and a Plan B = to have a plan which you will use if things happen the way you expect and a back-up plan in case things go wrong
6 weigh up the pros and cons = to consider the advantages and the disadvantages of something

2 9.3 Tell students that they will hear four different conversations about different decisions. Play the recording for them to say who they think the speakers are. Then ask what decisions the conversations concern.

1 a football coach and player (Playing in a football match.)
2 a teacher and a student (Choosing what to study.)
3 a father and daughter (Going on holiday with friends.)
4 a head teacher and student (Deciding where to go on the school trip.)

VOCABULARY (Continued)

3 9.4 Play the recording for students to complete the sentences. Pause after each section of the recording that gives the answer to allow students writing time. Stronger students may be able to do this from memory, or after hearing the whole sections again. Check answers in full group.

1 propose **2** selections **3** considering **4** evaluate
5 intention **6** judging **7** consult

4 Students complete the task in pairs. Conduct class feedback.

1 proposal/proposition **2** select **3** consideration
4 intend **5** evaluation **6** judgement **7** consultation

extra

Ask students to write example sentences for some of the new words in the task to show their meaning and use. Elicit some sentences from the class.

In the exam we may need to write a proposal.
The captain is going to select the team for next week's swimming competition later today.
The teacher takes our coursework into consideration when she writes our reports.
What do you intend to do about the plans?
The estate agent is giving my dad an evaluation of what our house might be worth.
A lawyer charges a lot of money for a consultation!

5 Students first read the title of the article and predict what they might read about. They then quickly read through the article to check their ideas. Elicit that it's about teenagers being more involved in big decisions than in the past. Write the words *decision, research* and *mind* on the board and elicit a collocation that students already know with each verb. Then read through the collocations in the box with the class. They complete the text with the correct words before comparing answers with a partner. Conduct class feedback.

1 based **2** revealed **3** According **4** involve **5** speak
6 challenge

extra

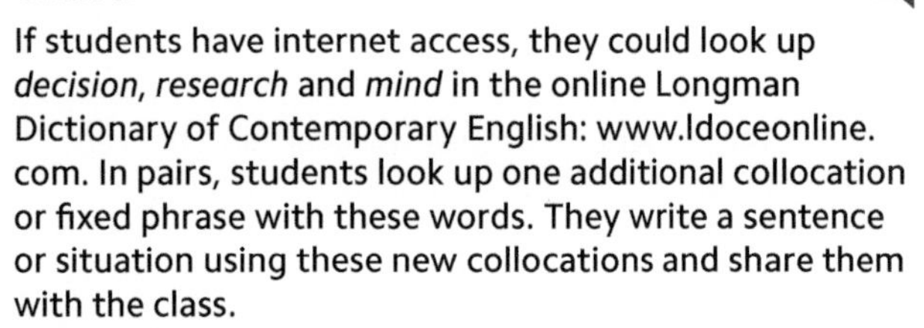

If students have internet access, they could look up *decision, research* and *mind* in the online Longman Dictionary of Contemporary English: www.ldoceonline.com. In pairs, students look up one additional collocation or fixed phrase with these words. They write a sentence or situation using these new collocations and share them with the class.

Speak up

6 Students discuss the question in pairs. Circulate and note interesting points to bring into general discussion, also any language points you may wish to look at with the class later.

Possible answers

Ideas include decisions that are too complex for younger children to fully understand, such as moving house, choosing a good school, or how to spend a household budget.

Fun footer

Read out the statement with the class. Divide the class in half with the pairs in one half discussing and noting arguments in favour of the statement and those in the other half points against. If appropriate, students could research facts to support their ideas online. Students then debate the issue in open group but must try to keep to their allocated point of view. At the end of the discussion ask students if any of them have changed their original ideas.

To finish

Students close their books. Write these words on the board: *speak, sleep, carry out, mind, decision, research, plan, weigh, torn, second.* Elicit from each student in turn a phrase or collocation using one of the words. If a student cannot give a phrase, they have to drop out. Remind students that for several of the words, there will be more than one phrase. The last student to remember a phrase wins.

Presentation tool:	Unit 9, Vocabulary
Workbook / Online Practice:	p91
Photocopiable activity:	9B, 9C
Audioscript:	SB p183
Extra Practice App	

LISTENING SB p124

To start

Write the word *milestone* on the board. Ask: *What does this word mean?* Say that it has two meanings, one literal and one metaphorical. Elicit that it is a stone that marks the number of miles from one place to another on a road. However, the word is also used to describe important moments in people's lives. Elicit some important milestones throughout a person's life, for example, someone's first steps as a baby, first word as a toddler, first day at school, passing their driving test, reaching the age of being an adult, getting married, having a baby.

Power up

1 Read through the experiences. Put students into small groups to discuss the two situations, and decide why they might be important. They should consider whether they chose to do the things themselves, and how they felt. As feedback, take one idea for each situation from each group. Write these on the board and take a vote on which situation they think would be the most difficult to deal with. They will probably say staying away from home, but if they have other ideas don't push them into deciding on this one.

Possible answers

1 The first time I stayed away from home was when I went on a school summer camp. It was my decision, and I was really excited about it. I was with all my friends, so I didn't feel lonely.

2 I remember a time once when my teacher just told me to come to the front of the class and say something. I hadn't prepared anything, so I was really surprised. I didn't know what to say, and I felt very embarrassed.

Listen up

2 9.5 Tell students that they're going to listen to a student experiencing his first time away from home. Play it through for them to listen for whether it was a good or bad experience for the boy.

His summer went generally well.

exam task: multiple choice

3 e 9.6 Go through the exam tip box about this part of the exam. Remind students that they will hear all the information they need to choose the correct answer in the recording, and they should not make assumptions about any answer based on their own ideas or experiences. This could cause them to choose the wrong option. Give students time to read through all the questions. Then play the recording and ask them to answer the questions. They should check their answers in pairs. If necessary, play the recording for a third time.

1 C (*What is special about the youth citizen course is that you can choose something different for each week of the course.*)
A is incorrect: it's not only sports that the course offers.
B is incorrect: he doesn't say that this is the aim of the course.

2 A (*But to be honest I was a bit worried at the thought of not being with my friends …*)
B is incorrect: he doesn't say he was disappointed, just that he was nervous.
C is incorrect: he said he gets bored in the summer, not on the course.

3 C (*I knew it would be hard but I didn't expect the rest of the group to be so brilliant. At one point I panicked but they all kept shouting to encourage me.*)
A is incorrect: he doesn't say he was surprised.
B is incorrect: he knew he would be frightened because he was afraid of heights.

4 B (*One of the leaders said his intention was to help us find a hidden passion. I think I discovered mine was for public speaking …*)
A is incorrect: he didn't appreciate it – he just says one of the leaders said he wanted to help the participants find a hidden passion.
C is incorrect: he said he discovered his talent for public speaking, but not that it was important

5 C (*I've got skills that I wouldn't have gained on the usual summer camp … if you feel you need something else, give this a go. You'll discover that you're capable of a lot more.*)
A is incorrect: he says if they want to do sports then they should go to a sports camp, but that if they need something else to go to this kind of camp.
B is incorrect: he says three weeks is a long time away from home, but doesn't say they'll be homesick

6 A (*It was my suggestion that we raise money for the local skate park …. we held a music event and the others cooked food to sell. My parents hadn't seen this side of me before because I normally let other people make decisions for me.*)
B is incorrect: he says it must have been annoying that he didn't stop talking.
C is incorrect: he says the others cooked.

7 B (*I think I'll be good at helping people especially those who are shy like me …*)
A is incorrect: he says he'll do the course again before he goes to university.
C is incorrect: he says he met friends from all over the country, not that he wants to travel more himself.

4 Students can discuss the question in the same groups. Conduct class feedback to discover the most common opinions about whether they would like to do the course.

1 Yes, it made him try new things.
2 Overcoming a fear of heights, giving a presentation (and realising he was good at it) and making the decision to do something in the community.
3 Students' own answers.

5 Check that students know the meaning of the words in the box. Then ask them to do the exercise in pairs.

1 adrenalin **2** community **3** convince **4** homesick **5** hidden **6** struggle

LISTENING (Continued)

Speak up

6 The questions pick on the main ideas students have discussed in this section. Once students have discussed them all, ask all the class: *Are you 'doers' or 'thinkers'?* Elicit how the majority of the class would describe themselves, and why they think of themselves in this way.

Possible answers

1 I don't like it when other people make decisions for me. It makes me feel small, like I have no power.

2 A 'doer' is someone who does things instead of just thinking or talking about them. A 'thinker' is someone who likes to plan things and consider them carefully before acting.

Fun footer

Read through the footer and elicit from students what they think it means. Explain that there are two fixed phrases in the footer. Ask: *What are they? What do they mean?* Elicit *at the eleventh hour* and *at the last possible moment*, and that they both mean 'it is almost too late'. Ask students: *Do you usually leave things until the last possible moment? Or do you like to do things well in advance?*

To finish

Ask students to write their own sentences using words from Ex 5. They should exchange their sentences with another pair and check if they have used the words correctly.

Consider asking students to read the Grammar file about cleft sentences on page 158 in preparation for the Use of English 1 lesson.

Presentation tool:	Unit 9, Listening
Workbook / Online Practice:	p92
Audioscript:	SB p183
Extra Practice App	

USE OF ENGLISH 1 SB p125

To start

Remind students that they've been working on using a range of language, and that it's a good idea to be able to say the same thing in different ways. Write these sentences on the board:

Peter was late. It was Peter who was late.

Ask students: *Do these sentences mean the same thing? Or are they different?* Elicit that they have the same meaning, but the emphasis is slightly different. In the first sentence, the information is simply factual, whereas in the second sentence the emphasis is on Peter and highlighting the fact that he – and not someone else – was late.

Tell students that the second sentence is called a cleft sentence, and it's a good technique for varying the way they say or write something and highlighting what the important information is. Read out the following sentences and elicit the cleft sentence beginning with *It was …* .

- *Clara won the competition. → It was …* (Clara who won the competition.)
- *Karl finished the homework first. → It was …* (Karl who finished the homework first.)
- *Susan played tennis better than anyone else. → It was …* (Susan who played tennis better than anyone else.)

explore **grammar** → SB p158

1 Cleft sentences can be difficult for students to understand at first. For this reason, go through the explore grammar box carefully. All the examples come from the listening. Ask students to underline the important information in the first two examples to help them remember it.

<u>It was my parents who decided</u> I should do a youth citizen programme over the summer. (= My parents decided, not me.)
What is really amazing is <u>how much confidence I gained</u>. (= I gained so much confidence. This was amazing.)

If you want to give them more examples, ask them to turn to the Grammar file on page 158 and go through the examples there. They can do Exs 5–6 on page 159 for homework.

2 Do the first example together with the class. If they seem to be having difficulty, do the whole exercise together with the class, explaining the structure as you go.

1 It wasn't until recently that I was interested in art.
2 What I love are the clothes (that) she wears.
3 It was my friends who made the cake for the party.
4 What I did was (to) take lots of photos while I was there.
5 It was our teacher who offered to help us with the project.
6 What we need is extra time for this exercise.
7 What I don't like in winter is the weather.
8 What happened was (that) too many people tried to help with the plans.

extra: fast finishers 

Write these sentence starters on the board. Fast finishers complete the sentences with their own experiences and ideas.

It wasn't until recently that I …
What I really love is/are …
What I real hate is/are …

3 This gives them further practice in using cleft sentences. Give your own example before putting students into groups. Go round and monitor their use of the structure as they think of their own examples, and correct if necessary. Don't conduct class feedback, unless you want to highlight a particularly good example that you've heard. If students have been having difficulty, then give your own answers to all of the sentences, so that they can hear good examples.

Possible answers

1 What I really enjoyed today was having lunch outside in the sun.
2 It was my friends who told me about the film.
3 What was good about last weekend was (that) I managed to see my best friend.
4 It's always my teacher who gives us interesting homework.

exam tip

4 Remind students that occasionally, there may be two possible answers that would fit the gap and are grammatically correct. These might be words like modal verbs with a similar meaning (e.g. *could/might*), linkers (e.g. *since/because*) or words such as *after/following*. However, even if students can think of two words, they must not write them both in the gap. They must choose the word they are sure is correct. This means it is really important that they read the whole sentence containing the gap and concentrate on the words before and after it as this will give them clues as to what the missing word is. Ask them to read the text quickly to see what it's about. Elicit that it's about a surprise birthday party. Ask: *What do you think goes in gap 6?*

The words *after* and *following* would both fit the gap, as they have a similar meaning and would both fit grammatically. In the exam, either word would be marked correctly, but if candidates write both words in the gap they will not get the mark. They must decide on the best answer.

exam task: open cloze

Most of the items tested here relate to cleft sentences which are the focus of the lesson.

5 **e** Students complete the rest of the task in pairs. Tell them to think especially about cleft sentences, and to think about the way the sentences in the text are formed. Once they've finished, elicit their answers with the whole class and highlight the cleft structures. You could mention that in the actual exam, there would not be so many cleft structures in a single text.

1 is (part of the cleft construction *What is worse is that …*)
2 who/that (part of the cleft construction *it's often your best friends who decide*)
3 was (part of the cleft construction *It was during my stay that*)
4 did (part of the cleft construction *What they did was to organise*)
5 had (part of the past perfect)
6 after/following (only one of these answers should be given)
7 what (part of the cleft construction *what slightly bothered me was*)
8 it (part of the cleft construction *it was the thought that mattered*)

Speak up

6 This picks up on the general topic of the text. Ask students to make notes on their ideas before they discuss the questions. They should think of where they could use cleft sentences, and prepare these in advance. Then put students into small groups and ask them to discuss the questions using their prepared cleft sentences where possible.

Possible answers

1 I went to a surprise party when I was 18. What was interesting about it was that it was for me! Nobody told me about it. It was my father who organised it, and it took place at my grandparents' house. All my family were there.
2 Ideas include: the person being surprised isn't happy about it; someone spoils the surprise by telling other people in advance.
3 I'd be really happy if my friends wanted to organise a birthday for me. But I wouldn't let them do it without me. I'd want to be involved in all the preparations. I'd especially want to be in control of who was invited, and who wasn't!

To finish

For homework, ask students to write a short paragraph about a party they have been to which they did or did not enjoy. They should include one cleft sentence in their paragraph. In the next lesson, they can exchange their paragraphs with a partner for any comments and corrections.

Presentation tool:	Unit 9, Use of English 1
Workbook / Online Practice:	p93
Grammar reference and practice:	SB p158
Extra Practice App	

USE OF ENGLISH 2 SB p126

To start

Ask students: *How did you choose the clothes you're wearing today. Did you buy them yourselves? Why did you decide to wear them today?*

1 Put students into pairs to discuss the questions. You could also discuss situations where students have to wear clothes they don't like in full group, if you feel they would enjoy this.

Possible answers

1 Normally, I make all my own decisions. But in school, I have to wear a uniform, and I don't have much control over that. I also do a part-time job on Saturday mornings. I don't have to wear a uniform for that, exactly, but I have to wear a white shirt and grey trousers.

2 I don't really like wearing very smart, formal clothes. But for some occasions, like job interviews or weddings, I have to.

2 9.7 Tell students that the four people they are going to listen to have very different opinions about clothes. Play the recording as students decide on the speakers' opinions. They should compare their answers in pairs.

1 C **2** D **3** B **4** A

explore vocabulary 1

3 9.8 Tell students that they are going to think about the language each speaker used, in particular, collocations connected with the topic of clothes. Elicit any that they know any already. Then go through the explore vocabulary box. Point out that these are collocations with verbs, and they are useful ways of discussing the topic. Play the recording and ask students to decide which speaker used each collocation in the box.

Speaker 1: experiment with new looks, have an issue with something, have a crazy dress sense

Speaker 2: stand out in a crowd, pick up bargains, put an outfit together, look really cool

Speaker 3: feel under pressure to wear something, wear a particular brand or label, follow the crowd

Speaker 4: throw on clothes, be obsessed with style and image

4 Students do this in pairs. Remind them that it is useful to learn collocations because using them is a good way to sound natural and show that they can use a range of language.

1 experiment with new looks
2 have an issue with
3 feel under pressure to
4 obsessed with style and image

Put students into small groups to discuss the four questions. They will probably be interested in giving their own opinions, so allow enough time for them to have the discussion. For questions 3 and 4, elicit what the whole class thinks.

explore vocabulary 2

5 Remind students taking the exam that they have to show a range of vocabulary, and using collocations can help them do this. They must also be able to use words in their correct form. Write the following words on the board that come from the listening. Ask students if they can come up with other forms of the words.

- *obsessed* (obsession, obsessive)
- *pressure* (press, pressured)
- *follow* (follower, following)
- *crowd* (crowded)
- *particular* (particularly)

Go through the explore vocabulary box. Point out that all the words here change from a noun to an adjective. Point out the suffixes in bold. Remind them that suffixes go at the end of words, and can help indicate what type of word it is (an adjective, verb, etc.). A prefix goes at the beginning of a word, and can change its meaning completely.

unintelligent, non-judgemental, unambitious, unsuspicious, unconfident, impatient, unstylish

exam task: word formation

6 **e** Tell students that they are going to change the capitalised words in the text to their correct form. First they read the title and predict the topic. Then they skim the article to check their predictions. Elicit that the article is about virtual dressing or fitting rooms, and a new way of trying on clothes and developing a style of dressing. Go through the exam tip. Point out that even though some words in English do keep the same form, in this exam task, students will always have to change the word they are given. Ask them to do the exercise in pairs. They should first identify the form of the word they are given, and then the form they need in order to fit in the gap. They will need both prefixes and suffixes.

1 trendy (noun to adjective)
2 conventional (noun to adjective)
3 measurements (verb to plural noun)
4 enables (adjective to verb)
5 undressed (verb to negative adjective)
6 combination (verb to noun)
7 influential (noun to adjective)
8 experimental (noun to adjective)

To finish

Ask students to discuss in pairs: *What do you think of the idea of virtual shopping? Does it take away the fun of going shopping with friends? Would they do it themselves?*

Presentation tool:	Unit 9, Use of English 2
Workbook / Online Practice:	p94
Audioscript:	SB p183
Extra Practice App	

SPEAKING SB p127

To start

Remind students of the discussions they have had about clothes. Ask: *Do you think it's a good idea to spend a lot of money on clothes? Why/Why not?*

Power up

1 Students should discuss the questions in pairs. Tell them that these are the type of personal questions that they might be asked in the Speaking test Part 1.

Possible answers

1 I prefer shopping alone. It's easier and I can make decisions a lot more quickly.
2 I usually buy the same types of clothes, from the same shops, because I know that I will like them.

2 Students can do this in pairs. Encourage them to check with you, or in a dictionary, if they don't know what certain words mean.

busy – quiet
casual – formal
cheerful – moody
messy – neat
old-fashioned – trendy
patterned – plain
smart – scruffy

alternative

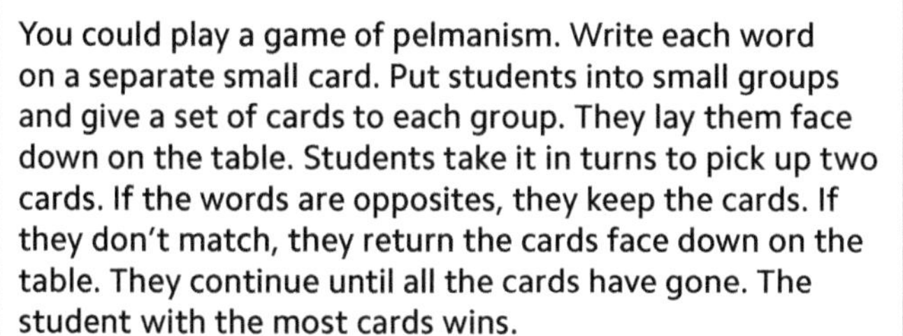

You could play a game of pelmanism. Write each word on a separate small card. Put students into small groups and give a set of cards to each group. They lay them face down on the table. Students take it in turns to pick up two cards. If the words are opposites, they keep the cards. If they don't match, they return the cards face down on the table. They continue until all the cards have gone. The student with the most cards wins.

3 Focus students' attention on the photos. Elicit answers from the class.

Suggested answers

Top photo: formal, neat, patterned, plain, smart
Bottom photo: casual, cheerful, patterned, plain, trendy

exam tip

4 9.9 Go through the exam tip. Remind students of the importance of dealing with both parts of the task. Each part allows them to show different types of language. Comparing the photos allows them to use the language of comparison and contrast and linkers, and answering the question allows them to use the language of speculation. In the exam, the interlocutor will time them and stop them after they have been speaking for a minute, even if they haven't covered both parts of the task. This is why students should practise doing the task in a minute so they get used to how long each part takes. Ask students to say what two things they must do in Part 2.

compare the photographs
say what the people might be finding difficult about their day out shopping

5 9.10 Play the recording as often as students need to complete the table. Highlight the fact that the students should compare the photographs, rather than simply describe them. This means that they have to link and contrast their ideas clearly. When they answer the question, they should be speculating, and using language such as modal verbs.

Similarities: people shopping
Differences:, relationship, the mood of the people, type of shop, type of clothes, location
What might be difficult:
Photo 1: the girl looks moody, she might be shopping with her mum, and finding it difficult
Photo 2: choosing clothes

6 Students complete sentences for themselves. When they compare their answers, they should explain the reasons for their ideas by referring to the photographs. In the exam they should always talk about the people in the photographs, not themselves.

Possible answers

1 Both photos show women looking for some new clothes.
2 Another similarity is they all have a lot of clothes to choose from, and are touching them and seeing how they look.
3 In the first photo, the people look quite serious, whereas in the second photo, the two girls are having fun.
4 Another difference is that the people in the first photo are different ages, and one person isn't looking for clothes for herself.
5 Shopping might be difficult for the person in the second photo because there are so many clothes to choose from.

exam tip

7 9.11 This question is about the situation in the photographs, although the students should give their own opinion about them. It may be asking which place or situation they would prefer, or whether they enjoy doing something shown in the photographs. The student should give a clear answer with reasons, but not speak for too long. Point out that this isn't another long turn!

Which of these days out shopping would you prefer?

useful language: talking about preferences

8 This language is useful for the question that a student is asked after their partner's long turn. This is because the student is asked about their own preference related to the topic of the photographs . After students have looked at the language, give them time to discuss their answers to the exam question in pairs.

Possible answers

Ideas include: talking about shopping with friends or with someone else; buying formal clothes or casual clothes; shopping in different types of store.

SPEAKING (Continued)

Speak up

exam task: **long turn** ➥ SB p163

9 **e** Put students into pairs and refer them to the photos on page 172 and page 174. Ask students to time themselves, so that they speak for one minute. Get students to record their long turns on their phones. They should then listen again to their turns, and assess how well they used linkers in their comparison of the photos, and how well they organised their long turn.

Possible answers

Page 172

A: Both of these photos show people eating with other people. The first photo shows some friends eating together, whereas the second one shoes a family having a meal. One difference is the location. The friends are eating outdoors, and the family are sitting around a table indoors. They might be at a restaurant, because the situation looks quite formal. Another difference is that the friends are eating out of what look like pizza boxes. They've probably bought the pizza from a take-away restaurant. They're obviously enjoying being together and being outdoors in the sunshine. The family are enjoying being together, too, and they seem to be having a conversation. They aren't enjoying any food, because there isn't any on the table yet.

B: I'd prefer to eat take-away food outdoors with friends. It's more relaxed, and probably cheaper, too.

Page 174

B: Both of these photos show people outdoors, and one other similarity is that there are only two people in each situation. The first photo shows two young people, who could be friends or brother and sister. They've been skateboarding, and now they're just relaxing. The second photo shows two people camping, and they're a bit older. One difference is that the people in the second photo are busy doing something. They're preparing food. In the first photo, however, the people have already done something. They might even be going home soon, whereas in the second photo, the people are probably going to spend the night outdoors.

A: If I had a choice, I'd do something like in the second photo. I like camping, and there's nothing better than eating outdoors on a warm evening.

Speaking extra

10 This is useful practice, but remind students not to describe the photos but to compare them. They should link their ideas and not focus too much on the details of the photographs. You could ask students to find their own pairs of photographs for homework and bring them into class for the other students to compare and discuss in the next lesson.

Fun footer

Read through the footer. Ask students: *Do you think this is true or not?* Elicit that a wrong decision can be funny or can have dramatic consequences. Ask students: *Have you ever made any bad decisions that have turned out to be funny or had dramatic consequences. What happened?*

To finish

Tell students that they are going to practise expressing preferences using language from Ex 8. Give them the following topics for them to compare with a partner, and to say which they prefer.

- *Shopping online or shopping in store.*
- *Buying clothes alone or buying clothes with a friend.*
- *Studying alone or studying with a friend.*

Presentation tool:	Unit 9, Speaking
Workbook / Online Practice:	p95
Speaking file:	SB p163
Audioscript:	SB pp183–184

WRITING SB pp128–129

To start

Tell students that they are going to write an essay about celebrities. Ask the class: *Are you generally interested in celebrities?* Conduct a short survey of those celebrities that are most popular among the class. You could also put categories up on the board and ask students to suggest celebrities they know about or are interested in in these categories: *sport, fashion, film, music, television*.

Power up

1 Students discuss the questions in pairs. You could use this as an extension of the 'To start' activity.

Possible answers

Some celebrities are often popular because they are especially attractive or funny, or because they are role models for young people. Other celebrities can be popular for exactly the opposite reasons: that they are shocking, or bad role models, and watching their lives can be interesting in the same way that a soap opera might be.

2 You could either ask students to continue their discussion in their groups or pairs, or do this as a class activity. Elicit students' ideas, and write them on the board. As it will feed into the essay writing, it is important that all the students hear the ideas.

Possible answers

Celebrities can influence the clothes that teenagers wear, the cars they want to drive, or jobs they choose. If celebrities are involved in advertising, they could influence the things teenagers want to buy. Celebrities can have a positive or negative effect on teenagers, depending on whether they themselves behave well. Celebrities who have a negative press can influence teenagers in a bad way.

Plan on

3 Students read the task. Check what they have underlined. Remind them to include a point of their own.

Write an essay using all the notes and giving reasons for your point of view.
Celebrities have a big influence on the decisions teenagers make. Is it a good or a bad thing?
1 behaviour
2 hobbies and interests
3 (your own idea)

4 Students work together to think of a third point. Remind them that it must be clearly different from the first two points, and that it must be relevant to the task. If students like it, they could work in a mind map by putting the central question in the middle and brainstorming their own ideas. Conduct brief class feedback from one or two pairs only, so that they are encouraged to use their own ideas when they write their essay.

Possible answers

fashion, hairstyles, language, career choices, political decisions, food and drink

5 Students read the essay and identify the third point.

Fashion trends, and having an impact on the way teenagers look.

explore language

6 Go through the explore language box before asking students to do Ex 6 in pairs. Remind them that using the right reference words makes their writing more interesting and easier to read. Students do Ex 6 in pairs. Conduct class feedback. Suggest that students highlight the words in the text that the referencing word refers to.

1 celebrities
2 the influence on teens' behaviour
3 the influence on teens' behaviour
4 developing a similar interest
5 adopting fashion trends

7 Students do the exercise in pairs. Conduct feedback, and discuss any possible answers.

1 this **2** they **3** it **4** This **5** it **6** this/that

Write on

8 Students read the task, underline the key information and think of a third point.

Write an essay using all the notes and giving reasons for your point of view.
Some people think that advertising has the greatest influence on the decisions teenagers make about style. Do you agree?
Write about:
1 parents
2 music
3 (your own idea)

Conduct feedback on possible ideas for a third point.

Possible answers

celebrities, friends, cost, where they live, availability (in shops)

exam tip

9 Go through the exam tip. Before you ask students to identify the words and phrases used in the essay to avoid repetition, ask if they can suggest any ideas for the words given themselves. Then ask them to work in pairs to mark the essay. Conduct class feedback.

celebrity: idol, film star, musician, footballer, well-known personalities
fans: follower, supporters
teenagers: teens, young people
influence: influential, positive effect, considerable impact, encourage

Students work together, using the points in Ex 9 as a checklist as they do so. Suggest that they always plan their paragraphs, as this will help them organise their ideas clearly and will make sure that they don't forget anything they need to include. Remind them that the style should be semi-formal.

WRITING (Continued)

exam task: **essay** ➥ SB p165

10 e As they write, monitor and help if necessary.

Model answer

Many things can have an impact on what teenagers buy. It's not the case that advertising is the only thing which affects teenagers' decisions, and indeed, it might not be the most important influence.

Parents, of course, have a big impact on what teenagers wear, although not usually in a positive way. Teenagers often want to wear the opposite to what their parents do, and make conscious efforts to look different.

For a very long time now, pop stars have been at the forefront of new fashions and trends. What's also true is that fans of certain genres of music can signal to other fans what they like by the style of clothes they wear.

Finally, friends probably have the greatest influence of all on what teenagers choose to wear. Most people want to look like they are part of a group, and we often make a deliberate effort to try and fit in with our friends.

In conclusion, I'd say that there are many things which positively or negatively influence teenagers' style decisions. In general, I believe that what our friends wear has the greatest impact.

Improve it

11 This activity, along with Exs 12 and 13 could be done for homework. Encourage students to check dictionaries or an online thesaurus to find similar words and phrases. Point out that it is not wrong to use the same words or phrases more than once in an essay, but they should try to avoid over-using the same words too often.

12 Point out that it is good to use referencing words, but their essay must also be clear and easy to follow. If there are too many, it can be unclear what they refer to.

13 Students check their work carefully for mistakes. Point out that they should always do this after a writing exercise, especially in an exam situation. When assessing students' work, refer to the checklist in Ex 9. Make sure that students have organised their ideas clearly, included a third point, and provided examples and reasons to support their ideas. Make sure that their conclusion follows their argument logically.

To finish

Ask students to look at the photos on pages 128 and 129. In pairs they should discuss what they like and don't like about the way each person dresses. Ask the class to vote on which person they think is the best and worst dressed.

Presentation tool:	Unit 9, Writing
Workbook / Online Practice:	p96
Writing file:	SB p165

SWITCH ON SB p130

Does smell sell?

1 Ask students when they last went shopping and what they bought. Then put them into pairs to discuss the questions. Conduct class feedback and compare influences. You could extend this by asking: *Are you ever pushed into buying something on your friends' advice?*

Possible answers

I was feeling hungry; I was feeling sad and needed cheering up; I was in a good mood; I recognised a product from a TV ad which I liked; I liked the look of the product; I liked the atmosphere in the shop; I liked the smells in the shop; I liked the music; I remembered that I needed the product; the packaging was attractive; the product was on offer.

2 ▶ Play the video clip for the students to answer the questions. Ask: *What is unusual about this supermarket?* Elicit that it uses a scent machine to fill the air with different smells in different departments.

1 $500,000,000,000 (five hundred billion US dollars)
2 75%
3 $99 per month

3 ▶ Play the clip again for students to name the different scents, which include grapefruit, rosemary and focaccia (a type of bread), chocolate and smoked meat. They then answer the question. Elicit answers.

1 They felt happy.
2 They felt hungry.
3 It reminded them of home.

4 Students discuss the question in full group.

The supermarket hopes to make the customers feel hungry and so buy more or 'open their wallets'.

The idea has been a success because sales have improved by 7% in the last month.

extra 

Put students into small groups to debate this question: *Do you think it's right for shops to use such techniques to persuade us to buy thing?* You could ask half each group to find reasons to support the statement and half to find reasons to oppose it. Students should be more focused on objectively debating the topic, rather than giving their own opinions.

Possible reasons for why it is allowable: It makes shopping a more pleasant experience in the same way that hearing happy music does. It is no different in my view from using persuasive language to encourage us to buy. We live in a consumer society whether we like it or not. The economy depends on us buying products, so it is fair enough for shopkeepers to encourage us to buy.

Possible reasons for why it is not allowable: The lovely smells make us think that the produce is really fresh and tasty whereas they are being manufactured by a machine, so they are selling customers a lie. It is 'subliminal' or taking advantage of us without us being aware.

Project

5 Put students into groups and explain the project. They are going to design a social media campaign for a new product or service and present it to the class. Talk through the stages.

The students in the groups can research campaigns individually online and discuss what they have found with their group in the following lesson to choose one to analyse in depth. Alternatively, they can brainstorm in their groups in class and decide which to analyse. The groups discuss the reasons for the campaign's success. They could list the aspects of the campaign and rank them in order of the contribution each made to the overall success.

Groups brainstorm a new product to promote. Give some examples if necessary: perfume, food, clothing, gym equipment, etc. Groups use the information gathered from their research to design an advert for the product. Suggest that they think about visuals, music, slogans, etc. Roles can be allocated and further development work done at home.

Groups present their campaign to the class. They can use video clips and recordings of music along with an oral presentation by one or more members of the group. The class votes on what was the most persuasive campaign, or the one most likely to be a success.

extra

1. Students can explore the psychology of advertising in more depth, researching what is meant by 'subliminal' and which ads employ subliminal techniques. They can choose one example to analyse in more depth and present to the class.
2. Students research some adverts in English and discuss what contributes to a successful or unsuccessful advert (including things like slogans, images, celebrities, attractive people, humour. etc.) They create a profile of the advert using their own analysis and information about it from online research. This should include any background information, interesting points about the creation of a particularly successful advert, how it was filmed, how people reacted to it, etc.

Presentation tool:	Unit 9, Switch on
Switch on videoscript:	TB p175

INDEPENDENT LEARNING SB p130

Skill review

1 Give students time to think about their strongest skill. In pairs, they say why they think this is their strongest skill and how they have improved it during the course.

2 Students then think about which is their weakest skill and note down the difficulties they have. They can compare their notes with a partner to see if they have identified the same things.

3 In pairs, students check back through the book to find tips that could help them both to improve. They note the appropriate tips down for themselves. If practical and not too sensitive, students can share relevant tips with the whole class.

4 If time allows, ask students to look back at the eight previous sections to identify the most important things they have learned from them. They should complete the sentences and if appropriate, discuss them with a partner or in full group. Alternatively, you may wish to make time to talk to each student on a one-to-one basis about their progress and suggestions for future work. Focus on positive aspects of their work and give practical advice about how to improve each skill. You can use examples of their written work to point out recurring mistakes but always encourage self-assessment of areas in which they need to improve. Point out that students who analyse their own shortcomings are far more likely to improve on them than those who are simply told what they should focus on.

Possible answers

1. My reading skills have improved because now I can read more quickly than I used to be able to, and I can scan texts for detailed information, rather than reading slowly, line-by-line.
2. In future when I do listening exercises, I'm going to pay attention to deciding what I need to listen out for before I listen, and to try and predict the kinds of thing that speakers will say.
3. My strength in speaking is speaking fluently and for a long time. I would also like to learn how to improve my accuracy, and to make fewer mistakes when I talk.
4. In future, when I do writing exercises, I'm going to pay attention to reference words like *it* or *they*, and how I can make my message clearer by using linkers more effectively.

UNIT CHECK SB p131

This Unit check covers vocabulary related to knowing, thinking and deciding, fixed phrases, relative clauses and cleft sentences.

Practice

1 **1** based **2** challenge **3** speak our minds **4** follow the crowd **5** issue **6** make up **7** reveals **8** stand out

2 **3** 9.12 and 9.13 **1** addictive **2** patient **3** foolish **4** obsessed **5** suspicious **6** faulty **7** confidential **8** ambitious

Review

1 **1** who's (who is) **2** who's (who has) **3** whose **4** who's (who has) **5** whose **6** whose

2 9.14 She needs to choose which extra language she's going to learn.

3 **4** 9.15 **1** looking **2** sent **3** Being **4** replacing **5** Having **6** taught

5 The open cloze type task here allows for a dash (-) if a word is not necessary. There is not this option in the Cambridge exam.
1 –/that/which **2** that/which **3** it **4** when **5** who/that **6** which/that/- **7** whose **8** –/if/when **9** that/which **10** what

6
1. It was his smile that she loved the most.
2. What I find difficult about learning English is the pronunciation.
3. What I did was to list all the pros and cons of each choice.
4. What happened was that she sent the text to the wrong person.
5. What she enjoys most about Greece is the lovely food.
6. It was last summer when I first met Harriet.

7 **Possible answer**
Jacob is a good friend who I met last year when I was at a football camp. I met him in Manchester, where he and his family come from. He has an older brother, who also plays football. He has short dark hair which is really curly. He's quite tall and very fast, which is why he's good at football. What I like about Jacob is that he always makes me laugh and he's never moody.

GRAMMAR FILE SB p159

1 **1** who **2** when **3** where **4** whose **5** which **6** when

2
1. Where's the bag that/which/– I put the shopping in?
2. I'm going camping with Alicia, whose younger sister you know.
3. Isobel, who is a good friend of mine, has decided to study abroad next year.
4. Have you got the book that/which/– I lent (to) you yesterday?
5. Here's a photo of the apartment where we stayed when we were on holiday.
6. That's the student whose short story won first prize in a national writing competition.
7. Mathew gave me some flowers for my birthday, which was very kind of him.
8. On Friday, when my exams are over, I'm going out with my friends. / I'm going out with my friends on Friday when my exams are over.

3 Sentences 2, 3, 7, 8

4 **Suggested answers**
1. The decision to reduce the lunch break is not popular with students.
2. Having enjoyed our trip to Valencia so much, we've decided to go back again this year.
3. Told to make a decision quickly, Mia chose to go with team A.
4. The research carried out into how we make decisions under stress revealed interesting findings.
5. Being unable to pick a winner, the judges gave two artists joint first prize.

5
1. was/were the special effects in the film.
2. is to be more involved in making family decisions.
3. because he's too young that Rob didn't vote in the election.
4. until yesterday that we decided about the trip.
5. when she looked at her phone that she realised what time it was.
6. was (to) weigh up the pros and cons before she made the decision.
7. was (that) Kate changed her mind and decided not to meet Alex.
8. is consult your doctor before starting the training programme.

6 **1** After **2** Being **3** was **4** whose **5** who **6** What **7** Having **8** that/which/–

Presentation tool:	Unit 9, Unit check
Workbook / Online Practice:	p97
Audioscript:	SB p184
Extra Practice App	

A matter of taste 10

READING
topic: having an open mind
task: multiple choice

USE OF ENGLISH
open cloze
key word transformations
multiple choice cloze
word formation

LISTENING
topic: giving advice
task: multiple choice: short texts

SPEAKING
topic: free time
tasks: interview; long turn; collaborative task; discussion

WRITING
topics: eating together; a weekend trip; a music magazine
tasks: email, article or review

Lead-in SB p133

Ask students to look at the picture and ask for their immediate reactions. Ask students to describe the photograph and say which of the two ice creams they would go for. Take a class vote on the favourite ice cream. Read through the quote, *I don't always like the same things as my friends*, and ask students: *Is this generally true for you?* Elicit some examples of things that students like, but their friends don't.

Focus students' attention on the unit title, *A matter taste of taste*, and tell students that has two meanings. Give an example: *I love the <u>taste</u> of freshly baked bread. My friend and I have very different <u>tastes</u> in music – she loves pop and I love jazz.* Elicit that one meaning of the word is related to the flavour of something in our mouth. The other meaning refers to the kinds of thing someone likes, and can refer to clothes, art, music, other people, etc. Give some examples of phrases using the word *taste* and elicit what they mean: *He's got no taste!* (He likes strange things). *This food has a good taste.* (It's delicious.) Move on to discussing questions 1–3 as a class.

Possible answers

1 I like to try new things, especially food from other countries. But I tend to eat very similar things, because the shops where I live don't have a big variety of food.
2 It's very important for people to learn how to cook. Not only does it save money if you can cook for yourself, but you can learn a lot about food, and what's in it. If you can cook your own food, you will probably eat more healthily.
3 I tried some vegetables from Korea called *kimchi*. It was very hot, spicy cabbage. I think it's a very healthy food. I liked it very much, and I wish I could have it more often.

READING SB pp134–135

To start

With books closed or lesson covered, students work in pairs to name as many fruits and vegetables as they can in two minutes. They should then choose which three they think are the most consumed in the world and rank them. Conduct class feedback and see which fruit or vegetable students think is the most consumed. Students uncover the page and see from the picture and the article that it's the banana. Elicit some reasons why the banana might be so popular.

Power up

1 Elicit how much students know about bananas. In pairs, they do the true/false quiz. Conduct class feedback.

1 T
2 F There is a type of banana called *Goldfinger* (the name of a James Bond film) and it tastes like an apple.
3 T
4 T
5 F They grow from a bulb/root in the ground. In fact what we normally call a banana tree is in fact a 'tree-like plant'.
6 F There are bananas that are not yellow. There are red, purple and pink bananas.

Read on

2 Refer students to the words in the box. Elicit any ideas that students have on the topic of bananas. Remind them to use language for speculation.

There might be a law about …
Perhaps some people make clothes from bananas.
It might be that …

3 Focus students' attention on the title of the article, *It's time to start taking bananas seriously*, and the photos. Elicit students' ideas about what they can see in the photo. Ask: *Why don't some people take bananas seriously?*

4 Students read the article quickly to check their ideas. They should also find out how the words in Ex 2 relate to the topic of bananas. Conduct class feedback.

A law was introduced in America banning people from dropping banana skins in public places.
Parts of the banana plant can be turned into textiles.
Bananas can be used to create electricity.
Leather shoes can be polished with banana skins.
Teeth can be whitened by rubbing banana peel on them.

exam task: multiple choice

5 e If necessary, revise tips from previous units on how to approach this Reading task. Students complete the task individually within a time limit of 15 minutes. Conduct class feedback.

1 B (*At that time there were no litter bins or street sweepers; banana peels were often thrown onto the streets. These rotten peels became extremely slippery and resulted in many people falling over and injuring themselves.*)
A is incorrect. All we learn is that they became a favourite street food.
C is incorrect. The reference to a 'law' is that one was created to ban people from dropping peel.
D is incorrect. There is no reference to this.

2 D (*But as I have found out, bananas' role as food is only one side of the story.*)
A is incorrect. The writer is already aware that bananas are entertaining.
B is incorrect. Bananas are less important than wheat, rice and milk.
C is incorrect. He refers to the size of bananas, not their shape.

3 D (*So what are these unexpected uses of bananas? Firstly, did you know that <u>banana peel</u> works brilliantly as a shoe polish? <u>It</u> can also be used …*)
A is incorrect. *Usefulness* is a quality. It can't be used to do something.
B is incorrect. *It* is referring backwards in the text, not forwards.
C is incorrect. *It* is referring backwards in the text, not forwards.

4 B (*Unlike the cotton production industry, which involves chemicals and ridiculous amounts of fresh water, textile production from bananas …*)
A is incorrect. *Forget about* is not related to cotton's influence.
C is incorrect. The reference to Japan and Southeast Asia is related to their use of bananas and is presented as a fact and not something the cotton industry could follow.
D is incorrect. It is the production of textiles from bananas, not cotton, that is almost carbon neutral.

5 C (*The idea came from a desire to make use of the mountain of unwanted bananas that needlessly go to waste because the fruit are too bruised or small to reach the shops.*)
A is incorrect. There is no reference to making a profit.
B is incorrect. There is no reference to finding a new source, just a desire to use up old bananas.
D is incorrect. The use of unwanted bananas will not reduce the amount.

6 D (*But in time, who knows, maybe you'll be reading articles like this wearing banana-based clothes in a banana-powered building*)
A is incorrect. The writer thinks it's possible that people might be using bananas in a different way in the future.
B is incorrect. There is no reference to this. The writer will think twice, but he isn't encouraging others to do the same
C is incorrect. There's a possibility, but no certainty.

6 In pairs students find the words and phrases in the text. Check answers together.

1 gag **2** crop **3** portion **4** potential **5** stems **6** decomposing **7** bruised **8** flaw

extra

Ask students to write sentences of their own to record the new items for homework. Remind them that the sentences should be memorable, show the meaning of the item, and show how the item is used structurally in a sentence. Ask students to share some of their sentences with the class in the next lesson.

Sum up

7 In pairs, students summarise the main topic of each paragraph in one sentence or phrase. Conduct class feedback.

Possible answers

Paragraph 1: This paragraph explains the history of why bananas have a funny reputation.

Paragraph 2: Bananas are a very popular food around the world.

Paragraph 3: They can be used in unexpected ways, for example as a shoe polish.

Paragraph 4: Bananas can also be used in the textile industry, and have been for a very long time.

Paragraph 5: They can also be used as a form of energy, although this hasn't been fully developed yet.

Paragraph 6: The full potential of bananas may only be realised in the future.

alternative

Students write their summary sentences individually, and then read them out to a partner, who has to guess which paragraph it refers to.

Speak up

8 Students discuss the questions in groups. Elicit their ideas and comments.

Possible answers

1 I think it's amazing that bananas might be used to produce energy. We need to find alternative energy sources, and although I don't think bananas are the answer, it's good to know that scientists are thinking of possible alternatives like this.

2 I think that from a young age, we enjoy it when people fall over or hurt themselves, as long as nothing serious happens. It might be because there's a feeling of fear whenever people actually hurt themselves, and laughing when other people aren't really injured is a form of relief.

Fun Footer

Read the joke with the class. Ask students to go online and research additional facts about bananas to report to the class. Alternatively, they could research any interesting facts about another fruit or vegetable of their choice.

To finish

For homework, students write an email to a friend about the article, summarising the main points. They can read out their texts in the next class or hand them in for correction.

Presentation tool: Unit 10, Reading
Workbook / Online Practice: pp102–107
Extra Practice App

USE OF ENGLISH 1 SB p136

To start

Ask students: *Do you like cooking? If yes, what do you enjoy cooking most? If not, why not? Would you like to be able to cook well?*

1 This could be quite quick if they don't watch any TV chefs, but they may have heard of some famous chefs. If not, move on quickly.

Gordon Ramsay is an example of a British chef who was featured in Unit 1. He has many restaurants which have received awards, including 16 Michelin stars, but he is most well-known for his TV shows in the UK about cooking. These, like *Hell's Kitchen* and *Ramsay's Kitchen Nightmares* are popular all over the world.

2 Tell students they're going to read about a famous chef. Ask them to scan the article to find out why he became a chef. Would this have inspired them to do the same thing?

He was inspired by the sound of knives sharpened on stone …

exam task: open cloze

3 **e** Before they do Ex 3, remind students that they should read the whole text first before they fill in any gaps, and that they should concentrate on the words immediately before and after each gap. In this part, they are looking for parts of structures, prepositions, phrasal verbs and so on.

1 at (part of the phrase *at university*)
2 only (part of the phrase *not only … but also*)
3 being (part of a passive form)
4 to (*decide* is followed by the infinitive)
5 for (a period of time – for five years)
6 which (a relative pronoun referring back to the competition)
7 up (part of the phrasal verb *come up with*)
8 such (part of the structure *such a … that*)

exam task: key word transformation

In this task all the items are related to the unit topic of food.

4 **e** Before students do Ex 4, elicit four crucial things they must be careful of when they're doing this exercise:

1 not to write more than five words.
2 not to change the given word.
3 to make sure that their sentence means the same as the given sentence.
4 to check all spelling is correct.
5 the food was (still) being (The past perfect continuous passive is used for an action happening at the same time as another continuing action in the past. It is passive as the preparation of the food is the focus, not who is preparing it.)

Ask them to do the exercise individually, and then in pairs. Ask: *Did you remember to check all four points to be careful of?*

1 regrets not learning/regrets not having learnt (*Regret* + *-ing* form is used as this is about a regret in the past.)
2 I were you, I'd/I would (*I were you, I'd* is used to give advice.)

USE OF ENGLISH 1 (Continued)

3 accused Rollo of leaving/of having left (The reporting verb *accuse* is followed by the *-ing* form.)
4 the first time I've/I have (The present perfect is used to talk about a period of time up to now, in this case the speaker's life up to this point, as this is the first time they've done this.)
5 the food was (still) being
6 has been said (*It has been said* is a passive reporting structure. It's not important who has said the restaurant is really good.)

Speak up

5 **Ask students to discuss the questions in pairs. You could ask them to also discuss their favourite food, and take a class vote on the most popular.**

Possible answers

1 I live in a big city, and it's possible to find restaurants and supermarkets with food from around the world. I enjoy eating Chinese, Italian and Middle Eastern food, for example.
2 TV cookery programmes are very popular now. There is a famous show about baking, in which contestants compete to make the best cakes. I think it's popular because people like watching people try hard, or make mistakes, and it can also be educational.

game on

Put students into groups to play this game. You could start them off by demonstrating the game with one or two students. Ask one students to suggest something to eat beginning with A. They say *apple*. You say: *Yes, one point*, then *banana*. Ask another student to suggest a word connected with food beginning with C. They say something like *cabbage*. You say *Yes, one point*, and then *dinner*. Then ask them to start again in their groups and to continue until they have finished.

Fun footer

Read through the proverb and elicit what it means: if there are too many people involved in something, it doesn't work very well and the result is not so good. Ask: *Do you have any similar sayings in your own language? Do you think the proverb is true?*

To finish

Write the following sentence on the board: *What are some of the advantages of cooking your meals at home? How about the disadvantages?*

Divide the class into two groups. Tell one group they should think about the advantages and the other group they should focus on the disadvantages. Give them a few moments to think of some ideas, then run a debate. Take a vote at the end on whether there are more advantages or disadvantages.

Presentation tool: Unit 10, Use of English 1
Workbook / Online Practice: pp100–101
Extra Practice App

USE OF ENGLISH 2 SB p137

To start

Ask students: *Is the appearance of food important to you. Do you prefer to eat a plate of food that looks colourful and is well presented or are you happy as long as it tastes good?*

1 **Ask students whether they ever take photographs of their food (in a restaurant or at home) and post them online. Ask: *Why do you do this? Do your friends do it? What do you think about it?* Encourage them to give reasons.**

Possible answers

I once made some pasta with black squid ink sauce. It's popular in parts of Italy, and I thought I'd make it. When I'd made it, I thought it looked really interesting. It was black spaghetti, with some yellow cheese on top. I posted it online, and all my friends wanted to know what it was, and how it tasted.

2 **Ask students to scan the text. What do they think the title of the article, *No photos please!* refers to?**

A famous chef, Heston Blumenthal, objects to people taking photos of food in his restaurant.

exam task: multiple-choice cloze

3 **e** **Before they do the task, remind students that they should read the whole text first. As they go through choosing the correct option, they should read the whole sentence before and after the gap. In this part of the test, they are looking for collocations, phrasal verbs and so on.**

1 C sense of smell (collocation)
2 C despite having had a difficult start (this is the only one that fits grammatically and also regarding the punctuation)
3 D gaining … qualifications (collocation)
4 C work out … ideas (phrasal verb)
5 A lose his temper (a collocation that means 'get angry')
6 D point of view (a collocation that means 'opinion')
7 A paying attention to (collocation)
8 B drives him … mad. (a collocation that means to make somebody angry)

4 **Students read the article quickly to see what students can do in the summer school.**

They can learn to cook and also learn foreign languages, e.g. English, French, Spanish and Italian.

exam task: word formation

5 e Students do the task in pairs. Remind them to read the whole article before they make any changes to the words, and that they must look out for negatives and plurals. When you conduct feedback, ask them to explain the change they have made to each word and why. You could ask them to spell their word aloud for practice, and remind them that in the exam, spelling must be correct. Remind them to be careful of any double letters (e.g. *successfully, dramatically*).

1 combination (verb to noun)
2 creativity (verb to noun)
3 personal (noun to adjective)
4 dramatically (noun to adverb)
5 confidence (adjective to noun)
6 participants (verb to plural noun)
7 successfully (verb to adverb)
8 unlikely (verb to negative adjective)

Speak up

6 Ask students to discuss the questions in pairs. Conduct feedback on the dish students would cook for a competition, and find out if they have similar ideas.

Possible answers

1 This would be a great way to find out about food from different countries, and how other people eat. It's always worth discovering more about food, as this can help you eat more healthily.
2 I'd choose to make a cake. I enjoy baking, and also, it's possible to decorate cakes in completely different ways or make them in different, attractive shapes. I think this is more creative than many other types of food. Also, most people love cakes, so it might help the judges choose me!

To finish

Put students into small groups. Ask them to talk about a local restaurant they like, what kind of food it serves, and why they would recommend it to other people. Conduct class feedback and find out if the students like the same restaurant.

Presentation tool: Unit 10, Use of English 2
Workbook / Online Practice: pp100–101
Extra Practice App

LISTENING SB p138

To start

Write the following statement on the board: *I think listening is the hardest part of learning English.*

Ask them to think about whether they agree with this statement or not. They should give their reasons. See whether everyone in the class agrees. Ask: *What can you do about it?* Elicit suggestions such as practising by watching films and programmes in English. Also, students should try to relax when listening – it's not always necessary to understand every word.

Power up

1 Go through all the points, and ask students to choose ones they agree with. Put them into pairs to discuss the options. Conduct class feedback.

Students should have ticked:
Read through the questions and options
Think about what each different situation might be
Underline key words

Listen up

exam task: multiple choice: short texts

All the conversations are related to the unit topic of food, unlike in the Cambridge exam.

2 e 10.1 As this is the last Listening test practice in the book, you could just let students do the task with no additional help. Give them time to read all the questions, and then play the recording.

1 A (*Perhaps one of your friends might be free? I can't think of anyone myself, so I'd be really grateful if you could ask around.*)
B is incorrect. He's not asking for help – he says he would have asked, but he knows she's going to be performing.
C is incorrect. He's giving information, but that is not why he's calling.
2 C (*Since these foods contain high levels of salt and sugar, I wouldn't recommend eating them every day. Once a week is fine …*)
A is incorrect. She's not advising specific meals to avoid.
B is incorrect. She mentions benefits of convenience, but isn't discussing them in detail.
3 C (*After a few minutes, I was OK. I was really lucky.*)
A is incorrect. He doesn't say it spoilt the evening – he says he enjoyed it and in fact, they had a free meal
B is incorrect. He says that they weren't to blame.
4 B (*I was stuck at home getting bored. I wanted to paint but it was too messy*)
A is incorrect. She doesn't say this – she says she wanted to paint, but she hadn't thought of writing before.
C incorrect. She just says her friends love her blog and her recipes.
5 A (*The forecast for Saturday isn't brilliant though, and I'm a bit nervous about that.*)
B is incorrect. He says he's not sure if he's invited enough people but not that he's forgotten anyone.
C is incorrect. He says he's sure nobody will go hungry, so he's certain there's enough food.

LISTENING (Continued)

6 B (*I've wondered whether the judges had their favourites in the past but I don't think they did last night.*)
A is incorrect. The girl says that it must be terrifying for them but the boy says they shouldn't go in for competitions if they can't cook under pressure.
C is incorrect. They boy says the presenters have made mistakes, but only the girl says they are doing a good job.

7 A (*Food can look quite different when taken from above or below, so make sure you try out a variety of angles before you make your choice.*)
B is incorrect. He says you might think you need more equipment but you only need good light
C is incorrect. He doesn't say this – he says a clean white plate is better than busy colours

8 C (*I just hope that everyone who's excited about it now will actually help out when the time comes.*)
A is incorrect. She doesn't say this – only that she has to do her work as well
B is incorrect. She doesn't say she's worried about having time to study – just that she has exams to study for

Speak up

3 Students should discuss their ideas in pairs. Conduct class feedback. Write students' ideas on the board and ask them to vote on the five most popular tips.

Possible answers
Ideas could include: build more exercise into your daily routine; avoid using a car for short trips; try not to sit so much; cook for yourself; make sure you include more fruit and vegetables in your diet.

Fun footer

Nominate a student to read the footer. Ask students if they know where the word *sandwich* comes from.

background

It is said that the word 'sandwich' comes from the Earl of Sandwich who lived in England in the 18th century. He loved playing cards and didn't want to stop playing in order to eat a meal. Having a sandwich was an easy way of making him a snack.

To finish

Put students into small groups. Ask them to tell one another whether they eat healthily or not, and why. Ask: *Do you eat the recommended amount of fruit and vegetables every day? What do you think is easy or difficult about doing this?*

Presentation tool:	Unit 10, Listening
Workbook / Online Practice:	pp110–112
Audioscript:	SB p184
Extra Practice App	

SPEAKING SB p139

To start

Write the following statements on the board.

1 *The hardest thing about the Speaking test is thinking of things to say.*
2 *I'm afraid of making mistakes when I speak.*

Discuss these issues with the class. Ask them if they can think of ways of solving these problems. Elicit suggestions along the lines of the ones below.

1 Try to follow news on the internet or on TV. You could also discuss old exam topics with other students, and keep a note of any interesting ideas from texts you read in class.
2 Making mistakes when you speak is not always important, as long as the mistakes don't prevent communication. It's often better to just keep speaking and not to worry, especially when you practise. This means talking in class whenever possible and not being too hard on yourself.

Power up

1 Students should discuss different ways of preparing for the Speaking test in general. Collect their ideas and write them on the board.

Possible answers
Ideas include: listening to English on TV or radio; talking with friends in English; revising vocabulary; practising talking about photographs; discussing different things with a partner using phrases for agreeing and disagreeing.

extra: whole class 

Put students into four groups, and give each group a different part of the Speaking test to discuss. They should think of ways of preparing for their part, then share their ideas with the rest of the class. The class could decide together on how they could practise for the Speaking test with other students.

Part 1: Prepare questions and practise talking about your school, holidays, hobbies, friends, favourite sports, etc. You could roleplay social situations, e.g. meeting new people, travelling, starting a new school and think about what you might talk about in these situations. Try to be spontaneous and not rehearse too much for this part.

Part 2: You could use photos from the book to practise talking for one minute. Select photos from magazines or use photos on your phone, e.g. two different holiday photos or social events. You could compare the holidays/ social events, etc. and say what you liked or disliked about them. You could also practise timing each other (and maybe recording each other) so that you have an idea of how long one minute is. You should also think about how you would respond to the topic so that you can think about the question you will be asked after your partner has finished his or her long turn.

Part 3: Practise discussing topics in small groups. Take turns to disagree or agree with each other and remember you need to listen carefully to the others and not just respond to the task. You must be prepared to contribute when necessary. You should get into the habit of always explaining your opinion using evidence or examples to back up your ideas.

Part 4: For the final part, work in pairs. Brainstorm topics, e.g. learning new skills, school trips, doing extreme sports, etc. Then prepare questions on one of those topics and then ask the questions to other students to elicit their opinions. You can then add things to what your partner has said, or disagree with them.

Speak up

exam task: interview

➥ SB p162

2 e Give students two minutes to ask and answer the questions. This gives them a sense of how long Part 1 of the Speaking test will last. Remind them to give details, but not too many, and not to interrupt their partner when they are answering their question. In this part, they don't interact with their partner, only with the interlocutor. If you would like to set this up as exam practice, then put students into groups of four. Give two of the students the roles of examiner, and the other two students the roles of candidates. One of the examiners asks the questions to each of the candidates alternately, and the other examiner listens and gives feedback. After two minutes stop them and allow time for feedback on how the candidates did, using the criteria below. Then repeat the task swapping the roles.

Assess how well the 'candidates' did the following. Did they:

- answer the question? (They must always say things which are relevant.)
- give details to support their answer?
- say too little or too much? (Either of these is not a good technique in the exam.)
- try to interact with their partner? (They shouldn't do this in Part 1 of the exam.)

Possible answers

Speaker 1

1 I'm from Rome, the capital of Italy.
2 I usually spend time either with my friends, or other people from my school.
3 I enjoy English most. I like it because it helps me communicate with different people from around the world.
4 I hope so. I have a long summer holiday, and I think we're going to visit my family in a town called Vasto. That's where we usually spend our summers.

Speaker 2

1 I'm from a town in Japan called Narita.
2 Yes, his name is Hiro. We've known each other for about three years.
3 I have. I went to Hawaii on holiday. It was a one-week holiday, and we had a great time on the beach.
4 I'd love to visit Australia. It's a long way from where I live, but I've heard so much about it, and many of my friends have been there, too.

3 Students practise making their own questions for Part 1. It's useful if they do this exercise in groups of 3, so that one student can listen and give feedback.

Possible answers

Which member of your family do you get on with most?
How long have you known your best friend?
What extra-curricular school activities do you enjoy doing?
What do you do in your free time?
Where did you go for your last holiday?
What special occasions do you celebrate in your country?
Do you have any plans for the future?

exam task: long turn

➥ SB p163

4 e Although students do this in pairs in the exam, ask them to do this exercise in groups of three. The third student times each 'candidate' talking about their pictures (it should be a minute), and listens to what they say. They then ask the listening candidate the follow-up question, and allow about 30 seconds for this. They should give feedback to their candidates on how they did. Conduct class feedback and comments from the third student on how the others managed their long turns. Remind students of the importance of addressing both parts of the long turn (comparing the photos and answering the question) and of filling the minute.

Possible answers

Page 139

A: Both photos show people eating food outdoors. The first photo shows people sitting in the snow, whereas the second one shows people in a much warmer environment, sitting at tables. Another difference is that the people in the first photo seem to be eating food that they have prepared themselves. They might be on some sort of hiking expedition. The second photo shows people eating food that has been prepared for them. One similarity is that both photos show people in groups, and they all look like they are enjoying what they are eating.

B: I'd much prefer to eat at a restaurant. I wouldn't like to sit in the snow eating my lunch!

Page 173

A: These two photos show people making food. They have a lot of things in common. For example, it looks like the people making the food are good cooks, and are confident in what they are doing. But there are lots of differences. The first photo shows two people, who might be related, making food at home. It doesn't look like they are making food for a lot of people. In contrast, the second photo shows someone making food outdoors, possibly at some kind of festival. He's preparing an enormous amount of food, which people are buying, and will probably eat while walking around.

B: I enjoy making food at home for other people. I like having friends around, and preparing meals for them.

SPEAKING (Continued)

exam task: **collaborative task** ➥ SB p164

5 **e** Remind students that in Part 3, the important thing is to have a good discussion. Ask them to suggest three things they should do and three things they don't have to do in this part. Elicit the following ideas.

They don't need to:

- talk about all the prompts.
- agree with all their partner's ideas.
- agree on the decision.

They should:

- ask each other for their opinions, and agree and disagree.
- add ideas to what their partner has said.
- support their ideas with evidence and examples.

6 Although students do this in pairs in the exam, ask them to do this exercise in groups of three. The third student times the discussion (it should be two minutes), and listens to what the 'candidates' say. They should give feedback to their candidates on how they did. They should consider whether the candidates interacted well, and were able to give reasons for their opinions. Conduct class feedback and comments from the third student on how the others managed their discussion. Remind students that they should not dominate the conversation, but genuinely interact with their partner.

Possible answers

A: OK, so let's think about speaking on local radio first. Why do you think someone would be interested in this?

B: I'm not sure they would be. It might be interesting for students to interview a guest, but it probably wouldn't be interesting for the visitor. How about visiting important buildings?

A: Yes, I think that would be a good idea. Especially if you live in an area with famous architecture. I think most people would find that interesting. And they could eat out, too.

B: Most people enjoy trying new, local food, don't they? OK, so let's talk about joining a sports club, too.

A: I guess, if you're really into sports, this could be interesting. But it's not really something you'd want to do when you visit a place, is it?

B: I agree. But watching a band would be a good idea.

A: Sure. It's a nice way to spend an evening out, and do something more fun and sociable.

exam task: **discussion** ➥ SB p164

7 **e** This is the decision phase of the task. Students should do it in groups of three, and the third student should time the discussion (one minute). Conduct feedback on the decision each group reached. Give class feedback, and remind them that there is no right or wrong answer and that they can discuss prompts they didn't have time to consider in their first discussion if they like. Remind them that they do have a minute for this, and that they should try to have a real discussion to fill the time and not just make an instant decision without giving reasons for their choice.

Possible answers

A: Right, so which two activities would be most interesting? I think we've talked about visiting important buildings, eating locally and watching a band. Which two would you choose?

B: I think eating locally and watching a band would be the most fun, wouldn't they?

A: You're right. But maybe when you visit a new place you want to experience something that can only be experienced in that place. Maybe experiencing the band could be done just by listening to some music online.

B: Yes, so eating, and walking around interesting buildings can only be done when you're really there.

A: Great, so let's choose those two things, then.

8 Students could do this in their same groups of three, with the third student playing the role of the examiner and asking the questions. Remind students that in this part, they can interact with their partner, and add to what they have said or disagree with their opinion. Once they have discussed all the questions, ask the third student in each group to report back to the class on the ideas their 'candidates' discussed. The assessment in this part should take into account how well the students interacted and the kind of language they used to express their ideas. As in the whole Speaking part of the exam, there are no right answers so students are not marked on their ideas, only the language they use to express them.

Possible answers

1 I would definitely like to do most of these things, and if there was someone who could show me the best places to see or eat locally, then that would be great. It's always better if you can get local advice, rather than try to rely on a guidebook. And when you have local people showing you around, you can learn a lot about a new country.

2 I think it helps you understand the world in more depth. You get to see how other people live, eat and work, and this puts everything else into perspective. You start to realise that what people do in your own country isn't the only way of doing things.

3 Some people are only comfortable with what they already know. They don't like to take risks, perhaps. Some people might not see the point of trying anything new, if they have already found something that they are happy with. They might think it's a waste of time to deliberately keep searching for new things.

To finish

Discuss the Speaking test with the whole class. Ask: *Which parts do you find most difficult?* Elicit suggestions for ways they could help themselves.

Presentation tool:	Unit 10, Speaking
Workbook / Online Practice:	pp113–115
Speaking file:	SB pp162–164

WRITING SB pp140–141

To start

Write the following statement on the board, and discuss students' reactions to it: *Writing is hard because I'm afraid of making mistakes.* Elicit any strategies that students have found useful so far in the course, for improving their writing.

Power up

1 Students discuss the questions in pairs. Use this as an extension of their discussions in the 'To start' section.

Possible answers

1 In my language, you can be more emotional. Things like punctuation and paragraphs are very different. In English, you have to write in a more organised way, and there are stricter rules about paragraphs and punctuation.

2 Read different types of books or articles; make a note of useful vocabulary; plan carefully before you write; get into the habit of checking for mistakes after you have finished.

Plan on

2 Students discuss how other students approach writing tasks. Ask: *Which one is most like you, and why?*

Possible answers

The third one is most like me. Maybe it's not the best way, because I know I ought to plan things before I start writing. But I like my method too, because I usually go back later, check my work, and maybe write a new version.

3 You could do this with the whole class. Conduct class feedback.

Possible answers

First comment

Positive: reading the task twice; underlining the important words.

Possible improvements: make notes before starting to write, brainstorm ideas and plan what vocabulary to use.

Second comment

Positive: making notes and adding ideas; using notes to guide the writing.

Possible improvement: plan what vocabulary to use.

Third comment

Possible improvement: take more time to think about the task; underline key words; brainstorm ideas; plan what vocabulary to use.

4 The table is a useful way of thinking about the different demands of different types of writing. Although this refers to these specific tasks, suggest students keep a copy and use it for any task and for revision.

Article:

Purpose: describe, give opinion

Reader: young people, teens

Style: interesting, lively, engaging

Email:

Purpose: give opinion, advise or persuade

Reader: friend

Style: friendly, sensitive to any problems

Review:

Purpose: describe (people and music), make recommendations

Reader: young people, teens

Style: informative, interesting, engaging

5 Ask students to think carefully about how they choose what to write about. Remind them that there are model answers in the Writing file at the back of the book. Students underline the key words in each of the tasks. Conduct class feedback.

5

1 Article

How important is eating with family and friends?

Do people take enough time to eat together? What sort of meals do you share with family and friends? Is it important to you? Why/Why not?

2 Email

Hi

I've just joined a climbing group and I've been invited on a weekend trip. It sounds fun but I'm very nervous because I'm not as good as everybody else. Do you think it's a good idea? Maybe I should wait until I get some more practice.

I don't know what to do. Can you help?

3 Review

We're looking for reviews of new bands for teenagers. In your review you should describe the members of the band, the kind of music the band plays and where they play. Would you recommend the band to people your age?

6 Focus students' attention on the tasks, and ask them to read them in more detail. Elicit the main topic of each task, and which ones seem most interesting.

Article: food, family

Email: sport, travel, new experiences

Review: music, bands

7 Put students into small groups to think of ideas. Go round and monitor their discussions, and make suggestions if necessary. If you want to give them practice in writing articles straightaway, ask them to write the article after they have discussed the questions in Ex 7. Otherwise, ask them to go on to do Ex 8 in pairs.

WRITING (Continued)

8 **Put students into pairs to think about the email and review tasks in detail. Conduct class feedback.**

Possible answers

Email
What type of trip is it?
Who's going?
Why is Callum worried about it?
What advice could be given?
Review
What's the name of the band?
Who are the people in it?
What type of music do they play?
Where do they perform?
What's good about them?
Why should other teenagers go to see them?

Write on

The article task in the Cambridge exam is not usually styled with bullet points.

9 **e** **Individually, students choose a task and write an answer. Give them around 40 minutes to do this, so that they have time to plan the structure of their work, and any vocabulary they would like to use.**

Possible answers

1

Eating is one of the greatest pleasures in life, especially with other people. Meal times allow us not only to share food, but also to share experiences and important news.

Often, however, people eat alone. Busy lives or just different lifestyles mean that we find ourselves eating in front of a computer or TV, or having a quick snack in the street.

It's not always easy to have meals with other people, but I think it's important to get together and do this at least once a week, and not only for special occasions. I try to have my evening meals with my family. I think this is important, as it gives us a chance to be together and find out how everyone is feeling, and what they have been doing. It's also possible that eating with others is healthier. We tend to spend more time preparing the food, and choosing healthy ingredients.

All in all, eating with family and friends is a great social activity. It might even make us fitter and happier than if we just eat alone all the time.

2

Hi Callum,

Thanks for your email and I'm sorry that you're feeling nervous. It's good, though, that you've been invited on a trip! That means that the climbing group want you to be with them!

If I were you, I wouldn't worry about not being as good as everybody else. After all, everyone has to start somewhere, and I'm sure not everyone in the climbing group is as good as you think they are.

Also, you said that you wanted to wait until you get some more practice. Don't you think that actually going on the trip would be a good way to practise? What's more, you can practise with lots of friends around you, who can show you what to do, and how to improve.

It sounds like you are mostly worried about being embarrassed in front of your new friends. I'm sure they wouldn't have invited you if they were the type of people who would laugh at you. So, my advice is to go, and have fun!

Speak to you soon,

Alison

3

One of the best new bands that I've seen recently are called the Green Dragons. They are a local band, and it's possible that they will become famous soon. So if you want to see a good new band before everyone else does, now's your chance!

The Green Dragons are a traditional rock band, and all the members are women. They write amazing lyrics about how it is to grow up, and find your identity, and what it means to be a young woman in today's world. If this sounds very serious, it's not. The band write brilliantly happy songs that never fail to make you feel good.

They usually play small gigs, but they have also started playing in festivals. This is the best way to hear them – in open spaces, with lots of happy people outdoors.

I'd definitely recommend this band to anyone who likes rock music, but wants to experience something a bit different. Also, if you're feeling in a bad mood, or just want cheering up, this is a great band to check out.

Improve it

10 **Students should spend at least five minutes going over their work. Point out that they shouldn't think of their work as being finished at this point, and not to be afraid of going back and changing anything.**

11 **Put students into pairs to read each other's work. Encourage students to make comments on how well the writing gets a message across, and whether or not it feels like a proper article, email or review. Students can hand their work in for assessment. When assessing writing, concentrate on whether the answer is relevant and sticks to the point. You could also comment on whether it is well organised, and check that there are not too many basic mistakes.**

game on

This is a relaxing activity to end the lesson. Before you ask students to write a paragraph about their own name, you could ask some general questions about the importance of names. Ask: ***Do you think a name is important? Why/ Why not? Should names be chosen as soon as a baby is born, or later on once their personality is established?***

Ask students to write their paragraph. They should make their paragraphs as interesting as possible. Collect the paragraphs, and give them randomly to different students. Students then read them and identify the writer.

To finish

Ask students to work in pairs and discuss any problems they think they have with the Writing paper. Conduct class feedback and make suggestions for helping students to improve their writing. Elicit ideas such as: check the key requirements of the task before you even plan; decide on the appropriate style you need to write in; take time to plan paragraphs; after writing, check your work for basic grammar and spelling mistakes.

Presentation tool:	Unit 10, Writing
Workbook / Online Practice:	pp108–109
Writing file:	SB pp165–170

SWITCH ON VIDEOSCRIPTS

Unit 1

Narrator: Gordon Ramsay is a renowned British chef who wants to recruit a Head Chef for a new restaurant. He has invited some of America's best young chefs to take part in a competition for the role. Today, he'll be asking them to test their senses.

Gordon: As a chef, we always rely on our senses, right?

Chefs: Yes, chef!

Gordon: The sense of taste is obviously the most important. But our sense of hearing – crucial. Our sense of smell helps us to identify aromas, fragrance. And then, our sense of sight. There is one sense that I left out. Today, I'm gonna be testing your sense of touch.

Narrator: A member of each team will go head to head.

Gordon: I will be placing an ingredient inside the box and then I'll ask you to put your arm inside the hole to feel around and try and guess what's inside. Hands through, gently.

Anthony: I'm a little apprehensive about just jamming my hand into an unknown place.

Zac: Come on Ant, you got it, baby.

Jon: You use it all the time.

Susan: You know this, Cindy.

Ja'Nel: You know just what that is.

Mary: You know it, girl!

Cyndi: It's definitely gross! I mean, for it to be slimy and wet, it can be anything.

Gordon: On the count of three, shout out the answer. One. Two. Three!

Both: Eggs.

Gordon: Good job. Hands in – gently!

Anthony: Quinoa, maybe but it's mush – it's potato, it's gotta be something in between the two and …

Gordon: One. Two. Three!

Both: Polenta.

Gordon: Nice!

Ja'Nel: Yeah, good job!

Gordon: Very, very nice!

Jon: Wow, you guys are awesome.

Narrator: The contestants' sense of touch has been fairly reliable. Now Gordon has a final test for the young chefs.

Gordon: So it's time for: the blind taste test! Time to put your palettes to work. Ready?

Contestants: Yes Chef!

Narrator: The blind taste test is one of the key methods that Gordon Ramsay uses to evaluate his chefs.

Gordon: Turkey.

Anthony: Just don't say "chicken".

Zac: Turkey.

Mary: It's really dry, but the flavour is really weird. Egg yolk?

Gordon: Did she just say, "egg yolk" for turkey?

Cyndi: Turkey and egg yolk don't even have the same texture, Mary!

Gordon: Turkey.

Mary: Urgh!

Gordon: Pistachio.

Susan: Oh, yeah.

Jon: Super easy.

Anthony: Cashews, chef.

Cyndi: Come on, Ja'Nel.

Ja'Nel: Pistachio?

Narrator: The teams are tied so it all rests on this last ingredient.

Gordon: Cauliflower.

Zac: White radish.

Gordon: Wrong. Cauliflower. If Susan gets this right, the red team have won.

Ja'Nel: Come on, Susan. Come on, Susan. Come on, Susan.

Cyndi: Oh my god, please.

Susan: Cauliflower.

Reds: Yes!

Mary: Yeah!

Gordon: Good job, you've just won it for your team.

Cyndi: Yes!

Narrator: These sensory tests have been revealing. Ja'Nel guessed 3 out of 4 ingredients thanks to her sensitive palette. But Anthony's sense of taste let him down completely. As Gordon Ramsay thinks taste is a chef's most important sense, it's interesting that no-one has achieved a perfect score. These tests have shown that when it comes to identifying foods, multiple senses are involved – even experienced chefs require more than just their tastebuds.

Unit 2

Narrator: It may not look like the typical holiday location but many people are keen to visit when they recognise it as planet Tatooine, from the world-famous *Star Wars* series. Despite the possible sandstorms and guaranteed Saharan heat, people from all over the world choose to make the long and difficult journey to this peculiar destination.

Man 1: You're actually seeing the things that you've had in your mind for, like, over 25 years, watching the video over and over again. And finally you're here and you can touch it, and you can feel it, and you can smell it, and – it's just amazing.

Narrator: The underground buildings are hundreds of years old and were originally designed to protect citizens from invaders.

Man 2: George Lucas basically chose this place because of its alien look. The architecture in … in Tunisia is … is unique. You don't find it anywhere else in the world.

Narrator: Filmmaker George Lucas travelled to Tunisia to shoot the first film in the saga in 1977 and chose Sidi Driss, in Matmata, as Luke Skywalker's home. The film crew did their work and left. But *Star Wars* became an international hit. Millions of fans around the world feel a connection with this location, even though they have never seen it in real life. Those that do make the journey are not disappointed.

Man 3: It's fantastic, you know it's still in really good condition cons … surprisingly.

Man 2: Look at this, it's … it's real, we can touch it, we can feel it …

Man 4: It kind of just brings the … the *Star Wars* universe a little closer and the fans together.

Narrator: But it's not only *Star Wars* fans who are able to appreciate this unique location.

Woman 1: I've never seen the *Star Wars* films but, uh, I think this place is strange.

Narrator: Before they leave, fans enjoy a home-made version of the films' famous "Bantha milk". This moment will be part of the the story they will tell about the place.

Man 1: Cheers mates.

Everybody: Cheers! Cheers!

Narrator: The journey to Sidi Driss may have been long, but it has been worth it for these fans, who will remember the experience for the rest of their lives.

Man 5: Purely, uh, magic!

Unit 3

Narrator: Philip Mellin is a 16-year-old shepherd. He's grown up on a dairy farm in Yorkshire, which also has 500 sheep. It's a lot of responsibility for Philip and his mother Carol, and a lot of hard work. However, this summer, Philip's finished secondary school and things are about to change.

Philip: Now I've left school, I feel on top of the world.

Narrator: Working on the family farm is all Philip has ever wanted to do for a living. However, the dairy business has not been doing well, so he and his mother have taken the decision to stop milking altogether and sell the cows.

Philip: Now we're coming out of the cows, um, obviously we'll need another way of making money. So, my idea is that we're to train dogs.

Narrator: Philip plans to train and sell these dogs to help farmers manage their flocks of sheep. So that these dogs have something to train with, however, Philip must maintain his own flock. An important part of looking after sheep is trimming their wool in a process called shearing, and Philip needs to learn how it's done.

Man 1: There's one over the backbone, and I'm gonna do another one, round this shoulder, as its right leg comes up.

Narrator: It's not long before Philip's first attempt, and he does the job well. After some training, it's time to take the shears to his own flock. Following a tricky start, Philip finishes shearing the first of his own sheep, and Carol is happy with his progress.

Carol: I think it's good that he's found something that's really challenging to get his teeth into and from what I've seen so far, he's doing a really good job of it.

Narrator: Now Philip has some training under his belt, he can turn his attention back to preparing his new business. He needs a premises, and plans to convert the empty cow shed into dog kennels. It's going to be expensive, but Philip knows how to strike a deal.

Philip: Thirty!

Man 2 [on the phone]: Well, make it forty-five and we'll split the difference.

Philip: Forty, and you've got a deal.

Narrator: After a few weeks of hard work, the kennels are complete. What's more, Philip has done it all himself.

Philip: Yeah, it's gone alright. It's gone much better than I thought it would have done.

Narrator: Now that Philip's set up, there's just one thing that he needs – a dog.

Man 3 [over PA system]: Four thousand four! Four thousand … !

Narrator: Luckily, there's a dog auction in town.

Philip: I've seen two in t'catalogue, um, which I like, so, I'll … I'll have a look at 'em when they're runnin', and see what I think.

Narrator: Philip picks his favourite and bids successfully. Carol is impressed.

Carol: Looks a nice dog actually, doe'n't it?

Narrator: But after five days, it's a different story. The dog is very friendly and Philip is wondering if, in fact, it's too friendly.

Phillip: It's all over me, it's been all over me since day one. And it's … it's too much all over me, so we'll just have to see how it goes.

Narrator: For his first dog, however, Philip's not done badly, and Carol's thinking about the future.

Carol: I'm just letting him throw his thoughts into it because at the end of the day it will be his business, won't it?

Narrator: It's been a significant summer for Philip. He's taken control of his destiny, reshaping the family business into something he can continue to grow, and making the transformation from schoolboy to man of the farm. There aren't many people who can say they're living the dream at 16 years old. Philip, however, just might.

Unit 4

Narrator: Shanghai, New York, Dubai, Vancouver. Many large cities are well known for their easily identifiable skylines. In London, numerous skyscrapers soar high over the streets below and have become part of the city's personality. Not as permanent as it seems however, the skyline is in constant development and plans for the city keep aiming higher and higher. In this craze for tall buildings, some skyscrapers stand out for the wrong reasons.

Man: Yesterday, uh, people were filming this bike saddle, that had actually caught alight, and the smoke was rising up off of there. But also, em, you know, it just gets so hot, you put your hand out into the light and immediately it's like, uh, scorching you straight away. It's really intense heat.

Narrator: The Walkie Talkie tower, nicknamed due to its distinctive shape, is a very good example of a city project that architects and urban planners didn't think through. The consequence – when the sun shined on its curved glass front, it acted as a giant heat collector, focusing a large area of sunshine on one small area of ground. Solar physicist Simon Foster explained the phenomenon.

Simon: If, when you look up at the building you should see it's like, kind of, parabolic we call it, you see, it's in the shape of a wok. If you've ever seen like a satellite dish what it does is it reflects radio waves down onto that receiver. Well, you can do the same with light. So as the light comes in, instead of it being reflected on a straight mirror back in the same direction, it gets bent down onto a curve, a focus – and we are right in the focus. So all that energy that's hitting up there, huge building, is being focused down onto this tiny little region here.

Narrator: Shop owners had to deal with tiles cracking in the heat and customers complaining of smoking furniture.

Shop owner: We didn't notice it until one of our customer, they, uh, they came in and then they said "you have a very serious problem" and they actually showed us, uh, the … the chair which was burning and then the carpet was, like, smelling very bad, and I was like "what's going on here?".

Simon: This has actually, it got up to 92.6 degrees. That's Celsius.

Narrator: One of the news reporters at the scene didn't bother to go into the café for his lunch – it was hot enough to fry an egg outside.

Simon: Having a curved surface like this reflecting sunlight is completely well known so I'm very surprised this wasn't taken into consideration.

Interviewer: And so what can be done about it?

Simon: You could coat it in some sort of surface that either scatters the light out; the other thing is you could re-orientate all the panes of glass and they're not gonna wanna do that.

Narrator: And although it took them a few months, the developers found a permanent solution. The 37-storey building was fitted with shades to deflect the sunlight. Although the building's new look isn't as shiny as the architects intended, the Walkie Talkie still plays its part in the dramatic London skyline.

Unit 5

Narrator: This is 16 year-old Sam Roper. He's a passionate cyclist and – this year – the youngest entrant to Yorkshire's notorious Three Peaks Challenge. The gruelling course covers a distance of 38 miles, with a combined climb of over 1,500 metres across the three peaks of Pen-y-Ghent, Whernside, and Ingleborough. Sam's competed in races before, but nothing quite like this.

Sam: The Three Peaks differs, uh, to, like, my normal cross-country races just because it … it's so much longer and a much, much harder race. And it'll definitely be a, uh, like a technical and a physical challenge.

Narrator: The Challenge is renowned for being the toughest cyclocross event in the UK. And history has shown that, if bad weather strikes, this race can quickly become treacherous. However, Sam has trained for every eventuality. He's even brought in eight-time Challenge champion Rob Jebb for some last-minute training! This weather is perfect. Hopefully it'll stay like this for the race. It's race day, and the weather has turned. Even defending champion Rob doesn't like the look of it!

Rob: I think it's gonna be the wettest one I've done for a long, long time. Uh, it could be real tricky.

Narrator: Sam, however, is more focused on what he should be wearing.

Sam: Rob said that he was only riding just in a short jersey and a pair of shorts so it's probably good advice from Rob there.

Narrator: Sam lines up with the rest of the cyclists and then …

Man 1: Go!

Narrator: In this wet weather, the ground is slippery and unpredictable. Crashes happen often, with some involving head injuries. Sam seems to be doing well, until …

Man 2: Oh!

Claire: He's over!

Narrator: Sam's landed on his head. He seems okay though, and gets back on his bike. But not for long.

Man 1: You alright?

Sam: I can't see properly out of one eye, it's all blurry.

Narrator: Sam has to stop, and asks his mum, Claire, for advice.

Claire: You alright? Have you … have you got concussion?

Sam: Well I might do yeah …

Narrator: Sam continues, despite his knock on the head affecting his sight.

Claire: I'm not sure if he should continue or not really. Um, he won't want to give up but we'll … we'll just follow him along, make sure he's okay.

Narrator: Sam's in the final stages of the course, and pushing harder than ever. Despite the weather and his injury, Sam's raced a second place in the junior category. It's a great result for a first-timer. It looks like his gamble in finishing the race with a potential concussion has paid off. So, how does he feel?

Sam: That was probably one of the hardest things I've ever done. It was absolutely ridiculous.

Narrator: With the difficulties of the race fading into memory, he's exhausted but proud of his achievement. For Sam, the risks of the Challenge go hand-in-hand with its rewards.

Sam: Most of the way round I thought it was absolutely horrible and I'd never, ever, ever do it again. But, uh, thinking about it now …I probably would come back and give it another go.

Unit 6

Narrator: From action cameras to capture movement in extreme sports to heat sensitive filming equipment used in the dead of night, technology aids filmmakers wanting to convey their own unique points of view in their films.

Rob: My name is Rob Spence, and I'm a cyborg. I have a prosthetic eye with a, uh, camera, right in the eye.

Narrator: Rob, a documentary filmmaker, lost one of his eyes in an accident and decided to have a camera put in its place. Now he uses it to film his own experiences and those of others like him. He has turned his disability into a very special tool.

Rob: I go around the world with my bionic eye and film bionic people. I film other cyborgs, the top cyborgs. Arms, legs, I am now filming your bionic hand with my bionic eye.

Man: It's pretty cool.

Rob: So basically, in here, is a battery, a camera and a wireless transmitter. It's transmitting to this receiver, which in turn I can output this video into any kind of video recorder.

Narrator: What makes Rob's eye such a special piece of filming equipment is the very personal, very human feel it adds to his footage.

Rob: The eye also tracks, it moves, you see blinking and glancing, which is a very actual human point of view. I also get video feedback when I'm looking at my own monitor.

Narrator: Rob is convinced the future will take him even further. His vision might not be great now but it has one very significant advantage – it can be upgraded.

Rob: Unlike you puny humans I can upgrade, so next year it'll be better and better and then eventually you'll be in the dust while I'm using my night-vision, telescopic, HD, thermal-vision, augmented-reality supereye.

Rob: Now, they call me Eyeborg.

Unit 7

Narrator: There is a strong connection between the stories that people pass on through word of mouth, from generation to generation and from one civilisation to the next, and the objects that inspire these stories. TV host and researcher Julia Bradbury is on her way to Manchester to find out about such an object.

Julia: I love this story because it's current, it's actually happening now. Apparently, there is an ancient Egyptian relic that is turning of its own accord at a museum in Manchester which is where I'm heading. Nobody know why it's happening, it's a bit of a mystery.

Narrator: It may seem unbelievable, but at the museum, they have the footage to prove it. Julia is on her way to talk to Egyptologist Campbell Price and check it out! When they realised the statue was moving, they set up a time-lapse camera.

Julia: Look at that! Clear, as day!

Narrator: The statue is indeed turning, while the others remain still.

Julia: Let's get back to the actual little statue itself.

Campbell (overlapping): Yeah.

Julia: Um, what … what does it stand for, where … where is it from, what's its history?

Campbell: So, it belonged to a man called Neb-Senu, and he lived about 4,000 years ago.

Narrator: There is a hieroglyphic inscription on its back asking for offerings for his spirit in the afterlife.

Campbell: The Ancient Egyptians believed that statuettes could be alternative homes for the spirit.

Julia: OK, I've seen the footage.

Campbell (overlapping): Uhm.

Julia: I've discussed things with you. Now, show me the mummy.

Campbell: OK.

Narrator: The story of the revolving figure in its solid glass case was all over the news and social media. Some suggested it might be the spirit of singer and dancer Michael Jackson while others blamed it on Neb-Senu himself, turning the statue around to get people's attention. Julia has arranged a meeting with Joyce Tyldesley to find out why ancient Egypt is such a powerful source of inspiration.

Joyce: I think we're almost pre-programmed to believe strange things about ancient Egypt. People have seen films, they've read about Tutankhamun and when you read about Tutankhamun it's very difficult to break away from the idea that there's a curse there.

Narrator: According to legend anyone who dared go anywhere near the boy king's final resting place, soon fell victim to the curse. In the 1920s the legend gained traction because some of the people who were involved in finding the tomb died not long after it was broken open and the press attributed their deaths to the curse.

Julia: And then we're brought back to our little rotating man and all of these ingredients just pulled together, didn't they? And created this big story out of a … out of a tiny object.

Joyce: Absolutely, yes.

Narrator: There did turn out to be a rational explanation as to why the statue was spinning. The outside vibrations created by footfall and even buses going past the museum, together with the slightly convex base of this particular statue caused it to slowly turn around. Sound expert Stephen Gosling has measured the vibrations and is one hundred percent sure.

Julia: Is this conclusive?

Stephen: Yes.

Julia: You'd stake your life on it?

Stephen: Yes.

Julia: Can't ask more than that, Steve.

Narrator: A rather unexciting ending to this particular story. But Ancient Egyptians left us many reminders of their civilisation with stories behind them we can only imagine.

Julia: We're steeped in Egyptian culture and that's one of the reasons why this story gathered such momentum around the world. So next time you're out and about, keep your eyes peeled for Sphinxes, pyramids, obelisks – they're everywhere apparently!

Unit 8

Narrator: The crowd is cheering as loudly as at any sporting event but this competition is more science than sport. It's all about robots. The annual robotics competition by FIRST: For Inspiration and Recognition of Science and Technology – a non-profit organization encouraging young people to take an interest in science subjects and careers.

Woodie: When you get 30,000 people together in a place like the St. Louis dome to celebrate a whole group of people who have built things, it makes a very positive statement about the complexity and the sophistication and the respect that goes to people who can create real things.

Narrator: High school students from around the world built these robots in just six weeks.

Guy: We are the first team from Israel to accomplish, uh, um, to reach the Einstein field. And it's very exciti … exciting for us to play with all the big teams. Uh, and we came here to have fun and represent our, uh, country.

Narrator: This year's challenge was called Recycle Rush. They started with some parts and a task. They had to build robotic carts that could pick up and stack plastic containers on top of one another. Then, they had to place a recycling bin at the very top. The higher the pile, the more points they won! As a team, they had to collaborate on every aspect – the design, the build and the business plan. All in a very short time frame, with the ultimate aim of earning the maximum number of points in the competition. Today was the climax of those efforts and time came for each team to see the results of their hard work. Only the strongest teams made it to the final rounds. For some, it was over sooner than they'd hoped, but they are still happy with the experience.

Bethany: I really got into it. It showed me that engineering, technology, science and math can be so much more than just paper doing problems. It showed me that it can be exciting, it can be just as fun as any sports any time.

Narrator: In the last round, the teams involved made the most of the final seconds. And it was team 118 "The Robonauts" who came out at the very top!

Christopher: I feel amazing right now. We've been striving to get this world championship for 18-19-20 years and counting. It's always … it's always escaped us but now, now it hasn't.

Mason: Oh, look, we just got a trophy out here, … Isn't that awesome? It's amazing. Yeah, it's … it's easy. I mean the robot we're building is as complicated as some of the stuff we're trying to send to space.

E.J.: What I want these kids to get out of it, um, is just what FIRST is about. You're inspiring them to do something with their lives, to be interested in STEM – science, math, technology. I'm into robots, I'm into cars. Like I said, I work at Tesla, we built a giant robot. I want these kids to be able to see professionals doing those things day in, day out. See that we're normal people and see where they can go.

Narrator: This year's competition is over but teams all over the world will soon be getting ready for the next one!

Unit 9

Interviewer: What does it smell like in the produce section here?

Man 1: Hmm … Kind of fruity.

Girl: Yeah.

Narrator: The aromas in the aisles at this Brooklyn supermarket are intense, but the smells aren't just coming from the products on the shelves.

Interviewer: So, do you think the smell in here is coming from these grapefruits?

Man 1: That's an interesting question. I know with modern technology it could come from a lot of sources.

Narrator: This savvy shopper just might be on to something.

Interviewer: See that little black machine behind you?

Man 1: Wow. What is that thing?

Interviewer (overlapping: Do you have any idea what that is?

Man 1: It's blowing a breeze so … it's … it's kind of funky. Don't tell me it's a grapefruit scent a … airer, what do they call the … aerator?

Narrator: Actually, they're called scent air machines, and this supermarket has five of them, each piping out a different smell, including grapefruit in the produce section …

Man 1: I think it's a grapefruit, isn't it? Or is it not a grapefruit?

Girl: Yeah, it is.

Narrator: … chocolate in the candy aisle …

Woman 1: It, uh, improves our mood you know.

Interviewer: It makes you happy?

Woman 1: Yeah.

Woman 2: Yes.

Narrator: …and rosemary focaccia by the bakery.

Man 2: It's a smell like at home.

Narrator: What looks like part of a typical ventilation system is part of a marketing campaign that targets a shopper's sense of smell.

Merchandise coordinator: The machine is really small so it's good for us. No … nobody can see …

Narrator: The store's merchandise coordinator says she installed the machines two months ago, after hearing about them overseas.

Merchandise coordinator: I think because of these machines, it makes customer more, like, hungrier.

Narrator: The goal is simple: make customers hungry and, in turn, open up their wallets.

Interviewer: Does the smell make you hungry?

Man 2: Yeah.

Woman 3: Yeah!

Narrator: In fact, sales in the produce department have gone up at least seven percent, and with each machine costing ninety-nine dollars a month, this market thinks it's made a good investment.

Interviewer: And so far so good.

Merchandise coordinator: Yes, so far so good, everybody's enjoying it, everybody loves it.

Narrator: In the US, consumers spend an estimated five hundred billion dollars a year on food, and with smell accounting for seventy-five percent of what we taste, there's no denying a psychological effect.

Expert: The sense of smell is so primal, it goes into an outer part of the brain before it can all register, and it's unconscious, wonderful thing that happens to you, so that sense of smell actually translates later into: "Oh! I wasn't even hungry but now I want popcorn!"

Narrator: But it isn't the smell of fresh popcorn that's overwhelming these shoppers.

Interviewer: Where we're standing, what are you smelling?

Woman 4: Uhm … I smell some s … I guess smoked meat.

Interviewer: What if I told you that smell was actually being pumped out of that little black machine over there?

Woman 4: That would be great! I understand … it… it working!

Interviewer: It's working?

Woman 4: Yeah.

Interviewer: Yeah.

Woman 4: It's working.

Narrator: So it seems in this store the machines are bringing in dollars and making scents.

Interviewer: Are you gonna buy a grapefruit today?

Man 1: Um … I know they're good for me. We didn't come for grapefruits but, uh, it's a …

Interviewer: Possibility?

Man 1: Yeah.

Girl: Yeah.

Man 1: It's … it's a good fruit.

Interviewer: You can have this one.

Man 1: Oh, thank you!

WORKBOOK ANSWER KEY

UNIT 1

Reading

1 1 dull **2** reluctant **3** overwhelming **4** pretty **5** dismiss **6** worthwhile **7** pigeonhole **8** willing **9** cosy

2 2 Have stories to tell, not stuff to show

3 1 F (*He* refers back to Thomas Gilovich)
2 C (*Firstly* introduces the answer to the question at the end of paragraph 2)
3 G (*They* refers back to *how people felt*; *missing an experience more than losing out on an object* refers back to *choosing not to do or buy something*; the sentence following the gap gives an example to support the research)
4 B (*experiences define who you are* refers back to *the effect on identity*)
5 A (*a difficult situation* refers back to *an experience has made someone unhappy*; *turn into a funny story* refers back to *make that person feel more positive*)
6 E (the whole sentence refers back to the idea of *how you want to spend your money*; *them* in the sentence following the gap refers to *objects* in sentence E)

4 1 to **2** with **3** to **4** about

5 1 possessions **2** stuff **3** regret **4** missed **5** last **6** keeping

Grammar

1 1 B **2** A **3** B **4** B **5** A **6** A **7** B

2 1 We **haven't known** each other for long, but we get on very well.
2 correct
3 correct
4 I'm hot because **I've been running** round the park
5 I broke my phone two days ago so I **haven't messaged** my friends for ages.
6 correct
7 All my friends **spend** every Saturday afternoon at the football.
8 correct

3 1 looks **2** are you looking **3** I don't really enjoy **4** haven't done **5** have you tried **6** I've never been (*I never am* is not possible because of the incorrect word order; the frequency adverb would come after *be*: *I am never*) **7** are standing **8** I'm getting **9** I've had **10** you're always walking

5 1 are always telling **2** does, mean **3** says **4** cross/'re crossing **5** 've been working **6** isn't going **7** 've been trying **8** Has, ever said **9** means **10** has, helped

Vocabulary

1 A thrilled 8
B petrified 2
C tense 7
D relieved 5
E determined 4
F sympathetic 1
G offended 3
H moved 6

2 1 understanding **2** anxious **3** strong-willed **4** terrified **5** insulted

3 1 insulted **2** understanding **3** terrified **4** anxious **5** sympathetic **6** delighted

4 1 miss out **2** put off **3** trying out **4** getting, across **5** take off **6** add to

5 1 up, in **2** after, back **3** on **4** over, on/on with **5** away, out **6** up

Listening

1 C to give information about a special category of people

2 1 sight *In the first talk in the series on senses, we looked at sight.*
2 cells *This is someone with a higher density and number of cells for taste compared with the average.*
3 limit *This was the biggest shock for me when researching this talk – that being a supertaster can actually limit the range of foods you enjoy.*
4 quarter … *that leaves about a quarter of us who have a very strong reaction to the bitter taste.*
5 (about) seventy *So our sense of smell and taste fade over time, especially after reaching about* seventy.
6 sophisticated *What most people don't realise is that we need the receptors in the nose to work with the taste buds to produce the sophisticated range of flavours we get from our diet.*
7 chemical *Humans have about 350 different receptor genes for smells. Their job is to recognise the chemical pattern given off by different foods.*
8 one trillion/a trillion *Estimates vary as to how many individual smells humans can detect, but one study suggests it's as many as one trillion.*
9 tried the test. *Many people from the team here at the Science for Life office all tried the test and I was really hoping to get supertaster status, but I'm sorry to say I was the worst taster of the whole group.*
10 the worst *I was really hoping to get supertaster status, but I'm sorry to say I was the worst taster of the whole group.*

3 A sour **B** sweet **C** bitter **D** salty

4 1 savoury **2** strong **3** watery **4** hot **5** fussy

5 1 sweet **2** bitter **3** strong **4** watery **5** spicy **6** hotter

Use of English 1

1 1 more **2** than **3** much **4** so **5** too **6** as **7** most **8** much **9** of

2 1 more **2** than **3** as big as **4** well **5** more **6** too long **7** good enough **8** better and better **9** so loudly

3 1 the funniest **2** the most disappointing **3** even better **4** the best **5** The closer **6** the more convinced **7** wasn't/was not near enough **8** as quickly as **9** a lot less cool

4 1 speak Russian more fluently than (comparative form with adverb)
2 left too late (*too* + adverb)
3 is (just) as tall as/is the same height as (comparative phrase *just as … as* with affirmative verb; *as … as* with noun phrase)
4 don't know anyone kinder (comparative form with *anyone*)
5 can run far/much faster than (comparative form with adverb *faster* and adverb of degree *far* or *much*)
6 the more accessible they (double comparative to show continual change)

Use of English 2

1 1 fitness **2** deafness **3** childishness **4** difference **5** laziness **6** fashionable **7** hopeful/hopeless **8** enthusiastic

2 1 athletic, impressive **2** scientific, artistic **3** moves, foolish

3 1 direction **2** rhythm **3** humour/fun **4** adventure/fun **5** achievement

4 1 successful (noun to adjective)
2 dreadful (noun/verb to adjective)
3 comfortable (noun to adjective)
4 repetitive (verb to adjective)

5 confidence (adjective to noun)
6 competitive (verb to adjective)
7 improvement (verb to noun)
8 accessible (noun/verb to adjective)

Speaking

1 Speaker 1: B not comparing both photos
Speaker 2: E asking the other student questions
Speaker 3: C asking the examiner for vocabulary
Speaker 4: D hesitating a lot
Speaker 5: A not using a range of language

3 1 show **2** similar **3** similarity **4** differences **5** whereas **6** celebrating **7** achievement **8** anxious **9** direction **10** better

Writing

1 1 B **2** B, D, F
3 A the reviewer's recommendation 4
B brief details about the subject 1
C the reviewer's experience 2
D more information/examples 3

2 1 C **2** F **3** E **4** A **5** D **6** B

3 1 it's not really worth the money **2** it's perfect for anyone without **3** thoroughly recommend **4** won't regret it **5** it's well worth trying **6** I wouldn't recommend it to

4 1 air-conditioned **2** all-inclusive, all-day **3** brightly-lit **4** first-class **5** old-fashioned **6** three-day **7** well-organised, well-known, well-lit

5 1 instructor **2** location **3** atmosphere **4** audience **5** activity **6** cost **7** problem

6 1 absolutely delicious **2** truly fascinating **3** really dreadful **4** extremely dull **5** totally terrifying

7 Model answer

Putting the fun back into festival

Are you looking for a great way to enjoy yourself this summer? It's well worth trying the ForTeen Festival. It's a five-day event that takes place every year in the first week of August. What makes it special? It's specifically for 14–18-year-olds.

One of the best things is the entertainment. It's perfect for anyone interested in bands, clothes, movies or gadgets. There are performances and talks by well-known musicians and speakers. The festival also offers workshops and one-hour lessons so you can have a go at something new.

It's a very well-organised festival, located a few kilometres from the centre. The area is divided into zones for music, technology, fashion and cinema. So you can go for what you love, or try a bit of everything. Air-conditioned buses run every 15 minutes to the festival and the area is accessible to wheelchairs.

Just one day at ForTeen is fantastic, but if you have time, an all-inclusive ticket is really worth the money. I would highly recommend the event to students of my age. Check out the programme for this year. You won't regret it.

Unit check

1 1 'm walking **2** calls **3** know **4** 's shouting **5** wants **6** say **7** don't even know **8** are you talking about **9** runs off **10** 'm standing **11** has just happened

2 1 the **2** lot **3** than **4** more **5** enough **6** most **7** as **8** too

3 1 the better your marks **2** wasn't as easy as **3** are far more adventurous than **4** aren't old enough **5** is the best time

4 1 put off **2** get, across **3** trying out **4** take off **5** are, adding to/have, been adding to **6** miss out

5 1 achievement, excitement **2** difference, existence **3** laziness, tiredness **4** competitive, creative **5** enthusiastic, sympathetic **6** knowledgeable, changeable

UNIT 2

Reading

1 1 boom, freak out **2** awe-inspiring, live up to expectations **3** exotic, superb **4** medieval, appeal to **5** feature, have access to **6** vast, incredible

2 C family and lifestyle

3 1 B *I haven't checked it out with my family yet. I'm trying to pick the right moment …*
2 A *In the last couple of years, the trip has been pretty tedious because it's tough finding fun things to do.*
3 C *I have never gotten along too well with my cousins, even though we're all in our teens.*
4 A *I had no idea what was coming next. My mom freaked out, her final words were, 'No way!'*
5 C *Can I please go to grandma's instead?*
6 D *Maybe they think I'll do something stupid.*
7 B *I found myself at a space museum to keep my brother smiling and a farm for my animal-mad sister!*
8 A *I was thinking of working over the summer, just to top up my allowance.*
9 D *We message each other all the time …*
10 C *Dad said yes and mom said maybe so things are still up in the air.*

4 1 join in **2** opt out **3** count me out **4** sort out **5** be in for a treat **6** checked it out with **7** chill out **8** up in the air

5 1 chill out **2** joining in **3** 'd be in for a treat **4** have, checked it out with **5** to sort out **6** opt out **7** count you out

Grammar

1 1 B **2** A **3** A **4** B **5** A **6** B **7** B

2 1 were walking, crashed **2** took off, 'd/had been waiting **3** was going to skype, was **4** had, swum, stepped **5** was reading, missed, had to **6** used to spend, would collect

3 *Would* can replace *used to* in sentences 2 and 4.

4 1 B **2** F **3** A **4** D **5** C **6** E

5 1 went **2** 'd never travelled **3** missed **4** didn't get on **5** 'd been writing **6** was due to stay **7** was going to have **8** 'd been looking forward **9** 're used to having **10** 'd already made **11** didn't think

Vocabulary

1 1 dressed up, live up to **2** Think up, doesn't conjure up **3** gave up, 'll, end up

2 1 over, moon **2** high, list **3** down, dumps **4** blown away **5** fell, love **6** got, swing

3 1 down in the dumps **2** fall in love with **3** (you) to get into the swing of things **4** blew you away **5** (feel) over the moon **6** high on the/your list

4 1 cheap travel **2** make reservations **3** package tours **4** make sure **5** extremely helpful **6** travelling light **7** takes such a long time **8** enter all the details **9** keeps a record **10** improve my travel experience

Listening

1 1 E **2** D **3** F **4** C

2 1 B *fairly typical categories; books for under-fourteens, books for fourteen to sixteen-year-olds; stories for animal-lovers, books about aliens.*
2 A *what brings them together is a very strong sense of place. Each book is set in a different part of the world*
3 C *we just voted for the first book as a group and since then each person has chosen a story and so the next destination.*

4 B Life of Pi … *turned out to be a great starting point. It's so thrilling that everyone loved it!;* The Old Man and the Sea … *divided the group. Some members enjoyed it, but others felt it lacked plot.*
5 A *Er, I don't want to say too much more in case your listeners are reading it or want to read it.*
6 C *I just couldn't put this one down … .The plot was so thrilling I had to read right to the end in a single weekend.*
7 C *you get to understand the experiences of people you would never meet … You really do get a global view.*

3 1 corners **2** trip **3** pack **4** starting **5** expedition **6** have **7** global

4 1 pack a suitcase **2** having adventures **3** be taken to the far corners of the globe **4** round-the-world trip **5** be a great starting point **6** joining, on an expedition **7** get a global view

Use of English 1

1 1 correct
2 That was **the** airline that lost all our luggage.
3 Where's **the** best place you've ever visited?
4 You find out so much about a place if you explore on ~~**the**~~ foot.
5 correct
6 correct
7 Have you ever been to **the** Netherlands?
8 I love (**to**) travel. I wish I could go abroad more often.
9 correct
10 It's great to get away for the weekend once in **a** while.

2 1 the, – **2** a, a, the **3** the, a **4** the, a **5** The, the **6** a, the

3 1 –, –, the, the, –, a **2** The, –, the, -, The, The, – **3** a, –, the, A/The, The

4 1 the/- **2** a **3** An **4** a **5** – **6** a **7** a/the **8** the **9** – **10** a **11** the **12** the **13** a **14** the **15** an/the

Use of English 2

1 1 warming, disasters **2** with, tourism **3** damage, have, think **4** achieved, on **5** At, no

2 1 collapsing **2** done a lot of harm **3** taking such a risk **4** tourist season **5** foreign visitors **6** make a living **7** run into problems **8** quality of life

3 1 with **2** on **3** of **4** for **5** about

4 1 to pay for **2** complained about **3** disagreed with **4** was afraid/scared of **5** decide on

5 1 B (the other nouns can't follow *take* in this context)
2 D (the other phrasal verbs don't fit the context)
3 A (the other adjectives don't fit the context)
4 C (the other phrasal verbs don't fit the context)
5 D (the other verbs don't collocate with *harm*)
6 A (the other verbs don't collocate with *jobs* in this context)
7 B (the other adjectives don't fit the context)
8 B (collocation is *quality of life*, a fixed expression)

Speaking

1 1 C **2** D **3** B **4** A **5** B **6** C **7** D **8** A

2 Question 2

3 1 C **2** B **3** D **4** A

4 1 like, because; question one **2** as; question seven **3** for; question three **4** so, such as; question eight

5 1 catch **2** repeating **3** say **4** sure **5** honest **6** used **7** sure

6 1 I'm sorry, I didn't quite catch that.
2 Would you mind repeating that?
3 Sorry, can you say that again, please?
4 That's an interesting question. I'm not really sure of the answer, but I think I'd say flying is the best way to travel.
5 To be honest, I've never been abroad, but I'd like to go to New Zealand because my favourite movie was filmed there.
6 I used to love just playing on the beach, but now I prefer spending time in cities.
7 I'm not really sure which school I'll be at, but I'll still be studying English.

7 Model answer

I definitely prefer my capital city because there's so much for teenagers to do there such as sports events and music festivals.

I'd go for a summer beach holiday, I think, as I'm not very good at skiing. I love doing things like swimming and relaxing with my family in the sunshine.

Australia, definitely! Three of my cousins live there, but I don't see them very often because of the distance.

I used to look forward to going to the water park on holiday every year. I loved all the activities, for example the water games and swimming races.

Although I'm quite confident, I don't think I'd like to travel alone because I would miss my family.

Writing

1 1 both
2 an eye-catching title ✓
questions that address the reader directly ✓
lively, colourful language ✓
an interesting conclusion ✓
a personal example or anecdote ✓
a new paragraph for each topic/event ✓

2 1 After we'd finally found a space on the beach, the sun went in.
2 By the time I found my ticket, the inspector had made me pay again.
3 As soon as we reached/had reached the coast, we ran into the sea.
4 I'd been trying to find my friend before I suddenly spotted her across the square.
5 Even though we had a few arguments, we still had a great time.
6 She didn't get back until late because her flight was/had been delayed. / Because her flight was/had been delayed, she didn't get back until late.
7 My brother wasn't well on the last day, so we cancelled the trip.
8 Since it was such a fantastic place, we've booked to go there again.

3 C My dream holiday turned nightmare

4 Paragraph B

5 1 cruising **2** burning **3** flew **4** crashed **5** shouted **6** hit the brakes **7** jumped **8** speeding

6 Conclusion A

7 Model answer

A flight I'll never forget

Do you know that feeling of excitement you get before an important journey? That's exactly how I felt before I flew alone for the first time. But not everything went according to plan …

On my sixteenth birthday, my parents agreed I could go to a music festival later that year. We'd decided that the easiest way to get to the event was to fly, so I'd been saving for an air ticket for months. Then the day finally arrived. I got to the local airport two hours early. I was certainly not going to miss this flight!

I'm not scared of flying, so was full of confidence as the plane climbed into the sky. However, minutes later something went wrong. There was a huge bang and the plane suddenly shook. Panic spread and people started screaming. I learned later we'd been hit by a bird and an engine had been damaged.

Luckily, the pilot was able to get us back to the airport. And my dad felt so sorry for me that he drove me to the festival. It certainly was a summer to remember!

Unit check

1 **1** had **2** 'd wanted **3** didn't message **4** saw **5** were going **6** were just doing **7** was always getting **8** did you make **9** met **10** were having **11** invited **12** 'd been planning **13** used to **14** get used to

2 **1** an, a **2** The, – **3** –, – **4** a, –, the, a/the **5** A, the **6** A, a/the, the **7** a, the **8** the, –

3 **1** down in the dumps, think up **2** blown away by, live up to **3** give up, into the swing of things **4** dress up, high on my list

4 **1** have fun **2** Keep a record of **3** run into **4** cause severe damage to **5** tan easily **6** a few everyday words **7** have an impact on

UNIT 3

Reading

1 **1** gearing up **2** pilot scheme **3** siblings **4** distractions **5** collaboration **6** win-win situation **7** support

2 **2** a journalist who writes about technology

3 **1** C *What teenager in the world hasn't thought of staying at home on a schoolday and sending an avatar to class instead? But what about young people who want to go to school, but can't?… Meet AV1, the avatar that allows students to attend school even when they are off sick.*

2 B *AV1 is the brainchild of a Norwegian robotics company appropriately named No Isolation.*

3 A *The built-in camera allows the ill student visual access to the activity in the classroom. However, the student is not visible to the rest of the class or the teacher. This is to protect their privacy…*

4 A *Contributions to the class are made through the robot with the student's own voice.* This refers back to *the student's own voice* and forward to *She describes AV1 as '… the voice' of the ill student at school.*

5 D *The students who are in school also need to feel they can relate to the avatar. Karen Dolva explains, '… This is supposed to be their friend.'*

6 B *It is an amazing opportunity for people with challenges similar to those I face, to be able to go to school, attend classes, … The most important thing is that Marthe gets to attend classes and that she is a part of the group, … .*

4 **1** long-term **2** much-needed **3** built-in **4** real-time **5** life-size **6** water-resistant **7** full-time

5 **1** life-size **2** water-resistant **3** long-term **4** full-time **5** built-in **6** much-needed

Grammar

1 **1** has already been planned **2** prediction **3** timetable **4** at **5** based on what I know **6** won't **7** before **8** in progress, duration **9** future

2 **1** A **2** A **3** B **4** A **5** B **6** B

3 **1** 'll be hanging out **2** 'm due to start **3** Are you working **4** 'll have earned **5** 'll have been helping **6** 'll be doing **7** 'll have started **8** won't have been studying **9** 'm unlikely to need **10** you make

4 **1** we're moving **2** about **3** will have started **4** will already know **5** I'll make **6** walk **7** will be thinking **8** going to be **9** will be **10** get **11** you'll feel **12** you'll be enjoying

Vocabulary

1 **1** experiment, handout **2** discipline, detention **3** syllabus, timetable **4** attendance, grades

2 Be: creative / self-employed / your own boss / responsible
Have: a good salary / control over your own time / a lot of pressure / time off
Work: independently / shifts / part-time / as a team

3 **1** a self-employed **2** off **3** responsible **4** independently **5** as **6** being **7** part-time **8** have **9** over **10** salary

4 **1** up with **2** up for **3** up on **4** up with **5** on with **6** out of

5 **A** 3 goes along with **B** 6 keep out of **C** 1 measure up to **D** 4 go in for **E** 2 get away with **F** 5 given up on

Listening

1 B Take your teen to work

2 **2** engineer, local company offices, visit to construction site **3** media/magazines, magazine studio **4** food scientist; lab/laboratory **5** lawyer, office, court

3 Speaker 1 D *But the best part was writing a job advert. That really helped me see what skills you need to get an interview.*
Speaker 2 G *The work is a lot more varied than I thought.*
Speaker 3 B *… it was pretty clear no one knew what to do with a thirteen-year-old.*
Speaker 4 H *We did have a go at a taste test, but it was something I'd already done at school. What I really wanted was to see some of the food under development, but that wasn't possible.*
Speaker 5 E *I might even be changing my mind about my career.*

4 **1** B **2** E **3** H **4** F **5** D **6** G **7** C **8** A

5 **1** 'll follow/'re going to follow in their footsteps **2** had a go **3** opened my eyes **4** talked us through **5** was stuck **6** came over to **7** dropping me off **8** turned out

Use of English 1

1 **1** suitcases **2** rubbish **3** journey **4** armchair **5** money **6** skills

2 **1** no **2** many **3** bit **4** many **5** few **6** a

3 **1** most **2** all **3** no **4** many **5** deal **6** little **7** each **8** several **9** a few

4 **1** a large number of (fixed expression to parallel *many*)
2 is little time/isn't much time (*time* is uncountable in this context and needs *little* or *not much* to parallel *few* and a third person singular verb)
3 a large amount of damage (*a large amount of* followed by uncountable noun damage to parallel *badly damaged*)
4 to do a bit of (infinitive after *it's better*, plus fixed expression to parallel *a little*)
5 will have no problem/won't have any problem (fixed expression to parallel *will be easy*)
6 Every parent wants (*every* followed by singular countable noun and third person singular verb)

5 **1** most (followed by a plural countable noun without another determiner)
2 number (followed by pronoun which stands for a plural countable noun)
3 No (followed by a plural countable noun without another determiner)
4 all (affirmative statement followed by a plural countable noun without another determiner)
5 lots of (with the positive meaning of *some* followed by a plural countable noun)
6 few (with the negative meaning of *not many* followed by an object pronoun)
7 a few (followed by plural countable noun)
8 each (followed by an uncountable noun without another determiner)

Use of English 2

1 **1** G **2** B **3** E **4** H **5** A **6** D **7** C **8** F

2 **1** to **2** for **3** between **4** with **5** on **6** for

3 1 C (*succeed* followed by preposition *in*)
2 A (preposition *in* collocates only with *specialise*)
3 A (*refer* followed by preposition *to*)
4 A (preposition *on* collocates only with *insist*)
5 B (*cope* followed by preposition *with*)
6 D (preposition *from* collocates only with *benefits*)
7 C (*depends* followed by preposition *on*)
8 D (preposition *to* collocates only with *leads*)

4 1 apologise **for** doing something **to** a person
2 agree **with** a person **about/on** an issue/question
3 care **for** a person who can't look after themselves,
4 ask **for** an object you want about a topic/issue
5 play **with** an object

5 1 for, with/to **2** for, about **3** for, to

Speaking

1 1 E **2** C **3** A **4** D **5** B

2 1 Shall we start with this one?
2 How do you think a sponsored walk helps you?
3 What do you think about that?
4 How about the benefit from helping an older person?
5 I think collecting litter teaches you teamwork, don't you agree?
6 OK, what about this one?

3 A collecting litter with a group
B being a guide in a local museum

4 Speaker A performs better.
Speaker B's mistakes:
not responding fully to the other speaker's comments ✓
not using a very polite tone ✓
using very direct language ✓

5 1 F **2** D **3** E **4** B **5** A **6** C

6 1 F **2** T **3** F **4** F **5** T

Writing

1 1 formal or semi-formal **2** your point of view supported by reasons/evidence, complex sentences with appropriate linking words
3 introduction with a general statement about the topic 1
a paragraph about the first point in the notes 2
a paragraph about the second point in the notes 3
a paragraph about your own idea 4
a conclusion with a summary of your ideas 5

2 1 Neither my mum nor my dad did.
2 both Spanish and German at school.
3 either walk to school or (we could) wait for the bus.

3 2 school's performance **3** teacher's handouts
4 parent's involvement

4 The topic is educating boys and girls separately.
1 E **2** A **3** B **4** D **5** F **6** C

5 Model answer:

Classes in most schools are based on age despite big differences between students born in the same year. Is this the best way to educate young people?

It is often thought that students of the same age learn well together. However, being the same age doesn't mean you have the same abilities. One fourteen-year old could be brilliant at maths and another might find it difficult. Likewise, two fifteen-year olds may have different skills in sport or music. Another important point is motivation. In a class of different ages, the older ones can motivate the younger ones to achieve more. Moreover, the older students benefit by showing what they have learned and gaining self-confidence. From my own experience, I believe mixed-age groups encourage teamwork. I'm part of an orchestra with a big age range and we all work together. Collaborating across age groups is also more like real life.

To sum up, I agree that mixed-aged classes help students learn better. By being in the same age group they may miss out on challenge and motivation. Working with different ages is also better preparation for the world of work.

Unit check

1 1 A **2** B **3** B **4** C **5** C **6** A **7** C **8** A

2 1 No **2** all **3** Lots **4** Few **5** number **6** teachers' and students' **7** several **8** both

3 1 Neither **2** either **3** Both

4 1 handout **2** detention **3** grades **4** attendance
5 experiment

5 1 a job **2** off sick **3** your progress **4** drawbacks **5** a skill
6 your friends

6 1 apologise for **2** choose between **3** depend on
4 believes in **5** benefited from **6** succeeded in

7 1 for **2** with **3** in **4** to

USE OF ENGLISH, UNITS 1–3

Part 1

1 D (only answer D is followed by the preposition *on*)
2 A (collocates with *take* to form the expression *take the risk*)
3 B (forms the phrasal verb *end up* which means *be in a particular situation after an unplanned event*)
4 D (only answer D is followed by the preposition *with)*
5 A (collocates with *adventure* to form a fixed expression)
6 C (only answer C is followed by the preposition *in*)
7 B (collocates with *be … on your list* to form an idiom)
8 C (collocates with *tourism* to form the phrase *mass tourism*)

Part 2

9 be (infinitive, forms part of future continuous: *will be* + *-ing*)
10 too (*too* + adjective to mean *more than necessary*)
11 neither (conjunction, part of phrase *neither … nor*)
12 an (indefinite article before a vowel sound)
13 have (auxiliary, forms part of present perfect continuous: *has/have been* + *-ing*)
14 more (comparative form of adverb *easily*)
15 of (determiner *a number of* + plural countable noun)
16 up (forms phrasal verb *dress up* which means put clothes on someone/something to change their appearance)

Part 3

17 scientific (noun to adjective)
18 difference (verb to adjective)
19 accessible (verb/noun to adjective)
20 visible (noun to adjective)
21 comfortable (noun/verb to adjective)
22 painful (noun to adjective)
23 deafness (adjective to noun)
24 foolish (noun to adjective)

Part 4

25 is as enjoyable as singing (*as* + adjective + *as* to say that two things are the same in some way)
26 the furthest/farthest we had ever (superlative *the* + *-est* + past perfect with *ever*)
27 after/once/when she had looked (past perfect after a time expression to show the sequence of past actions; *look* collocates with *at*)
28 will have been flying (future perfect continuous *will have been* + *-ing* for an action happening during a period up to a specified time in the future)
29 a great deal of (determiner *a great deal of* + uncountable noun)
30 are only a few (*only* + *a few* + plural countable noun to mean *not many*)

UNIT 4

Reading

1 **1** defaced, imposing **2** issues **3** amenities **4** increasingly **5** ancestral **6** insulated, simulated

2 A the use of the city for different forms of entertainment

3 **1** C *Performing right next to a spectator, right in the middle of their hometown makes the magic somehow personal.*
2 D *So take a walk through the city and you might be thrown into a whole new dimension.*
3 A *Moving on when the crowd starts heckling with insults or the weather turns bad is all part of the job – as is being moved on by the authorities.*
4 C *Medieval kings and queens often employed a magician as an entertainer or healer.*
5 B *Each audience is unique, making the artist change their performance to suit the likes of the crowd.*
6 C *But viewers weren't always convinced by TV magic, suspecting that it may all be down to camera work.*
7 D *The artists' names or 'tags' that covered urban settings in the 1970s were seen as pure vandalism.*
8 B *Performing without a permit is often illegal …*
9 D *Some argue that street art has its roots in prehistoric cave paintings, developing over time from the examples of graffiti found in ancient Greece and Rome.*
10 A *It's possible to earn a reasonable living and some even turn professional having learned their craft on the streets.*

4 **1** heckling **2** down on their luck **3** learned their craft **4** spare a thought for **5** stunts **6** be down to **7** attract your attention **8** making a mark **9** survived a troubled past **10** in vain

5 **1** down on their luck **2** down to **3** survived a troubled past **4** stunts **5** attract, attention **6** make their mark/make a mark **7** learned our craft

Grammar

1 **1** D, F **2** B **3** E **4** C **5** A

2 **1** need, check **2** walk, always get **3** don't, 'll **4** could, I'd be **5** been staring, wouldn't have walked **6** I'd set, were **7** move, I'll visit **8** hadn't told, might have been waiting

3 **A** a threat 3
B some advice 6
C an instruction 1
D a promise 7
E a criticism 5

4 **1** B **2** B **3** A **4** B **5** A **6** B

5 **1** do you feel **2** wanted **3** 'd been born **4** don't, skate **5** were **6** would you create **7** would you have done

6 **1** have, to **2** were, have **3** hadn't, would **4** is, be

Vocabulary

1 **1** inner-city + well-connected **2** handy + overcrowded **3** remote + secure **4** express + winding

2 **1** country cottage **2** apartment block/complex **3** tourist spots **4** power station **5** public transport **6** leisure complex

3 **1** weather conditions **2** sales department **3** city walls **4** market square **5** window shopping **6** road markings

4 **1** air quality **2** city life **3** street lighting **4** rainwater **5** footsteps **6** air temperature

5 **1** city life **2** street lighting **3** air temperature **4** rainwater

Listening

1 **1** to his son's school **2** very impressive **3** at the start **4** difficult **5** small rural **6** on Saturday and Sunday **7** modern **8** on the next day

2 **1** B *Please wait at school and I'll get there as soon as I can. … Whatever you do, don't start walking or we'll miss each other.*
2 C *Lucinda has just updated her profile. Check out the pictures she's uploaded. … Has she posted anything else? Just a few more images and a note to say 'come and see me soon'.*
3 B *I thought I'd better be near college, … So you have a room on campus? That's right. I don't have to travel to lectures …*
4 C *I got a free pass for the morning in return for handing out 250 of these leaflets.*
5 A *… join us this Friday morning for a peaceful demonstration outside the council offices … Join us in the main square at 8.30 on Friday. We will then march to the council offices to hand in our petition*
6 B *… we were busy all weekend. … why do people in the country get up so early? … So there wasn't time to get bored. … I fell asleep on the sofa in the afternoon.*
7 B *What I enjoyed most was finding out how what they grow gets from the farm to our plate.*
8 A *I suppose we could walk in and get a lift back. … OK, let's go in on foot.*

3 **1** Don't bother going **2** have you found, more or less what I expected **3** I'd better be **4** I don't suppose you would **5** just off the main square **6** Do you fancy coming **7** remember

4 **1** Do you fancy **2** remember **3** just off **4** I'd better be **5** have you found **6** more or less what I expected **7** I don't suppose you would **8** don't bother

Use of English 1

1 **1** D **2** E **3** F **4** A **5** B **6** C

2 **1** You can borrow my bike provided that you take good care of it.
2 correct **3** correct
4 I'll let you have the bigger bedroom on condition that you keep it tidy.
5 Take a jumper in case it gets cold on the way back from town.
6 correct
7 The city will have a housing crisis unless it builds more affordable homes./The city will have a housing crisis if it doesn't build more affordable homes. **8** correct

3 **1** lived **2** wasn't **3** wouldn't show **4** could **5** hadn't come **6** wouldn't talk **7** had/'d trained **8** hadn't worn

4 **1** had a room of my own, wouldn't leave her stuff everywhere
2 hadn't gone red, would leave me alone
3 'd been more careful, would forgive me

5 **1** provided (linker, precedes *that* to introduce a conditional clause)
2 case (linker, follows *in* to introduce a conditional clause)
3 Unless (linker, meaning *if not* introduces a conditional clause)
4 long (linker, part of fixed phrase *as long as* introduces a conditional clause)
5 if/when (linker, introduces a conditional clause)
6 on (linker, part of fixed phrase *on condition that* to introduce a conditional clause)
7 could (modal verb, in past simple after *I wish*)
8 had (auxiliary verb, in past perfect after *If only* to express a past regret)

Use of English 2

1 **1** like **2** as **3** like **4** like **5** like **6** as

2 **1** A on, B in **2** A in, B out of **3** A on, B in **4** A in, B out of

3 **1** in, out of **2** On, by **3** at, on **4** by, by **5** By, at

4 **1** mind **2** one **3** person **4** real **5** order **6** part **7** place **8** date **9** order **10** hold

5 1 A (collocation *describes it as*)
2 D (fixed prepositional phrase *in good time*)
3 B (fixed prepositional phrase *at (no) risk*)
4 D (fixed prepositional phrase *for a start*)
5 A (fixed prepositional phrase *in place*)
6 C (fixed prepositional phrase *in reach of*)
7 B (fixed prepositional phrase *out of sight*)
8 D (fixed prepositional phrase *for good*)

Speaking

1 1 B, H **2** D, J **3** A, G **4** F, L **5** C, I **6** E, K
2 1 experience, imagine; question four
2 As, frankly; question two
3 In, I believe; question one
3 1 If you ~~would~~ ask me, …
2 I'd ~~have~~ definitely say that …
3 To be honest ~~you~~, …
4 I'm pretty sure ~~of~~ that …
5 I'm absolutely ~~too~~ convinced that …
6 This is just ~~own~~ my opinion, but …
4 Students 1 and 4.

Writing

1 1 B, C, D, F
2 1 catch a train **2** takes your breath away **3** make excuses **4** losing sleep **5** made; a difference **6** makes your day **7** tell the difference
positive 1, 2, 5, 6 negative 3, 4, 7
3 1 lost track of **2** make the most **3** be honest with you **4** lost patience **5** took control **6** made such a mess of **7** made a fuss
4 2 Hi (Miguel) ✓ **3** Dear (Ewa) ✓
5 1 Thanks ~~much~~ again.
2 All the best ~~you~~.
3 It was great to hear ~~of~~ about your holiday.
4 Hope that ~~can~~ helps.
5 I've just read about your ~~a~~ good news
6 Take ~~you~~ care!
7 Thanks ~~you~~ for your message.
8 Bye ~~soon~~ for now!
Sentences 3, 5 and 7 can be used in the first paragraph. The others are all for ending the email.

6 Model answer

Hi Piotr

Thanks for your message. Of course I'll help with your project. Here's the information about where I live.

The biggest thing that's changed is the transport system. They've taken cars out of the centre and installed electric trams. If they hadn't, we'd all be sitting in traffic every day just to get to school! It's really made a difference to the whole town. Another improvement is that there's less litter now. The council lost patience with people who were always making a mess when having a barbecue on the beach. They started fining them and now everyone tidies up.

You asked about what should have been done differently. Well, the new cinema has been a waste of money. A lot of local people have lost interest in cinema because of Netflix, but the silliest decision was the location. It's miles out of town, but you can't catch public transport there. So when you've made up your mind which film to see, you still need to organise a lift. If only someone had taken charge of the transport links!

Anyway, I hope that helps.

All the best

Anna

Unit check

1 1 C **2** G **3** A **4** F **5** B **6** D **7** E
2 1 unless **2** when **3** in case **4** that **5** could **6** hadn't built
3 1 as **2** had **3** was/were **4** like **5** case **6** long **7** would/could
4 1 well-connected **2** secure **3** overcrowded **4** express **5** inner-city **6** winding **7** remote **8** handy
5 1 entrance gates **2** water level **3** play area **4** weather conditions **5** housing crisis **6** traffic sign
6 1 out of, by, on **2** in, at, On **3** by, at, on **4** in, by, out of **5** on, in, in
7 1 on board **2** a flight **3** the right thing **4** arrangements **5** something funny

UNIT 5

Reading

1 1 rooting for **2** superior **3** yelling **4** relieve **5** boast **6** nil **7** jinx **8** rivals
2 Picture A (the football fan)
3 1 C *Three generations of the same family united in their love for their team.… But if a team or sport isn't in your family DNA, how do you know who to root for?*
2 A *Local sportspeople are a source of civic pride and provoke fierce loyalty in their fans, even when the sporting performance is less than perfect.*
3 D *On occasions, a person can be simply so impressed by an individual sportsperson that they adopt the sport.… Dream teams can also have the same effect.*
4 B *They shout their support loudest when times are good and the top trophies are being won, but are nowhere to be seen when the bad times hit.*
5 C *If team-switching makes you a fake fan, so does peer pressure. No one should support a team or player because they are told to.*
6 B *I enjoy the tight connection that being in a fan family offers me. The support we show our team is an extension of the support we show for each other.*
4 1 an affinity **2** fierce loyalty **3** to back **4** through thick and thin **5** a diehard fan **6** to rub off on you

Grammar

1 1 a noun **2** let **3** *to*-infinitive **4** can't **5** promise **6** it comes after a preposition
2 1 A managed B succeeded
2 A let me B allow me
3 A suggested B offered
4 A force B make
5 A capable B able
6 A feel like B want
3 1 telling **2** sharing **3** running **4** to do **5** training **6** them to take
4 1 motivating **2** listening **3** to push **4** to encourage **5** to sustain **6** returning **7** not to listen **8** following

Vocabulary

1 1 opponents **2** training **3** a trophy
2 1 a tournament, a championship **2** fans, spectators **3** coordination, training **4** prize money, a silver medal **5** the rival team, an opponent
3 1 B (the other verbs do not fit the context)
2 D (the other verbs aren't followed by *for* in this context)
3 A (the other verbs do not fit the context)
4 C (*take part in* is a fixed prepositional phrase)
5 D (only *championships* collocates with *enter* in this context)

6 B (only *titles* collocates with *compete for* in this context)
7 A (the other verbs do not fit the context)
8 C (the other nouns do not fit the context or grammar; *team*, *teammate* and *team player* are countable and would require an article *a*; only *teamwork* is uncountable and doesn't need an article)

4 1 on **2** on **3** off **4** out **5** out

5 1 E **2** B **3** A **4** C **5** D

6 1 F **2** B **3** C **4** A **5** E **6** D
send off and *put off* are separable verbs

Listening

1 C to introduce people to a sport they may not know about

2 1 B *I've had conversations where people have thought I've said football and they launch into a long description of Liverpool's latest match. It's funny to see their face when I say, 'Not football, floorball!'*
2 C *Well, the first thing to say is that it's played only indoors, so it makes it a perfect all-year-round sport.*
3 B *You may do only a short turn in the game, score, but then come off and be replaced with someone with different skills and more energy. This is what makes the sport so thrilling because you can change the style of play at any time.*
4 C *... you need a lot less power to get across the field of play. This means a successful player relies more on tactics than strength in floorball.*
5 B *What got me interested was the fact that we can play in mixed teams. I think it's really old-fashioned to divide up sports, you know, with the lads playing football in one place and the girls netball in another.*
6 A *... it doesn't upset me if people think it's uncool. ... It suits me to do my own thing and not to play the same old games as everyone else.*
7 A *I can see it continuing to grow where there are already a number of established clubs and fans.*

3 1 new one on **2** launch **3** death **4** job **5** bother **6** do **7** Since when **8** much

4 1 new one on me **2** good job **3** Since when **4** pretty much **5** bother **6** do your own thing **7** freezing to death

Use of English 1

1 1 brought **2** Had **3** didn't **4** leave **5** to go **6** go

2 1 becoming **2** starting **3** to catch **4** to cheer/cheering **5** to book **6** supporting/to support **7** to mention **8** playing
Both *-ing* and infinitive are possible in sentences 4 and 6.

3 1 B **2** A **3** A **4** B **5** A

4 1 play **2** asking **3** stay **4** practising **5** to change **6** developing **7** to focus **8** saw

5 1 regret to tell/regret to inform (*regret* + *to*-infinitive to mean *I'm sorry I have to tell you this.*)
2 time I got (*It's time* + past tense to talk about something I should do)
3 would rather play basketball (*would rather* + infinitive without *to* to talk about preferences)
4 had better buy (*had better* + infinitive without *to* to give advice)
5 went on playing (past of *go on* + *-ing* form to mean *continued*)
6 try to attend (*try* + *to*-infinitive to mean *make an effort*)

Use of English 2

1 1 exhaustion, expectation, connection (*expect* forms the noun with *-ation*, the other two with just *-ion*)
2 difference, embarrassment, amusement (*differ* forms the noun with *-ence*, the other two with *-ment*)
3 assistance, appearance, achievement (*achieve* forms the noun with *-ment*, the other two with *-ance*)
4 behaviour, frustration, motivation (*behave* forms the noun by dropping the final *-e* and adding *-iour*, the other two by dropping the final *-e* and adding *-ion*)
5 question, decision, trade (*decide* forms the noun by dropping the final *-e* and adding *-sion*, the other two have the same form for the verb and the noun)

2 1 improvement **2** guidance **3** qualifications **4** design (no change) **5** comfort (no change) **6** production **7** discovery **8** decision **9** expectations

3 1 misbehave, **im**polite **2 Re**payment **3 re**arrange, **un**expectedly **4 Dis**honest, **im**moral **5 mis**understood, **ir**relevant **6 In**visible, **il**legal

4 1 illogical, inexpensive **2** disapprove, nonsense **3** nonverbal, unfamiliar **4** irresponsible, irrelevant

5 1 misunderstand **2** commitment **3** unaffordable **4** refundable/refunded **5** incredibly **6** nonsense **7** inconvenience **8** disappearance

Speaking

1 Photo 1: indoors, teamwork, competitive, coach, pre-match talk, team kit
Photo 2: outdoors, fresh air, everyday clothes, relaxed, equipment
both: physical exercise, friendships, sociable

2 1 Perhaps it's the final of a tournament. Photo 1
2 It looks like a kind of park. Photo 2
3 Maybe they're just hanging out after school. Photo 2
4 It may not be the beginning of the match. Photo 1

3 1 may **2** looks **3** probably **4** might **5** looks like **6** get **7** have

4 1 Unlike, probably **2** Both, different **3** might, whereas **4** may, much **5** actually, could **6** Perhaps, important
1 Unlike the **friends**, who are **not** com**pe**ting with each other, the **team** are **pro**bably thinking about the **score**.
2 Both groups **may** spend a lot of time to**ge**ther, but for different **rea**sons.
3 The **team might** be **wor**ried about making **mistakes** in front of spec**ta**tors whereas for the **friends** it doesn't **matt**er if they do something **wrong**.
4 As they're playing to **win**, the **team may** not en**joy** the activity as much as the group of **friends**.
5 In the **second** photo, the **friends** are actually **u**sing the **equip**ment, but in the **first** it **could** be half-**time** or during a **pre**-match **talk**.
6 Perhaps the **friends** don't need to think about motiva**va**tion whereas for the **team** that's an im**por**tant part of the ac**tiv**ity.

5 1 notice **2** looks **3** equipment **4** background **5** main **6** definitely **7** benefit **8** getting **9** hand **10** appear **11** beat **12** good

6 B what you think the advantages are of doing sport in these different ways.

Writing

1 Do you <u>feel stressed</u>?
We want <u>articles on how people deal with stress</u>. Tell us <u>what</u> things <u>you do to beat stress</u> and <u>how</u> they make <u>you feel better</u>. The best articles will appear on our site next month.

2 1 stressful **2** Stress **3** stressed **4** out **5** under

3 1 A **2** F **3** E **4** C **5** D **6** B

4 1 taking **2** try **3** getting **4** worrying **5** staring **6** feel **7** to make **8** get

5 1 main paragraphs **2** conclusion **3** introduction **4** main paragraphs **5** main paragraphs **6** introduction **7** conclusion **8** main paragraphs

6 **1** get up **2** get, down **3** get round to **4** get back to **5** get through **6** Get together
A 6 **B** 4 **C** 1, 5 **D** 2 **E** 3

7 A and C

8 **Model answer**

From stressed to best

What do teenagers have in common? We all suffer from stress sometimes. Schoolwork, exams and relationships can all get us down, but there are ways of dealing with stress.

First of all, you have to recognise what makes life stressful for you. If you know which situations are a problem, you can control them. For me, I'm most under stress when I meet new people. I get nervous and I talk too much, so I've learned to ask a question and then just listen. That helps me not take over the conversation and I can get to know the person.

Another problem is my shared bedroom. My sister is younger than me and we argue about silly things. That's when I need to take a break from her. Listening to music while I'm out walking clears my head and reduces stress levels. By the time I get home, I'm ready to spend time with my sister again.

All in all, we have to understand that we can never escape stress completely, but by learning to deal with it we can get through life healthier and happier.

Unit check

1 **1** to sign up **2** wear **3** talking **4** to make **5** to think **6** to consider **7** to join **8** coming **9** doing

2 **1** it's time, finished **2** 'd rather ride **3** 'd better see **4** 'd rather, didn't tell **5** It's time to blow

3 **1** forget **2** spent **3** playing **4** getting/doing **5** so **6** had **7** allow **8** learned/knew

4 **1** worked out **2** showing off, count on **3** gets me down, get through **4** get up, get back to **5** get together, taken on

5 **1** inexpensive, irresponsible **2** behaviour, embarrassment **3** amusement, nonsense **4** disapprove, illogical **5** application, irrelevant

UNIT 6

Reading

1 **1** exploits **2** miniature **3** blur **4** narrative **5** sequence

2 B The article is written for a general, non-scientific reader. ✓
D The writer's aim is to help the reader understand problems faced by dyslexics. ✓
E The style used is mainly factual and neutral. ✓

3 **1** F (*This amounts to 700 million* and the figure refers back to *one in ten people* in the previous sentence)
2 C (*understanding an individual's frustration with reading is even more challenging* refers back to *it's hard to imagine being unable to work out letters; That's why …* in the sentence after the gap explains what a designer has done to help non-dyslexics understand)
3 A (*In this way …* refers back to *… it slows down a non-dyslexic's reading; … the time and effort required* refers forward to *have to work* in the sentence after the gap)
4 B (*Sensing movement* refers back to *the letters seem to jump around* and is the first example of a problem dyslexics have. The second example is introduced in the following sentence with *A further characteristic is …*)
5 E (*However* introduces the contrast with the statement that the coding is clever; it refers back to the coding/simulation)
6 G (*Equally important is* introduces another example of what is needed for dyslexics after the two examples given in the previous two sentences)

4 **1** run in **2** better appreciation **3** slows **4** wrong, round **5** go back, start **6** take, granted **7** overcome **8** achievers

5 **1** go back to the start, slowed, down
2 take, for granted, overcome, challenge

Grammar

1 **1** F **2** T **3** F **4** T **5** T **6** F

2 **1** being **2** wasn't **3** will **4** be **5** is **6** built/constructed **7** hadn't **8** being **9** has **10** be

3 **1** is said to be the best singer of her generation
2 is claimed that the result of the election was unfair
3 are reported to have got married in secret
4 was shared by millions of people all over the world
5 were made to wait for hours, were allowed into the stadium
6 were shown to the visitors, were shown the most interesting parts of the city

4 **1** has, been associated **2** 's, thought **3** are, being offered **4** was persuaded **5** was being guided **6** was allowed **7** were replaced **8** was lit/was being lit **9** get, distracted **10** don't have to be left **11** must be kept **12** be integrated

Vocabulary

1 **1** B **2** C **3** A **4** A **5** C **6** C **7** B **8** C

2 **1** up, above **2** outside, out of **3** across, opposite **4** among, between **5** next to, near **6** into, inside **7** under, below

3 **1** towards **2** beneath (this is more formal than under/underneath) **3** beside/by **4** by **5** round **6** above

4 **1** speeded **2** occasionally **3** at **4** momentum **5** daily **6** throughout

5 **1** last, good **2** late, on **3** middle, by **4** point, time **5** with, no **6** every, sooner

Listening

1 A how he became interested in sound maps ✓
C the benefits of sound maps ✓
E suggestions for making your first sound map ✓
G a different way of producing a local map ✓

2 **1** drama *I first got into sound maps when I was at school – surprisingly not in geography classes or even music sessions, but as part of a drama course.*
2 (the) technology *But I'm happy to say that now the technology has really moved on, so today anyone can add sounds to a map.*
3 memories *But the thing that I find fascinating is how sound helps you to remember. People often say that a sound recording of a place brings back stronger memories than looking at a traditional map or photo.*
4 equipment *The audio quality on most modern smartphones is good enough, so there really isn't any need for costly equipment.*
5 description *And just one piece of very basic advice the key thing is to know what you've got, so don't forget to include a brief description for every audio file.*
6 tools *One of the most user-friendly tools is called, appropriately, Map Maker.*
7 (own) street *I've found that the majority of people take up sound mapping in their spare time after producing recordings of their own street.*
8 interviews *The most valuable information I've ever got on an area has been in interviews with residents who live at different points along the route.*
9 unbelievable *It's unbelievable how a quick search online will take you maps from all over the world with everything from the sounds of a market to a beautiful singing voice.*
10 Nature Zone *But the one I go back to, almost on a daily basis, is Nature Zone. The range of animals and locations is so wide, you could never get bored.*

3 1 F **2** B **3** H **4** E **5** C **6** G **7** A **8** D

4 A: So what are we going to do for this project? We need ideas that will increase tourism.

B: People expect clear information with one tap of a screen. Things have moved **on** from the days of paper maps and leaflets.

A: You're right. I can't **get** over the number of sites that have too much information. People can't choose what to do so they don't **have** a go at anything at all.

B: So maybe we should focus on a smaller area, you know, just keep it **local**.

A: Wouldn't that be a bit boring? The key thing is to get people interested in this area. We'd need something that would really bring the place to **life** for them.

B: How about creating a top ten list of things to do in and around the city? Some could be right in the centre and others more **off** the beaten track. With just ten, we focus on fewer activities, but in more detail.

A: Nice! Let's get started.

Use of English 1

1 1 D **2** A **3** E **4** C **5** F **6** B

2 1 B **2** A **3** A **4** B **5** A

3 1 'd get/would get, built **2** get, to understand
3 'm having/'m going to have, taken out

4 1 repaired **2** have **3** updating **4** do **5** getting

5 1 can get your phone unlocked/can have your phone unlocked (*can* followed by *get/have* without *to* + object + past participle)
2 had my appendix taken out (past form of *have* + object + past participle)
3 to get the tickets sent (*to get* (infinitive of purpose) + object + past participle)
4 having stories told (*-ing* form of *have* after *like* + object + past participle)
5 have my clothes made/get my clothes made (infinitive form of *have/get* after *like to* + object + past participle)

Use of English 2

1 1 strength **2** accuracy **3** length **4** failure **5** arrival
6 happily **7** daily **8** weight **9** enthusiasm **10** variety
Mystery word: naturalist

2 1 poisonous **2** industrial **3** strengthen **4** length
5 confident **6** dramatically

3 1 weight, height **2** exciting, occasionally **3** depth, width
4 environmental, inhabitants **5** widen, deepen

4 1 conservationist (abstract noun to personal noun of role/job)
2 critically (noun to adjective to adverb)
3 behavioural/behaviour (noun to adjective, or compound noun)
4 deadly (adjective to adverb)
5 educator (verb to personal noun of role/job)
6 heighten (noun to verb)
7 shortage (adjective to noun)
8 passionate (noun to adjective)

Speaking

1 2 discuss the benefits of the different activities ✓
5 give reasons for your opinions ✓
7 listen and respond to your partner's opinions ✓
9 ask your partner questions to clarify their opinion ✓

2 1 D **2** B **3** A **4** C **5** E

3 1 if **2** definitely **3** so **4** In **5** more **6** do

4 They choose the walk and the competition.

5 1 So then **2** do you think **3** that leaves, make up our minds
4 Are we both in favour **5** we'll go with

6 1 aren't there **2** isn't it **3** does it **4** do they

Writing

1 B the accuracy of information available today

2 1 Wikipedia ✓
3 social media ✓
4 product reviews ✓

3 1 In **the** first place, it's important to know why this information was sent to you.
2 Texts are not always what they seem – **for** instance, some adverts look like information documents, but they are actually selling a product.
3 On **the** whole, I'd say that you can trust what you read, but you still need to be careful.
4 With reference **to** Wikipedia, it's clear when the information is not accurate or complete.
5 As far **as** I'm concerned, it's getting harder to know which information is reliable.
6 People need to know who produced the information. What**'s/is** more, they need to understand why.

4 2 There are a number of things you need to check. First of all, it's important to know if the text is written in a neutral way.
3 Some documents are full of mistakes. For this reason, we're only allowed to use reliable sites for homework.
4 There is so much news on social media. In my view, it's important to be selective.
5 On the one hand we are fortunate to have information at our fingertips, but on the other hand we need to be cautious.
6 There are different ways of checking information. For example, comparing against two or three other documents is a good technique.

5 1 Generally speaking, I think people ignore online advertising.
2 In my opinion, getting advice from someone I know is best.
3 Regarding the news, it's important to check different sources.
4 In conclusion, learning to manage information is an important skill.
5 Articles are written from many different points of view.

6 1 access **2** It is said **3** on an hourly basis **4** widen your range of **5** tend to **6** huge variety **7** bear in mind **8** sole

7 Model answer

Every day, we receive a huge amount of information from a wide range of sources. It's important that we can trust what we read and hear.

Firstly, regarding articles, it depends if you're reading for information or entertainment. Content for a school project, for example, needs to be checked for accuracy. So it's a good idea to compare details from different sources. However, in my view, when reading an article for fun, accuracy is less important.

Secondly, with reference to advertisements, I believe you need to be cautious about their content. Generally speaking, advertisers want to make money, so you need to know what the real benefits of a product are.

Finally, product reviews provide useful information, but only if the writer gives an honest opinion. On some websites, reviewers are paid so they may write positive comments even though the product was fairly ordinary. What is more, a celebrity review can make a product seem more attractive than it really is.

In conclusion, on the one hand we're lucky to have all this information available, but on the other hand we need to know who produced it and why.

Unit check

1 **1** are held **2** is being filmed **3** have already been sold **4** was destroyed/had been destroyed **5** will be updated **6** be promoted **7** being invited **8** is said

2 **1** be done **2** gets, completed **3** had, built **4** got, planted **5** have, made **6** need painting/need to be painted **7** having, constructed **8** got, taken

3 [top row] Vicky Kyle Ali Jake
[bottom row] Claire Rani Misha Su

4 **1** strengthen, privacy **2** anxiety, beneficial **3** accidentally, guilty **4** shortage, applicants **5** collector, pleasure **6** tolerant, fortunate

USE OF ENGLISH, UNITS 1–6

Part 1

1 A (collocates with *other day* to form the time expression *every other day*)
2 A (collocates with *round to* to form the phrase *get round to*)
3 B (collocates with *in the … of* to form the time phrase *in the middle of*)
4 D (only answer D collocates with *on*)
5 C (collocates with *a record* to form the expression *keep a record*)
6 A (collocates with interest to form the expression *lose interest*)
7 B (collocates with … *the point of* to form the time phrase *on the point of*)
8 C (only answer C works in this context to form the phrase *in reach*)

Part 2

9 got/had (past form of *have/get* from structure *have/get something done* to describe something bad that has happened to a person)
10 case (noun, part of the phrase *in case* to talk about things that people do to be prepared for a future situation)
11 been (verb, part of passive modal structure; (modal) + *have been* + past participle)
12 by (preposition, part of prepositional phrase *by hand*)
13 taking/stealing (verb pattern *regret* + *-ing* when the meaning is *wished you hadn't done something*)
14 them (pronoun, verb pattern *advise* + object + *to*- infinitive)
15 only (adverb, part of phrase *if only* + past simple to talk about things we are not happy with)
16 have (verb, part of third conditional + modal structure – *if* + past perfect + *might/mightn't, could/couldn't* + *have* + past participle)

Part 3

17 unexpected (verb to adjective plus negative prefix)
18 accidental (noun to adjective)
19 confidence (adjective to noun)
20 frustration (verb to noun)
21 failure (verb to noun)
22 Appearance (verb to noun)
23 strengthen (adjective to verb)
24 enthusiasm (adjective to noun)

Part 4

25 would not have (part of third conditional structure; *if* + past perfect + *would/wouldn't have* + past participle)
26 to give up playing (verb pattern *decide* + *to* infinitive; phrasal verb *give up* meaning *stop doing something* + *-ing* form after the preposition)
27 had better not (*had better (not)* + infinitive without *to* to give advice)
28 didn't mean to tear/did not mean to tear (verb pattern *not mean* + *to* infinitive meaning *it wasn't my intention to …*)
29 is believed to have run (part of a reported structure with the passive; *it is said/believed*, etc. + *that* + clause)
30 not old enough (not + adjective + *enough* to mean *not sufficient*)

UNIT 7

Reading

1 **1** realised **2** daydream **3** make-believe **4** appeal **5** genuinely **6** deliver **7** memorable **8** spooky

2 **1** Lin and Jake **2** Jake and Simon **3** Simon **4** a publisher/publishing company

3 **1** B *I was by no means an overnight success, but over time my fan base grew.*
2 D *Just because fanfiction has a huge audience doesn't make it right.*
3 C *… we do keep a close eye on the main fanfiction sites, just to see which genre is most popular and who are the up-and-coming writers.*
4 A *Having their comments helps me shape what happens next …. It's that ongoing interaction that distinguishes fanfiction from other forms of writing.*
5 C *Fanfiction is often seen as second best, as if the writers are just imitators of 'real' authors. I don't see it like that.*
6 B *And once a story is out in the world, it's really owned by the readers, so I can't control it.*
7 D *Most of these writers remain anonymous on Wattpad, …*
8 A *It was when I found that other fans were as dissatisfied as me with the same book, that I decided to make my version available online.*
9 B *All I can say is my sales haven't suffered.*
10 D *I contacted my publisher to see if we could get all the stories related to my work taken down.*

4 **1** E **2** H **3** G **4** F **5** A **6** B **7** D **8** C

5 **1** take on **2** make a name for themselves **3** keeps, going **4** overnight success **5** seen as second best **6** set about **7** keep a close eye 8 up-and-coming

Grammar

1 **1** past, needs **2** can **3** don't change **4** pronoun, tense **5** if or whether **6** a question word

2 **1** The survey asked how often ~~did~~ we read classic literature.
2 She said we could ~~have~~ download the book for free.
3 The journalist asked if ~~that~~ he had always been keen on writing.
4 I explained that I'd ~~had~~ already seen that episode the day before.
5 My classmate refused to tell ~~to~~ me the answer.
6 The tutor wanted to know what ~~if~~ genre we were interested in.
7 The writer said ~~us~~ it was going to be his last book for teenagers.
8 The students wanted to know how many stories he ~~does~~ writes a year.

3 **1** (that) she would see us both later at the leisure complex
2 (that) it was/is the worst programme she'd ever seen
3 (that) they were reading a great new story at their book club at that time/then
4 (that) he'd left his Kindle on the sofa there, but then he couldn't find it
5 (that) we all had to write a paragraph plan before we started that task
6 (that) he'd been watching a film when I/we texted the night before/the previous night

7 (that) she was going to publish her first book of short stories the following year
8 (that) they might go to the book festival the following/next day

4 1 why Gina had chosen to write 2 if/whether it was true, herself 3 if/whether she ever ran out of ideas for her
4 how long it took 5 if/whether Gina might start writing
6 when Gina's books were going to be made

5 1 had 2 They 3 why 4 previous/past/last 5 if/whether
6 told/informed 7 are/were 8 me

Vocabulary

1 1 ebook 2 ending 3 illustrations 4 novel 5 paperback
6 passage 7 print 8 publisher 9 series

2 1 H 2 E 3 G 4 D 5 C 6 F 7 B 8 A

3 1 cheer, up 2 go for 3 figure out 4 leave out 5 give in
6 fall for 7 take in 8 look up

4 1 make up 2 read out 3 use up 4 bring in 5 stand for
6 point out 7 live for 8 join in

Listening

1 A making a request by phone 8
B different ways of enjoying movies 1
C a change in programming 6
D a description of feeling nervous 3
E how to be a writer 4
F advice from a teacher 5
G a contest for young storytellers 7
H a change in writing style 2

2 1 B *... why bother going all the way out to the leisure complex when we can watch it here? ... Action movies are made for the big screen. ... You'd never get all that on a computer screen. ... you can't stop and start the movie like you can in your own living room.*
2 C *I've no idea what happened. I couldn't figure out why he took an instant dislike to the book. I was left wondering why it was all so one-sided.*
3 A *What if I mess up and I can't remember the words? Or I get the notes all wrong? The band have been rehearsing for weeks. I come on at such an important part in the whole show .... I just keep imagining opening my mouth and no sound coming out.*
4 A *... what's helped me is just being myself. There are so many talented writers ..., it's tempting to imitate their style, but you really have to create your own voice.*
5 B *However, there was one big problem that was common to everybody the length of your conversations.*
6 C *You're kidding! So they're carrying on all the storylines and making another series?*
7 B *The difference this time round is that we want to encourage fresh talent, so if you've entered before, I'm afraid you won't be allowed to compete this year.*
8 C *Would it be possible to get my money back on the extra ticket?*

4 1 feel 2 bother 3 look 4 kidding 5 messed 6 such
7 got 8 took 9 from

Use of English 1

1 1 encourage 2 agree 3 deny 4 suggest 5 congratulate
6 threaten 7 admit 8 boast

2 1 E 2 A 3 G 4 C 5 F 6 B 7 H 8 D

3 1 congratulated me on winning
2 warned me against signing/warned me not to sign
3 promised to read/that she would read/promised me that she would read
4 insisted that we did/insisted on doing
5 recommended that I got/recommended getting/ recommended me to get
6 invited me to go
7 complained that he/she should have won/complained about not winning

4 1 admitted (that) she had borrowed/admitted to borrowing/ admitted borrowing (verb + *that* + clause / verb + preposition + *-ing* / verb + *-ing*)
2 promised to sign/promised (that) they would sign (verb + *to* infinitive / verb + *that* + clause)
3 refused to take (verb + *to* infinitive)
4 boasted about writing/boasted (that) he had written (verb + preposition + *-ing* / verb + *that* + clause)
5 told us not to use (verb + person + *not* + *to* infinitive)
6 congratulated Eddie on getting (congratulated verb + person + preposition + *-ing*)

Use of English 2

1 1 in 2 by 3 on 4 by/at 5 On 6 In

2 1 for 2 in 3 at 4 at 5 for 6 at 7 By 8 on

3 1 of, surprised 2 to, clever 3 at, involved 4 of, successful
5 horrified, of 6 experienced, to 7 interested, to

4 1 D (the other adjectives aren't followed by *of*)
2 A (fixed prepositional phrase *on demand*)
3 C (the other adjectives aren't followed by *of*)
4 A (fixed prepositional phrase *according to*)
5 B (fixed prepositional phrase *by choice*)
6 B (the other adjectives aren't followed by *at*)
7 D (*attached* collocates with *to* and is the only answer that fits in this context)
8 C (fixed prepositional phrase *by day*)

Speaking

1 1 E 2 F 3 A 4 C 5 D 6 B

2 1 They are discussing question 4.
2 They are discussing question 6.

3 1 completely agree with 2 up to a point
3 you have a point 4 think so, too 5 don't really think so
6 agree more 7 absolutely right 8 what you mean

4 1 sure 2 agree 3 don't 4 that 5 isn't 6 true 7 really
8 think 9 Perhaps 10 about 11 wouldn't 12 agree

Writing

1 1 A 2 D

2 A give the background to the situation 2
B introduce the situation and main characters 1
C bring events to a conclusion 4
D build the tension before the climax to the story 3

3 1 appeared 2 had seen 3 was, going 4 had made
5 'd been chatting 6 'm/am going to invite 7 nodded
8 was standing 9 met

4 1 as quick as a flash 2 whispered 3 close to tears

5 1 terribly 2 totally 3 unbearably 4 surprisingly 5 incredibly

6 1 spooky ancient stone 2 cool white cotton
3 beautiful round gold 4 shy young Spanish

7 **Model answer**

As soon as I found the old letter, I knew what I had to do. I'd come across it when we'd moved to a new house. It had been sitting in a dusty old box for years.

I was about to throw the box in the bin, but then the address on the letter caught my eye. It was for a person in a nearby town. 'Why write a letter, put a stamp on the envelope, but not send it?' I said to myself.

Turning over the envelope, I realised it was open. I took a deep breath and read the first line 'My dear sister Ellen, I'm sorry from the bottom of my heart about our argument.' It was horribly sad to think that Ellen might never have known about the apology.

After checking the address online, my mum realised that Ellen lived less than an hour away. As quick as a flash, she said, 'Get in the car! Let's deliver the letter right now!' When Ellen opened the door, she was incredibly surprised to see us. And she was close to tears when she read her sister's words.

Unit check

1 1 (that) she was going to drama school the following/next year
2 (that) they hadn't caught up on the first episode yet/by that time/by then
3 (that) she wouldn't bother finishing that story
4 what the worst programme on TV was at that moment/then
5 who had won best actress at the award ceremony the previous night/the night before
6 if/whether it took/takes a long time to learn my/our lines

2 1 congratulated me on getting
2 promised to come and see me/promised that she would come and see me
3 admitted dropping/admitted that she had dropped
4 invited me to come along
5 advised me not to pay/advised me against paying

3 1 reminded Katy to take **2** apologised for missing my
3 denied borrowing my/(that) she had borrowed my
4 warned us not to expect

4 1 main character **2** special effects **3** unexpected twists
4 rave reviews **5** weak storyline **6** complicated plot
7 happy ending **8** final scene

5 1 fall for **2** Cheer up **3** go for **4** left out

6 1 of **2** to **3** at/by **4** for **5** on **6** in **7** to **8** in

UNIT 8

Reading

1 1 slouching **2** make allowances **3** dribbling **4** heading
5 crash course **6** streaming **7** lunatic **8** muttered

2 1 The article is written from a teenager's point of view. ✓
3 The main aim is to highlight a problem in family life. ✓
4 The writer has done some research for the article. ✓

3 1 C *Glancing down at the screen, I see that yet again my face is all over social media.… I wasn't ready for the picture, didn't ask for it and the last thing I wanted was for it to go online.*
2 A *I know I should be happy that she felt proud of me, but I just wish she would pick her moments with the camera.*
3 D *And even for someone born into the so-called digital age, I was amazed by the facts and figures.*
4 B *But I had reckoned on a bit less sharenting now I'm in my teens.*
5 A *In a world where adults are telling us to respect others and think before we act, how does that fit with them taking photos of their kids' every move? One of my friends has her social media accounts monitored twenty-four seven by her parents, but her family posts images of her online without a second thought.*
6 B *… and pretend the digital revolution never happened.*

4 1 went ahead **2** cute **3** pick your moments
4 anything but trendy **5** gets me **6** their kids' every move
7 without a second thought **8** have my say

5 1 have our say **2** go ahead **3** without a second thought
4 my every move **5** anything but trendy **6** gets me **7** cute
8 pick their moments

Grammar

1 1 B **2** B **3** A **4** B **5** A **6** B

2 1 were able to **2** be educated **3** should have been **4** can't
5 may **6** have walked **7** wasn't allowed to **8** could

3 1 weren't able to/were not able to
2 can't have met/cannot have met/couldn't have met/could not have met
3 needn't have bought/need not have bought/shouldn't have bought/should not have bought
4 ought to have looked
5 don't have to get/do not have to get
6 must be turned

4 1 can make **2** might be unfriended **3** must have done
4 ought not to have posted **5** Could I have been **6** can be interpreted **7** might lose **8** have to be **9** might be able
10 may have been **11** might have gone **12** can't have been

Vocabulary

1 1 cheerful **2** eccentric **3** defensive **4** flamboyant
5 irresponsible **6** courageous **7** arrogant **8** cooperative

2 1 thoughtful, stubborn **2** anti-social, courteous
3 possessive, demanding **4** talkative, immature

3 1 admiration **2** honesty **3** loyalty **4** sympathy
5 willingness **6** discipline **7** flexibility

4 1 don't have, to have **2** will/'ll keep **3** to keep/to have kept
4 had **5** kept

5 1 'm beginning to have serious doubts **2** keep a secret keep her mouth shut **3** couldn't keep her mouth shut/a secret
4 have nothing to do **5** 're having a bad day **6** started having difficulty **7** keeps in touch

Listening

1 D

2 Speaker 1: G *As the 'baby' of the team, the older members have kind of taken me under their wing, you know, really taken care of me.*
Speaker 2: H *To be honest, I wasn't very keen, but the others stressed how much they needed a fourth member, so I gave in.… We won by miles and then I got hooked and we haven't looked back.*
Speaker 3: C *… I found a local club and asked if I could join. They were a talented and established team and there I was a complete beginner, so the answer was no.*
Speaker 4: E *That's why I formed the club, to bring people my age together to have fun in a different way.*
Speaker 5: A *At first, I joined just to help out with costumes and lighting, … And then someone dropped out and they needed a stand-in. It was only a small part, but I found I really enjoyed it.*

3 1 G **2** A **3** F **4** H **5** D **6** C **7** E **8** B

4 1 desperate to **2** by miles **3** performing live
4 won't look back **5** in her **6** glued to
7 took me under their wing **8** a regular

Use of English 1

1 1 We lost touch when I changed schools despite **~~of~~** being very close for years.
2 The festival will always be one of my happiest memories in spite of **~~have~~** the awful weather.
3 Despite the **~~even~~** fact that we argue all the time, my twin is my best friend.
4 I don't think I'm spoiled in spite of **~~I'm~~** being the youngest.
5 Not only were we born on the same day, but we **~~too~~** also have the same middle name.
6 Not only did she **~~was~~** unfriend me, but she also talked behind my back.

2 **1** A **2** B **3** A **4** B

3 **1** Not only does she talk behind your back, but she also tells lies.
2 Not only did he ignore my messages, but he also unfollowed me.
3 Not only is she fun to be with, but she's also a loyal friend.
4 Not only had I given her advice, but I'd also lent her some money.
5 Not only have you been late every day this week, but you have also missed three deadlines.
6 Not only were they playing loud music, but they were also shouting at the top of their voices.

4 **1** did I forget **2** but I also **3** spite of being
4 despite the fact that **5** was I messaging
6 despite the confusion

5 **1** despite not having done/despite not doing (*despite* + *-ing*)
2 only did he behave (inversion of auxiliary and subject in simple past after *not only*)
3 despite the music not being (*despite* + *-ing*)
4 spite of her illness/spite of being ill (*despite* + noun/ *despite* + *-ing*)
5 despite the fact that (*despite* + *the fact that* + clause)

Use of English 2

1 **1** A to fill, in B will/'ll fill, in on
2 A haven't, been getting along B 've/have, got along with
3 A to hang out B to hang out with/hanging out with
4 A came across as B (to) come across

2 **1** put me off **2** carry on **3** get over **4** speak up **5** clear up

3 **1** up **2** took **3** with **4** to **5** get **6** on **7** stood **8** look

4 **1** have, waste **2** bear, have **3** attention, strength **4** pick, deep **5** goal, in

5 **1** D (The other phrasal verbs don't fit this context.)
2 A (*set* collocates with *a goal*)
3 C (The other phrasal verbs don't fit this context.)
4 B (The other phrasal verbs don't fit this context.)
5 A (*hand* collocates with *give someone a*)
6 C (The other phrasal verbs don't fit this context.)
7 A (*take* collocates with *a deep breath*)
8 D (*lose* collocates with *have nothing to*, forming the fixed expression *have nothing to lose*)

Speaking

2 **A** reading out the whole task aloud – 2
B not sounding very interested – not needed
C not discussing the topic together – 3
D not deciding on the first topic together – 1

3 **1** Shall **2** think **3** you're **4** point **5** moving on **6** mean **7** Do **8** let's

4 discussed changing school, becoming a vegetarian and unfriending
changing school and unfriending are chosen

5 **1** It's quite difficult to decide. **2** I'm not quite sure. **3** Sorry, I've changed my mind. **4** Yes, maybe that choice wasn't the best one.

6 **1** O **2** O **3** S **4** D **5** O **6** S **7** O **8** D

Writing

1 **1** A **2** C **3** B

2 **1** set up **2** creating **3** to have **4** introducing **5** to put together **6** providing

3 **1** F **2** A **3** E **4** C **5** D **6** B

4 **1** such an, that **2** so few **3** such a lot of, that **4** so **5** so little **6** so many

5 **1** Dear Ms Hillier **2** I'm writing **3** will **4** such **5** could have **6** so **7** be shown **8** Finally **9** so few **10** to introduce **11** reach **12** With best wishes

6 **Model answer**

Dear Mr Leeson

I'm writing to offer you some fundraising suggestions for the new teenagers centre. It's going to be such a great place.

Since we need to appeal to people of different ages, why don't we organise a sponsored walk? That is something everyone can do, even if they aren't sporty. We could raise more money by asking local businesses to take part.

Secondly, how about a sale of things that people don't need any more? So many of us have clothes, books and DVDs around the house that we don't use. These could be sold and the money could help us reach our target.

Finally, as music is so popular, it might be a good idea to have a weekend festival. If we had different styles of music from different cultures, I think the whole community would go for that. We could also have food on sale to help increase the profit we make.

In my opinion, the main thing is to have activities that everyone can take part in and to attract as many volunteers as possible.

I hope my ideas are useful.

Best wishes

[name]

Unit check

1 **1** must have got **2** should be **3** might have been delayed **4** shouldn't have been **5** ought to **6** 'll be able to **7** can be fixed **8** have to unfriend

2 **1** living **2** so **3** does he borrow **4** not **5** In spite of **6** such **7** that **8** little

3 **1** shouldn't **2** so **3** need/have **4** have **5** can't/couldn't

4 **1** with **2** in **3** up

5 **1** stand **2** out **3** clear **4** mouth **5** attention **6** waiting **7** waste **8** come

UNIT 9

Reading

1 **1** founder **2** short-sighted **3** a split second **4** Beware **5** filter **6** skip **7** gets, crammed **8** poised

2 **1** B **2** C **3** B

3 **1** E (*So* introduces the information about the new experiment as a result of *few studies* having been done; *experiment* links to *Its aim* in the following sentence.)
2 B (*Most* refers back to *thirty questions*; *serious issues* links to *Examples included*… in the following sentence.)
3 G (*Then* introduces the next stage in the experiment; *flipped the virtual coin* links to *heads* and *tails* in the following sentence.)
4 A (*This was true* refers back to people being *substantially happier* in the previous sentence.)
5 F (*wasn't completely scientific* links to *wasn't fully representative of the general population* in the following sentence.)
6 C (*do nothing* links to *preference for the status quo* in the following sentence.)

4 **1** tested **2** major **3** on **4** make **5** faced **6** over (and over) **7** out fine

5 **1** turns **2** with **3** life **4** act **5** tried **6** make **7** worked

Grammar

1 **1** That's the decision <u>that</u> I regret most.
2 When <u>you are</u> making up your mind, don't be rushed into a decision.
3 The person whose advice I listen to most is my older brother.

4 People <u>who are</u> faced with too many decisions often don't decide anything at all.
5 The problem page, <u>which is part of my favourite magazine</u>, often has useful tips.
6 I don't want a friend who isn't there for me during the bad times.

2 1 who/that **2** when **3** (when/that) **4** whose **5** (why/that)

3 1 Do you remember that time we took the wrong road and got lost?
2 These are the trainers I wish I'd never bought.
3 Max is the student whose twin brother decided to dye his hair purple.
4 My friend, who has been a vegetarian for five years, decided to eat meat again.
5 This is the café that/which serves over 100 different drinks.
6 I went to the school where my mum had been a teacher./ I went to the school my mum had been a teacher at.

4 1 who are **2** who was **3** that were **4** which had been **5** that is **6** that had been

5 1 Impressed **2** Having tried on **3** Wearing **4** encouraged **5** Coming **6** Having packed

6 1 that/which **2** when **3** who/that **4** whose **5** Having **6** why **7** making **8** which

Vocabulary

1 1 is torn between two choices **2** sleep on it **3** is having second thoughts **4** have a Plan A and a Plan B **5** to speak out about

2 1 propose **2** consideration **3** evaluate **4** judgement **5** select **6** evaluation **7** proposition **8** consult **9** intend mystery word: selection

3 1 speak **2** come **3** own **4** mind **5** change **6** on **7** According to **8** involve **9** reveals **10** make **11** challenge

4 1 between **2** weigh **3** cons **4** out **5** were **6** came **7** mind(s) **8** carries/has

Listening

1 B give up social media temporarily

2 1 A *The school wanted to trial a period of no-phone use at home .... So my parents put me on the scheme*
2 C *Before I'd be checking my phone every few minutes, moving across different apps to keep up with who was saying what. ... It was as if the world was going on and I was missing out.*
3 B *... everyone was trying to take my mind off my phone by suggesting nice food, games, or walks.*
4 B *... to fill the time, I went back to things I used to enjoy like drawing and painting.*
5 C *Now I'm able to keep focused on what I'm doing for longer ...*
6 A *You can't say to anyone who's addicted to being online, 'Just turn your phone off.' ... They need to want to cut down.*
7 C *... I'm pleased to say it doesn't rule my life like before. ... I keep a check on how long I'm spending online and if it gets past twenty minutes, I stop and do something else.*

3 1 E **2** A **3** G **4** D **5** C **6** B **7** H **8** F

4 1 spare **2** bit **3** knew **4** reaching **5** myself **6** take **7** wonder **8** detox

Use of English 1

1 1 D **2** B **3** C **4** F **5** A **6** E

2 1 What happened was (that) my battery ran out so I couldn't text.
2 It was just yesterday when/that I received the invitation.
3 What I don't understand is their way of thinking.
4 It's my parents who pay for most of my clothes.
5 What surprises me is how much everything costs.
6 It wasn't until I was sixteen that I was allowed to stay over at my friend's.
7 What we did was (to) weigh up the pros and cons and then decide.
8 What you should do is (to) think things through before you make a choice.

3 1 I really like is **2** happened was (that) **3** my parents who **4** about them is **5** did was (to) make

4 1 according (part of the phrase *according to*)
2 What (introduces cleft sentence *What* + clause + *be* + phrase)
3 it (introduces cleft sentence *it* + *be* + important phrase)
4 do (use of auxiliary in cleft sentence to emphasise the verb *to Google*)
5 which/that (relative pronoun referring back to *world*)
6 who/that (relative pronoun referring back to *people*)
7 whose (relative pronoun indicating possession and referring to Tania's personality)
8 is (part of cleft sentence *What* + clause + *be* + infinitive)

Use of English 2

1 has a crazy dress sense. 4
is obsessed with style and image. 1
looks as if they have thrown on their clothes. 3
is happy to follow the crowd. 6
wants to wear a particular brand or label. 5
is good at picking up bargains. 2

2 1 experiment **2** put **3** pressure **4** looks **5** issue **6** out in

3 1 imaginative, judgemental **2** bossy, independent **3** suspicious, stylish **4** intelligent, risky **5** ambitious, confident **6** faulty, developmental **7** obsessed, confidential

4 1 messy (noun to adjective) **2** patience (adjective to noun)
3 obsessively (noun to adjective then adverb)
4 development (verb to noun) **5** interactive (verb to adjective)
6 innovation (verb to noun)
7 environmental (noun to adjective)
8 essential (noun to adjective)

Speaking

1 2 say what is similar and different about the pictures. ✓
5 answer the question after talking about the pictures. ✓
6 speculate about the people's reasons for shopping in this way. ✓

2 1 S **2** O **3** S **4** D **5** D **6** O **7** D

3 Both photos show; Another similarity is; Both pictures show ...; On the other hand, ...; For me, ...; I'd say that ...

4 1 though **2** may **3** could **4** so **5** Perhaps **6** be going **7** must **8** because

5 1 C, F **2** A, D **3** B, E

6 C Which of these ways of shopping would you like best?

Writing

2 image and style and leisure activities; image and style repeats point 1 in the notes and leisure activities repeats point 2.

3 Sentences1 and 2 repeat the words *teenager(s)*, sentences 2 and 3 *make their own choice*, and *choice*.

4 1 this, them **2** that/it **3** this, they **4** this/that, they, their **5** these

5 **1** A themselves B make up
2 A way B projects
3 A freedom B given
4 A get B in
5 A what B whoever

7 **Model answer**

For teenagers making their own choices is part of growing up. However, it's too simplistic to say that young people should always choose for themselves. It depends on the age of the person and the type of decision.

Developing a style is part of a young person's identity. It can be fun to dress creatively and project an image that's different. However, a very extreme look can be problematic. For example, a teen with tattoos or piercings may be excluded from school.

Teenagers need to have the freedom to select their own hobbies, as this develops their skills and confidence. In spite of this benefit, safety is also important. Young teens in particular shouldn't be allowed to take up dangerous activities without adult help.

Finally, the right to make new friendships is essential. It helps teenagers manage relationships and understand their own personality. Despite this, young people need advice when they fall out or if another teen is a bad influence.

In conclusion, it's only by making choices that young people can start to develop. I think they need the freedom to decide for themselves, but also help and advice.

Unit check

1 **1** which **2** Being **3** whose **4** up for **5** Bored **6** Having **7** why **8** which

2 **1** Items bought can only be exchanged not refunded.
2 The boy wearing jeans and a top works in the shop.
3 What I hate about shopping is trying stuff on.
4 It was last week when I started my part-time job.
5 It's Annie who has the most clothes.
6 What I did was borrow my brother's jacket without asking.

3 **1** that/which **2** when **3** who/that **4** What **5** to **6** Having **7** it **8** After

4 **1** (Ellen) E **2** (Tim) G **3** (Katrina) A **4** (Simon) B **5** (Melanie) D

5 **1** sleep **2** make **3** mind **4** Coming **5** involve **6** pros **7** torn **8** reveals **9** base **10** decision

USE OF ENGLISH, UNITS 1–9

Part 1

1 A (only answer A works in this context to form the phrase *complicated plot*)
2 B (only answer B collocates with *at* to form the expression *surprised at*)
3 C (collocates with *have nothing to … with* to form the expression *have nothing to do with*)
4 A (forms the phrasal verb *come across as*)
5 D (forms the phrasal verb *reach out to*)
6 A (collocates with *take … in* to form the expression *take part in*)
7 B (forms the prepositional phrase *at the top of your voice*)
8 D (collocates with … *something in common* to form the expression *have something in common*)

Part 2

9 did (auxiliary verb, part of the linking phrase *not only … but also* for emphasis; requires inversion of the subject and verb in the first part of the sentence and the auxiliary *did* in the simple past)
10 which (relative pronoun referring back to *origami* in a non-defining relative clause)
11 what (*part of* a cleft sentence for emphasis; *What* + clause + *be* + word/phrase/topic)
12 who (relative pronoun referring back to *girl* in a non-defining relative clause)
13 have (verb, part of past modal structure; *must/can't have* + past participle used to speculate about a past situation)
14 spite (part of the linking phrase *in spite of* used to express concession and contrast)
15 so (part of structure for emphasis; *so* + adjective/adverb + *that*)
16 out (forms phrasal verb *hang out with* meaning *to spend time with*)

Part 3

17 behaviour (verb to noun)
18 hopeless (noun/verb to adjective)
19 irresponsibly (negative prefix, then adjective to adverb)
20 patience (adjective to noun)
21 encouragement (verb to noun)
22 communicative (verb to adjective)
23 judgemental (noun to adjective)
24 disorganised (negative prefix, then verb to adjective)

Part 4

25 got used to (part of the structure *get used to* + *-ing* meaning *become accustomed to*)
26 never forget winning (verb pattern *forget* + *-ing* meaning *will always remember*)
27 must be returned (modal verb + passive structure; modal *could, should, must*, etc. + *be* + past participle)
28 it was my mother who (part of a cleft sentence for emphasis; *It* + *be* + important word/phrase/topic)
29 unless it builds (*unless* in first conditional sentence meaning *if not*)
30 got bitten by the dog (passive formed with *get* to talk about something undesired; *get* + past participle; *by* to show who/what did the action)

UNIT 10

Reading and Use of English

Part 1

1 A (*lead* is the only verb followed by the preposition *to*)
2 B (collocates with … *a negative effect* to form the expression *have a negative effect*)
3 D (*typical* is the only adjective followed by the preposition *of*)
4 C (forms the prepositional phrase *at your best*)
5 B (*put up with* is the only phrasal verb that works in this context)
6 B (*benefit* is the only verb followed by the preposition *from*)
7 C (collocates with *have an … with* to form the expression *have an issue with*)
8 A (collocates with *get it* … to form the expression *get it right*)

Part 2

9 for (phrasal verb *stand for* meaning *be an abbreviation for*)
10 the (definite article when there is only one of something)
11 on (prepositional phrase; *on offer*)
12 little (determiner + uncountable noun)
13 how (quantifier *how much*)
14 What (cleft sentence structure; *What* + clause + *be* + word/phrase/topic)
15 so (linking phrase *so that* to talk about purpose/result)
16 be (passive infinitive; *to be* + past participle)

Part 3

17 official (noun to adjective)
18 incorrect (adjective with negative prefix)
19 accuracy (adjective to noun)
20 selection (verb to noun)
21 participants (verb to plural noun)
22 absolutely (adjective to adverb)
23 variety (adjective to noun)
24 appearance (verb to noun)

Part 4

25 such a good singer (*such a/an* + adjective + noun + *that*)
26 as long as students (*as long as* used in the first conditional to talk about things that are or will be possible only if something else happens or is done)
27 went on to become (verb pattern *go on* + *to*-infinitive meaning *to do/start something after completing something else*)
28 had been walking (past perfect continuous for an action that was happening over a period of time before another action in the past)
29 are believed to have reached (reported structure with the passive; *is/are believed/said*, etc. + *to* + *have* + past participle)
30 congratulated me on/for winning (reporting verb *congratulate* + object + *on/for* + *-ing*)

Part 5

31 B *The girls' department is also where you'll find the skirts and dresses, but couldn't they just appear alongside the jeans, hoodies and other unisex items? Do we actually need different departments according to gender?*
32 D *This was met with mixed reactions. Some parents welcomed the unisex approach while others threatened to stop using the store altogether.*
33 C *However, the range available online and on the high street suggests that the same colours and symbols are used for girls of all ages. There's still a lot of pink to be seen, along with images of fantasy creatures like unicorns and mermaids.*
34 A *So a group of boys did just that* (refers back to *wear a skirt* in the previous sentence)
35 D (supported by designer's liking of men's clothes and her own unisex range)
36 C *A T-shirt for boys went on sale with the slogan 'Little man, big ideas'; the corresponding top for girls read 'Little girl, big smiles'. In a world where little girls can grow up to be astronauts and boys hairdressers that just seems rather behind the times.*

Part 6

37 E (sentence exemplifies the benefit to the science community; *make it possible* links back to *wouldn't normally be able to collect*)
38 G (gives the result of the previous sentence, linking *measurable results* to *aren't just playing at being scientists*; the following sentence supports the idea that the volunteers' work is valuable)
39 B (sentence answers the question that precedes it and links to the result in the following sentence)
40 D (sentence links back to the need for work on several groups of birds; *cameras* links forward to *analyse the images*)
41 F (*Some* refers back to *teams of teenagers* and forward to *It was their opportunity*)
42 A (*these amateurs* refers back to *teenagers* earlier in the paragraph; the following sentence gives the reason why they were given the equipment)

Part 7

43 B *This young entrepreneur got into the world of commerce almost by accident …*
44 A *And he only gets annoyed when people say that business must be interfering with his childhood.*
45 C *He hopes to help make the commercial world more accessible for other teenagers.*
46 D *She makes sure she knows what people are willing to pay but also how she can make a profit.*
47 B *Inspiration struck after watching a father struggling to help his young son on his bike in the park.*
48 C *… he sometimes gets mistaken for just a junior in the company rather than the owner.*
49 D *Too young to use eBay, she turned to Depop, a trading platform set up for teenagers.*
50 A *When he made a recent presentation to 200 conference delegates, he didn't bother with notes.*
51 B *Sky admits that she didn't imagine the product would be successful at all …*
52 C *… Matthew took full advantage of technical knowledge that older people lacked.*

Listening

Part 1

1 A *What let it down for me was the menu – all they had were the usual dishes when I was hoping for something a bit more imaginative.*
2 A *… my aunt ran on and gave me a kiss. I went bright red and now it's all over social media.*
3 C *This time you have to work in teams of four, that's both boys and girls working together. Your designs need to be in the form of an online project, with drawings but not a model.*
4 B *My plan is to go travelling for twelve months and see something of the world.*
5 C *But what makes her stand out is her ability to create her own lyrics. In a world where companies employ professional songwriters to create tracks for artists, it's good to know that Kerry can do this herself.*
6 A *… so I'm a bit concerned about getting there by myself this time. It's quite a long way.*
7 C *but the most unbelievable thing is that the completion date has been brought forward and the whole thing will be ready in less than eighteen months. So all 20,000 spectators will be sitting in brand new seats … sooner than any of us thought.*
8 B *Girl: … I can't complain about the staff. Boy: Me neither. They've all made us feel really welcome. Girl: I know. It really helped me get over my first-day nerves.*

Part 2

9 confidence *I chose filming instead of acting because I don't have much confidence in myself.*

10 notices details *You see, I believe that to produce a successful movie you need to be someone who notices details.*

11 thriller *... I won a competition. You might think that a person of that age would go for a simple cartoon or a comedy as their first film, but I wrote and directed a thriller*

12 irritated *what irritated me a little was that the adult judges thought young film-makers wouldn't achieve much.*

13 conversations *my imagination often gets working when I overhear conversations in day-to-day situations*

14 trained actors *I tend not to use trained actors. Once they've had drama lessons, they aren't so spontaneous and instinctive*

15 twins/two twins/twin sisters *I met the people for the key roles in the movie I'm making now. I was walking down a street ... and twin sisters were walking towards me.*

16 story *... but remember, the best films all have an absorbing story.*

17 strangers *... strangers will always give you a more honest opinion*

18 English *I'm about to start my English degree in about four weeks*

Part 3

19 H *And it's really helped me decide what career I'd like to do. It's journalism for me ...*

20 A *... I was finding there was too much to get through. ... the articles were great, just too long and dense.*

21 F *... you get pop-up after pop-up trying to sell you stuff. ... Give me good articles online and leave the promotions for when I go shopping.*

22 B *It's being able to access these ideas from young people from other cultures that I appreciate most about the site.*

23 D *... at first, my reaction was positive. ... But I've found that over time, it's lost its appeal.*

Part 4

24 B *The fact is I suffered from different food allergies which affected what I could eat. I had to cut out sugar and dairy products like milk and cheese, for example.*

25 C *I've never been that keen on red meat so an average evening meal might be chicken and broccoli.*

26 A *But the truth is I was fed up with eating the same thing every week. It can get pretty tedious when everyone else has a full range of ingredients to enjoy.*

27 C *And in the end I got tired of emailing recipes so I put them all into a blog.*

28 A *I think I've achieved a large number of readers because my recipes work for everyone.*

29 B *It's not that I get nervous, I'm just not very keen on looking at myself on screen.*

30 A *So to any teenager who's into cooking, I'd say have fun in the kitchen and make what you like.*

SPEAKING: SUCCESS CRITERIA

The following information aims to help teachers and students gain a better understanding of what Cambridge First candidates need to do in order to achieve a pass in the exam (Solid), or higher grades (Good and Acing it!) in the Speaking paper. The categories are based on the marking criteria for the Cambridge First exam. These tables can be used by teachers when assessing speaking, or by students when peer or self-assessing their performance in speaking tasks. They can also use them to set goals to help them advance their speaking skills.

Part 2: Individual long turn

+ = Solid plus whatever is in the *Good* or *Acing It!* box.

	SOLID	GOOD	ACING IT! ✓
GRAMMAR			
Range	Uses a range of simple grammar (e.g. basic tenses).	+ Uses a little complex grammar (e.g. relative clauses, passive forms, verb patterns).	+ Uses a range of complex grammar (e.g. relative clauses, passive forms, verb patterns).
Accuracy	Uses simple grammar to convey meaning with a good level of accuracy.	+ Uses complex grammar with some accuracy.	+ Uses complex grammar with good accuracy.
VOCABULARY			
Function	Compares, contrasts and reacts to the photos.	+ Uses a number of phrases appropriately and often accurately e.g. *Both of the photos show …/ This photo shows … but this photo shows …/This photo reminds me of …*	+ Uses a range of phrases appropriately and often accurately. E.g. *Both of the photos show …/This photo shows … but this photo shows … /This photo reminds me of …*
Range	Uses everyday vocabulary to talk about familiar topics.	+ Uses a good range of vocabulary.	+ Uses a good range of vocabulary; talks about a range of familiar topics.
Accuracy	Uses everyday vocabulary accurately and appropriately.	+ Errors don't often affect understanding.	+ Errors don't usually affect understanding.
DISCOURSE MANAGEMENT			
Fluency	Can talk about the photo for one minute.	+ Only a little hesitation.	+ Very little hesitation.
Relevance	Content is relevant to the photos.	+ Little repetition of ideas.	+ Very little or no repetition of ideas.
Development of ideas and organisation	Ideas about the photos are organised clearly.	+ Ideas are developed e.g. by giving reasons and examples.	+ Ideas are developed e.g. by giving reasons and examples; ideas are usually coherent.
Cohesion	Uses linkers to connect ideas about the photos (e.g. *but, while, also, as well as that*).	+ Uses a range of linkers and a few discourse markers (e.g. *Anyway, So, I mean, Well*).	+ Uses a good range of linkers and some discourse markers (e.g. *Anyway, So, I mean, Well*).
PRONUNCIATION			
Clarity of pronunciation	Sounds are pronounced clearly; stress is placed correctly in words and sentences; intonation is appropriate.	+ Overall, the speaker is usually intelligible to the listener.	+ Overall, the speaker is almost always intelligible to the listener.
INTERACTIVE COMMUNICATION			
Response	Listens and responds to partner's description of the two photos when prompted by the examiner.	+ Response is to some degree related to their partner's description. E.g. *I agree with what Anna said about …*	+ Response is related to their partner's description. E.g. *I agree with what Anna said about …*

Part 3: Collaborative task

+ = Solid plus whatever is in the Good or Acing It! box.

	SOLID	GOOD	ACING IT! ✓
GRAMMAR			
Range	Uses a range of simple grammar (e.g. basic tenses).	+ Uses a little complex grammar (e.g. relative clauses, passive forms, verb patterns).	+ Uses a range of complex grammar (e.g. relative clauses, passive forms, verb patterns).
Accuracy	Uses simple grammar to convey meaning with a good level of accuracy.	+ Uses complex grammar with some accuracy.	+ Uses complex grammar with good accuracy.
VOCABULARY			
Function	Gives and justifies opinions about the given prompts; speculates.	+ Uses a number of phrases appropriately and often accurately, e.g. *In my view … because/I believe that … because/One reason is that …/It could be that …*	+ Uses a range of phrases appropriately and often accurately, e.g. *In my view … because/I believe that … because/One reason is that …/It could be that …*
Range	Uses everyday vocabulary to talk about familiar topics.	+ Uses a good range of vocabulary.	+ Uses a good range of vocabulary; talks about a range of familiar topics.
Accuracy	Uses everyday vocabulary accurately and appropriately.	+ Errors don't often affect understanding.	+ Errors don't usually affect understanding.
DISCOURSE MANAGEMENT			
Fluency	Can give an opinion and reasons for an appropriate length of time.	+ Only a little hesitation.	+ Very little hesitation.
Relevance	Content is relevant to the task.	+ Little repetition of ideas.	+ Very little or no repetition of ideas.
Development of ideas and organisation	Ideas about the prompts are organised clearly.	+ Ideas are developed e.g. by giving reasons and examples.	+ Ideas are developed e.g. by giving reasons and examples; ideas are usually coherent.
Cohesion	Uses linkers to connect ideas about the prompts (e.g. *That's because, …/As well as that, …*).	+ Uses a range of linkers and a few discourse markers (e.g. *Anyway, So, I mean, Well*).	+ Uses a good range of linkers and some discourse markers (e.g. *Anyway, So, I mean, Well*).
PRONUNCIATION			
Clarity of pronunciation	Sounds are pronounced clearly; stress is placed correctly in words and sentences; intonation is appropriate.	+ Overall, the speaker is usually intelligible to the listener.	+ Overall, the speaker is almost always intelligible to the listener.
INTERACTIVE COMMUNICATION			
Initiation and response	Starts discussion, responds to what partner says and develops the conversation, e.g. by agreeing or disagreeing or asking a question.	+ Usually responds appropriately.	+ Always responds appropriately and links ideas, e.g. *You just said that … Well, I agree because …*
Negotiation	Discusses some or all of the prompts and works towards reaching a decision.	+ Works towards a decision fairly easily.	+ Works towards a decision easily.

Part 4: Discussion

+ = Solid plus whatever is in the Good or Acing It! box.

	SOLID	GOOD	ACING IT! ✓
GRAMMATICAL RESOURCE			
Range	Uses a range of simple grammar (e.g. basic tenses).	+ Uses a little complex grammar (e.g. relative clauses, passive forms, verb patterns).	+ Uses a range of complex grammar (e.g. relative clauses, passive forms, verb patterns).
Accuracy	Uses simple grammar to convey meaning with a good level of accuracy.	+ Uses complex grammar with some accuracy.	+ Uses complex grammar with good accuracy.
LEXICAL RESOURCE			
Function	Gives and justifies opinions in answer to the questions; speculates.	+ Uses a number of phrases appropriately and often accurately e.g. *In my view … because/I believe that … because/One reason is that …/It might be …*	+ Uses a range of phrases appropriately and often accurately. E.g. *In my view … because/I believe that … because/One reason is that …/It might be …*
Range	Uses everyday vocabulary to talk about familiar topics.	+ Uses a good range of vocabulary.	+ Uses a good range of vocabulary; talks about a range of familiar topics.
Accuracy	Uses everyday vocabulary accurately and appropriately.	+ Errors don't often affect understanding.	+ Errors don't usually affect understanding.
DISCOURSE MANAGEMENT			
Fluency	Can give an opinion and reasons for an appropriate length of time.	+ Only a little hesitation.	+ Very little hesitation.
Relevance	Content is relevant to the task.	+ Little repetition of ideas.	+ Very little or no repetition of ideas.
Development of ideas and organisation	Ideas about the prompts are organised clearly.	+ Ideas are developed, e.g. by giving reasons and examples.	+ Ideas are developed, e.g. by giving reasons and examples; ideas are usually coherent.
Cohesion	Uses linkers to connect ideas in answer to the questions (e.g. *That's because …/As well as that …*).	+ Uses a range of linkers and a few discourse markers (e.g. *Anyway, So, I mean, Well*).	+ Uses a good range of linkers and some discourse markers (e.g. *Anyway, So, I mean, Well*).
PRONUNCIATION			
Clarity of pronunciation	Sounds are pronounced clearly; stress is placed correctly in words and sentences; intonation is appropriate.	+ Overall, the speaker is usually intelligible to the listener.	+ Overall, the speaker is almost always intelligible to the listener.
INTERACTIVE COMMUNICATION			
Initiation and response	Starts discussion, responds to what partner says and develops the conversation, e.g. by agreeing or disagreeing or asking a question.	+ Usually responds appropriately.	+ Always responds appropriately and links ideas, e.g. *You just said that … Well, I agree because …*
Discussion	Discusses the question and negotiates towards an outcome, e.g. agreement or disagreement.	+ Asks questions to open the discussion up.	+ Asks questions to open the discussion up and takes the discussion into new areas.

WRITING: SUCCESS CRITERIA

The following information aims to help teachers and students gain a better understanding of what Cambridge First candidates need to do in order to achieve a pass in the Writing paper (Solid), or higher grades (Good and Acing it!). The categories are based on the marking criteria for the Cambridge First exam. This information can be used by teachers when marking written work, or by students when peer or self-assessing written work. They can also use it to set goals to help them advance their written skills.

Essay

The examples given in this table come from the example Solid, Good and Acing it! essays below.

+ = Solid plus whatever is in the Good or Acing it! box.

	SOLID	GOOD	ACING IT!
CONTENT			
Task fulfilment	Discusses the two points given in the question and adds one idea of their own.	+ Develops the ideas in sound depth.	+ Develops the ideas in good depth.
Relevance	The content is relevant to the question and clear to the reader.	+ Few irrelevances or omissions.	+ No irrelevances or omissions.
COMMUNICATIVE ACHIEVEMENT			
Introduction	Starts with an introduction which introduces the topic. E.g. *Which is better for children? The city or the countryside?*	+ States what the essay will argue or discuss e.g. *it is better to grow up in an urban area than the countryside.*	+ Gives some background information to the topic and states what the essay will discuss e.g. *Over 50% of people around the world live in cities these days.*
Conclusion	Ends with a conclusion which restates the main point(s) of the essay and comes to a conclusion. E.g. *In my opinion, it's better to grow up in the city than the countryside but it is also important for children to go to the countryside.*	+ Summarises both stated options and reasons why e.g. *To conclude, it is better to grow up in the city than in the countryside due to the public services and transport system there.*	+ Leaves the reader with something to think about. E.g. *cities must provide safe green areas for children to play in.*
Tone	Uses neutral language to present opinions and reasons e.g. using passive forms (e.g. *a car is needed),* not using contractions (e.g. *it is also important),* avoiding informal language (e.g. *lots of),* avoiding we/I where possible (e.g. *You can find)*	+ The tone is often consistent throughout the letter/email but there may be some inconsistencies.	+ The tone is usually consistent throughout the letter/email but there may be some inconsistencies.
Conveying ideas	Expresses simple ideas clearly which the reader can mostly understand.	+ Expresses a few complex ideas which the reader can usually understand.	+ Expresses some complex ideas which the reader can usually understand.
ORGANISATION			
Paragraphing	Essay is divided into logical paragraphs.	+ The ideas within each paragraph are ordered logically i.e. topic sentence to introduce the main idea (e.g. *urban areas have more public services than towns)* followed by supporting ideas (explanation, examples, reasons e.g. *Children grow up with a school and healthcare close*).	+ The ideas within each paragraph are ordered logically e.g. topic sentence + supporting ideas; ideas are linked between paragraphs e.g. *Furthermore, On the other hand.*
Cohesion	Ideas in paragraphs are linked through the use of linkers (e.g. *but, However*), referencing and substitution (e.g, *these services*).	+ A variety of linking is used, often appropriately and accurately.	+ A variety of linking is used, usually appropriately and accurately.
LANGUAGE			
Grammar	Uses a variety of grammar with good accuracy. Errors don't stop the reader from understanding the essay.	+ Uses a little complex grammar, often accurately.	+ Uses some complex grammar, generally accurately.
Vocabulary	Uses everyday vocabulary mostly appropriately e.g. *public transport.*	+ Uses some less common vocabulary with some accuracy. (e.g. *urban areas, high priced).*	+ Uses some less common vocabulary with good accuracy. (e.g. *urban areas, run a car, close proximity*).

Essay task

'It is better to grow up in the city than the countryside.' Do you agree?

Notes

Write about:

1 nature
2 public services
3 ... (your own idea)

Example answer – Solid

Many people live in the city these days. Which is better for children? The city or the countryside?

There are more public services in the city. You can find many schools and hospitals there. Children need these services in their lives much.

We can use lots of buses and trams to get around in the city but in the countryside a car is needed. Public transport is better for society. There's public transport in the city.

However, the countryside has more nature than the city. Children can be more freedom in the countryside and also more safety. City life is not as safe.

In my opinion, it's better to grow up in the city than the countryside but it is also important for children to go to the countryside and enjoy some nature too.

Examiner comments	
Content	Discusses the two points and adds a third one. The writer doesn't develop the ideas fully. Why do children need those services? Why is public transport better for society? The essay is just under 140 words which suggests a lack of development.
Communicative achievement	There's an introduction, a main body and a conclusion. The introduction introduces the topic but doesn't state the argument the essay will make, or state that it will discuss both arguments before coming to a conclusion. The writer comes to a conclusion and restates the main points. The tone is generally objective but it isn't always consistent (contractions, choice of words, objectivity (e.g. *there's public transport / lots of buses / You can find* vs *We need*).
Organisation	Essay is divided into logical paragraphs but the information within the paragraphs could be organised better. Ideas are generally linked within paragraphs (e.g. *but, and also, these services*).
Language	A range of simple grammar is used generally correctly (e.g. modal verbs, present simple, comparatives); everyday vocabulary is mostly used appropriately (e.g. *public transport, buses, trams*), errors don't affect communication (e.g. *in their lives much / can be more freedom / more safety*).

Example answer – Good

More and more people live in the city these days. City life can be stressful but, in my view, it is better to grow up there than the countryside.

The first reason is that urban areas have more public services than towns and villages can. Children grow up with a school and healthcare close. This helps them to be inteligent and healthy.

Public transport is much more convenient in cities. There are regular buses and trams. Families in the countryside have to own a vehicle which can be more high priced than public transport and cause a big damage to the environment. Cities have buses and trams people can use.

There is a downside though. It's more difficult for children to see nature in a city. Visiting a park isn't anywhere near as good as visiting the countryside. There you can enjoy the safety and freedom. It's much easier to be with nature there.

To conclude, it is better to grow up in the city than in the countryside due to the public services and transport system there. However, cities cannot give the same kind of green areas for children to play in as the countryside does.

Examiner comments	
Content	Discusses the two points and adds a third. The ideas are developed quite well but there is some repetition of ideas i.e. *cities have buses and trams you can use / It's much easier to engage with nature there.*
Communicative achievement	There's an introduction, a main body and a conclusion. The introduction introduces the topic and states what the essay will argue. The conclusion restates the main points of the essay and reasons. The tone is generally neutral but there are a few inconsistencies (e.g. *it's more difficult/anywhere near as good*).
Organisation	Essay is divided into paragraphs and each paragraph has a topic statement and then supporting points. Ideas are generally linked within paragraphs (e.g. *This helps/There you can/However*).
Language	Simple structures are generally used accurately. There are also complex sentences (e.g. *which can be more costly, due to the public services*); there is some less common vocabulary used appropriately (e.g. *urban areas, downside, high priced*), errors are minor and don't affect communication (e.g. *inteligent, a school and healthcare close, a big damage*).

Example answer – Acing it!

Over 50% of people around the world live in cities these days; a number which is expected to rise in future. Although city life can be stressful, in my view, it is better to grow up in an urban area than a rural area.

The first reason is that urban areas provides more public services than towns and villages can. Children grow up with a school and healthcare in close proximity which helps them to lead a better educated and healthier life.

Furthermore, public transport is better in cities. There are regular buses and trams. Families in rural areas have to run a car which can be more costly and much more worse for the environment than public transport.

On the other hand, it is more difficult for children to experience nature in a city. While there are green areas, visiting those is not the same as enjoying the safety and freedom that walks in the countryside give you.

To conclude, it is better to grow up in the city than in the countryside due to the public services and transport system there. However, cities must provide safe green areas for children to play so that they can enjoy some of the same benefits that rural areas offers.

Examiner comments	
Content	Discusses the two points and adds a third. The ideas are developed well and can be clearly understood by the reader.
Communicative achievement	There's an introduction, a main body and a conclusion. The introduction introduces the topic and states what the essay will argue. It also adds some background information (i.e. *Over 50% of people around the world live in cities these days*). The conclusion restates the main points of the essay and reasons. It also leaves the reader with something to think about (i.e. *cities must provide safe green areas for children).* The tone is generally neutral throughout.
Organisation	Essay is divided into paragraphs and each paragraph has a topic statement and then supporting points. Ideas are generally linked within paragraphs and between paragraphs (e.g. *Furthermore, On the other hand*).
Language	Simple structures and some more complex structures are generally used accurately (e.g. *visiting those is not the same as enjoy the safety and freedom that*); there is some less common vocabulary used appropriately (e.g. *urban areas, run a car, close proximity, safe green areas*), errors are minor and don't affect communication (e.g. *urban areas provides, much more worse, rural areas offers*).

Email/letter

+ = Solid plus whatever is in the Good or Acing it! box.

	SOLID	GOOD	ACING IT!
CONTENT			
Task fulfilment	Answers all the questions in the email, e.g. *I suggest you take a bus tour of the city while you're here.*	+ Develops the ideas in sound depth, e.g. *I suggest you take a bus tour of the city while you're here as you'll get to see all of the main attractions in the area.*	+ Develops the ideas in good depth, e.g. *I suggest you take a bus tour of the city while you're here as you'll get to see all of the main attractions in the area for a really cheap price. I'm sure you'll love it!*
Relevance	The content is relevant to the question and clear to the reader.	+ Few irrelevances or omissions.	+ No irrelevances or omissions.
COMMUNICATIVE ACHIEVEMENT			
Opening and closing	Opens and closes the email/letter appropriately, e.g. *Dear Mr Smith/Hi Kerry/Yours sincerely/All the Best*. The purpose for writing is made clear, e.g. *I am writing to apply for .../I've got some exciting news for you.*	As Solid.	As Solid.
Tone	Selects an appropriate tone, depending on the writer's relationship to the reader. Formal letters/emails have a formal tone, e.g. *I am writing to complain about a product I recently purchased.* Informal letters/emails have an informal tone, e.g. *You'll never guess what happened to me last week!*	+ The tone is often consistent throughout the letter/email but there may be some inconsistencies.	+ The tone is usually consistent throughout the letter/email but there may be some inconsistencies.
Functions	Uses phrases to convey functions such as inviting, thanking, suggesting, e.g. *Would you like to come to my party next week?/Thanks so much for the tickets./Why don't you come with me?*	+ The phrases are usually used appropriately and accurately.	+ The phrases are mostly used appropriately and accurately.
Conveying ideas	Expresses simple ideas clearly which the reader can mostly understand.	+ Expresses a few complex ideas which the reader can usually understand.	+ Expresses some complex ideas which the reader can usually understand.
ORGANISATION			
Paragraphing	Email/letter is divided into logical paragraphs.	+ The ideas within each paragraph are ordered logically, e.g. topic sentence to introduce the main idea + supporting points, e.g. explanation, examples, reasons.	+ The ideas within each paragraph are ordered logically, e.g. topic sentence + supporting ideas; ideas are linked across paragraphs, e.g. *In addition to that/On the other hand.*
Cohesion	Ideas are connected using linkers (e.g. *Anyway, Mind you*), referencing and substitution (e.g it, this, one).	+ A variety of linking is used, often appropriately and accurately.	+ A variety of linking is used, usually appropriately and accurately.
LANGUAGE			
Grammar	Uses a variety of grammar with good accuracy. Errors don't stop the reader from understanding the email/letter.	+ Uses a little complex grammar, often accurately.	+ Uses some complex grammar, generally accurately.
Vocabulary	Uses everyday vocabulary mostly appropriately.	+ Uses some less common vocabulary with some accuracy.	+ Uses some less common vocabulary with good accuracy.

Email/letter task

You have received an email from an English-speaking friend.

From: Darren

Subject: Visit to your town

Some of my friends are visiting your city with school next month. They'd love to go sightseeing while they're there. What kinds of things would you recommend for them to do? How can they get to those places?

If you could let me know, I'll pass on the information to them.

Thanks!

Darren

Write your email in 140–190 words

Example answer - Solid

Hi Darren,

Thank you very much for your email. I'm happy that your friends are coming to stay in my city. It's a lovely place so I think they'll enjoy it. I went shopping in the city centre last week and it was fun.

I think your friends should to go to the zoo. You can find some interesting animals there and the zoo look after them well. Your money will help animals too.

Close to the city there's a water park. It's great fun. It's quite expensive so your friends will need to save money but I'm sure they'll love it. Hopefully the weather will be nice when they come.

The best way to get to these two places is on bus. Your friends should get on at the bus station in the city centre and pay the driver. It's very easy. You can access the timetable on the bus website address is bigbluebus.uk.

I hope your friends will have a good time.

All the best,

Verity

Examiner comments	
Content	Answers both questions in the task. The ideas could be developed better, especially about how money helps animals and what's at the water park. The line about shopping is irrelevant.
Communicative achievement	The purpose of the email is given in the first paragraph and there is an ending although the tone is a little formal. Appropriate phrases of suggestion/recommendation are used. The ideas conveyed are generally simple.
Organisation	The email is divided into paragraphs and the information in each paragraph is logically ordered. There is some simple linking (e.g. *so, there, them, too, these two places*).
Language	A range of simple grammar is used generally correctly; everyday vocabulary is used appropriately (e.g. *interesting animals*) but not really any complex vocabulary. Errors don't affect communication (e.g. *should to go, look after*).

Example answer - Acing it!

Hi Darren,

It was great to hear from you. I hope things are good with you.

So, your friends are visiting. Well, there are a lots of different things to do in my city so they're going to have a fun time. I'd definitely recommend the zoo. There are some unusual animals there which you can learn about. The animals are really well looked after and profit from customers is used to help animals in the wild.

About five minutes outside the city, there's a water park which I'm sure your friends will love. It's huge with some exciting rides. It's not cheap but it's worth the money. You have to be accompanied by an adult if you're under 16 so a teacher will need to go with them.

You asked about transport. Well, I'd suggest the bus. Your friends will be able to get one to both the zoo and the water park. They run regularly and tickets aren't expensive. They should to be able to find the timetables online.

I hope your friends have a fantastic time. Let me know how they get on.

Verity

Examiner comments	
Content	Answers both questions in the task. The ideas are developed in good depth and all the information is relevant.
Communicative achievement	The email is opened and closed appropriately. The tone is consistently informal throughout. Appropriate phrases of suggestion/recommendation are used (e.g. *I'd recommend; I'd suggest*). Some complex ideas are conveyed.
Organisation	The email is divided into paragraphs and the information in each paragraph is logically ordered. There is a variety of linking (e.g. *and, so, get one to, They run regularly*).
Language	A range of simple grammar is used generally correctly (e.g. present simple, future predictions, first conditional) as well as some more complex grammar (e.g. relative clauses, variety of passive forms); everyday vocabulary is used appropriately (e.g. *transport, worth the money*) and there is some less common vocabulary too (e.g. *profit, accompanied by, get on*). Errors don't affect communication (e.g. *a lots of, The should to be able to.*).

Article

+ = Solid plus whatever is in the Good or Acing it! box.

	SOLID	GOOD	ACING IT!
CONTENT			
Task fulfilment	Includes all information required in the task, e.g. What's the best way to get around your city? Why is it the best way? How could transport in your city be improved?	+ Develops the ideas in sound depth, e.g. *Anyone visiting my city should use the metro system. It's cheap and convenient.*	+ Develops the ideas in good depth, e.g. *Anyone visiting my city should use the metro. It's cheap and convenient and almost everyone uses it. Don't be left out!*
Relevance	The content is relevant to the question and clear to the reader.	+ Few irrelevances or omissions.	+ No irrelevances or omissions.
COMMUNICATIVE ACHIEVEMENT			
Attracting the reader	Attracts and keeps the reader's attention, for example by asking a rhetorical question or making a bold statement, e.g. *The Moscow metro. This is the only thing you'll need to get around my city.*	+ Is mostly organised clearly so the reader understands it.	+ Is fully organised clearly so the reader fully understands it.
Evaluation	Offers an opinion.	+ The opinions are mostly supported with examples and reasons.	+ The opinions are fully supported with examples and reasons.
Tone	Uses an informal tone to engage the reader through a variety of modifiers and adjectives, emphasis and rhetorical questions,e.g. *Would you like to stand in a small space surrounded by lots of others? The buses are just so crowded here. It's best to avoid them.*	+ The tone is often consistent throughout the review but there may be some inconsistencies.	+ The tone is usually consistent throughout the review but there may be some inconsistencies.
Conveying ideas	Expresses simple ideas clearly which the reader can mostly understand.	+ Expresses a few complex ideas which the reader can usually understand.	+ Expresses some complex ideas which the reader can usually understand.
ORGANISATION			
Heading	The article has a heading, e.g. *The greatest story you've never heard of.*	+ The heading is mostly appropriate to the content of the article and attracts the reader's attention.	+ The heading is fully appropriate to the content of the article and fully attracts the reader's attention.
Paragraphing	The article is organised into paragraphs.	+ The ideas within each paragraph are ordered logically, e.g. topic sentence to introduce the main idea + supporting points, e.g. explanation, examples, reasons.	+ The ideas within each paragraph are ordered logically, e.g. topic sentence + supporting ideas; ideas are linked across paragraphs, e.g. *On top of that/Of course it's not all positive.*
Cohesion	Sentences are linked through the use of formal linkers, e.g. *What's more;* organisational patterns, e.g. *Can you guess why that is? It's because…;* referencing and substitution, e.g it, this, one.	+ A variety of linking is used, often appropriately and accurately.	+ A variety of linking is used, usually appropriately and accurately.
LANGUAGE			
Grammar	Uses a variety of grammar with good accuracy. Errors don't stop the reader from understanding the article.	+ Uses a little complex grammar, often accurately.	+ Uses some complex grammar, generally accurately.
Vocabulary	Uses everyday vocabulary mostly appropriately.	+ Uses some less common vocabulary with some accuracy.	+ Uses some less common vocabulary with good accuracy.

Article task

You have seen this announcement on an English-language website.

Articles wanted!

How do you get around your city? What's the best way? How could transport in your city be improved?

Write an article answering these questions. We'll publish the best ones on our website.

Write your article in 140–190 words.

Example answer – Solid

Getting around my city

One of the benefits of city life is transport. There are so many different ways to get around. In my city, you can take the metro, take a train or get a bus. You can even cycle in one of the many cycle paths if you want to get some exercise.

There are advantages and disadvantages with each type of transport but in my view, the metro is the best of them all. The trains can be expensive and the buses get stuck in traffic. The metro is quick, cheap and convenient. There's a metro stop just a hundred metres from my front door.

Of course, nothing is perfect, is it? The metro stops at 11pm which isn't great for people who work in the evenings or in the night. I'd love it if the metro could go all night so that everyone can use it.

Examiner comments	
Content	Answers all of the questions in the task. Develops the ideas in sufficient depth although the idea in the third paragraph could be developed more fully. The mention of cycle paths is irrelevant as they aren't public transport.
Communicative achievement	The article starts with a statement. It offers an opinion and uses a fairly informal tone although it's not always consistent (e.g. the first line of paragraph 2 is quite formal). There are some adjectives (e.g. *quick, cheap and convenient*), emphasis (e.g. *so many different ways*) and a rhetorical question (e.g. *Of course, nothing is perfect, is it?*).
Organisation	There's a title but it's quite generic. It's not particularly relevant or engaging. The review is organised into paragraphs. Sentences are linked (e.g. *can even cycle, but in my view, use it*).
Language	A range of simple grammar is used generally correctly (e.g. present simple, *can, there is/are*, first conditional); everyday vocabulary is mostly used appropriately (e.g. *different ways, get some exercise, get stuck in traffic*), errors don't affect communication (e.g. omission of *the* before *transport* in the first line, and prepositions *in one of the many paths, disadvantages with, in the night*).

Example answer – Acing it!

Metro magic

The metro. This is the only thing you need to get around my city. It's quick, it's convenient and it's reasonably priced. It's also super modern and really clean. Even if you use it at night, you'll feel safe. Everyone who uses it loves it!

Of course there are alternative form of transport available. There's a network of trains which are more expensive then the metro and doesn't stop at all the main tourist spots. It's better for commuters who want to travel to and from the city.

There are also the buses but let me ask you a question. Would you stand in a small space surrounded by fifty people? No? Then the buses aren't for you. They're so packed that it's best to avoid them. If only the buses were bigger and ran more frequently, they'd be great to use. That's something I'd love to see.

Until that happens, I'd say that any visitor to my city should give the busses and trains a miss and get a daily metro card that allow them to travel all around the city. They won't regret it.

Examiner comments	
Content	Includes all of the ideas in the task. Develops the ideas in good depth. The content is relevant to the question and clear to the reader.
Communicative achievement	The article starts with an eye-catching phrase and then a bold statement. It offers an opinion and uses a consistently appropriate tone. There's a variety of adjectives (e.g. *convenient, super modern*), emphasis (e.g, *so packed that*) and a rhetorical question (e.g. *Would you stand in a small space … ?*).
Organisation	There's an appropriate and attractive title. The article is organised into paragraphs and ideas within the paragraph are organised effectively i.e. the idea is introduced and then further details are given. Sentences are linked (e.g. *This is the only thing; There are also buses; Until that happens*).
Language	A range of simple grammar is used correctly (e.g. present simple, first and second conditionals, *so … that*, comparatives) and there is some complex grammar too (e.g. relative clauses, *if only …, Until that happens …*); everyday vocabulary is used appropriately (e.g. *reasonably priced, a network of trains, commuters*) and some less common vocabulary is used with good accuracy (e.g. *tourist spots, packed, give them a miss*); errors don't affect communication (e.g. *form of transport, are more expensive then the metro, busses*).

Review

+ = Solid plus whatever is in the Good or Acing it! box.

	SOLID	GOOD	ACING IT! ✓
CONTENT			
Task fulfilment	Includes all information required in the task, e.g. How did the main characters change during the story? Was this change for the better or worse?	+ Develops the ideas in sound depth, e.g. *Elise became much more confident throughout the story which was very positive.*	+ Develops the ideas in good depth, e.g. *Elise became much more confident throughout the story as she realised that she was a good dancer. This was positive as it helped her achieve her dreams and become a professional dancer.*
Relevance	The content is relevant to the question and clear to the reader.	+ Few irrelevances or omissions.	+ No irrelevances or omissions.
COMMUNICATIVE ACHIEVEMENT			
Introduction	Attracts the reader's attention by asking a rhetorical question or speaking directly to the reader, e.g. *What's the best place to make a film? I bet it's not where you think it is!*	+ Is mostly organised coherently so the reader understands it.	+ Is consistently organised coherently so the reader fully understands it.
Evaluation	Evaluates as well as describes, i.e. strengths and weaknesses, giving personal opinions.	+ The evaluation and opinions are mostly supported with examples and reasons.	+ The evaluation and opinions are fully supported with examples and reasons.
Summary and recommendation	Ends with a summary of the main points of the review and a recommendation, e.g. *This is the best film I've ever seen. Make sure you don't miss it.*	+ The summary and recommendation mostly come from ideas in the main body of the review. The reader understands them.	+ The summary and recommendation all come from ideas in the main body of the review. The reader understands them.
Tone	Uses an informal tone to engage the reader through a variety of modifiers and adjectives, emphasis and rhetorical questions, e.g. *The location of the film was absolutely incredible./ Can you guess what happened next?*	+ The tone is often consistent throughout the review but there may be some inconsistencies.	+ The tone is usually consistent throughout the review but there may be some inconsistencies.
Conveying ideas	Expresses simple ideas clearly which the reader can mostly understand.	+ Expresses a few complex ideas which the reader can usually understand.	+ Expresses some complex ideas which the reader can usually understand.
ORGANISATION			
Heading	The review has a heading, e.g. *The greatest story you've never heard of.*	+ The heading is mostly appropriate to the content of the review and attracts the reader's attention.	+ The heading is fully appropriate to the content of the review and fully attracts the reader's attention.
Paragraphing	The review is organised into paragraphs.	+ The ideas within each paragraph are ordered logically, e.g. topic sentence to introduce the main idea + supporting points, e.g. explanation, examples, reasons.	+ The ideas within each paragraph are ordered logically, e.g. topic sentence + supporting ideas; ideas are linked across paragraphs to create a coherent review, e.g. *Just like the acting, the cinematography is stunning.*
Cohesion	Sentences are linked through the use of informal linkers, e.g. *What's more;* referencing and substitution, e.g it, this, one.	+ The linking is mostly appropriate and accurate.	+ The linking is always appropriate and accurate.
LANGUAGE			
Grammar	Uses a range of grammar mostly accurately.	+ Uses a range of complex grammar mostly accurately; makes only minor errors.	+ Uses a wide range of complex grammar mostly accurately; makes only very minor errors.
Vocabulary	Uses common and less common vocabulary mostly appropriately.	+ Uses a good range of vocabulary mostly accurately.	+ Uses a wide range of vocabulary accurately.

Review task

You have seen this announcement in an English-language magazine.

We're looking for reviews of films where the main character changed in some way during the story. Write a review of the film and tell us how the main character changed and if it was for the better or not. Tell us whether or not you'd recommend this film to others.

We'll publish the best reviews in our magazine.

Write your story in 140–190 words

Example answer - Solid

A fantastic film!

Do you like exciting films? Then you should watch Lost in the City. It's a thrilling film about a young boy. He gets lost in New Delhi. He tries to find his mum. However, lots of dangerous things happen to him so he isn't safety. I went to see it in the cinema and really enjoyed it.

At first, Arjun is a shy boy but at the end of the film he's strong. He's a survivor. Unfortunately, he's also serious. He's not funny any more and we can see that he's not a child in his mind now. This is a disapointment. He can't just have fun any more.

I think everyone should watch Lost in the City. It is possible to download it or rent it from a website. It's not perfect but it's exciting and it has a good ending. The little boy is a good actor. I hope we see him in other films. Watch this film. You'll learn a lot.

Examiner comments	
Content	Answers the two questions in the task. Develops many of the ideas but reasons aren't fully given as to why the reader should watch the film in the final paragraph. The lines about seeing the film at the cinema and downloading the film aren't very relevant to the task.
Communicative achievement	The review starts with a question for the reader. The conclusion gives a recommendation. The writer evaluates the film. However, the tone is too formal in places (e.g. *However, It is possible to, a disappointment*).
Organisation	There is a title but it is generic and not very attractive. The review is divided into logical paragraphs and ideas within paragraphs are logically ordered. Ideas are generally linked (e.g. *Then, However, Unfortunately, rent it, this film*).
Language	A range of simple grammar is used generally correctly (e.g. present simple, simple verb patterns, *should*) but there is little complex grammar. Everyday vocabulary is used appropriately (e.g. *thrilling, a survivor, a good ending*). Errors don't affect communication (e.g. *safety, in the cinema, disapointment*).

Example answer - Acing it!

You'll get lost in this film

Do you have two hours to spare? Then you must watch Lost in the City, an inspiring film about an eight-year-old boy called Arjun who gets lost in the large city of New Delhi. He spends the whole film trying to get home to his mum. It's a thriller, as Arjun faces a lot of danger.

At the beginning of the film, Arjun is a quiet and cheeky little boy. As the film progresses, he has to change in order to survive. He becomes tougher and more confident which help him to live. However, he also loses his sense of humour because of the serious of his situation. This is a negative change. He is no longer a sweet, innocent child.

Lost in the City is a must-see film. It's a story about not giving up. The middle part is a little slow but there are several thrilling parts and the ending is fantastic. The acting is excellent too. I can't think of a better way to waste the couple of hours.

Examiner comments	
Content	Answers the two questions in the task. Develops the ideas in good depth. The content is all relevant.
Communicative achievement	The review starts with a question for the reader. The introduction and ending are clear and well organised. The writer evaluates the film and uses an appropriate tone throughout.
Organisation	The title is relevant and attractive. The review is divided into logical paragraphs and ideas within paragraphs are logically ordered. There is a variety of linking (e.g. *Then, This is a, but, too*).
Language	A range of simple grammar is used generally correctly (e.g. present simple) and some complex grammar is used too (e.g. relative clauses, verb patterns, sentences with two clauses). Everyday vocabulary is used appropriately (e.g. *an inspiring film, becomes tougher, sense of humour, not giving up, several thrilling parts*), and some less common vocabulary is used too (e.g. *faces a lot of danger, sweet, innocent child, a must-see film*). Errors don't affect communication (e.g. *quiet and cheeky, serious of his situation, the couple of hours*).

Story

+ = Solid plus whatever is in the Good or Acing it! box.

	SOLID	GOOD	ACING IT! ✓
CONTENT			
Task fulfilment	Continues the first line of the story and includes the ideas given in the task.	+ Develops the ideas in sound depth.	+ Develops the ideas in good depth.
Relevance	The content is relevant to the task and clear to the reader.	+ Few irrelevances or omissions.	+ No irrelevances or omissions.
COMMUNICATIVE ACHIEVEMENT			
Title	Includes a title.	+ Title is fully relevant to the story.	+ Title is fully relevant to the story and attracts the readers' attention.
Engages the reader	Uses language to engage the reader e.g. descriptive language (adjectives and adverbs), direct and indirect speech.	+ Uses a range of language.	+ Uses a wide range of language.
Story ending	Story has a clear ending.	+Ending is logical.	+ Ending is logical and interesting.
Conveying ideas	Expresses simple ideas clearly which the reader can mostly understand.	+ Expresses a few complex ideas which the reader can usually understand.	+ Expresses some complex ideas which the reader can usually understand.
ORGANISATION			
Beginning, middle and end	Story has a beginning, middle and end.	+ These are clear.	+ These are clear and logical.
Paragraphing	The story is divided into coherent paragraphs.	+ The paragraphs reflect the beginning, middle and end of the story.	+ The paragraphs reflect the beginning, middle and end of the story. The ideas within each paragraph are organised logically.
Cohesion	Actions within the story are ordered using time linkers and/or tenses (e.g. past simple/past perfect). Sentences are linked through the use of linkers (e.g. *although, as well as that*), referencing and substitution (e.g. *it, this, one*).	+ A variety of linking is used, often appropriately and accurately.	+ A variety of linking is used, usually appropriately and accurately.
LANGUAGE			
Grammar	Uses a variety of grammar with good accuracy. Errors don't stop the reader from understanding the story.	+ Uses a little complex grammar, often accurately.	+ Uses some complex grammar, generally accurately.
Vocabulary	Uses everyday vocabulary mostly appropriately.	+ Uses some less common vocabulary with some accuracy.	+ Uses some less common vocabulary with good accuracy.

Story task

You have seen this announcement on a short story website.

We're looking for good short stories!

Why not write a story for our website? Your story must begin with this sentence:

When Mark's alarm went off, he remembered that today was an important day.

Your story must include:

- an interview
- a mistake

Write your story in 140–190 words

Example answer – Solid

A silly mistake

When Mark's alarm went off, he remembered that today was an important day. Today was his first ever job interview. It was his dream job and he wanted to make a good impression. He had a light breakfast, showered and then dressed in his suit.

He left home nice and early. He got in the car and drove to the company's main offices. He arrived twenty minutes before his interview. However when he got to reception the receptionist said him that he was in the wrong place. The interview was in a different location twenty minutes from here.

Mark couldn't believe it. He immediately returned his car and drove as fast as he could towards the correct place. Every traffic light was red and all pedestrian wanted to cross the road on a pedestrian crossing. It was a nightmare! Finally he arrived at the right place. He even had one minute to calm down and prepare for the interview. Phew!

Examiner comments	
Content	Continues the first line of the story and includes the ideas given in the task. Develops the ideas in sufficient depth. With around 28 spare words, the writer could give more description to develop some ideas more.
Communicative achievement	There's a title but it's quite generic. It's not particularly relevant or engaging. The story has some descriptive language (e.g. *a good impression, a light breakfast, as fast as he could*) but there isn't a lot of variety and there aren't any examples of direct or indirect speech. The ending is fine but not as exciting as it could be.
Organisation	The story is divided into logical paragraphs. The story is told using only the past simple with three examples of time linkers (*then dressed in his suit, immediately returned, Finally he arrived*).
Language	A range of simple grammar is used generally correctly (e.g. past simple); everyday vocabulary is mostly used appropriately (e.g. *make a good impression, in the wrong place, It was a nightmare!, pedestrian crossing*); errors don't affect communication (e.g. lack of commas after *However/Finally, dressed in his suit, said him that, returned his car, all pedestrian*).

Example answer – Acing it!

One mistake can cost you your dream

When Mark's alarm went off, he remembered that today was an important day. He had applied for his dream job and today he had his interview. He put on the posh new suit he'd bought last week and got to the office with twenty minutes to spare.

Mark presented himself to the receptionist. "Hello", he said smiling. "I'm here for the job interview." The receptionist looked puzzled. "I'm sorry", he said. "The interview isn't here. It's at our South Road site, twenty minutes from here." Mark couldn't believe it. How had he made such a basic mistake?

Without taking a breath he turned, got back in his car and drove speedily towards South Road. Just before he arrived, he had to stop and let a woman cross a pedestrian crossing. The woman spent so long on her phone while crossing that Mark screamed angrily at her to hurry up. She stopped and stared at him before finally moving.

Mark managed to get to the offices on time. He walked into the interview room and you've guessed it he came face to face with the woman he'd just shouted at.

Examiner comments	
Content	Continues the first line of the story and includes the ideas given in the task. The ideas are developed in good depth and all the information is relevant to the task.
Communicative achievement	The title is relevant and engaging. The story has a wide range of descriptive language (e.g. *posh new suit, drove speedily, screamed angrily*) as well as direct speech.
Organisation	The story is divided into logical paragraphs. The order of actions is told using the past simple and past perfect (*suit he'd bought last week, How had he made such a basic mistake?*), as well as time linkers (*Without taking a breath, Just before he arrived*). There's a variety which helps to engage the reader.
Language	A range of simple grammar is used generally correctly (e.g. past simple and past perfect) as well as some more complex grammar (e.g. sentences with two or three clauses; participle clause, e.g. *Without taking a breath*); everyday vocabulary is mostly used appropriately (e.g. *managed to get to, with twenty minutes to spare*) and there is some less common vocabulary too (e.g. *posh new suit, looked puzzled*). Errors don't affect communication (e.g. lack of commas in some clauses, e.g. after *Without taking a breath*, around *you've guessed it*.).

Report

+ = Solid plus whatever is in the Good or Acing it! box.

	SOLID	GOOD	ACING IT!
CONTENT			
Task fulfilment	Includes all information required in the task, e.g. Say what aims the club has met, how it met them and what you recommend for the future.	+ Develops the ideas in sound depth.	+ Develops the ideas in good depth.
Relevance	The content is relevant to the question and clear to the reader.	+ Few irrelevances or omissions.	+ No irrelevances or omissions.
COMMUNICATIVE ACHIEVEMENT			
Introduction	Starts with an introduction which states the aim of the report and how data was collected, e.g. *This report gives information about the college's restaurant. To prepare for this report, I interviewed thirty students.*	+ Is mostly organised clearly so the reader understands it.	+ Is organised clearly so the reader fully understands it.
Conclusion and recommendations	Ends with a conclusion which restates, draws conclusions and makes suggestions, e.g. *All in all, the restaurant offers value for money. However, there are some items which students believe are too expensive. I therefore suggest that the manager reduces these prices.*	+ The conclusions and suggestions mostly come from the main body of the report. They are clear to the reader.	+ The conclusions and suggestions all come from the main body of the report. They are clear to the reader.
Tone	Uses a neutral tone, e.g. *This report describes the opinion of students at our school.*	+ The tone is often consistent throughout the report but there may be some inconsistencies.	+ The tone is usually consistent throughout the report but there may be some inconsistencies.
Evaluation	Evaluates as well as describes, e.g. benefits, issues, solutions.	+ The evaluation is mostly supported with examples and reasons.	+ The evaluation is fully supported with examples and reasons.
Conveying ideas	Expresses simple ideas clearly which the reader can mostly understand.	+ Expresses a few complex ideas which the reader can usually understand.	+ Expresses some complex ideas which the reader can usually understand.
ORGANISATION			
Heading/sub-headings	Report has a heading, e.g. *Report on the college restaurant.* The report is divided into sections, with each section sitting under a sub-heading.	+ The sections and sub-headings are mostly appropriate and describe what is in the section.	+ The sections and sub-headings are always appropriate and describe what is in the section.
Paragraphing	Within each section, the report is divided into coherent paragraphs.	+ The ideas within each paragraph are ordered logically, e.g. topic sentence to introduce the main idea + supporting points, e.g. explanation, examples, reasons.	+ The ideas within each paragraph are ordered logically, e.g. topic sentence + supporting ideas; ideas are linked across paragraphs to create a coherent report, e.g. *As previously stated …*
Cohesion	Sentences are linked through the use of more formal linkers, e.g. *However, Furthermore,* referencing and substitution, e.g *it, this, one*).	+ A variety of linking is used, often appropriately and accurately.	+ A variety of linking is used, usually appropriately and accurately.
LANGUAGE			
Grammar	Uses a variety of grammar with good accuracy. Errors don't stop the reader from understanding the report.	+ Uses a little complex grammar, often accurately.	+ Uses some complex grammar, generally accurately.
Vocabulary	Uses everyday vocabulary mostly appropriately.	+ Uses some less common vocabulary with some accuracy.	+ Uses some less common vocabulary with good accuracy.